JOURNAL FOR THE STUDY OF THE NEW TESTAMENT
SUPPLEMENT SERIES
215

Executive Editor
Stanley E. Porter

Sheffield Academic Press
A Continuum imprint

New Light on Luke

Its Purpose, Sources and Literary Context

Barbara Shellard

Journal for the Study of the New Testament
Supplement Series 215

Copyright © 2002 Sheffield Academic Press
A Continuum imprint

Published by
Sheffield Academic Press Ltd
The Tower Building, 11 York Road, London SE1 7NX
370 Lexington Avenue, New York, NY 10017-6550

www.SheffieldAcademicPress.com
www.continuumbooks.com

British Library Cataloguing-in-Publication Data

A catalogue record for this book is available from the British Library

Typeset by Sheffield Academic Press
Printed on acid-free paper in Great Britain by MPG Books Ltd, Bodmin, Cornwall

ISBN 1-84127-236-1

All other things to their destruction draw
Only our love hath no decay… (John Donne)

This study is dedicated to the memory of my husband, Roland Derrick Shellard, who gave me the courage to face adversity and thereby enabled me to face a new and challenging life without him, and to that of my father, John Ernest Brigden, who financed my academic career in the first place. I owe both of them an incalculable debt.

CONTENTS

ACKNOWLEDGMENTS

So many people have contributed in differing ways to the writing of this study that I shall find it difficult to single out individuals for special thanks. It nevertheless seems proper to begin with the staff of my college, St Hilda's, Oxford University, and in particular to the present Principal, Elizabeth Llewellyn-Smith, the previous Principal, Mary Moore, Kathleen Wilkes, Anne Elliott, and Doreen Innes, all of whom have been especially supportive.

Regarding my chosen field of research, theology, I should like to express my gratitude to my supervisor, Robert Morgan, for his many suggestions of profitable areas of study and his tireless support of my ideas; to Christopher Rowland, whose thoughts on apocalyptic were, appropriately, a revelation to me; and to John Fenton, who initially accepted me to read theology and has throughout encouraged my enthusiasm. It also seems fitting here to thank Susan Lake, the Librarian at the Theology Faculty, for all her help; and also my fellow-students, many of whom helped me to formulate my ideas. Particular thanks are owed to Paula Gooder, Ian Boxall and Chris Joynes, and especially to Mark Goodacre, whose doctoral thesis was contiguous with my own in many respects, and who constitued my most valued and valuable 'background resource'.

Other friends, too, have helped in various ways, extending from technical help with my wordprocessor (from my father-in-law, Derrick Shellard, and also—and especially—Laurie Powell and Neil Jeffries, who have provided ongoing back-up), through practical and emotional support (most obviously from my mother-in-law, Elizabeth Shellard, and friends including Caroline Bolton, Laura Lauer, Claire Sands, Lorraine Essam, Ann Hussey, Ken Lane, Anne O'Hagan, Marion Payne, Jill Powell, Liz Marshall, Jo Wild, Beverly Varley and Chris Webb, all of whom helped in different ways), to the absolutely essential back-up care of my children and my dog (and here I am especially grateful to my mother, Dorothy Brigden: without her, none of this would have been possible!). I must also express my thanks to my children, Dominic and Corrina, who have accepted cheerfully the (relative) financial hardship which accompanies having a mother who chooses to be a student. They have endured with good humour the hours I have spent at my desk, and the consequent erratic timing of meals, etc., and have shown themselves more than willing to shoulder some of my more pressing domestic responsibilities.

I must also express my thanks to the British Academy, which helped to fund my research, to Timothy Higgins, Rector of St Mary's, Aylesbury, who supported me through many crises, and to John Morrison, now Archdeacon of Oxford, who nurtured my interest in theology in the first place and is therefore indirectly the cause of all that has since followed.

ABBREVIATIONS

AB	Anchor Bible
Aeg	*Aegyptus*
AnBib	Analecta biblica
ANRW	Hildegard Temporini and Wolfgang Haase (eds.), *Aufstieg und Niedergang der römischen Welt: Geschichte und Kultur Roms im Spiegel der neueren Forschung* (Berlin: W. de Gruyter, 1972–)
ATR	*Anglican Theological Review*
AUSS	*Andrews University Seminary Studies*
BETL	Bibliotheca ephemeridum theologicarum lovaniensium
BGBE	Beitrage zur Geschichte der biblischen Exegese
BTB	*Biblical Theology Bulletin*
BZNW	Beihefte zur *ZNW*
CBQ	*Catholic Biblical Quarterly*
CQR	*Church Quarterly Review*
CRINT	Compendia rerum iudaicarum ad Novum Testamentum
CTA	A. Herdner (ed.), *Corpus des tablettes en cunéiformes alphabétiques découvertes à Ras Shamra–Ugarit de 1929 à 1939* (Paris: Imprimerie nationale Geuthner, 1963)
ETL	*Ephemerides theologicae lovanienses*
Exp	*The Expositor*
ExpTim	*Expository Times*
FzB	Forschung zur Bibel
FRLANT	Forschungen zur Religion und Literatur des Alten und Neuen Testaments
GNS	Good News Studies
HeyJ	*Heythrop Journal*
HNTC	Harper's NT Commentaries
HTKNT	Herders theologischer Kommentar zum Neuen Testament
HTR	*Harvard Theological Review*
JB	*Jerusalem Bible*
JBL	*Journal of Biblical Literature*
JHS	*Journal of Hellenic Studies*
JRS	*Journal of Roman Studies*
JSNT	*Journal for the Study of the New Testament*

JSNTSup	*Journal for the Study of the New Testament*, Supplement Series
JSPSup	*Journal for the Study of the Pseudepigrapha*, Supplement Series
JTS	*Journal of Theological Studies*
KEK	H.A.W. Meyer (ed.), *Kritisch-exegetischer Kommentar über das Neue Testament*
NEB	*New English Bible*
NovT	*Novum Testamentum*
NovTSup	*Novum Testamentum*, Supplements
NTS	*New Testament Studies*
OTP	James Charlesworth (ed.), *Old Testament Pseudepigrapha*
OTS	*Oudtestamentische Studiën*
PGM	K. Preisendanz (ed.), *Papyri graecae magicae*
PRS	*Perspectives on Religious Studies*
PWSup	Supplement to August Friedrich von Pauly and Georg Wissowa (eds.), *Real-Encyclopädie der classischen Altertumswissenschaft* (Stuttgart: Metzler, 1894–)
RB	*Revue biblique*
RSR	*Recherches de science religieuse*
RSV	Revised Standard Version
SANT	Studien zum Alten und Neuen Testament
SB	Sources bibliques
SBL	Society of Biblical Literature
SBLBS	SBL Biblical Scholarship in N. America
SBLDS	SBL Dissertation Series
SBLMS	SBL Monograph Series
SBLSP	*SBL Seminar Papers*
SBS	Stuttgarter Bibelstudien
SE	*Studia Evangelica I, II, III* (= TU 73 [1959], 87 [1964], 88 [1964], etc.)
SJ	Studia judaica
SJT	*Scottish Journal of Theology*
SNTSMS	Society for New Testament Studies Monograph Series
TDNT	Gerhard Kittel and Gerhard Friedrich (eds.), *Theological Dictionary of the New Testament* (trans. Geoffrey W. Bromiley; 10 vols.; Grand Rapids: Eerdmans, 1964–)
TLZ	*Theologische Literaturzeitung*
TTod	*Theology Today*
TU	Texte und Untersuchungen
TW	Theologie und Wirklichkeit
UNT	Untersuchungen zum Neuen Testament
WUNT	Wissenschaftliche Untersuchungen zum Neuen Testament
ZNW	*Zeitschrift für die neutestamentliche Wissenschaft*

INTRODUCTION

There is normally a close relationship between a writer's use of sources and his or her purpose: the two are interlinked and when possible should be considered together. This tenet of literary criticism forms the basis of the present study. Moreover, our awareness of the way authors have transformed their material increases our appreciation of their creative skills. Thus, for example, we cannot properly recognize either Chaucer's literary talent or his purpose in *The Knight's Tale* unless we consider it in relation to Boccaccio's *Teseida*, which served as his main source; and our understanding of Chaucer is further enriched when we perceive not only how he has imaginatively recast and reinterpreted Boccaccio, but also how he has woven into it strands from his other reading.[1] This reading forms part of his 'literary context', and, along with other contemporaneous works of the same genre, provides the intellectual milieu within which we can appreciate it more fully. In the same way, a study of Luke's treatment of his sources and the literary background against which his work should be set is essential for an adequate assessment of him, and it helps us to perceive more clearly his purpose in writing.

Of course, if we are not sure what sources a writer has used, we can only construct hypotheses and test them by the sense they make of the data. But hypotheses about extant sources are more susceptible of testing than those involving sources which (if they existed) are now lost. The present study will therefore focus primarily on the relation of Luke–Acts to other works in the New Testament, although those that provide a literary context regarding classical historiography, rhetoric and apocalyptic (which is an important—though insufficiently acknowledged—influence on Luke's thought) will of necessity be touched on too.

I shall propose that a careful comparison of Luke with the other Gospels

---

1. E.g. the *Roman de la Rose* and Boethius's *De Consolatione Philosophiae*. Even when Chaucer's main source is some other work and these two are not used directly, odd words and phrases, which often occur in different contexts, reflect their all-pervasive influence.

suggests that when, in his prologue, he mentions *many* other narratives about Jesus, he is not merely using a rhetorical overstatement to mean two, Mark and the hypothetical Q;[2] he is referring to at least three.[3] He has, indeed, used all the other now canonical Gospels to compose his own, as he may arguably have used some (if not all) of Paul's epistles in the composition of Acts. I shall also suggest that consideration of the way he has done so enables us to draw some inferences about his interests and his overall purpose which significantly enlarge our understanding of his work.

The first part of this study will consider when and where Luke–Acts was written. As a preliminary, however, it is necessary briefly to discuss its dating in relation to that of the other writings involved, since it has to be shown that any suggestion made concerning the order of their composition is actually possible. The arguments here are inconclusive and hotly contested, with proposals for the dates of the Gospels ranging from a decade or so after the crucifixion to the middle of the second century. I am assuming that, as most believe, Mark was the first of the canonical Gospels to be written, c. 70 CE.[4] Allowing some time to elapse between the composition of Mark and its elaboration and complete revision by the author of Matthew, this means that Matthew should probably be dated somewhere in the eighties, as is proposed by many scholars, when tensions with Judaism were leading to the expulsion of Jewish Christians from synagogues.[5]

2.	It is a matter of debate whether the word διήγησις can properly be applied to a collection of sayings such as Q.

3.	Cf. L. Alexander, *The Preface to Luke's Gospel* (SNTSMS, 78; Cambridge: Cambridge University Press, 1993), contra H.J. Cadbury, 'A Commentary on the Preface of Luke', in F.J. Foakes Jackson and K. Lake (eds.), *The Beginnings of Christianity*, II (London: Macmillan, 1922), pp. 489-510. Alexander says (p. 114) that πολλοὶ implies many sources, not just two. For Luke to have used it with this meaning would have been deliberately misleading; and conventions were not normally followed blindly, in total disregard of the facts.

4.	The arguments of M. Hengel, *Studies in the Gospel of Mark* (trans. J. Bowden; London: SCM Press, 1985), pp. 1-30, in favour of its composition c. 69 in Rome, when the destruction of Jerusalem was inevitable, but not yet realized, and Rome itself was in upheaval, are strong (pp. 28ff.); but a dating a few years later and a different location (such as Syria) are also possible.

5.	Even if the 'cursing of the Noṣrîm' (Christians) belongs to a later period, as is argued by R. Kimelman, '*Birkat Ha-Minim* and the Lack of Evidence for an Anti-Christian Jewish Prayer in Late Antiquity', in E.P. Sanders (ed.), *Jewish and Christian Self-Definition*, II (London: SCM Press, 1981), pp. 226-44, it nevertheless seems likely that Jewish Christians, as *minîm*, suffered exclusion at least from full participation in synagogue worship much earlier, perhaps in the mid- to late eighties. See W. Horbury,

There is less of a consensus about the other two Gospels. Patristic sources without exception regard John's as the latest to be written, but the earliest statement to this effect is that of Irenaeus[6] and the testimony of the early Fathers is not generally considered reliable in such matters. Although the Gospel must precede c. 120–130 CE if the Rylands papyrus fragment is rightly dated, many scholars nevertheless date it well into the second century, on the assumption that the ideas dominating its theology, especially its very high Christology, require a long period of development. But we know from the example of Paul that sophisticated theological reflection and a high Christology are not necessarily late, any more than a lower Christology must inevitably be early, as the views of the Ebionites[7] and, later, Arius, testify. R.E. Brown[8] estimates its composition to be c. 90 CE; Hengel,[9] too, even though he believes that the final editing of the Gospel did not take place until just after c. 100 CE, thinks that most of the material belongs to the period 90–100 CE. There is no evidence to exclude a dating in the early nineties, which is the position I accept in this study.

Dating Luke–Acts has presented critics with even more problems. There is no certain use of Luke's Gospel until c. 130 CE, although there is a family resemblance to other works usually dated to the late first or very early second centuries, such as 1 Peter, Ephesians, *1 Clement, Hermas,* and possibly James. Because of this, and because Luke–Acts reflects issues that preoccupied the Church at the turn of the century, such as the importance of repentance/forgiveness, the affirmation of the apostolic tradition in the missionary activity of the early Church, and the need to oppose docetic ideas about Christ and to resist the temptation to apostasize, Luke–Acts would seem to belong ideologically to the end of the first century. I shall take it as a working hypothesis for the following study, which accords with the admittedly scanty evidence, that Luke–Acts was written c. 100 CE, probably at Rome, even though the final revision of Acts may have been prevented by the death of the author, who would by then have been in his late sixties, and who was perhaps attached to the fringes of the Pauline mission in his youth.

'The Benediction of the Minim and early Jewish–Christian Controversy', *JTS* NS 33 (1982), pp. 19-61.

6.   Irenaeus, *Against Heresies* 3.1.1.

7.   See Irenaeus, *Against Heresies* 1.26.1-2.

8.   R.E. Brown, *The Community of the Beloved Disciple* (New York: Paulist Press, 1979), p. 59.

9.   M. Hengel, *The Johannine Question* (trans. J. Bowden; London: SCM Press; Philadelphia: Trinity Press International, 1989), pp. 81ff.

Chapter 1

CLEARING THE GROUND: THE GENRE,
DATE AND LOCATION OF LUKE–ACTS

1.1 *Genre*

The genre of the Gospels has been the subject of much discussion: even if
they are broadly conformable to the category of biography, they are lives
of a special type.[1] Luke–Acts in particular poses special problems: even
while we might believe that Luke's Gospel itself is a βίος, Acts is not a
'life' in any sense;[2] it is a history which in some respects combines the
detail of a monograph with the sweep of a more general review of early
Christianity. Sterling[3] argues, persuasively, that it is an apologetic history
like those of Josephus, whereby Christianity is defined internally and
externally and set into the wider context of Hellenistic culture.

Genres were fairly flexible in the ancient world,[4] and the categories of
historiography and biography often overlapped, in any case.[5] Character
was important in both (this was as true in the Hellenistic world as in
Jewish historiography); and both of necessity also included reviews of
events which affected, or were affected by, important people. Biography

---

1.   In this respect, even if we disagree, we can understand why some scholars have
argued that they are *sui generis*.

2.   C.H. Talbert, *What is a Gospel?: The Genre of the Canonical Gospels*
(Philadelphia: Fortress Press, 1977), tries to fit Luke–Acts into the category of 'succession narratives', which he suggests were derived from the sources of Diogenes
Laertius's later *Lives of the Eminent Philosophers*, but evidence of most of these
sources is lacking, and only six of Diogenes's 82 recorded lives fit the pattern Talbert
wishes to apply to Luke–Acts.

3.   G.E. Sterling, *Historiography and Self-Definition: Josephos, Luke–Acts and
Apologetic Historiography* (NovTSup, 64; Leiden: E.J. Brill, 1992).

4.   See J.A. Darr, *On Character Building: The Reader and the Rhetoric of Characterization in Luke–Acts* (Louisville, KY: Westminster/John Knox Press, 1992), pp. 22ff.

5.   An obvious example is Tacitus's *Agricola*. See also R.A. Burridge, *What Are
the Gospels?* (SNTSMS, 70; Cambridge: Cambridge University Press, 1992), p. 245.

normally focused on the lives of prominent people who were to be remembered and maybe emulated;[6] it perhaps allowed the author a greater
freedom in handling material than did history. Plutarch, for example, to
streamline his narrative, felt free to abridge by conflating similar items; to
compress, telescope and displace material; to group thematically related
items together; to alter historical data if necessary; and to fabricate contexts for the speeches he composed.[7]

Attempts to define the genre of Luke–Acts too rigidly and specifically
have not been successful, either because there are too many examples to
afford an adequate generic classification, or because there are too few parallels available for comparison.[8] It is probably best to regard Luke–Acts as a
'history' in the widest sense, a record of 'the things that have been accomplished among us' (Lk. 1.1), with the Gospel concentrating more on the life
of the founder of Christianity (and therefore more nearly approximating to
biography), and the second volume on presenting the growth of the movement he inspired.[9] Barr and Wentling[10] see Acts as synthesizing the
selectivity of a βίος with the breadth and lack of specific personal focus of
a history, just as it synthesizes Hellenistic and Jewish models.

The question of genre is important because it affects how one reads a
work. For this reason, Pervo's[11] classification of Luke–Acts as a historical
novel is unsatisfactory, because the word 'novel' suggests fictionality, and

6.   Many βίοι presented accounts of figures who provided moral examples to the
reader and who were thus to be admired, but these were a sub-type rather than a special
genre of 'encomium biography', contra P.L. Shuler, *A Genre for the Gospels: The
Biographical Character of Matthew* (Minneapolis: Fortress Press, 1982).

7.   See C.B.R. Pelling, 'Plutarch's Method of Work in the Roman Lives', *JHS* 19
(1979), pp. 74-96; *idem*, 'Plutarch's Adaptation of Source Material', *JHS* 20 (1980),
pp. 127-40.

8.   Thus prologues, although perhaps originally characteristic of histories, occurred
at the beginning of biographies and even scientific works, as is argued by Alexander,
Preface.

9.   See W.C. van Unnik, 'Luke's Second Book and the Rules of Hellenistic Historiography', in J. Kremer (ed.), *Les Actes des Apôtres: Tradition, Rédaction, Théologie*
(BETL, 48; Leuven: Leuven University Press, 1979), pp. 37-60.

10.   D.L. Barr and J.L. Wentling, 'The Conventions of Classical Biography and the
Genre of Luke–Acts: A Preliminary Study', in C.H. Talbert (ed.), *Luke–Acts: New
Perspectives from the SBL* (New York: Crossroad, 1984), pp. 63-88.

11.   R.I. Pervo, *Profit with Delight: The Literary Genre of the Acts of the Apostles*
(Philadelphia: Fortress Press, 1987). Similarly, S.M. Praeder, 'Luke–Acts and the
Ancient Novel', in K.H. Richards (ed.), *SBLSP*, 20 (Chico, CA: Scholars Press, 1981),
pp. 269-92.

Luke–Acts was certainly not intended fictionally, as Luke's prologue makes clear. Acts may have been written in part to delight the reader:[12] Pervo rightly draws attention to many incidents which are entertaining in themselves, such as the picture of the weeping widows showing Peter examples of Dorcas's needlework, or Eutychus dropping asleep during one of Paul's lengthier sermons and falling out of the window. But it was written primarily to convey the truth as Luke saw it, to instruct, and in this respect we should compare not ancient novels but the works of Isocrates, Livy, Sallust, Tacitus, Josephus, and Dionysius of Halicarnassus.[13]

Luke is careful to conform his two volumes to the requirements of ancient historiography; this is indicated at the outset by his choice of the word διήγησις instead of Mark's εὐαγγέλιον, and by his stress on accuracy, careful research, and truth.[14] It is therefore important that we judge him by the standards of his time, not those of our own.[15] Critics like Pervo, who censure his factual inaccuracies and the freedom with which he treats his likely sources, and see these as evidence that he is not to be regarded as a historian, forget that ancient historians were primarily trained not in history but in rhetoric, which formed the basis of their educational system.[16] They aimed to convince the reader of the truth of their account of events, and the speeches they wrote were appropriate for the circumstances rather than verbatim records.[17] There was not any conflict with the

12. *Delectatio lectoris* was a responsibility ancient historians were aware of, too; see Cicero, *De Partitione Oratoria* 31-32; Tacitus, *Annals* 4.32.1, 33.2-3. On this topic, see T. Woodman, 'Self-imitation and the Substance of History', in D. West and T. Woodman (eds.), *Creative Imitation and Latin Literature* (Cambridge: Cambridge University Press, 1979), pp. 143-55, especially pp. 152ff.

13. See, for example, Dionysius, *Roman Antiquities* 1.1-3; or Livy, *Histories* Preface 9-10.

14. See D.E. Aune, *The New Testament in its Literary Environment* (Cambridge: James Clarke & Co., 1988), p. 116.

15. A similar point is made by T. Woodman, 'Self-imitation', pp. 152-53, concerning Tacitus. Woodman suggests that Tacitus has based the details of his description of Germanicus's visit to the site of Varus's defeat (*Annals* 1.61-62) on that of Vitellius's visit to Cremona, which he had earlier recorded (see *Histories* 2.70). This is an example of a device which Woodman terms 'substantive self-imitation'. It was not regarded as conflicting with historical truth, even if the details themselves did not reflect what actually happened.

16. See G.A. Kennedy, *A New Testament Interpretation through Rhetorical Criticism* (Chapel Hill, NC: University of North Carolina Press, 1984).

17. Thus, the speech of Claudius recorded by Tacitus, *Annals* 11.23ff. is much shorter than the inscribed version.

principle of historical truth, as the ancients saw it, when Dionysius
exaggerated details for rhetorical effect,[18] nor when Josephus increased the
numbers given in his source.[19] Aune says:

> Plausibility was the primary means of separating truth from falsehood,
> rather than the critical analysis of sources, and the main requirement of
> narrative... To claim that the evangelists wrote biography with historical
> intentions does not guarantee that they preserved a single historical fact.[20]

It must be stressed that Luke seems to have regarded himself as a
historian. Although the terminology of his prologue is to some degree
conventional, it is nevertheless most suited to the aims of a historian, as
Callan has shown.[21] The evangelist coordinates differing chronographies
at the beginning of his Gospel (Lk. 3.1-2), which is a historical technique;
in addition the letters he includes accord with contemporary historiographical practice and are appropriate for the given circumstances. The letter of
Lysias to Felix in Acts 23.26-30, for example, is typically Hellenistic in
form and expression; and the Apostolic Decree of Acts 15 reflects Hellenistic conventions and employs a vocabulary consistent with the decisions
of a provincial assembly.[22] Moreover, Luke provides accurate information
when possible about the places mentioned in his narrative, and he names
the various civic authorities of towns like Philippi, Thessalonica, and
Ephesus, and even identifies particular individuals such as Gallio, Procon-
sul of Achaia, all of which details have been confirmed by recent
research.[23] In this context, it is worth noting that the language of Acts
19.38-39, especially the impersonal third person plural verb form, resembles that of an edict of Rutilius Lupus, Prefect of Alexandria in 115 CE.[24]
Luke has studied official documents and imitates their phraseology.

---

18. See Dionysius, *Roman Antiquities* 8.89.1-2.

19. Cf. Josephus, *Ant.* 12.24 and *Aristeas* 19.

20. Aune, *Literary Environment*, p. 84.

21. T. Callan, 'The Preface of Luke–Acts and Historiography', *NTS* 31 (1985), pp.
576-81.

22. Thus Aune, *Literary Environment*, p. 128.

23. See, among others, A.N. Sherwin-White, *Roman Society and Roman Law in
the New Testament* (Oxford: Oxford University Press, 1963); C.J. Hemer, *The Book of
Acts in the Setting of Hellenistic History* (Tübingen: J.C.B. Mohr [Paul Siebeck],
1989).

24. See *CPJ* 435. This papyrus is discussed by A. Fuks, 'The Jewish Revolt in
Egypt, A.D. 115–117, in the Light of the Papyri', *Aeg* 33 (1953), pp. 131-58; *idem*,
'Aspects of the Jewish Revolt in A.D. 115–117', *JRS* 51 (1961), pp. 93-104.

The speeches Luke provides are 'in character', too, as we would expect of a Hellenistic historian;[25] we may compare the thoroughly Semitic atmosphere and language of the early chapters of Acts with the fulsome Greek periods of the lawyer Tertullus. Indeed, speeches are suited to speaker, audience and occasion so well that it is impossible to rule out the possibility that Luke may have derived them from some early source; they are what one assumes would have been said in the circumstances.[26] Aune concludes:

> Hellenistic historians found a wealth of discourse material in their sources...
> Since Luke wrote about events of the previous generation, it is unlikely that
> he found speeches in written sources. His options were three. (1) To
> interview those present or (if he was present) to recall the substance of what
> was actually spoken; (2) to freely improvise speeches according to the
> principle of appropriateness; or (3) to combine research and memory with
> free composition. Luke followed the last route.[27]

The actions Luke records, too, which are lively and dramatic, are to an extent representative and paradigmatic—what, given the circumstances, one would expect to have happened. Although Luke repeats items that he regards as particularly important,[28] Pervo[29] notes that Luke normally presents just one full-scale account of a type of incident; there is one developed synagogue sermon in Luke 4, one major Pauline sermon to Jews (Antioch) and one to Gentiles (Athens), one riot, one Apostolic Council and one shipwreck (Paul himself, at 2 Cor. 11.25, refers to three).[30] The

---

25. Thucydides, *A History of the War between Athens and Sparta* 1.22.1 was (mis)interpreted by later historians such as Ephorus to mean that speeches should be appropriate rather than accurate. Polybius objected to this practice (see *History* 12.25a.5-b.1), but it seems to have been common; see Dionysius, *On Thucydides* 18, 20, 37, and especially 34, where Dionysius, in this context, refers to a historian's 'felicity of invention'; or Lucian, *How to Write History* 58. A.J. Woodman, *Rhetoric in Classical Historiography* (London: Croom Helm, 1988), notes that Sallust 'puts speeches into the mouths of the various personages in all three [of his historical] works' (p. 117). See also the full discussion by C. Gempf, 'Public Speaking and Published Accounts', in B.W. Winter and A.D. Clarke (eds.), *The Book of Acts in its First Century Setting*, I (Grand Rapids: Eerdmans, 1993), pp. 259-304.

26. See C.K. Barrett, *Luke the Historian in Recent Study* (London: Epworth Press, 1961), pp. 29ff.

27. Aune, *Literary Environment*, p. 125.

28. Thus there are three accounts Paul's conversion, and two of Cornelius's vision.

29. Pervo, *Profit*, p. 21.

30. We may compare Sallust, who although he varies his accounts of battles and

shipwreck is especially interesting because of the many classical parallels to the details Luke includes, such as the prolonged storm, the rallying speech and the running aground of the ship.[31] His account is not, however, to be taken as fictional, even if none of the three shipwrecks Paul actually experienced precisely resembled it. The evangelist knew that Paul had undergone shipwreck, and since plausibility was what mattered, he provided a very vivid description of one, perhaps using the many sources at his disposal for such incidents. Aune[32] notes that Luke, who elsewhere uses the word πλοῖον for 'ship', chooses the obsolete ναῦς at Acts 27.41, pairing it with the poetic verb ἐπικέλλω; the two words also occur together in Homer, *Odyssey* 9.148 (cf. 9.546), and this may be significant.

It has also been argued by Robbins[33] that first person narration (as in the 'we' sections of Acts) was a rhetorical device used by ancient writers to give immediacy to their accounts of sea-voyages. He can only find two examples from history to support his claim that it was considered stylistically appropriate for such material, however; and Polybius seems rather to imply that first person narration indicates direct personal involvement.[34] Luke's use of the first person plural suggests either that the author himself experienced the events narrated or that he intended us to think that he did.[35] The implication is that Luke himself was a companion of Paul. He was perhaps attached to the fringes of the Pauline mission while he was a youth, and these passages may derive from rough notes taken at the time, or from Luke's later ὑπομνήματα based on them,[36] which may thus have

sieges in his *Jugurthian War* normally has only one example of a type and includes details which confirm the characters of the generals concerned.

31. We should note that the sea-storms in Homer's *Odyssey* 5.291-473, 12.402-25, became the models for many later descriptions, from Virgil's *Aeneid* 1.34-179 onwards.

32. Aune, *Literary Environment*, p. 129.

33. See V.K. Robbins, 'By Land and Sea: The We Passages and Ancient Sea Voyages', in C.H. Talbert (ed.), *Perspectives on Luke–Acts* (Danville, VA: Association of Baptist Professors of Religion, 1978), pp. 215-42. Aune, *Literary Environment*, p. 124 discusses Robbins's contention in detail.

34. See Polybius, *History* 36.11-12; also the criticisms made by Lucian, *How to Write History* 29. Polybius (12.27.1-6; 12.28.6) and Lucian (47) both stress the importance of first-hand knowledge.

35. See Aune, *Literary Environment*, p. 124. The suggestion that Luke could have used another man's diary at this point on literary and stylistic grounds is rejected by J.M. Creed, *The Gospel According to Luke* (London: Macmillan, 1930), pp. xiv n. 1, xv.

36. The first stage of history writing in the ancient world was the conversion of the

been written long before the Gospel or the rest of Acts.[37] If Luke as a young man first met Paul at Troas, he would have known that Paul was active in Thrace, Macedonia and Achaia, even if he did not know the full details about what happened in places at which he was not present.

1.2. *The Date of Luke–Acts*

1.2.1. *A Brief Review of the Evidence*

The *terminus a quo* for the dating of Luke, regardless of whether he used Mark and Matthew/Q, is the fall of Jerusalem in 70 CE. Although some critics[38] have argued that Luke's description in chs. 19 and 21 is not to be regarded as a correction of Mark made on historical grounds, since all the details can be paralleled in the Septuagint, Esler[39] points out that not every siege involved constructing a circumvallation (Lk. 19.43-44), nor were many cities razed to the ground (Lk. 19.44) and 'trampled' by Gentiles, with their inhabitants being led off as captives (Lk. 21.24). These accurate, specific details, which can be paralleled in Josephus,[40] strongly suggest a date after Jerusalem's fall. It would be a remarkable coincidence for Luke to have chosen those very items from the Septuagint which formed part of the siege of Jerusalem and were omitted by Mark.

The *terminus ad quem* is much harder to determine. It is assumed by many that Luke–Acts, with its (relatively) positive attitude to Rome, must precede the latter part of Domitian's reign, when there was persecution of 'those who had drifted into the practices of the Jews'[41] (usually interpreted

author's notes into the ὑπομνῆματα, a preliminary sketch of events. (See Lucian, *How to Write History* 16, 48; Josephus, *Apion* 1.47-50.)

37. See Hemer, *Acts*, p. 354.

38. E.g. C.H. Dodd, 'The Fall of Jerusalem and the "Abomination of Desolation"', in C.H. Dodd, *More New Testament Studies* (Grand Rapids: Eerdmans, 1968), pp. 69-83. See also J.A.T. Robinson, *Redating the New Testament* (London: SCM Press, 1976); John Wenham, *Redating Matthew, Mark and Luke* (London: Hodder & Stoughton, 1991).

39. P.F. Esler, *Community and Gospel in Luke–Acts: The Social and Political Motivations of Lukan Theology* (SNTSMS, 57; Cambridge: Cambridge University Press, 1987), p. 28.

40. Josephus, *War* 5.491ff.; 6.413-17; 7.1-4. Josephus observes that it was not the original intention of the Roman forces to construct a circumvallation, which was not the normal course of action.

41. Dio Cassius, *Roman History* 67.14. It should be stressed that he is a hostile source with regard to Domitian, and it is therefore dangerous to rely too heavily on his evidence.

as including Christians). But there is little evidence of any widespread Domitianic persecution: things may have been uncomfortable and uncertain, but they were not fatal for many,[42] although there was always a danger of being informed against, since Christians could not participate in the emperor cult. The actions of Domitian against Christians probably did not differ significantly from measures which were enforced sporadically in earlier reigns, although it is possible that some Christians were the unintended victims of an internal power-struggle between Domitian and supposed political opponents like Flavius Clemens. Domitian himself died in 96 CE, and it was left to successors such as Trajan (98–117 CE) actively to enforce the emperor cult, but even though a few Christians died in Asia under Trajan[43] there was no systematic and deliberate persecution of them as such, although they were executed if, after being informed against, they persisted in their confession of faith.

Luke's avoidance of any reference to Paul's death at Roman hands may therefore perhaps reflect a context of potential persecution,[44] where Christians were under threat of similar treatment if they were discovered. Under these circumstances, it was prudent to be as conciliatory as possible and to avoid attracting any undesirable attention.[45] Texts like 1 Peter and *1 Clement* are even more positive in their attitude to Rome, despite the Neronian persecution in the sixties and difficulties with Domitian a generation later; this may be because both these emperors were popularly regarded as insane, and their actions could therefore be accounted abnormal. In the event, the situation seems to have worsened in respect of the emperor cult under the later Trajan, but Christians in the short reign of Nerva and also the early days of Trajan were not to know that.

Although the testimony of the early Fathers (which is considered below)

---

42. See *1 Clem.* 1.1.

43. See Pliny, *Epistles* 10.96. This letter dates from c. 112 CE, by which time some Christians were clearly being executed in Bithynia.

44. Cf. P. Lampe and U. Luz, 'Post-Pauline Christianity and Pagan Society', in J. Becker (ed.), *Christian Beginnings* (Louisville, KY: Westminster/John Knox Press, 1993), pp. 242-82 (259). Lampe and Luz think that Luke–Acts should be dated c. 100 CE. If Luke–Acts is to be dated in Trajan's reign, in view of the anti-Jewish polemic of much of Acts, the lack of any allusion to the Jewish revolt in Alexandria (115–117 CE) would seem to indicate a date at the beginning of the reign rather than the end: see E.P. Sanders and M. Davies, *Studying the Synoptic Gospels* (London: SCM Press, 1989), p. 17.

45. See R.L. Maddox, *The Purpose of Luke–Acts* (FRLANT, 126; Edinburgh: T. & T. Clark, 1985), pp. 96ff.

is contentious, it is often remarked that there is no certain[46] use of Luke before c. 130 CE,[47] nor of Acts before c. 180 CE. Acts 4.13, however, seems to be reflected in Justin Martyr, at *1 Apol.* 39.3; elsewhere, too, there appear to be echoes of Acts in Justin. There may also be a connection between Polycarp, *Phil.* 1.5 and some Western manuscripts of Acts 2.24: it is significant that both speak of God 'loosing the pangs of Hades', rather than the Septuagintal 'the pangs of death'. Both writers have thus made the same alteration/error, which is not found in Alexandrian texts of Acts, and that this shared error occurs only in Western manuscripts may itself be significant for the dating of Acts, since even if on some occasions the Western version preserves the correct reading,[48] it is clearly a later and tendentious revision.[49] The dating of Polycarp's letter is disputed, and although parts of it may be as late as 133 CE,[50] much may be earlier. If Polycarp does reflect Acts here, which must remain in doubt, and this reference should be dated to the earlier section (i.e. 112–115 CE), we would need to allow time for Acts to have been revised by a 'Western' editor, before reaching Polycarp. This would suggest that Luke–Acts cannot be too much later than 95–100 CE.

The testimony of the early Fathers to our canonical Gospels is itself a disputed question, as was noted above: although some think that *1 Clement* knew Luke–Acts, the evidence is very thin, and H.B. Green has argued

---

46. Some have seen Ignatius, *Smyrn.* 3.2 as a citation of Lk. 24.39. We cannot be sure, however, since the same combination of seeing and touching, which affirms the corporeality of the resurrection—an aim common to much early Christian apologetic—occurs elsewhere in the New Testament, too: for example, at 1 Jn 1.1 (where the same verb ψηλαφάω is used), and also at Jn 20.25.

47. It is more likely that Marcion used Luke than vice versa (contra the suggestion of J. Knox, *Marcion and the New Testament* [Chicago: University of Chicago Press, 1942], *passim*, so that we must date it before 140 CE, on the usual dating of Marcion).

48. E.g., at Acts 8.37, where there has been anablempsis of a line in the Alexandrian text.

49. This is convincingly argued by J.H. Ropes, 'The Text of Acts', in F.J. Foakes Jackson and K. Lake (eds.), *The Beginnings of Christianity* (5 vols.; London: MacMillan, 1920–33), III, pp. ccxv-cclvi, and B. Witherington, 'The Anti-feminist Tendency in the Western Text of Acts', *JBL* 103 (1984), pp. 82-84, contra F. Blass, *The Philology of the Gospels* (London: Macmillan, 1898) and latterly W.A. Strange, *The Problem of the Text of Acts* (SNTSMS, 71; Cambridge: Cambridge University Press, 1992).

50. See P.N. Harrison, *Polycarp's Two Epistles to the Philippians* (Cambridge: Cambridge University Press, 1936).

persuasively[51] that *1 Clement* may, on the contrary, have influenced Luke at Lk. 6.38 (cf. *1 Clem.* 13.2) and Lk. 17.1-2a (cf. *1 Clem.* 46.8): Green likewise finds Acts secondary to *1 Clement* at Acts 13.22 (cf. *1 Clem.* 18.1). He points out[52] that the Roman succession list, which names a Clement (usually identified as the author of *1 Clement*) as Bishop of Rome, is clearly anachronistic since there was no monoepiscopate in Rome until much later, as is borne out by both Ignatius's *Epistle to the Romans* and *The Shepherd of Hermas*. This means that we can no longer fix the date of *1 Clement* securely at 95–96 CE: it may be later, in which case Luke–Acts would be later still, although Green believes that it must have been in a state nearing completion when Luke encountered it.[53]

Citation of texts was very free at this time, and later writers usually relied on memory, as is evident from the Old Testament quotations of Paul and *1 Clement*. It is therefore not surprising that although the *Didache* refers to 'the gospel' at 8.2, 11.3, 15.3, the text does not coincide with any of our Gospels. The same is true of Justin Martyr: we should not assume that because he does not use the text familiar to us for the canonical Gospels, he did not know them—although the form of the text he knew may have differed significantly from ours.

In this context, J.C. O'Neill[54] has pointed out how many connections there are between the ideas of Luke and Justin Martyr,[55] although few would regard these as evidence that Luke and Justin are therefore to be dated at approximately the same time; a likelier explanation is that Justin used Luke.[56] In this respect, Käsemann's much-criticized description of

51. H.B. Green, 'Matthew, Clement and Luke: Their Sequence and Relationship', *JTS* NS 40 (1989) pp. 1-25; see especially pp. 9-11, 18, 21.

52. Green, 'Sequence', p. 2.

53. Green, 'Sequence', p. 24.

54. J.C. O'Neill, *The Theology of Acts* (London: SPCK, 2nd edn, 1970).

55. For example, the concept of the suffering messiah; the Ascension motif; salvation history (using the Old Testament as well as the story of Jesus, both of which demonstrate God's salvific actions); the use of prophecy to prove, not merely to assert, Jesus' Messiahship. Christological titles used by both are similar, too.

56. Similarly H. Koester, *Ancient Christian Gospels* (London: SCM Press, 1990), pp. 364ff. See *Dial.* 100.5 (cf. Lk. 1.35, 38); *1 Apol.* 50 (Lk. 24.25; 24.44; Acts 1.8-9). Justin's allusions, like Polycarp, often reflect Western text readings of Luke: cf. *1 Apol.* 17.4 and the Western text of Lk. 12.48; *Dial.* 88.3; *1 Apol.* 103.6 and the Western text of Lk. 3.22, which quotes Ps. 2.7 with reference to the baptism. In several places, Justin apparently conflates Luke with Matthew: *1 Apol.* 16.1, for example, combines Lk. 6.29 and Mt. 5.39-41; and *1 Apol.* 15.13-17 seems to conflate several Matthaean and Lukan verses.

Luke as 'early Catholic'[57] reflected an awareness, which is shared by several scholars including O'Neill, that many of the concerns of the second century church are apparent in Luke–Acts. We notice, for example, that although Luke does not consider the Church as the divinely appointed instrument of salvation, nor the apostolic succession and the ordained ministry,[58] he does seek to validate the apostolic tradition, which he grounds in the post-Resurrection instruction given to the disciples by Jesus. Similarly, his emphasis on the corporeality of Jesus' gestation, birth, death, burial and resurrection may well be aimed at counteracting docetic ideas. It may likewise be significant that Luke's interests so often seem ecclesiological;[59] the Mission of the Seventy (Two), for example, which seems to relate to the Gentile mission and the situation facing later missionaries, is much fuller than his Mission of the Twelve. Perseverance in faith, as well, is a Lukan motif which he adds to his Markan source at Lk. 8.15 (cf. Mk 4.20 and Mt. 13.23). Closely related is the fear of apostasy, which is reflected in Lk. 12.47-48.[60] Luke's rigorous attitude here has affinities with the same hard-line approach to the problem that we see in Hebrews, where it is said to be impossible for παραπεσόντας (Heb. 6.6: usually interpreted as meaning apostates) to repent again and be forgiven. It was obviously a live issue at the turn of the century, as was the whole question of post-baptismal sin and repentance. In this connection, we should note that Luke who, like *Hermas*, stresses the need for repentance and God's readiness to forgive, shows that even apostasy is in practice forgivable, as Lk. 22.31-34 demonstrates. Indeed, it is not clear that even the heinous post-baptismal sin of Simon Magus in Acts 8.19—one which was patently 'against the Holy Spirit'—is unforgivable if he repents (see v. 22). Luke leaves the question open, but the words of Peter and Simon's response imply that forgiveness is still felt to be possible.

In all these respects, Luke's affinities with the concerns of the Church at the beginning of the second century may be a better indication of the date of Luke–Acts than his employment of a Christology which reflects, in Acts, his aim to provide a historical narrative about the beginnings of Christianity. Townsend[61] argues persuasively that Acts makes sense if we

57. See E. Käsemann, 'Ministry and Community in the New Testament', in *Essays on New Testament Themes* (London: SCM Press, 1966), pp. 63-94.

58. We may contrast the Pastoral Epistles.

59. See, e.g., Lk. 10.1-12; 12.8-12; 12.46-48.

60. See also Lk. 12.10.

61. J.T. Townsend, 'The Date of Luke–Acts', in C.H. Talbert (ed.), *Luke–Acts: New Perspectives from the SBL* (New York: Crossroad, 1984), pp. 47-62.

see it as relating to many problems facing the early second-century Church, not just to those concerning Marcion, as was argued by Knox.[62]

With regard to the question of the dating of Luke–Acts, it may be significant that the historical details Luke gives normally relate to the circumstances existing at the turn of the century, rather than to a later period. Thus, for example, Sherwin-White notes that the degree of civic autonomy evidenced at Ephesus is only consistent with a dating in the late first and early second centuries; it would have been anachronistic very much later.[63] The whole sequence of Paul's trial, too, which represents the judicial process termed *provocatio*, was only in operation until approximately the last decade of the first century, after which time the procedure, *appelatio*, was slightly different and Luke's account would have been incorrect.[64] Likewise, the question of jurisdiction, which is reflected uniquely in Luke's Passion account (see Lk. 23.6-7), was important only at this period, when there was a move away from hearing cases in the *forum delicti*, where the crime was committed, to that of the *forum domicilii*, where the defendant lived.[65] The evidence we have of the change shows that it was only at the end of the first century and the beginning of the second century, when the new practice, which proved unworkable, was 'on trial', that the situation reflected in Luke–Acts can be historically substantiated. This, too, suggests that it should probably be dated to this period.

In this context, it should be noted that the govenor Felix's decision at Acts 23.34-35 to hear Paul's case himself, once he learned that the prisoner came from Cilicia, may also demonstrate the accuracy of Luke's knowledge. Cilicia was part of the larger province of Syria at this time; by 72 CE the two were separated.[66] Presumably the Legate of Syria would not have wished to waste time over a relatively minor dispute on the fringes of his province: Felix's action is thus entirely plausible. Acts may be tendentious, but although we cannot assume that the incidents, as Luke records them, are historically true,[67] studies by scholars such as J. Smith and W.M.

62. See J. Knox, 'Acts and the Pauline Letter Corpus', in L.E. Keck and J.L. Martyn (eds.), *Studies in Luke–Acts* (Philadelphia: Fortress Press; London: SPCK, 1966), pp. 279-87.

63. Sherwin-White, *Roman Society*, p. 84.

64. See Sherwin-White, *Roman Society*, pp. 57ff.

65. Sherwin-White, *Roman Society*, pp. 28ff.

66. Sherwin-White, *Roman Society*, pp. 55ff.

67. See H.W. Tajra, *The Trial of Paul* (WUNT, 2.95; Tübingen: J.C.B. Mohr, 1989), p. 2.

Ramsay[68] and more recent works by A.N. Sherwin-White, W. Gasque, C.J. Hemer, H.W. Tajra and R. Lane Fox[69] have confirmed the accuracy of many of the details Luke includes.[70] Hence, for example, Fair Havens, though unlikely to be known to any except someone who had sailed this route,[71] is attested in contemporary reports. Similarly, the family of Sergius Paulus is well-known through a series of inscriptions from Rome and Asia Minor, and there are references to a senator of Claudian date by this name who became a consul,[72] although we have no external evidence that he became a Christian. Gallio's proconsulship also (see Acts 18.12) has been confirmed by an inscription at Delphi dating from 52 CE. It is worth noting that neither proconsulship is mentioned in Tacitus's *Annals*, nor does Seneca refer to them. There is no evidence that archives were kept in provinces in the first century, and it would not have been easy to find out such a detail without access to Roman documents which are not likely to have been available to Luke.

In connection with the dating of Luke–Acts, it must be recognized that it is not necessary for us fully to harmonize Acts and Paul's epistles; it would have been consistent with the practices of the time, as we have seen above in Plutarch, for Luke to have modified the chronology of Paul's mission to some extent to suit his own purposes. At Acts 20.13-17, for

68. J. Smith, *The Voyage and Shipwreck of St Paul* (London, 4th edn, 1880); W.M. Ramsay, *The Bearing of Recent Discovery on the Trustworthiness of the New Testament* (London: Hodder & Stoughton, 1915).

69. Sherwin-White, *Roman Society*; W. Gasque, *A History of the Criticism of the Acts of the Apostles* (BGBE, 17; Tübingen: J.C.B. Mohr [Paul Siebeck], 1975); Hemer, *Acts*; Tajra, *Trial of St Paul*; R. Lane Fox, *The Unauthorized Version* (Harmondsworth: Penguin, 1991).

70. Thus contra E. Schürer, *The History of the Jewish People in the Age of Jesus Christ, 175 B.C.–A.D. 135*, I (revised by G. Vermes, F. Millar and M. Black; Edinburgh: T. & T. Clark; Naperville, IL: Allenson, 1973 [subsequently revised by G. Vermes, F. Miller and M. Goodman in 1987]), p. 375, Lane Fox, *Unauthorized Version*, pp. 39-40, says that since Caesarea was still under direct Roman rule, the presence of the 'Italian cohort' of Roman troops in the chief city residence of the governor would only have been incorrect during the reign of Herod Agrippa (41–44 CE), when the province returned briefly to direct rule.

71. See Hemer, *Acts*, p. 136.

72. See B.M. Levick, *Roman Colonies in Southern Asia Minor* (Oxford: Clarendon Press, 1967), p. 112; and also S. Mitchell, *Anatolia*. II. *The Rise of the Church* (Oxford: Clarendon Press, 1993), pp. 6ff.

example, Jewett[73] argues persuasively that there is evidence that the author has altered the details to accord with his own redactional ends: Luke wished to conceal the real reason for Paul's avoidance of Ephesus, which was probably continuing tension there and perhaps the hostility of the Roman authorities. He therefore chose to stress that Paul as a devout Jew was hurrying to Jerusalem for Pentecost, even though in that case the delay at Miletus is strange. The dating of the Jerusalem conference is another example of redactional modification which is impossible to reconcile with Pauline chronology. Luke wishes to show that Paul's missionary activities are all sanctioned by Jerusalem; hence his presentation.

Luke's normal practice is to select information he has about Paul's activities in any one place (such as Corinth), and then to gather it together and tell it 'in one burst'.[74] Afterwards, he refers to the place only in passing, even though some of the incidents recorded may actually have belonged to a later visit (which in the case of Corinth must have been c. 51–52 CE). Jewett estimates Paul's mission in Troas to have taken place c. 48 CE.[75] If Luke were a youth of 16 to 18 then, he would therefore have been born c. 30–32 CE. (He was clearly a grown man by the late fifties, the likely date of Philemon, if we identify him with Luke the physician.) Assuming that Luke–Acts was written c. 98–100 CE, the author would by then have been in his sixties, which does not present insuperable problems. Longevity, though uncommon, was not impossible in the ancient world: Polycarp was in his eighties when he was martyred.[76] There is no reason why Luke could not have written his final draft of Luke–Acts at 65 or so, using material he had in some cases written much earlier. It is perhaps worth observing that Acts itself bears signs of incomplete revision,[77] which

73. R. Jewett, *Dating Paul's Life* (Philadelphia: Fortress Press; London: SCM Press, 1979), pp. 15ff.

74. Thus G. Lüdemann, *Paul, Apostle to the Gentiles* (Philadelphia: Fortress Press; London: SCM Press, 1984), p. 17.

75. See Jewett, *Dating Paul*, p. 164. Other chronologies differ: using that proposed by M.D. Goulder, *A Tale of Two Missions* (London: SCM Press, 1994), pp. 190-93, Luke may have first met Paul a couple of years later than this.

76. The Anti-Marcionite Prologue, which is attached to the Gospel in a number of Latin manuscripts, records that Luke, who was a native of Antioch, died in Boeotia at the age of 84. It is conceivable that this information is at least partly accurate.

77. For example, Acts 18.19, which is meaningless in context; likewise, perhaps, Acts 3.16; 10.36-38. In addition, the function of the seven deacons, too, bears little relation to what Stephen actually does in Acts. See Strange, *Text of Acts*, pp. 176ff.

could suggest that its author's death may have interrupted the final editing of the text.

Many critics have regarded the publication of the Pauline letter collection (probably in the nineties) as a *terminus ad quem* for Luke–Acts,[78] since it is argued that it was the publication of Acts which revived interest in Paul and initiated the collection of his letters, although Luke was himself ignorant of them. I believe that the evidence in our possession suggests that such a view is mistaken, as will be argued below:[79] Luke did indeed know some, if not all, of Paul's letters, as is indicated by many items in his narrative, but since his purpose and his intended audience were different, he did not refer to them explicitly. Instead, he used them to provide a basis for much of his history of the early Church, treating them as creatively as he had done his other sources.

1.2.2. *Luke and Josephus*

Since the evidence offered by the early Fathers for dating Luke–Acts is inconclusive, some scholars have sought to determine it by an external check, the work of the historian Josephus; although whether or not Luke used Josephus is another contested issue. That Luke nowhere refers to the Jewish historian does not matter, because ancient writers rarely acknowledged their sources: Josephus himself never mentions Dionysius of Halicarnassus, even though his *Jewish Antiquities* is clearly modelled on Dionysius's *Roman Antiquities.* As far as *Jewish War* is concerned, there is some evidence that it was known to Luke: many features of his prediction of the fall of Jerusalem, which are unparalleled in the other Gospels, also occur in Josephus. It may be significant, too, that places like Nain and Emmaus, which are found only in Luke among the Gospels, are also found in Josephus.[80] Josephus had a detailed knowledge of the territory, he was an eye-witness of many of the events, and he had access to the *Commentarii* of Titus. It is intrinsically likely that Luke would have used him as a source and relied on his topographical information, even if he may have regarded some of Josephus's figures with justifiable suspicion.[81]

---

78. Thus E.J. Goodspeed, *New Solutions to New Testament Problems* (Chicago: University of Chicago Press, 1927).

79. See Chapter 2. The special problem presented by Ephesians is discussed in the *Excursus* to this chapter.

80. See *War* 4.511; 7.217.

81. The obvious example concerns 'the Egyptian': Josephus in *War* 2.261-63 refers to thirty thousand insurgents, of whom most were killed, although in *Ant.* 20.169-72 he

That Luke may well have used *Jewish War*, which was published between 75 and 79 CE, does not aid us in fixing a *terminus ad quem* for Luke–Acts, since few critics would date it any earlier than this, anyway.[82] Josephus's *Jewish Antiquities*, published in 93–94 CE, are another matter: if Luke can be shown to have used this work, then Luke–Acts cannot have been completed before it. Although M. Krenkel[83] overstated the case for the dependence of Luke on the *Jewish Antiquities*, with the unfortunate result that many critics have dismissed the evidence he offered altogether, there are nevertheless many significant points of contact between the two texts. This is apparent, for example, in Luke's treatment of the Herodian dynasty. Thus, whereas Mark at Mk 6.17 (likewise Mt. 14.3) calls Herodias the wife of Philip the tetrarch, Josephus in *Jewish Antiquities* explicitly says that Herodias was married to another half-brother of Antipas (confusingly also named Herod).[84] It was Salome, Herodias's daughter, who was married to Philip. Luke corrects Mark and Matthew at Lk. 3.19 and omits the reference to Philip, and like Josephus, he also acknowledges that this was not the only motive for the killing of the Baptist. Similarly, both Josephus and Luke refer to Felix's marriage to Drusilla,[85] and their accounts of the death of Herod Agrippa resemble one another in many respects,[86] both describing the king's gorgeous appearance and noting the blasphemy which he tacitly accepts, with dire consequences. Luke, however, omits all mention of the fateful owl, which was perhaps too magical, and prefers to substitute for Josephus's 'pains in the belly' the more scriptural 'devoured by worms'.

There are, however, significant differences between Luke and Josephus elsewhere. This is evident regarding the followers of the Egyptian: so, too, with the accounts of the rebels Judas and Theudas, where although Luke refers to the same two men in similar terms, he appears to have reversed

greatly modifies this: of four hundred men, two hundred were killed. Luke's figure of four thousand rebels is perhaps a compromise, although it has been suggested that it was a palaeographic error, with *War*'s Λ (thirty thousand) being read as Δ (four thousand).

82. For this reason, even though Luke's Parable of the Ten Pounds almost certainly contains an allusion to Archelaus, whose story was narrated by Josephus, we cannot thereby establish a date for Luke, since Josephus refers to Archelaus in both *War* 2.1-113 and *Ant.* 17.206ff.

83. M. Krenkel, *Josephus und Lukas* (Leipzig, 1894).

84. See *Ant.* 18.109.

85. See *Ant.* 20.141ff.; Acts 24.24.

86. Cf. *Ant.* 19.343-45; Acts 12.21-23.

their chronological order. It is often observed that Josephus, having described Theudas's rebellion,[87] proceeds to mention the execution of Judas's sons.[88] Luke's error here may perhaps reflect careless reading; alternatively, it may be the result of over-hasty note-taking, since we know that it was customary[89] for ancient writers to read their works aloud prior to publication and invite comment. If Luke had heard Josephus, he may have been in the same position as many a hard-pressed undergraduate, whose lecture notes cover the important points in the given order, but omit the vital connectives which relate them to one another.[90]

Luke's dependence on Josephus's *Jewish Antiquities* cannot therefore be regarded as proven, especially in view of the paucity of verbal parallels, but it still seems a strong possibility, especially if Luke–Acts were written in Rome, as will be argued below. We have no record of any other source which would have been so apposite to his purpose and which Luke could have used to provide the details the two share; this remains the most economical explanation of the connections between them.

There are also numerous verbal connections between Luke's prologue and the beginning of Josephus's *Against Apion*,[91] which was published 95–96 CE, although the difficulty here is that the vocabulary of a prologue was governed largely by convention.[92] Moreover, Luke–Acts and *Against Apion* share a common historiographical perspective,[93] and it is noticeable that they argue in the same way against pagan attacks.[94] In addition, even

87. *Ant.* 20.97-99.

88. See *Ant.* 20.102.

89. See Pliny, *Epistles* 7.17.

90. This explanation would also account for the discrepancy over Trachonitis: Josephus (*Ant.* 20.138) says it was added to Philip's tetrarchy along with Batanaea, and Luke (Lk. 3.1) says it was part of Philip's tetrarchy. The census of Quirinius is rather different. Luke is correct here about the individual responsible, but wrong about the date and the requirement to return to one's native city. (The need to explain Mary's and Joseph's presence in Bethlehem perhaps took priority here over historical accuracy.)

91. Thus παράδοσιν (*Apion* 1.53; cf. Lk. 1.2); παρακολουθέω in association with ἀκριβῶς (*Apion* 1.53; Lk. 1.3); the passive γενόμενοι together with αὐτόπτης (*Apion* 1.55; Lk. 1.2); ἄνωθεν (*Apion* 1.28; Lk. 1.3); ἐξ ἀρχῆς (*Apion* 1.30; cf. Lk. 1.2).

92. Thus I.I. du Plessis, 'Once More: The Purpose of Luke's Prologue (Lk. 1:1-4)', *NovT* 16 (1974), pp. 259-71 (261) notes that Lk. 1.1-4 is also quite close to *War* 1.1-17, especially 1.17.

93. See Sterling, *Historiography*, especially pp. 345ff.; p. 367.

94. Compare *Apion* 2.190-92 and Acts 17.24-29. The order here is similar: both begin by asserting God's sovereignty (*Apion* 2.190b; Acts 17.24a [though Luke

though Luke and Josephus.choose a Hellenistic form to present their material, they interpret it from a moralist's viewpoint in a thoroughly Jewish way, and stress God's providential care of his people and his continuing plan of salvation.[95] To sum up, from the evidence it seems more than likely that Luke used *Jewish War*, quite likely that he used *Jewish Antiquities*, and possible that he used *Against Apion*. This, too, supports a dating for Luke–Acts c. 100 CE, which has been indicated above on other grounds.

1.3. *The Place of Composition*

There remains the question of where Luke–Acts was written. In view of the many connections with works which were written at or to Rome, such as Hebrews, 1 Peter, *1 Clement*, and perhaps James, which have been noted by scholars, and the fact that Acts ends in Rome, the imperial capital must have a strong claim. If Matthew's Gospel had superseded Mark's at Rome in the nineties, as seems possible (though Mark's would presumably still have been known), both would have been available there as sources for Luke, to which he had direct access. Rome was at this time the cultural hub of the ancient world, and Luke would have encountered there the works of historians such as Josephus.

It is significant that concerns which we know occupied the Roman church, such as the question of continuing repentance, the need for unity (though without any indication of a fixed church order),[96] and perhaps also

---

develops the point concerning God's creative activity in greater detail in 17.25b, perhaps to refute Gnostic claims: Josephus ends by referring to God as Creator]); both refer next to his all-sufficiency (*Apion* 2.190c; Acts 17.25c); both follow this with some 'natural theology' (*Apion* 2.190d; Acts 17.26-27 [Luke includes a quotation at v. 28 to captivate his audience!]); both then stress the impossibility of representing God in a form made by man (*Apion* 2.191-92; Acts 17.29). See also F.G. Downing, 'Common Ground with Paganism in Luke and Josephus', *NTS* 28 (1982), pp. 546-59.

95. Both *Apion* 2.218 and Lk. 10.25 emphasize that the true purpose of the Torah is to lead to eternal life. Salvation in both texts is linked to caring for others and sharing one's possessions (cf. *Apion* 2.197; Lk. 19.9).

96. The implication of Romans 16—if it is indeed part of the Epistle to the Romans, which some have disputed—implies that there was not a single united Roman church, in the early days, but rather several smaller house churches. (Romans refers to at least three.) This may explain why there was probably no monoepiscopate there until the second century, as is suggested by J.S. Jeffers, *Conflict at Rome* (Minneapolis: Fortress Press, 1991), p. 130.

the need for fellowship and hospitality,[97] are emphasized much more strongly by Luke than by the other evangelists. Rome was almost from the first a mixed community (see Rom. 2.17; 11.3), and an inclusive Gospel such as Luke's, which, while stressing that salvation was always intended for the Gentiles, nevertheless emphasized its origin within Judaism, would have been particularly suitable for its needs.[98] Luke's 'theology of the poor', also, which reminded the rich in uncompromising terms of the requirement for active charity and help for the unfortunate, may indicate a relatively wealthy church, such as Rome, which was perhaps having to accommodate an influx of mainly Gentile poor workers or slaves from elsewhere in the Empire.

While Bauer[99] overstated the case for the efforts of Rome to extend its authority over other churches, since *1 Clement* more likely reflects Rome's concern to restore peace and harmony to a sister church which seemed in danger of going astray,[100] there is some evidence that Rome was eager to sanction 'orthodox' ideas from a relatively early date:[101] we recall that Marcion was excommunicated from the Roman church in 144 CE, and Valentinus a few years later was not elected bishop. In this context, it is significant that the old Roman Symbol, which was seemingly the first attempt to define orthodox Christian beliefs, and probably dates from the end of the second century, appears to be a summary of Luke's Gospel,[102] and Irenaeus in *Against Heresies* 3.14.2 (c. 185 CE) used Acts to counter heresy. Early tradition links Luke to Antioch, and he may indeed have lived there for some time, since Acts contains much detailed information

97. See *1 Clem.* 1.2; 10.7; 11.1; 12.1, 3; Hermas, *Mand.* 8.10 (twice); *Sim.* 9.27.2; Heb. 13.2; and 1 Pet. 4.9; and cf. Lk. 11.5-8; 14.12-14.

98. Cf. R.E. Brown and J.P. Meier, *Antioch and Rome* (Garden City, NY: Doubleday, 1983), where Brown describes the Roman church as 'containing a dominant Jewish/Gentile Christianity that had strong loyalties to Jerusalem and the Jewish tradition' (p. 204).

99. W. Bauer, *Orthodoxy and Heresy in Earliest Christianity* (Philadelphia: Fortress Press, 1971), pp. 95-129.

100. Cf. Jeffers, *Conflict*, p. 95. It may nevertheless be significant that Ignatius, *Rom.* 3.1 says that Rome 'taught others'.

101. Thus, although John's Gospel was popular in Asia Minor in the second century, it was regarded with suspicion by Rome for some time.

102. See F.J. Foakes Jackson and K. Lake, *The Beginnings of Christianity* (London: Macmillan, 1922), II, pp. 200ff., and also Kirsopp Lake, 'The Apostles' Creed', *HTR* 17 (1924), pp. 173-83. Lake believed that Rome was the likely place of origin of Luke's Gospel (Jackson and Lake, *Beginnings*, II, p. 204).

about this city even though the author was not present during Paul's stay there,[103] but if it did come from Antioch, it seems strange that Ignatius, who almost certainly knew Matthew's Gospel, was apparently unfamiliar with it.[104] On balance, not least because of the 'family resemblance' to other works such as 1 Peter, *1 Clement*, and Hebrews, it seems more probable that Luke–Acts was written in the capital, where the second volume leaves its author (Acts 28.16), although it is not unlikely that the final revision of the text of Acts was prevented by his death.

103. It was presumably because of these seemingly authentic details and later tradition that some Western manuscripts inserted a 'we' into Luke's Antioch account. Many later scholars have postulated an Antiochene source which was used at this point: this source may have been the author himself, at a later date.

104. Matthew's Gospel is probably to be located in Syria, and perhaps in Antioch. This is the conclusion of J.P. Meier, among others: see Brown and Meier, *Antioch and Rome*, pp. 22ff., especially p. 22 n. 51.

Chapter 2

THE NATURE OF LUKE'S INTENDED AUDIENCE

It has been shown above that Luke–Acts is to be placed in the tradition of ancient historiography, and its intention, in accordance with rhetorical practice, is to persuade. It is therefore necessary for us to consider the nature of the audience Luke was aiming to reach.[1]

2.1. *Romans*

Luke's is often termed the 'Gentile Gospel', and the salvation of the Gentiles[2] is 'a major theme from the first. We notice that Luke's attitude to the Gentile super-power Rome is relatively positive:[3] this is especially evident when it is contrasted with the fierce hatred of 'the Beast' or 'Babylon' which burns through Revelation. (It is also instructive in this context to compare Luke's portrayal of Paul's experiences at Roman hands as he travels in captivity to the imperial capital with those of Ignatius, as recounted in *Rom.* 5.1, although it is possible that Paul, as a Roman citizen, received different treatment.)[4] Although some Roman

1.   See Kennedy, *Rhetorical Criticism*, and also M.A. Powell, *What Is Narrative Criticism?* (Minneapolis: Augsburg–Fortress, 1990). Powell observes that since Luke–Acts reflects rhetorical techniques and its purpose is in part apologetic, its intended audience—not just its implied reader—must be considered.

2.   See, for example, Lk. 2.32, or Lk. 3.6, where only Luke extends the quotation of Isa. 40.3 (which is also used by Mark and Matthew) to Isa. 40.5: 'all flesh shall see the salvation of God'.

3   Contra critics such as Richard J. Cassidy, *Jesus, Politics and Society* (Maryknoll, NY: Orbis Books, 1978); or W. Swartley, 'Politics and Peace in Luke's Gospel', in Richard. J. Cassidy and Philip J. Scharper (eds.), *Political Issues in Luke–Acts* (Maryknoll, NY: Orbis Books, 1983), pp. 18-37.

4.   We should note that Paul's Roman citizenship is not confirmed in any of his epistles, although it seems at Acts 22.28 to be a source of pride to both Paul and his biographer, and one to which Luke expects us to respond positively. Luke may have

leaders may be corrupt, like Felix (see Acts 24.26), or cruel, like Pilate (see Lk. 13.1),[5] and many seem prepared to sacrifice justice to expediency, as does Festus in Acts 25.9 and perhaps Gallio in Acts 18.17, ordinary Romans such as the centurions Cornelius and Julius in Acts are treated with marked favour, and Roman law is afforded respect and approval:

οὐκ ἔστιν ἔθος Ῥωμαίοις χαρίζεσθαί τινα ἄνθρωπον πρὶν ἢ ὁ κατηγορούμενος κατὰ πρόσωπον ἔχοι τοὺς κατηγόρους τόπον τε ἀπολογίας λάβοι περὶ τοῦ ἐγκλήματος (Acts 25.16).

Christians can, in the main, have confidence in it, though not necessarily in individual Romans. Roman power and Roman law rescue Paul on several occasions,[6] even though Felix and Festus, like Pilate before them, eventually give way to Jewish pressure, and this necessitates Paul's appeal to Caesar.

The Romans are anxious, in Luke–Acts, to behave correctly to those subject to them; thus Jesus is sent to Herod because he is a Galilaean and hence under Herod's jurisdiction. Paul's declaration of his citizenship meets an immediate response and he is treated thereafter with scrupulous fairness. (The only time he is flogged, which was an illegal punishment for a Roman citizen before trial, is a mistake for which an immediate apology is made.)[7] The Romans are quite capable of recognizing innocence and detecting false information laid by malice, as is evident in both Luke and Acts, even if they will not always act to uphold justice when it does not serve their interests to do so. It is not surprising, therefore, that in Luke's presentation it is Herod's soldiers, not Pilate's, who mock Jesus. Indeed, Luke modifies the Passion narrative at Lk. 23.25 to exculpate the Romans and further incriminate the Jews, so that it seems that they themselves crucify Christ. Similarly, at the end of Acts there is no mention of the fact

had access to information not available to us on this point, if he was associated with the Pauline mission, or he may have inferred it from Paul's presence in the imperial capital; but it is also possible that it is a plot device to provide an explanation for Paul's journey to Rome, since ancient historians were expected to provide credible motivation for actions. Critics such as Klaus Wengst, *Pax Romana* (trans. J. Bowden; London: SCM Press, 1987), p. 102, have therefore expressed doubt whether there is any truth in Luke's claim that Paul was a Roman citizen, although others such as Tajra, *Trial of Paul*, think it probable (pp. 86ff.).

5.   We have no confirmation of this atrocity in any contemporary source, even one as consistently anti-Pilate as Josephus.

6.   See for instance Acts 18.15; 19.37-41; 21.35; 23.16-31.

7.   See Acts 16.39.

that the Emperor to whom Paul has appealed is none other than Nero. Luke closes with the statement that Paul lives for two years in Rome, teaching and preaching 'quite openly and unhindered'.[8]

Christians are implicitly encouraged not to seek confrontation with the Roman authorities: Luke does not wish to stimulate resistance to Roman power of the sort that had proved so disastrous to the Jews in the recent revolt. In this sense, his is an anti-revolutionary document. We notice that he is careful not to highlight any execution which takes place as a result of Roman activity. Thus he emphasizes the (relative) innocence of the Roman authorities regarding Jesus' death, despite the political nature of the punishment; and similarly Paul's and Peter's martyrdoms are never mentioned.

Many critics[9] have assumed that Luke's purpose was, in part, to convince Rome that Christians were politically harmless, as should have been evident all along: any trouble was to be attributed to the Jews, who were dangerous troublemakers, as the recent revolt had demonstrated. Luke is therefore careful to use the argument that it is necessary to obey God rather than men—which is far from reassuring, politically—only when the audience addressed is a Jewish one (see Acts 5.29). He does not wish to suggest that Christianity could pose any danger to the state.[10]

We should not conclude, however, that Rome and its representatives are idealized by Luke. He does not have any naïve, romantic view of political power. Thus, in Acts 4.27, Pilate is blamed for conspiring in the murder of Christ. He and Herod are linked together in an unholy alliance, as is intimated earlier at Lk. 23.12. In this context, the reference to benefactors (εὐεργέται)[11] at Lk. 22.25 may indeed be sarcastic, as Cassidy suggests.[12]

---

8.   The speech at Miletus has nevertheless made it plain that Paul is going to die: see especially Acts 20.24-25.

9.   For example, H.J. Cadbury, *The Making of Luke–Acts* (London: Macmillan, rev. edn, 1958); Hans Conzelmann, *The Theology of St Luke* (London: SCM Press, 1960).

10.   Thus Luke mutes the apocalyptic of Mark and Matthew, which could have undesired political implications: see Esler, *Community and Gospel*, pp. 58ff. Luke prefers to stress the pastoral aspect of πειρασμός, the need to remain firm in the faith and resist apostasy. In addition, unlike the author of Revelation, he plays down the kingship motif; it is only in a non-political, heavenly sense (Lk. 19.38) that Jesus comes as king. His messiahship, too, is consistently linked to suffering by Luke; Jesus is a suffering messiah, not a victorious Davidic one.

11.   See Frederick W. Danker, *Jesus and the New Age* (Philadelphia: Fortress Press, 2nd edn, 1988); *idem*, 'The Endangered Benefactor in Luke–Acts', in K.H. Richards (ed.), *SBLSP*, 20 (Chico, CA: Scholars Press, 1981), pp. 39-48.

Luke's attitude to Roman authority is less enthusiastic than that found in Romans, or the Pastoral Epistles, or 1 Peter, or *1 Clement*.[13]

For these reasons, Walaskay's[14] suggestion that Luke is here mounting a defence of Rome to Christianity is not wholly satisfactory. The same is true of the once widely held assumption that Luke is offering an *apologia* for Christianity to Rome.[15] (This proposal is open to the further objection that few Romans who were not already Christians would have been likely to read either volume.)[16] Both interpretations may nevertheless contain elements of truth: Luke strives to present both Christianity and Roman power in a positive way, and to stress that the two are not incompatible.[17] Thus, even while it seems clear that Luke–Acts is primarily aimed at 'insiders'[18] rather than at pagans, of the four canonical Gospels it is the one most evidently adaptable to missionary purposes.[19] We notice how careful Luke is to conform his narrative to the practices of contemporary

12. Cassidy, *Jesus.* Contra Wengst, *Pax Romana*, p.103, and Esler, *Community and Gospel*, p. 208, whatever may be the normal connotation of this word in the context of the relationship between Hellenistic rulers and their subjects, the use of καλοῦνται after it casts some doubt on whether Luke intends it to be taken thus here.

13. See Rom. 13.1-7; 1 Tim. 2.1-2, 6.1; Tit. 2.9, 3.1; 1 Pet. 2.13-17; *1 Clem.* 61.1-4, especially 61.1.

14. Paul W. Walaskay, *And So We Came to Rome* (SNTSMS, 49; Cambridge: Cambridge University Press, 1983).

15. This is especially true of the later chapters of Acts, which defend Paul, not Christianity; although the converse is also true, in that if Luke–Acts were intended as a defence brief for Paul, as some have suggested (for example, A.J. Mattill, 'The Purpose of Acts: Schneckenburger Reconsidered', in W. Ward Gasque and Ralph P. Martin (eds.), *The Apostolic History and the Gospel* [Exeter: Paternoster Press, 1970], pp. 108-22), then what about the whole of Luke's Gospel?

16. Similarly Barrett, *Luke the Historian*, p. 63.

17. Similarly Esler, *Community and Gospel*, p. 218. Esler sees it as 'legitimation' aimed at other Christians rather than 'apologetic' aimed at Rome. (Cf. the view of Sterling, *Historiography*.)

18. Esler, *Community and Gospel*, says, 'He often alludes to the Greek Old Testament in a way which would have been opaque, even unintelligible, to someone unfamiliar with its language and contents' (p. 25). The Septuagint itself would probably not have been an accessible resource to Gentiles who were not in any case used to frequent the synagogue; see Arthur Darby Nock, *Conversion: The Old and the New in Religion from Alexander the Great to Augustine of Hippo* (Oxford: Oxford University Press, 1933), p. 79.

19. O'Neill, *Theology of Acts*, pp. 177ff., regards Luke's intention as primarily evangelical.

historiography and to relate it to events in the world outside Judaea.[20] The events described were not 'done in a corner' (Acts 26.26), as Luke intends us to appreciate, and they are relevant to all since they concern our salvation:

ὃ ἡτοίμασας κατὰ πρόσωπον πάντων τῶν λαῶν,
φῶς εἰς ἀποκάλυψιν ἐθνῶν
καὶ δόξαν λαοῦ σου Ἰσραήλ (Lk. 2.31-32).

In this respect, the Theophilus of Luke's Prologue may be a symbolic figure, who represents any well-disposed 'lover of God'.[21] Luke, who is sensitive to the meaning of names (see Acts 4.36; 9.36; 13.8) would thus have chosen this one quite deliberately. His Gospel is inclusive, as is evident from his redaction of Mk 4.21/Mt. 5.15 at Lk. 11.33, and he does not want to shut anyone out.

Luke–Acts therefore has a double function, as Luke Johnson[22] observes, in that it provides a theodicy which shows that God first fulfilled the promises to Israel and then to the Gentiles. The significance of Rome should not be undervalued, but it is symbolic rather than 'apologetic', and this may be related to the wider question of the prestige and authority of the Roman church, especially if, as was argued above, Luke–Acts were itself written in Rome. The imperial capital is where the Church, as represented by Paul, realizes that its true role lies outside Judaism, so that it is able to become a world religion in its own right. Although there is a Christian presence in Rome already, as has been made clear in Acts 18.2, it is still rooted within Judaism: Paul takes the gospel to the Gentiles in the capital of the Gentile world. This is the significance of Paul's arrival in Rome, and it is also why Luke ends his story at this point.

20. See, e.g., Lk. 2.1-2; or 3.1-2.

21. This is also the conclusion of Susan R. Garrett, *The Demise of the Devil: Magic and the Demonic in Luke's Writings* (Minneapolis: Augsburg–Fortress, 1989), p. 115 n. 15: 'By addressing the discourse to "Theophilus"—i.e. to an eminent individual who has been instructed about Christianity and yet needs "assurance"—Luke implicitly casts all of his readers into this role'. At least one of Horace's *Epistles* (1.6) and some of his *Odes* (for example, 1.22) were probably written to fictional addressees, as their names suggest; it is therefore not impossible that Luke, too, might have invented one.

22. Luke T. Johnson, *Sharing Possessions* (Philadelphia: Fortress Press, 1981), pp. 204-205.

2.2. *Jews and God-fearers*

It must be emphasized that, although in the main the Jews reject the gospel, many 'myriads'[23] accept it, especially in the early days, and throughout Acts it is stressed that usually some respond. This is true even in Rome; note the imperfect tense of the verb πείθω at Acts 28.24. Conversely, although many Gentiles are converted, most are not—as Athens recalls— and some are actively hostile, as at Lystra, Philippi, and Ephesus. Paul, as presented by Luke, is not just the 'Apostle to the Gentiles': his message is wider and more universalistic in its appeal, and he consistently preaches to the Jews first.[24]

2.2.1. *God-fearers*

Christians nevertheless remain a very small minority everywhere, and the Gentiles who accept the gospel in Luke–Acts are usually idealized like the centurion of Luke 7, who has built a synagogue for the Jews, or his counterpart in Acts, Cornelius, who gives alms so liberally. (There is also the hospitable Lydia of Philippi; as usual, Luke wishes to give a female example, too.) Pagan idolaters such as the inhabitants of Lystra are regarded with abhorrence (see Acts 14.14) and anger (Acts 17.16).[25] The converts to Christianity whom Luke depicts normally revere the Lord: most are 'God-fearers',[26] who worship in the synagogue like the Jews.[27]

---

23. See Michael J. Cook, 'The Mission to the Jews in Acts: Unraveling Luke's "Myth of the Myriads"', in Joseph B. Tyson (ed.), *Luke–Acts and the Jewish People* (Minneapolis: Augsburg–Fortress, 1988), pp. 102-23.

24. Cf. Rom. 1.16; 2.10 etc.

25. See Jacob Jervell: 'The Church of Jews and God-fearers', in Joseph B. Tyson (ed.), *Luke–Acts and the Jewish People*, pp. 11-20. Jervell, however, overstates the case when he says, 'For "pure" Gentiles—pagans—the Church is not open' (p. 12). What of the jailer at Philippi, or Dionysius the Areopagite, or Sergius Paulus in Cyprus? (See also Acts 14.20; 17.34.)

26. Contra A.T. Kraabel, 'The Disappearance of the "God-fearers"', *Numen* 28 (1981), pp. 113-26, who maintains that there is no archaeological evidence of God-fearers in Diaspora synagogues, their existence is confirmed by Josephus in *Apion* 2.282; *War* 2.461-63; 7.45; *Ant.* 14.110, and supported by the archaeological evidence of an inscription from a synagogue in Akmonia, as Esler, *Community and Gospel*, pp. 36ff. and M.J. Cook, *Mission*, p. 120 n. 64 both note. See also the analysis by Gerd Lüdemann, *Earliest Christianity According to the Traditions in Acts* (London: SCM Press, 1989), pp. 155-56.

27. See, e.g., Acts 13.5; 14.1; 16.13-14; 17.2, 10, 17; 18.4. Luke's portrayal is

(We notice that Titius Justus, one of these non-Jewish worshippers of God, symbolically lives next door to the synagogue: such people are regarded by Luke as near-Jews, who share Jewish beliefs. The only difference is that unlike the proselytes whom Luke mentions at Acts 2.10; 6.5; 13.43, they have not undergone the ritual obligation of circumcision.)

The God-fearers often seem to have been relatively influential and wealthy, like Lydia in Acts or the centurion of Luke 7; the evangelist does not wish to give the impression that Christianity only attracted low-born riff-raff. One assumes that most were not anti-Roman, and therefore they would not have been sympathetic to attacks on a political system they presumably accepted and perhaps valued: in this context we have seen how careful Luke is not to criticize Roman law. God-fearers also obviously had a knowledge of Judaism, so that they were able to appreciate 'prophecy/fulfilment' arguments which presupposed a familiarity with Jewish Scriptures.[28]

God-fearers perform a symbolic, transitional function in Luke–Acts, as many critics[29] have noted. There is a progression from the Jews to what Sanders [30] calls 'the periphery'. In the gospel, this is represented by 'outcasts' like the tax-collectors and sinners, who are nevertheless still Jews, since in Luke's presentation the time of the Gentiles is after the resurrection. In Acts the gospel is given first to the Palestinian Jews (represented by the disciples gathered in Jerusalem at the beginning),[31] then at Pentecost to the Diaspora Jews in Acts 2.5-41, and also to the proselytes (though these are clearly of a lower status as converts, as is shown by the order in which they are placed in relation to the Jews in Acts 2.10 and 6.5), and then to the God-fearers before being offered to the Gentiles. The Ethiopian eunuch of Acts 8.25-39, who worships in the Temple, is the first of these God-fearers, and his conversion takes place—appropriately—on the road from Judaea to the Gentile Gaza: Luke uses symbolic geography

---

clearly an idealized one, since in Acts 17 the converts in Thessalonica are Jews and God-fearers, whereas in 1 Thessalonians (1 Thess. 1.9) they are idolaters.

28. This is evident in the conversions of both the Ethiopian eunuch (see Acts 8.32-35) and Cornelius (especially Acts 10.42-43) but it is also the case with Paul's speeches; see, e.g., Acts 13.47; 17.2-4, 11; 18.4-5. We notice that when Paul's audience is Gentile, as at Athens, proof-texts and Old Testament allusions are avoided and scriptural references concern the Creator of all rather than Jesus.

29. E.g. *Mission*, p. 120 n. 66.

30. Jack T. Sanders, *The Jews in Luke–Acts* (Philadelphia: Fortress Press; London: SCM Press, 1987), pp. 132ff.

31. Hence the significance of Lk. 24.47-53.

to structure Acts as well as his Gospel. God-fearers and the like are 'accept-able'[32] to God, says Luke, and God draws no distinction between those who act rightly,[33] whatever their origin, and Jews—which effectively sabotages the whole notion of Jewish election.

Esler[34] argues that Luke's was a mixed community of Jews and Gentiles, and that he is attempting to legitimate table-fellowship between these two groups, thus providing security (ἀσφάλειαν, Lk. 1.4) for both by retro-jecting a current dispute and showing that it had been decisively settled in apostolic times. The Cornelius episode, which bears on the issue of table-fellowship, is accordingly given much greater emphasis than the conver-sion of the Ethiopian eunuch, the real beginning of the Gentile mission.[35] Esler suggests that the Apostolic Decree of Acts 15 may thus represent a compromise agreement reached by Luke's community;[36] Luke is here reacting to a current church problem and offering pastoral guidance.

The God-fearers, who embody a compromise between Judaism and the Gentile world, are therefore of great importance. Cadbury observes: 'The Acts has so much to say about the 'God-fearers' or Gentiles who, without becoming full proselytes, had attached themselves to Judaism that some have naturally conjectured that the author himself followed this path out of paganism to Christianity'.[37]

In this context, it may be worth noting that when Peter at Acts 15.10 calls the Torah ζυγὸν[38] he concentrates on its oppressive weight; this is

32. δεκτός at Acts 10.35 is a word with cultic connotations, and its usage is deliberate

33. Cf. Rom. 2.10.

34. Esler, *Community and Gospel*, especially pp. 93ff.

35. The eunuch may, however, have been a proselyte, although we are not told so explicitly, since he worships in Jerusalem (Acts 8.27), in which case he would have been reckoned as technically a Jew.

36. Luke T. Johnson, 'On Finding the Lukan Community: A Cautious Cautionary Essay', in P.J. Achtemeier (ed.), *SBLSP*, 18 (Missoula, MT: Scholars Press, 1979), I, pp. 87-100, regards it as unproven that a specific Lukan community existed, and warns of the dangers of the 'mirror method'. The attempts of both Esler and Karris (Robert J. Karris, 'Missionary Communities', *CBQ* 41 [1979], pp. 80-97) to determine the precise nature of the Lukan community present us with a whole society in microcosm, since it apparently included Jews, Gentiles, proselytes, God-fearers, rich, poor, slaves, free-men, Romans, civilians and soldiers. It is difficult to see how such a broad spectrum helps our understanding.

37. Cadbury, *Making of Luke–Acts*, p. 272.

38. The 'yoke of the Torah' did not in itself have a negative connotation, but the

not, perhaps, how the ritual obligations therein laid down would have seemed to most Jews, who regarded the Torah as a God-given privilege. There is also evidence in Luke–Acts which could suggest Luke's ignorance of some Jewish customs: for example, only the women were purified after childbirth, not both partners, as at Lk. 2.22;[39] and he is mistaken about some of the details[40] attaching to a Nazirite vow, such as that undertaken by Paul in Acts 21.26-27, although to those unfamiliar with Jewish practices his account serves to present Paul, the ex-Pharisee, as both orthodox and Torah-observant, which was clearly Luke's intention. Even though neither of these items is particularly significant in itself, and may be attributable to an occasional looseness of style, taken together they offer support to the contention that Luke is writing from a Gentile perspective. Although in many cases the attitude to ritual minutiae seems to have been less rigid in the Diaspora than in Judaea (especially, one supposes, after the destruction of the Temple), mistakes of this type are probably less likely to have been made by one who was born a Jew.

2.2.2. *Jews*

The question of whether Luke was himself a Gentile rather than a (Diaspora) Jew is important, even if ultimately we can only hypothesize about it, since it may affect how we interpret his comments about the Jews. Thus D.L. Tiede[41] and Marilyn Salmon[42] observe that if Luke is writing as an 'insider', as both believe is the case, then his criticisms can be seen to belong to the prophetic tradition of fierce censure of the 'chosen people' for their obduracy, greed, luxury, wealth, lack of compassion, and so on which we find, for example, in Isaiah and Amos. Such statements are only to be interpreted as anti-Jewish if they are written by a non-Jew,[43] and this

image could nevertheless carry negative associations (especially, one supposes, to non-Jews).

39. Luke *adds* αὐτῶν to his citation of Lev. 12.6.

40. The time required for purification was at least three weeks, not one week.

41. David L. Tiede, *Prophecy and History in Luke–Acts* (Philadelphia: Fortress Press, 1980); *idem*, 'Glory to thy People, Israel', in Joseph B. Tyson (ed.), *Luke–Acts and the Jewish People* (Minneapolis: Augsburg–Fortress, 1988), pp. 21-34. 'Normative Judaism' is a later conception; in the first century it was thoroughly diverse, and may have included views as hostile to Jewish exclusivity as Luke's.

42. Marilyn Salmon, 'Insider or Outsider? Luke's Relationship with Judaism', in Joseph B. Tyson (ed.), *Luke–Acts and the Jewish People* (Minneapolis: Augsburg–Fortress, 1988), pp. 76-82.

43. We notice that only Jews such as Jesus, Peter, Stephen and Paul berate the Jews

raises the further question whether anyone as steeped in the Old Testament as Luke clearly was might not have thought of himself as a Jew, even if he was in actuality a proselyte or God-fearing Gentile. How we answer these questions will influence whether we see Luke's treatment of the Jewish rejection of Christ as savage and vindictive[44] or as profoundly tragic.[45] In this context, it is worth noting that whereas in Matthew's Passion narrative the Jews shout the terrible cry: τὸ αἷμα αὐτοῦ ἐφ᾽ ἡμᾶς καὶ ἐπὶ τὰ τέκνα ἡμῶν (Mt. 27.25) in Luke's they beat their breasts.

Luke's attitude to the Jewish people is complex: indeed, many would maintain that it is fundamentally inconsistent,[46] as he struggles to provide a theodicy which takes account of the fact that God's chosen people, to whom the Old Testament promises had been given, have nevertheless rejected their Messiah and his proffered salvation. Thus, while it is possible that the presentation of the Jews as the 'villains' of his narrative was to some extent thrust upon Luke as a consequence of his desire to emphasize that the Christians are politically harmless and the Romans basically fair-minded,[47] it is equally possible that it was, rather, the guilt of the Jews, as Luke saw it, which led him to portray the Romans as relatively innocent; they are two sides of the same coin. In either case, the Jews served to provide a scapegoat to account for the deaths of Jesus and early followers such as Stephen and James, and, indeed, the sufferings of later ones such as Paul. And since by the end of the first century localized and sporadic

directly in Luke–Acts, although the narrator's presentation of their frequent and murderous attacks on Paul constitutes a sustained, though implicit, polemic against them.

44. Thus, J.T. Sanders, *Jews*; *idem*, 'The Jewish People in Luke–Acts', in Joseph B. Tyson (ed.), *Luke–Acts and the Jewish People* (Minneapolis: Augsburg–Fortress, 1988), pp. 51-75. We may also compare the views of Ernst Haenchen, *The Acts of the Apostles* (trans. Bernard Noble; Philadelphia: Westminster Press, 1971).

45. Thus Robert C. Tannehill, *The Narrative Unity of Luke–Acts*, II (Minneapolis: Augsburg–Fortress, 1990); 'Rejection by Jews and Turning to Gentiles: The Pattern of Paul's Mission to Acts', in Joseph B. Tyson (ed.), *Luke–Acts and the Jewish People* (Minneapolis: Augsburg–Fortress, 1988), pp. 83-101.

46. Thus, Joseph B. Tyson, 'The Problem of Jewish Rejection in Acts', in Joseph B. Tyson (ed.), *Luke–Acts and the Jewish People* (Minneapolis: Augsburg–Fortress, 1988), pp. 124-37 (137) calls it 'ambivalent'.

47. We may compare the treatment of Josephus. Sterling, *Historiography*, p. 393, sees Josephus's apologetic with regard to non-Jews as directed primarily at Greeks, as Josephus himself says (see, for example, *Ant.* 16.174). But Josephus's message that outsiders should respect the antiquity and previous rights of the Jews is surely aimed at persuading Romans.

persecution of Christians was taking place, with action against them maybe resulting, in many cases, from information laid by Jewish informers,[48] this may well reflect the later situation and contemporary Christian reaction to it.

Luke nevertheless differentiates between individual Jews, like Paul and Barnabas, 'myriads' of whom respond in the early days (and of those who do not, some are still well-disposed, like Gamaliel or the devout Jews who bury Stephen), and 'the Jews' considered as a collective entity, who murder the prophets, Jesus, Stephen, and James, and repeatedly attempt to destroy Paul and his mission. Luke does not simply distinguish between the ordinary Jewish people and their leaders, however, although this is the impression one could draw from his Gospel; in two speeches in Acts[49] they are joined together in both responsibility and exoneration.[50] As Luke presents them, the Jews are at once sympathetic (Lk. 23.27), so that they may be exonerated *if* they repent, and also threateningly volatile, all alike calling for Jesus' execution at 23.18, so that they are nevertheless culpable. Luke does not intend us to infer that Jesus' death was not their fault.

2.2.3. *Luke's Treatment of the Pharisees*
Like the other evangelists, Luke is very much opposed to specific groups within Judaism such as the Sadducees, the Scribes, the Lawyers, and the Pharisees. We should note, however, that there seems to be some inconsistency in his treatment of the Pharisees, although much of the evidence is equivocal and susceptible of differing interpretations. Thus, while some would see their words at Lk. 13.31 as displaying a disinterested desire to save Jesus' life, it is more likely that the Pharisees are in league with Herod here since this is how Jesus himself interprets their behaviour at 13.32, and his is a supremely authoritative viewpoint.[51] Similarly, some have regarded the Pharisees' frequent invitations of Jesus to dinner as a further example of a more positive treatment by the evangelist, but in this context Darr[52]

---

48. A summary of the evidence for this suggestion, which is persuasive but not conclusive, is offered by Karris, 'Missionary Communities', p. 86.

49. See Acts 3.17; 13.27.

50. Thus J.L. Houlden, 'The Purpose of Luke', *JSNT* 21 (1984), pp. 53-65.

51. Similarly Luke T. Johnson, *The Gospel of Luke* (Sacra Pagina; Collegeville, MN: Liturgical Press, 1991), pp. 220ff., contra Sanders, *Jews*, p. 86. Moreover, Luke stresses that Jesus can perceive the thoughts of people at 6.8; 9.47.

52. Darr, *Character Building*, pp. 151ff. We may also compare John T. Carroll, 'Luke's Portrayal of the Pharisees', *CBQ* 50 (1988), pp. 604-21.

has argued convincingly that the *symposium* framework of the shared meals is significant. An ancient reader would respond to such a context by identifying Jesus with the virtuous philosopher/sage and the Pharisees (whom Jesus, appropriately, boldly opposed) as, by implication, wicked. In both these cases, Luke's presentation can therefore be seen as straightforwardly hostile.

It is nevertheless noticeable that Luke keeps the Pharisees out of his Passion altogether, unlike all the other evangelists (see Mk 12.13; Mt. 21.45; 22.15–23.39; Jn 18.3). If his intention is to vilify them as much as possible, it seems strange that he has missed an opportunity here. The real difficulty for this interpretation, however, is posed by the narrative of Acts, where the Pharisees are consistently presented as far less inimical to the Christians than are the other Jewish groups. In Luke's second volume Gamaliel, a leading Pharisee, successfully resists an attempt by the Sanhedrin to execute Peter and John; and Paul is able to enlist the Pharisees' support, after he has given an account of the circumstances of his conversion. Some of them even become Christians, as Luke tells us at Acts 15.5. One therefore infers that they are more open-minded and receptive to the gospel message than are the Sadducees, none of whom is reported as being converted.

Carroll[53] argues that Luke uses the Pharisees to legitimate Christianity and hence implicitly to mollify Jewish Christian anxiety that the Torah was being disregarded. His argument, which would explain why the Pharisees in Acts receive a treatment which differs from that in Luke's Gospel, is plausible. The result, however, is that there are unresolved tensions in Luke's presentation.[54]

To some aspects of Pharisaism—namely, its exclusivity, and its concern with what Luke seems to have regarded as trivial and unnecessary details[55] —Luke is nevertheless consistently hostile. Indeed, Sanders points out that Luke has introduced five instances of Pharisaic opposition of this type which are not in Mark or Matthew.[56] Luke rejects outright any narrowly

53. Carroll, 'Pharisees', p. 616.

54. Similarly J.A. Ziesler, 'Luke and the Pharisees', *NTS* 25 (1978), pp. 146-57, though Darr, *Character Building*, points out in Chapter 4 that we read Acts with our conception of the Pharisees already formed by their behaviour in Luke's Gospel.

55. Thus he omits Mk 12.28/Mt. 22.36, since he is not concerned with making a Rabbinic point concerning which is the Torah's greatest commandment, but with its salvific force (cf. Lk. 10.25).

56. Sanders, *Jews*, p. 89, cites Lk. 5.21; 11.53; the introduction to the parables in Ch.15; 16.14; and 19.39.

nationalistic interpretation of God's salvation, as is evident from the pro-grammatic 'Nazareth Manifesto' of Lk. 4.18-27. This is not what Israel's glory involves at all: to see the promises to Israel in these terms is to misunderstand them, as does Zechariah in Ch. 1, and Jesus corrects such an interpretation both in Luke 4 and at Acts 1.6, where we notice that he avoids the question of when 'the Kingdom' will be restored *to Israel*. The consolation (παράκλησις) of Lk. 2.25 is to be extended to others, too; at Acts 10.34-35, indeed, Luke strikes at the very basis of Judaism, since the implication is that God's people are now chosen not according to their race but their conduct. And the Law cannot save, as is evident from the Lukan Parable of the Pharisee and the Tax-Collector (Lk. 18.9-14); salva-tion is through faith in Jesus.[57]

2.2.4. *Luke's Attitude to the Cult*
Particularly bitter, and here again he is following the prophetic tradition,[58] is Luke's denunciation of the Jewish Cult, which in some senses encapsu-lated Jewish exclusivity at its most unacceptable, since not just non-Jews but also any who were physically imperfect, such as the blind, deaf, lame, and eunuchs, and also all women and children, were forbidden to partici-pate in sacrificial worship. It is significant that the adjective χειροποίητος, which has strong connotations of idolatry when used in the Septuagint, and which is used of the Temple by Jesus in Mk 14.58 (although Luke, like Matthew, omits it at this point), is also used by Stephen in this same context at Acts 7.48, in a fierce and thoroughly prophetic indictment. It is also used by Paul at Acts 17.24, and just as God initiates the Gentile mission through Philip and Peter, he seems to be driving the Christians out of the Temple,[59] since it is when he is praying in the Temple that Paul is sent by God to the Gentiles (Acts 22.17-21) and it is in the Temple that he is arrested. The Temple is certainly not a 'house of prayer for all nations' in Luke–Acts; when Luke drops the πασιν τοῖς ἔθνεσιν of Mk 11.17 this may not simply be because the Temple had been destroyed by the time Luke wrote.

And yet the Temple is also the heart of Jewish worship, and as such it is venerated by the leading characters of Luke–Acts, all of whom are devout and Torah-observant Jews. It is of crucial importance for the revelation of God's purpose in the birth narrative; Jesus never criticizes it in any way;

57. See, e.g., Lk. 1.69-79; 2.11, 30-32.
58. See, e.g., Amos 5.21-23 or Isa. 1.11.
59. This point is made by O'Neill, *Theology of Acts*, p. 81.

the early followers of the Risen Lord visit it daily to bless God (Lk. 24.53). And because it is part of Luke's purpose to show how Christianity evolved out of Judaism and is its fulfilment, in many respects the picture has to be a positive one. Thus Luke goes out of his way to show us Judaism at its best in figures like Zechariah, Simeon and Anna. They are not merely foils, as Kingsbury[60] suggests, nor are they intended (obliquely) to recommend later organized Christian worship. The Jews who recognize Christ are, as Luke takes care to stress, sincere and devout. Christianity to Luke is what Judaism is aiming at; the best Jews are Christians[61] and it is the Jews themselves who fail to keep the Law at Acts 7.53. Luke's hostility to the 'circumcision party' of Judaea, however, and perhaps to the Christian Pharisees of Acts 15.5 (who are maybe to be numbered among them), who wish to impose all the ritual obligations of Judaism on converted Gentiles in Acts 11.2; 15.1-2, is unwavering.[62]

The theme of prophecy/fulfilment structures the whole of Luke–Acts, and Luke's favourite verb δεῖ[63] hammers home the point that all is happening according to God's plan. Salvation, Luke would agree with John, is 'from the Jews',[64] and Luke is careful to emphasize the continuity between Christianity and Judaism not in order to secure acceptance of Christianity by Rome as a *religio licita*, a category which did not in fact exist,[65] but to show that Christians are the true heirs to the promises which the Jews have anticipated so eagerly and yet which, with tragic irony, they now reject.[66] The irony is not solely because there is a tension between Israel's expectation—a glorious victory over her oppressors—and the reality, that of her suffering, which will paradoxically achieve her salvation, as Moessner[67]

60. J.D. Kingsbury, *Conflict in Luke* (Minneapolis: Fortress Press, 1991), p. 24.

61. Thus Cook, 'Mission', pp. 110ff.

62. Thus Sanders, *Jews*, pp. 110ff. Cf. Gal. 2.12.

63. See C.H. Cosgrove, 'The divine "δεῖ" in Luke–Acts', *NovT* 26 (1984), pp. 168-90.

64. Jn 4.22.

65. See Esler, *Community and Gospel*, pp. 211ff., and R. Maddox, *The Purpose of Luke–Acts* (FRLANT, 126; Göttingen: Vanderhoeck & Ruprecht, 1982; Edinburgh: T. & T. Clark, 1985), pp. 91-93, contra Jackson and Lake (eds.), *Beginnings*, II, pp. 177-78, and also Burton Scott Easton, *Earliest Christianity: The Purpose of Acts* (revised by F.C. Grant; New York: Seabury, rev. edn, 1954), pp. 41-57. Ernst Haenchen in his 1971 commentary (Haenchen, E., *Acts*) also inclines to the same mistaken idea.

66. Thus Tannehill, 'Rejection', pp. 83-101.

67. David P. Moessner, 'The Ironic Fulfilment of Israel's Glory', in Joseph B.

proposes. 'The Jews' are, as they have always been, wilfully ignorant of the purposes of God, rejecting God's offer of salvation and persecuting those who mediate this message. There is a powerful ironic contrast, as Tannehill[68] notes, between the willingness of the Gentiles to hear and the deafness of the Jews: all flesh does not see the salvation of God (Lk. 3.6) because they choose to shut their eyes to it. As far as the Jews are concerned, Luke–Acts 28.26-27 ends on a deeply tragic note, in the bitter words of Isaiah 6.9-10:

ἀκοῇ ἀκούσετε καὶ οὐ μὴ συνῆτε
καὶ βλέποντες βλέψετε καὶ οὐ μὴ ἴδητε
ἐπαχύνθη γὰρ ἡ καρδία τοῦ λαοῦ τούτου
καὶ τοῖς ὠσίν βαρέως ἤκουσαν
καὶ τοὺς ὀφθαλμοὺς αὐτῶν ἐκάμμυσαν·
μήποτε ἴδωσιν τοῖς ὀφθαλμοῖς
καὶ τοῖς ὠσίν ἀκούσωσιν
καὶ τῇ καρδίᾳ συνῶσιν καὶ ἐπιστρέψωσιν,
καὶ ἰάσομαι αὐτούς.

Though individual Jews may still repent and believe in the gospel, Acts 28.28 has an air of finality. It is presumably mainly the Gentiles who come to Paul in Acts 28.30, and to whom he preaches the Kingdom of God and teaches about the Lord Jesus Christ. Luke's story closes with them, and thereafter, the future of the Church lies with the Gentiles.

2.3. *Christians*

There remains the probability that Luke's intended audience is a Christian one.[69] Luke's concerns are frequently pastoral ones; for example, he wishes to reassure Christians that even suffering is part of God's plan, and thus in Luke–Acts, both Jesus and Stephen die perfect martyrs' deaths.[70] As we have seen, too, his polemic is strong against those Christians who would compel Gentile converts to become Jews first,[71] although it seems

Tyson (ed.), *Luke–Acts and the Jewish People* (Minneapolis: Augsburg–Fortress, 1988), pp. 35-50.

68. Tannehill, *Narrative Unity*, II, p. 348.

69. The verb κατηχέω may imply that Theophilus, if he existed at all, had received instruction in the Christian faith.

70. We may compare 1 Peter, where there is a similar use of Christ as an example of innocent suffering which is intended to serve as a model for believers.

71. See, for example, Acts 15.1, 5; and also 21.20-27, where the consequence of the attempt to placate them is the capture of Paul.

to be the consequence of their beliefs for other Christians to which Luke objects, not the beliefs themselves. Likewise, Paul's speech at Miletus is less concerned with the difficulties Christians were experiencing from 'outsiders', be they Jew or Roman, than with pressure from those inside[72] the community who weaken it by their heretical ideas[73] and tear it apart.

Luke is in part aiming to give 'security' and 'confidence' by presenting the past apostolic age in ideal terms: it is unified and untroubled by false ideas or schism. Even though we can occasionally infer from the text that all was not as rosy as it seemed, Luke is anxious to emphasize that any disputes, such as that between the Hellenists and the Hebrews in Acts 6, are quickly resolved.[74] The Gentile mission in Acts is therefore begun by Philip and Peter, and it is sanctioned—as are all Paul's activities—by the irreproachably orthodox James. This serves both to legitimate the mission and to defend Paul against any charge of antinomianism;[75] the only direct criticisms of the Law in Acts are made by Peter and James, at Acts 15.10, 28. S.G. Wilson sums up: 'Luke's positive account of the Law is designed less to propagate or legitimate legal piety and more to defend the beleaguered reputation of Paul'.[76]

The contrast between Luke's presentation of Paul in Acts and what we can learn of him from his Epistles is nevertheless so glaring that many critics[77] have concluded that Luke cannot have used them, but this is to ignore the difference of genre and audience and also of purpose. Paul is writing letters to churches he himself has in most cases established: Luke is writing a narrative aimed at all. Paul is usually responding to some particular crisis within a specific church;[78] he discusses, instructs, cajoles,

72. Similarly Houlden, *Purpose*, p. 61.

73. See Acts 20.29-30, especially: ἄνδρες λαλοῦντες διεστραμμένα τοῦ ἀποσπᾶν τοὺς μαθητὰς ὀπίσω αὐτῶν (Acts 20.30).

74. Thus Tannehill, *Narrative Unity*, II, p. 81.

75. And therefore to defend him from Gnostic appropriation. As Houlden, *Purpose* (p. 62) observes, Luke is walking a tightrope on this issue, since if he is too anti-Jewish he will encourage the proto-Gnostics, but if he is too pro-Jewish this will alienate those who blamed the Jews for the deaths of Jesus and Stephen and maybe Paul.

76. Stephen G. Wilson, *Luke and the Law* (SNTSMS, 50; Cambridge: Cambridge University Press, 1983), p. 116.

77. For example, Ernst Haenchen, *Acts*; or Philipp Vielhauer, 'On the Paulinism of Acts', in L.E. Keck and J.L. Martyn (eds.), *Studies in Luke–Acts* (Philadelphia: Fortress Press; London: SPCK, 1966), pp. 33-50.

78. An exception is perhaps Romans, which is more of a theological treatise where Paul develops his ideas in some depth.

exhorts, upbraids and recriminates. Luke's much more irenic presentation aims to stress the unity of the early Church so that it can serve as a model for the very different situation faced by his contemporaries.[79]

Luke wishes to defend Paul: not in the sense that Acts is to be construed as a 'defence brief', but against charges of antinominianism levied by some sections within the Christian Church, and also perhaps by some outside it (both Jewish and non-Jewish) whose views may have been influential among contemporary Christians. Luke's Paul is a devout Jew; and the evangelist by his presentation is maybe seeking not only to placate Jewish Christians, but also to oppose heretical groups violently opposed to Judaism, some of which (such as the later Marcionites) regarded Paul as championing their wholesale rejection of the Old Testament.[80] Paul grounds his missionary preaching very firmly on Scripture, except when he is preaching to Gentiles, as at Athens. Christianity is the fulfilment of Old Testament prophecy and Old Testament hopes, as Jews who know their Scriptures should appreciate, and it is on this basis that he appeals to them: Jesus is the predicted Messiah, who must suffer and be raised from the dead, and in him the promised salvation is realized. Paul says nothing to which most Christians would not have subscribed; we are aware that Luke makes little attempt to present Paul's very distinctive theology in his speeches in Acts, which are usually of a missionary nature, and addressed to outsiders.

Luke prefers to present dramatically many Pauline ideas which he regards as especially important in the same way that he dramatizes the injunction to love your enemies in the Parable of the Good Samaritan. Thus, 'to the Jew first, and after, to the Greek' (e.g. Rom. 1.16) structures the missionary activity of Acts; that 'God shows no partiality' (Rom. 2.11) is the theme of the Cornelius episode (see Acts 10.34); that salvation is through faith, not Law (Gal. 2.16), is stressed in Lk. 18.14, and that faith is trust in Jesus, in Lk. 23.43; that salvation is found in him alone (Rom. 5 and elsewhere) is reflected in Acts 4.12; Acts 13.28-39; that grace abounds (Rom. 5.20-21) is apparent in the Prodigal Son; that Judaism, the true olive tree (Rom. 11.24), was the recipient of the Covenant and the promises

79. See Acts 20.29-31.

80. Knox, 'Acts', pp. 279-87, argues that Luke knew Paul's epistles, but deliberately avoided mentioning them, because they were used by Marcionites (or pre-Marcionites) whom he aimed to correct. We may note that other writers, too, such as Justin Martyr, were reluctant to cite Paul's letters, even though they almost certainly knew them.

(Rom. 9.4), is central to Luke's presentation in his birth narrative, and links with the overarching prophecy/fulfilment motif, since Gentile Christians are themselves, as was always intended, sharers in the promises (cf. Gal. 4.28; Rom. 4.16), even though most Jews, tragically, have now rejected them (Acts 28.26-28; Rom. 9-10).[81] Christianity in Luke's presentation is the legitimate (and legitimated) development of Judaism, not a new religion; and the time of salvation is *now*.[82]

It is also evident, however, that Luke is prepared to modify Paul's ideas in accordance with his own emphases in the same way that he has modified those in the other Gospels, as will be argued below. Thus the echo of the very Pauline 'justification by faith' at Acts 13.39 is combined with an un-Pauline (but entirely Lukan) reference to the forgiveness of sins; and Luke likewise reinterprets the 'natural theology' which Paul uses to emphasize that there is no excuse for unbelief (Rom. 1.20) to stress, instead, that the God proclaimed by Paul is the Creator of all (Acts 17.24-26). Some Gnostics believed that the Creator of the world—not the Creator of all— was a spiteful, envious demiurge; Paul's speech at Athens refutes such an idea.

In addition, Luke usually prefers to tone down the eschatological fervour which is frequently strong in Paul;[83] although we are aware that the evangelist does not obliterate every trace of imminent expectation, his main emphasis is on a still-unfolding history of salvation.[84] He omits altogether Pauline emphases which were uncongenial, such as Paul's conception of the relation of the Law to Sin, or his Christology which included pre-existence, or his belief in the cross as the ground of human salvation.[85] It is also noticeable that Luke plays down and relocates the collection for the needy in Jerusalem which may have led to Paul's arrest, referring to it very early on at Acts 11.29-30, although he clearly knew of its significance for Paul's later history (see Acts 24.17). Aiding the needy is very important to Luke, and he does not wish to suggest that it could prove so disastrous; in Acts, therefore, the arrest is provoked by a malicious

81. Cf. the similar connections noted by Peder Borgen, 'From Paul to Luke', *CBQ* 31 (1969), pp. 168-82.

82. Cf. 2 Cor. 6.2/Lk. 4.18-21; Gal. 3.8/Acts 3.25, although Luke's understanding of this theme is not the same as Paul's.

83. See, e.g., 1 Cor. 7.29-31; 1 Thess. 1.10; 4.13-17; Rom. 8.18-23; 13.12.

84. This idea itself has some foundation in Paul; see Romans 9-11, especially 11.25 (cf. Lk. 21.24c; Acts 3.19-21).

85. Acts 20.28 is a shadow of Paul's *theologia crucis*.

fabrication of some Asian Jews (which the reader knows from Luke's presentation to be untrue), concerning Paul's alleged disregard of the Law.[86]

Ethically, the Law (especially Deuteronomy) was congenial to Luke, and his Paul never utters any direct criticism of it, any more than does his Jesus; this is reserved for Peter and James, whose loyalty to Judaism few would question. There is never any suggestion that the Law is to be associated with Sin and Death.[87] No shade of criticism is to be detected in James's description (Acts 21.20) of the thousands of Christian Jews who remain ζηλωταὶ τοῦ νόμου. Luke's Paul is prepared to undergo a Nazirite vow to mollify them, just as earlier he has Timothy circumcised. In this context we should note that most of the problems Paul encounters are not with other groups within the Church,[88] but with the Jews. When Paul 'turns to the Gentiles' in Antioch, Corinth and Rome it is because the Jews have rejected the gospel. Moreover, Luke deliberately subordinates Paul to the authority of the Jerusalem church, which oversees his activities.[89] By linking Paul to the true tradition, which for Luke is embodied by this church since many of its members have been witnesses 'from the beginning', Luke binds the Pauline mission to the Christian Church's founder, Christ. It is a conciliatory—even if partly unhistorical—presentation, and it is designed to inspire confidence. To sum up, Luke may indeed have been writing for a 'mixed' audience of Jews and Gentiles like Rome, which seems the best explanation for his presentation, but nevertheless both groups were members of the same Church and were thus heirs to the same promises, and Luke–Acts is intended to strengthen and confirm their faith.

86. Similarly, Gerd Lüdemann, *Opposition to Paul in Jewish Christianity* (Minneapolis: Augsburg–Fortress, 1989), pp. 58-62. Although Luke characteristically combines the motifs of the Law and the collection at Acts 24.18, all the emphasis is on the former.

87. No other Christian writer makes this association; Paul is unique in this respect, and his views must have been deeply offensive to many Jewish Christians.

88. At Acts 11.2, it is *Peter* who clashes with the 'circumcision party', which is presumably a Christian group (we may compare Acts 15.5); but Paul's conflict at Acts 15.1-2 could be with Jews, not Jewish Christians.

89. We may contrast Marcion, who consistently elevates Paul and denigrates the Twelve.

Excursus

THE PROBLEM OF EPHESIANS

Ephesians, which few critics today regard as authentically Pauline, poses special problems in any consideration of Paul's epistles. The connections between it and Luke–Acts, which are numerous and striking, have been considered in detail by C.L. Mitton.[1] Mitton, too, assumes the priority of Luke–Acts, which he thinks has been used by the author (not Paul) of Ephesians. He notes, for example, that both Acts 2.4, 15 and Eph. 5.18 refer to being filled with the Holy Spirit (un-Pauline, and unique in Ephesians, but found five times in Acts), and compare this to inebriation.[2] Much of the evidence he offers, however, is reversible and some strongly suggests that the priority is rather that of Ephesians, such as the use of κληρονομία at Acts 20.32, which does not occur elsewhere in Luke but is part of the characteristic vocabulary of Ephesians (see, e.g., Eph. 1.18).[3] Similarly, Acts 20.24 is closely related to Eph. 3.2, 7, but Ephesians is probably dependent here on Col. 1.23, 25, and Luke may be conflating the two, since 'the gospel of God's grace' in Acts seems to be a message and Colossians refers to preaching and to the word of God. At Acts 20.28, too, as Mitton points out,[4] there is a sequence of uncommon words and ideas linking Acts and Ephesians 1.7, 14; 4.11. For example, there is περιποιήσις (Eph. 1.14)/περιποιέομαι (Acts 20.28), which in both cases is associated with the Holy Spirit. In Eph. 1.14, however, it is also joined with ἀπολύτρωσις, which is itself connected in v. 7 with the phrase διὰ τοῦ αἵματος αὐτοῦ; and at Acts 20.28 the verb is also linked with διὰ τοῦ αἵματος in a reference to the expiatory blood of Christ which is

1. C.L. Mitton, *The Epistle to the Ephesians: Its Authority, Origin and Purpose* (Oxford: Clarendon Press, 1951), pp. 198-220.
2. Mitton, *Ephesians*, pp. 205-206.
3. Mitton, *Ephesians*, p. 213. The idea itself is Pauline: cf. Gal. 3.18.
4. Mitton, *Ephesians*, p. 212.

unique and untypical of Luke.[5] There is also the shepherd/flock metaphor and metaphor and the use of ποιμαίνειν (Acts)/ποιμένας (Eph. 4.11). Luke seems to have been echoing different verses in Ephesians here.

Mitton concludes that since the connections between Ephesians and Acts are most evident in Acts 20.17-35, the speech to the Ephesian Elders at Miletus, either Luke has remembered what was said or the writer of Ephesians knew Acts, and concentrated on this particular portion of it.[6] Another possibility is, of course, that the writer of Acts knew Ephesians. Mitton stresses that Ephesians was written in imitation of Paul by a devoted disciple who knew the Epistle to the Colossians[7] very well; Ephesians reflects most of Paul's known letters and seems to be a summary of some key elements of Paul's thought which provides a guide for the writer's own day. It has been suggested by R.P. Martin[8] that this devoted disciple and skilful imitator may have been Luke himself;[9] he is mentioned in Colossians at 4.14, and this may be significant. If Luke were responsible for any of the other items in the New Testament canon, which must remain open to debate,[10] Ephesians, where the presentation of Paul and many of the ideas—especially the stress on purity of doctrine, unity, inclusiveness and tolerance—are reminiscent of Luke, would seem perhaps to be the likeliest candidate; and if this were the case, the difficulty of deciding which of the two texts is the earlier vanishes. Mitton estimates that Ephesians should be dated in the early nineties,[11] since he judges that

5. The use of διά in both cases, when we would perhaps have expected ἐν, is noteworthy, too.

6. Mitton, *Ephesians*, pp. 205ff.

7. It is worth pointing out that Mitton (pp. 214-15) believes that if Acts 26.16-18 is using a literary source, it seems to be dependent on Col. 1.12-14 rather than Eph. 1.7, 18; 2.2; 5.8, where the various items are scattered. Acts 20.24, too, seems to reflect Colossians.

8. Ralph P. Martin, 'An Epistle in Search of a Life-Setting', *ExpTim* 79 (1967), pp. 296-302.

9. Imitation was an important part of rhetorical training, at which Luke excelled.

10. The connections between Luke–Acts and Hebrews were noted by C.P.M. Jones, 'The Epistle to the Hebrews and the Lukan Writings', in D.E. Nineham (ed.), *Studies in the Gospels: Essays in Memory of R.H. Lightfoot* (Oxford: Basil Blackwell, 1955), pp. 113-43. That the evangelist wrote the Pastoral Epistles was suggested by J.D. Quinn, 'The Last Volume of Luke: The Relation of Luke–Acts to the Pastoral Epistles', in Charles H. Talbert (ed.), *Perspectives on Luke–Acts* (Danville, VA: Association of Baptist Professors of Religion, 1978), pp. 62-75; and also S.G. Wilson, *Luke and the Pastoral Epistles* (London: SPCK, 1979). Neither suggestion is persuasive.

11. Mitton, *Ephesians*, p. 260.

it is known by other writings such as 1 Peter, Hebrews and perhaps *1 Clement* (though the dates of all these are disputed). If Luke–Acts were completed soon afterwards, perhaps by the same person, this again would support a dating for Luke–Acts close to the turn of the century.

Chapter 3

LUKE AND MATTHEW: THE SYNOPTIC PROBLEM

3.1. *The Nature of the Problem*

Few critics dispute that Luke used Mark as his main source for narrative.[1] But Luke's source for the teaching material that he does not derive from Mark, much of which is shared with Matthew, is another matter. There is no clear consensus of opinion here, and it is necessary, as part of any investigation of Luke's relation to his sources, to consider critically the proposed alternatives.

For about one hundred years, most scholars accepted the hypothesis which posits an independent use by Luke and Matthew of Mark's Gospel and of a (lost) sayings source, Q[2]—though the precise content of Q, whether this was oral or written, a cycle of tradition or a single document, and also the amount of other non-Q material included by Matthew and Luke, have all been the subject of much debate. There have always been dissenting voices: thus some scholars have suggested that the connections between the Synoptic Gospels are to be explained by the oral transmission of material[3] which was reshaped and remodelled by differing Christian communities. But although it seems unwise to rule out altogether such a hypothesis, which in some cases offers a credible explanation for differences between the Gospels,[4] the contention that there was no literary relationship of any sort between them faces a problem in Luke's prologue,

1. But see W.R. Farmer, *The Synoptic Problem: A Critical Analysis* (London: Macmillan, 1964); D.L. Dungan, 'Mark: The Abridgement of Matthew and Luke', in D.G. Miller (ed.), *Jesus and Man's Hope*, I (Pittsburgh: Pittsburgh Theological Seminary, 1970), pp. 51-97. Luke's use of Mark is considered below, in Chapter 8.

2. The classic English statement of this view is that of B.H. Streeter, *The Four Gospels* (London: Macmillan, 2nd edn, 1930).

3. See, e.g., B. Reicke, *The Roots of the Synoptic Tradition* (Philadelphia: Fortress Press, 1986); B. Chilton, *Profiles of a Rabbi* (Atlanta, GA: Scholars Press, 1989).

4. E.g., the differing versions of the Lord's Prayer in Matthew and Luke.

which almost certainly refers explicitly to many (πολλοὶ) written sources,[5] and is surely refuted by the extent of the agreements between them in wording and order.

There are also scholars who, even while they accept that the remarkable closeness[6] of the Synoptic Gospels to one another implies a literary relationship between them, do not hold the view about that relationship set out so clearly by Streeter. In 1774 Griesbach proposed Matthaean priority and suggested that Mark conflated Matthew and Luke, and this view (which, assuming Luke's use of Matthew, did not require Q) has been defended and strengthened more recently by W.R. Farmer[7] and D. Dungan,[8] although they are faced with the formidable task of explaining why, for example, Mark in that case chose to omit items such as the Lord's Prayer[9] when he had an ideal opportunity to include it at Mk 11.24-25. They are also forced to postulate a dating for Mark that is later than Matthew and Luke.[10] Unless the other two Gospels are dated very early, which most scholars do not accept, this gives a date for Mark which seems somewhat at variance with the admittedly scanty historical references in the text, and especially with ch. 13, which most probably relate to the period around 70 CE. There seem to be no references belonging to a later period (except perhaps 12.33b).

5. The conjunction of ἀνατάσσομαι (compile) and διήγησις (a narrative) most probably relates to a written document. Reicke's contention (*Roots*, pp. 45, 71) that παρέδοσαν in Lk. 1.2 applies *exclusively* to the oral transmission of material is refuted by Cadbury, 'Preface', p. 497. Cadbury points out that Luke himself uses it with reference to written material at Acts 6.14; so does Justin Martyr in *1 Apol.* 66. (See also Alexander, *Preface*, pp. 82ff., especially pp. 85-86.)

6. Thus F.G. Downing, 'Redaction Criticism: Josephus's "Antiquities" and the Synoptic Gospels II', *JSNT* 9 (1980), pp. 29-48 (33).

7. Farmer, *Synoptic Problem*. Farmer has maintained this view in numerous later articles.

8. Dungan, 'Mark', pp. 51-97.

9. This point is made by many scholars; see, e.g., Sanders and Davies, *Synoptic Gospels*, p. 92.

10. Contra B.C. Butler, *The Originality of St Matthew* (Cambridge: Cambridge University Press, 1951), and Wenham, *Redating*, who also maintain Matthaean priority, but believe that Luke used Mark. Wenham dates Mark as early as c. 45 CE. If Mark is later than Luke, it is surely very strange that Marcion apparently preferred the latter, since one would have expected many of the distinguishing features of Mark's Gospel to have been congenial to him, such as the explicit rejection of points of Jewish Law and the absence of birth and resurrection accounts. But if Luke's was the most recently written Gospel, this would offer some explanation as to why his was chosen instead. (Matthew's would obviously have been unacceptable to Marcion.)

Nevertheless, in the last resort the strongest argument in favour of Markan priority remains literary, rather than historical: the difficulty of explaining Mark, if Matthew was the first Gospel, to which none of the Matthaean priorists has offered a convincing answer.

A different solution to the intractable 'Synoptic Problem' was proposed in 1915 by E.W. Lummis.[11] He, too, rejected the Q hypothesis but argued that Matthew used Mark, and that Luke used them both—a view later advocated by Austin Farrer[12] and recently developed by M.D. Goulder in his commentary on Luke.[13] It was pointed out by all three that we do not need Q as a source unless we assume that Luke cannot have known and used Matthew. There is a nice irony in the fact that B.H. Streeter, staunch champion of the 'two source hypothesis', stated very succinctly the core of the case against it, even though he failed to apply to the Synoptic question his strictures against other writers:

> There is another reason why writers…often misconceive the nature and value of…statements of Church writers, when these occur in a chronological series… They forget that the ancients read one another. Indeed, save in exceptional and more or less accidental circumstances, no ancient writer has survived at all unless his work was highly esteemed by those who followed after; and where a statement appeared in a previous writer of esteemed reputation, a later writer naturally accepted it on his own authority… Irenaeus derived material from Papias, Hegesippus, and Justin Martyr; Clement of Alexandria, Tertullian and Hippolytus used Irenaeus; Origen read most of his predecessors; and Eusebius…used *all* of these earlier writers… But even Eusebius rarely, if ever, perceived that a later writer was merely repeating, with his own comments or conjectural amplification, the statement of an earlier writer; and he thus sets their evidence side by side, as if they were independent witnesses, who corroborated one another's testimony. And not a few modern writers have followed his example.[14]

11. E.W. Lummis, *How Luke was Written* (dissertation, Cambridge University, 1915). Wenham, *Redating*, p. 44, observes that this approach, which Lummis 'pioneered', was worked out more fully by H.G. Jameson, *The Origin of the Synoptic Gospels* (Oxford: Basil Blackwell, 1922). The Griesbach hypothesis assumed Luke's use of Matthew; Lummis reconciled this with Markan priority.

12. A.M. Farrer, 'On Dispensing with Q', in D.E. Nineham (ed.), *Studies in the Gospels: Essays in Memory of R.H. Lightfoot* (Oxford: Basil Blackwell, 1955), pp. 55-88.

13. M.D. Goulder, *Luke: A New Paradigm* (Sheffield: JSOT Press, 1989).

14. Streeter, *Four Gospels*, pp. 16-17.

One can only say, *'De te, fabula!'* (literally, 'The story is told about you').
The same is true of the evangelists: there is therefore no need to postulate
a hypothetical 'Q' to explain the connections between Matthew and Luke
unless Luke could not have used Matthew or vice versa.

Some support for the Q hypothesis has, however, been provided by the
Gospel of Thomas, a Coptic text which was discovered complete at Nag
Hammadi in 1945. This seems indeed to be a random collection of 'Jesus
sayings', parables and so on, with no narrative framework and no Passion.
It is thus possible that some of Jesus' sayings were preserved in a written
form and that this/these document(s) provided a source/sources for
Matthew and Luke. Even if we maintain that the sayings recorded in *Gos.
Thom.* are modifications or variations of those found in the canonical
Gospels, we cannot reject too dogmatically the possibility of a common
written source, which fresh archaeological evidence might conceivably
validate. It remains true that one could prove the existence of Q in the light
of new discoveries: it is not possible to prove its non-existence.

The existence and extent of Q must therefore remain a matter for debate.
What we do have to compare with Luke's text are the Gospels of Matthew
and Mark—and here Alexander[15] has shown that ancient writers used their
sources in three main ways: first, by direct quotation (as we see frequently
in Matthew's use of the Old Testament, introduced by a phrase such as ἵνα
πληρωθῇ τὸ ῥηθὲν ὑπὸ κυρίου διὰ τοῦ προφήτου[Mt. 1.22]); secondly,
by using sources as a sort of rough copy to be polished up and stylistically
improved (evident, perhaps, in Matthew's and Luke's use of Mark); and
thirdly by rewriting them and integrating them into the writer's own work,
often following the original very closely, but not citing it directly—and
here the source would not normally be named, just as neither Matthew nor
Luke mentions Mark. Imitation was a recognized part of a writer's training
in rhetoric, in any case, and paraphrase was encouraged (thus Isocrates,
Panegyrics 7-9),[16] although there were differences of opinion as to how

15. See L. Alexander, *Luke–Acts in its Contemporary Setting* (DPhil thesis, Oxford
University, 1977), pp. 145ff. Alexander does not treat it in such detail in *Preface,* her
(published) 1993 version of this thesis.

16. Creative imitation ('emulation') of a model/source in the ancient world
involved transforming the original text. Imitation and emulation were very tightly
bound together; see Quintilian, *Institutio Oratoria* 10.1ff., and Dionysius of Halicarnassus, *Opera*, II, pp. 200-201 (ed. H. Usener and L. Radermacher and cited by D.A.
Russell, 'De imitatione', in D. West and T. Woodman [eds.], *Creative Imitation and
Latin Literature* [Cambridge: Cambridge University Press, 1979], pp. 1-16). Making a

closely the words of the original should be followed; Horace, for example, in *Ars Poetica* 133.5, criticized word-for-word adaptation.

In addition, Alexander points out[17] that manuscript transmission was so problematic in those days that what was intended as a copy might actually prove to be a very much revised edition, since the copier sometimes used the original wording, and sometimes paraphrased freely. In this context, we notice that there are numerous occasions when Luke's text and Matthew's are more or less identical;[18] there are others where the correspondence is quite close, although there are some variations in vocabulary;[19] and yet others when a comparison of the two shows the link to be mainly one of idea, since there has been a very free rewriting of the original (an example would be Luke's version at 11.21-22 of the Strong Man Bound). This may even involve reinterpretation, as seems to be the case with the Beatitudes and the Parable of the Lost Sheep; in such cases, it is very difficult, if not impossible, to decide the priority of either version.

3.2. *Luke and Matthew*

3.2.1. *Order*
Perhaps the main argument used to support Markan priority and the Q hypothesis is that from order; an analysis of the Triple Tradition material shows that Mark's placement is usually[20] supported by Luke or Matthew (or both); therefore the inference is that Mark is the middle term.[21] It is

source one's own (Horace, *Ars Poetica* 131) by adapting it and assimilating it to a new context and purpose, and building upon it, as Quintilian (*Institutio Oratoria* 10.1.108) believed that Cicero built upon Demosthenes, Plato and Isocrates, was a recognized practice. As Quintilian acknowledged (10.2.15, 28) this inevitably sometimes meant improving upon it: thus Macrobius in *Saturnalia* 5.14 regarded Virgil's encouragement of his shipwrecked companions (*Aeneid* 1.198ff.) as an improvement on Odysseus's speech (Homer, *Odyssey* 12.108). See also Longinus: *On the Sublime* 16.3ff.

17. Alexander, *Contemporary Setting*, pp. 145-46. She notes that this makes the detection and identification of sources difficult.

18. E.g. Mt. 6.24/Lk. 16.13; Mt. 3.7b-10/Lk. 3.7b-9; Mt. 12.43-45a/Lk. 11.24-26.

19. E.g. Mt. 11.8/Lk. 7.25; Mt. 6.25-33/Lk. 12.22-31.

20. But not always, especially *within* pericopes, as was shown by E.P. Sanders, 'The Argument from Order and the Relationship between Matthew and Luke', *NTS* 15 (1968), pp. 249-61.

21. See C.M. Tuckett, 'Arguments from Order: Definition and Evaluation', in *idem* (ed.), *Synoptic Studies* (Sheffield: Sheffield Academic Press, 1984), pp. 197-219. Tuckett stresses that although this argument can offer support to a synoptic theory, it

claimed that Matthew and Luke almost never agree on the placement of Q material; Streeter[22] suggested that if Luke had indeed used Matthew, the two Gospels would surely do so more often. But here we should observe that if Luke does use Matthew as well as Mark he treats the two differently. He tends to accept Mark's order for narrative (though with reservations, as is evident in the pericopes of the Rejection of Jesus at Nazareth and the Anointing of Jesus) but not so readily Matthew's order for teaching. He is also wary of Matthew's narrative material—there are thus wide differences between Matthew's and Luke's birth account, and likewise their treatment of the resurrection appearances.

Since Matthew structures most of the teaching material into five major discourses, it is usually assumed that Luke, whose architectonic principles are far harder to determine (especially in his central section, which is considered more fully in the next two chapters), must remain much closer to the possibly random sequence of Q.[23] To break up Matthew's satisfactory arrangement to no purpose seems otherwise an act of wanton and senseless destruction. However, since Q is hypothetical we cannot tell what its order was. And in any case Lummis,[24] Farrer[25] and Goulder[26] have all claimed that Luke in the main adheres quite closely to Matthew's order for teaching material, even if he often places that material in different contexts.[27] Thus three of Matthew's discourses[28] are found in a

---

does not prove it. Ultimately, we have to weigh up which explanation seems the most plausible.

22. The core of Streeter's argument is neatly summarized in Sanders and Davies, *Synoptic Gospels*, pp. 62, 66.

23. Not all scholars see Q as random: see, for example, A. Harnack, *The Sayings of Jesus: The Second Source of St Matthew and St Luke* (London: Williams & Norgate, 1908), p. 181. On Q and Luke, M.A. Powell, *What Are They Saying about Luke?* (New York: Paulist Press, 1989), p. 22, says (contra Harnack), 'The order of the sayings, which is best preserved in Luke…' Cf. D.R. Catchpole, *The Quest for Q* (Edinburgh: T. & T. Clark, 1993), p. 79. Creed, *Luke*, p. lxv, inclines to the same opinion, although he adds a caution: 'Luke's tendency to group together discourses which have some points of contact…may have disturbed the order of the source.'

24. Lummis, *Luke*, pp. 6-13.

25. Farrer, 'Dispensing with Q', pp. 82ff.

26. See, e.g., the discussion on the Sermon on the Plain, in Goulder, *Luke*, pp. 346ff. Also, see pp. 581-83, and elsewhere.

27. Goulder, *Luke*, p. 40.

28. As far as the other two Matthaean speeches are concerned, we note that Luke prefers to insert parables into his narrative at intervals, rather than gather them into a solid block like Matthew ch. 13; and he has already used much of Matthew ch. 18

condensed form but substantially in the same order in Luke. Lummis estimates that of the 215 verses common to Matthew and Luke, 98 are in exactly the same order in Luke,[29] and $^4/_7$ are in substantially the same order.[30] The difficulty here is that even though critics like Lummis and Goulder agree that an order can be discerned in Luke's use of Matthew's teaching material, they have different ideas as to what that order may be. Thus Lummis[31] proposes three separate ordered series, which would mean that Luke went through it once, and then repeated the process twice more; Goulder[32] instead sees a sequence of Matthaean order afterwards repeated in reverse. It seems unlikely that both could be true, and this may suggest that such systematic schemes owe more to the critic's ingenuity than to Lukan composition. It is perhaps best to conclude that Luke inserts teaching material at whatever point in his narrative seems most appropriate.

We may infer from Luke's treatment of his material that he dislikes long, uninterrupted blocks of teaching: the Lukan norm is from 12 to 20 verses.[33] He usually prefers to break the material up into smaller, more manageable units, and assign these to new contexts, where they either provide an example of teaching or link thematically with a topic he wishes to treat, so that the texts serve to comment on each other. This is probably the case at Lk. 10.21-24, where Jesus' thanksgiving to the Father and the concomitant—and very Johannine-sounding—statement about the mutual knowledge of Father and Son and the revelation of that knowledge to those with whom the Son chooses to share it is combined with the blessing of the disciples for the knowledge they have been granted. The stress on

---

earlier in the narrative in its Markan context. (Thus he uses Mark's account of disorder among the disciples at Lk. 9.46-48, although he also uses it later at Lk. 22.24-27, which could suggest he is following two sources.)

29. Lummis, *Luke*, p. 7.

30. Lummis, *Luke*, p. 9.

31. Lummis, *Luke*, pp. 9-10. Similarly, W.R. Farmer, 'A Fresh Approach to Q', in J. Neusner (ed.), *Christianity, Judaism and Graeco-Roman Cults*, I (Leiden: E.J. Brill, 1975), pp. 39-50. Farmer claims that Luke works forwards in Matthew several times.

32. Goulder, *Luke*, pp. 581-83.

33. Cf. Goulder, *Luke*, p. 40. C.M. Tuckett, 'The Existence of Q', in R.A. Piper (ed.), *The Gospel behind the Gospels* (NovTSup, 75; Leiden: E.J. Brill, 1995), pp. 19-47 (41) points out that Lk. 12.22-53 and Luke ch. 21 both exceed this norm: but in neither case does the uninterrupted teaching approach the length (nearly 110 verses) of the Sermon on the Mount, which challenges ready assimilation. The speech of Stephen in Acts, some 53 verses, is a review of Jewish history and does not tax the understanding in the same way: the same is true of Peter's evangelistic Pentecostal speech.

this kind of personal witness, which was required in ancient historiography,[34] is a strong theme in both Luke and John.

3.2.2. *Minor Agreements*

A weakness of the 'two source' hypothesis has always been the so-called 'minor accords', where Luke's wording agrees with Matthew's rather than Mark's in Triple Tradition passages, such as the use of Ναζαρά at Mt. 4.13 and Lk. 4.16 which is not found in Mark, nor elsewhere in the New Testament. (Some of these agreements are particularly significant, such as Προφήτευσον τίς ἐστιν ὁ παίσας σε at Mt. 26.68/Lk. 22.64, since Q has, by definition, no Passion, and thus agreements outside it suggest either that there has been textual assimilation or that there may be a direct dependence of one text upon the other.)[35] The accords between Matthew and Luke against Mark are very numerous: it has been estimated that there are about one thousand examples,[36] and very few apparently Markan sections are without them. Thus, for example, in their versions of the Healing of a Paralytic, both Matthew and Luke replace Mark's possibly vulgar κράβαττος (Mk 2.4, 9, 11 and 12) with κλίνης (Mt. 9.2, 6; Lk. 5.18; at Lk. 5.19, 24, too, Luke uses a diminutive of this, κλινίδιον). In addition, both alter Mark's ἐξῆλθεν ἔμπροσθεν πάντων to ἀπῆλθεν εἰς τὸν οἶκον αὐτοῦ; and both quite uncharacteristically[37] replace Mark's δέ at 2.6 with καί. Particularly difficult to explain are the occasions when both make what is arguably the same error; there is, for example, the word μωρανθῇ at Mt. 5.13/Lk. 14.34 which Jeremias[38] suggests may be the result of a mistranslation of the Aramaic word *tapel*, which means 'to be saltless'[39] but can also metaphorically mean to talk foolishly. Another possible instance is the alteration by both of the Septuagintal 'fear' to 'worship', using the same word προσκυνήσεις at Mt. 4.10/Lk. 4.4, although one could argue here that the error was in Q.

In addition, what some critics have termed 'Matthaeanisms'[40] occur in Luke's Gospel, albeit much less frequently than in Matthew. Thus at Lk. 13.28 there is the Matthaean favourite ὁ κλαυθμὸς καὶ ὁ βρυγμὸς τῶν

34. Cf. Aune, *Literary Environment*, pp. 81ff.
35. See Goulder, *Luke*, pp. 6ff.
36. Thus Sanders and Davies, *Synoptic Gospels*, p. 73.
37. Sanders and Davies, *Synoptic Gospels*, p. 70.
38. J. Jeremias, *The Parables of Jesus* (London: SCM Press, 1972), p. 168.
39. Thus, correctly, Mk 9.50.
40. Thus, Sanders and Davies, *Synoptic Gospels*, p. 93.

ὀδόντων (compare Mt. 8.12; 13.42, 50; 22.13; 24.51; 25.30); similarly, at Lk. 12.5 there is γέεννα (compare Mt. 5.22, 29, 30; 10.28; 18.9; 23.15, 33), although Luke usually prefers the Greek Hades[41] to this very Jewish abode of punishment; and at Lk. 3.7 we find γεννήματα ἐχιδνῶν (compare Mt. 37; 12.34; 23.33). Moreover, the designation ὑποκριταί, too, although it occurs three times in Luke (at Lk. 6.42; 12.56; and 13.15) is very much more common in Matthew.[42] We may perhaps infer that Luke's use of such expressions, which he clearly did not particularly like, shows his reluctance to omit altogether what were recorded by Matthew as sayings of the Lord: Luke therefore felt obliged to include at least one example of each, but he avoided as many as he could. The problem here is that it would be equally possible to argue that the sayings occurred in Q, and that Matthew, who liked them, used them more than once.

To account for all the minor agreements if we maintain the independence of Matthew and Luke, critics have resorted to numerous explanations, as we can see in Davies and Allison's[43] commentary on Matthew. The least contentious of these are the 'negative agreements', where Markan errors such as the identification of Abiathar are omitted, or Markan interpretations which Matthew and Luke both reject, such as Jesus' displays of anger or his irritation at the disciples' stupidity.[44] There are, however, other agreements which Davies dismisses, rather too hastily, as 'insignificant',[45] such as the use of καλεῖ for λέγει at the parallels to Mk 12.37,[46] or ἠδυνήθησαν for ἴσχυσαν at those to Mk 9.18,[47] or μετά for σύν at those to Mk 2.26.[48] Although the actual examples are unremarkable, their quantity is not, and it is surely surprising that Matthew and Luke would so often independently choose the same word when they alter Mark. Similarly, even if we regard some changes as independent stylistic corrections, such as the avoidance of κράβαττος, or of Mark's historic present and parataxis, we need to bear in mind that we often find Luke agreeing with

---

41. See Lk. 10.15; 16.23; Acts 2.27, 31.

42. See Mt. 6.2, 5, 16; 7.5; 15.7; 22.18; 23.13, 14, 15, 23, 25, 27, 29.

43. W.D. Davies and D.C. Allison, *A Critical and Exegetical Commentary on the Gospel According to St Matthew*, I (Edinburgh: T. & T. Clark, 1988), pp. 109-14.

44. Both clearly find the implication of Mk 4.38 uncongenial, too.

45. Davies and Allison, *Matthew*, I, p. 111.

46. See Mt. 22.45; Lk. 20.44.

47. See Mt. 17.16; Lk. 9.40.

48. See Mt. 12.4; Lk. 6.4. Luke frequently uses σύν, although Matthew seems to dislike it.

Matthew against Mark over the use of a particular word or construction with which he seems quite happy elsewhere,[49] such as the omission of καὶ ἐγένετο in the Parable of the Sower. In this parable, too, we notice that Matthew, who prefers participial constructions, at Mt. 13.9 drops Mark's relative pronoun plus indicative verb (Mk 4.9, ὃς ἔχει ὦτα ἀκούειν ἀκουέτω) and writes ὁ ἔχων ὦτα ἀκουέτω. Luke, who elsewhere uses the Markan construction (see Lk. 14.33), at this point changes Mark's version to agree with Matthew's. Lk. 8.8 begins with Matthew's ὁ ἔχων ὦτα and continues with *Mark's* ending ἀκούειν ἀκουέτω, so that what we have seems to be a conflation of the two.

Another example is provided by the cornfields incident: here both Luke and Matthew replace Mark's τοῖς σὺν αὐτῷ οὖσιν (Mk 2.26) with τοῖς μετ' αὐτοῦ (Mt. 12.4; Lk. 6.4), and both omit οὖσιν. Οἱ μετά + genitive is a Matthaean construction, occurring five times in his Gospel;[50] he never uses οἱ σύν + dative. Luke, however, only has the οἱ μετά construction on two occasions, of which this is one—normally he uses οἱ σύν.[51] When Luke acts against his usual practice in this way, it clearly suggests either a common written source or direct dependence: and given that the change is made by Luke, it suggests Matthaean priority to Luke.

Other explanations offered for agreements are scribal errors and alterations,[52] and the later assimilation of one text to another.[53] There are certainly examples of this, such as the insertion of vv. 2b-3 into Matthew Ch. 16, which was presumably suggested by Lk. 12.54-56, and adapted to suit the very different climatic conditions of the community using Matthew's Gospel; and the quotation of Ps. 2.7, including 'this day have I begotten thee',[54] in some Western texts of Lk. 3.22. (The alternative to this in most manuscripts is an allusion to Isa. 42.1—'in whom my soul

49. This point is made by N. Turner, 'The Minor Verbal Agreements of Matthew and Luke against Mark', in K. Aland (ed.), *SE I* (TU, 73; Berlin: Akademie Verlag, 1959), pp. 223-34.
50. See Mt. 12.3, 4; 25.10, 31 and 27.54.
51. See Lk. 5.9; 9.32; 24.24, 33; Acts 5.17, 21; 19.38; 22.9; 26.13.
52. Davies and Allison, *Matthew*, p. 113.
53. Davies and Allison, *Matthew*, p. 112. As was noted above, this is the explanation many critics have offered for the minor accord in the Passion at Mt. 26.68, Lk. 22.64.
54. J.A. Fitzmyer, *The Gospel According to St Luke* (2 vols.; AB; Garden City, NY: Doubleday, 1981), I, p. 485, notes that this text is only used elsewhere in the New Testament in the context of the Resurrection and exaltation of Christ (see Acts 13.33; Heb.1.5; 5.5).

delights', which is used by Matthew and Mark as well.) If all else fails, there is always the suggestion that Matthew and Luke used a different version of Mark from ours,[55] which is almost certainly true.[56] H. Koester's analysis[57] of Mk 1.40-44 and its synoptic parallels is typical: in v. 40, since both Luke and Matthew have κύριε, this must have been in the original copy of Mark which they used; in v. 41, the word σπλαγχνισθεὶς cannot have been in the original version of Mark, since it does not appear in Luke or Matthew; v. 43 (which neither uses) is clearly a later interpolation which was not available to them. Arguments like these, when pressed thus far, would mean that all three Gospels were identical in Triple Tradition passages. It seems to be assumed by some critics that none of the evangelists, and especially not Luke, could ever have used his sources creatively, as other ancient writers frequently did: they were by implication mere compilers who were adept at wielding scissors and paste, not writers or theologians.

3.2.3. *Overlaps and Doublets*
If we are to maintain the independence of Matthew and Luke, the many agreements would imply that there were several overlaps between Mark and Q.[58] Streeter, in his more detailed analysis of these,[59] expanded his original 5[60] to at least 16. This means that Q keeps growing, encompassing increasing quantities of narrative material as well as sayings.[61] An obvious example is the Beelzebul controversy, where there are a number of minor agreements between Matthew and Luke against Mark, such as εἰδὼς δὲ...αὐτῶν...εἶπεν...πᾶσα...ἐρημοῦται at Mt. 12.25, Lk. 11.17; or Mt. 12.27 and Lk. 11.19, which are almost identical. We can only assume that

---

55. Thus Koester, *Gospels*, pp. 276ff.

56. Scholars such as R. Bultmann, *The History of the Synoptic Tradition* (Oxford: Basil Blackwell, 1968), p. 328, and G. Strecker, *The Sermon on the Mount* (trans. O.C. Dean; Nashville: Abingdon Press, 1988), pp. 13ff., in a similar way suggest different versions of Q to explain variations between the Jesus sayings recorded in Matthew and Luke. Explanations such as this can always save the 'two source' hypothesis, but they are not testable.

57. Koester, *Gospels*, p. 212.

58. I offer my own interpretation of the main 'overlaps' in the following pages.

59. B.H. Streeter, 'St Mark's Knowledge and Use of Q', in W. Sanday (ed.), *Oxford Studies in the Synoptic Problem* (Oxford: Clarendon Press, 1911), pp. 165-83.

60. John the Baptist; the Temptation; Collusion with Satan; the Mustard Seed/Leaven; the Mission of the Twelve.

61. Thus Sanders and Davies, *Synoptic Gospels*, p. 91.

either Mark and a version of Q which included some narrative overlapped at this point, or that Luke has used Matthew. I shall examine this section in some detail to show that Lukan use of both Matthew and Mark seems the more probable explanation.

First, it is not difficult to find a reason why Luke might have relocated this sequence. Mark's placement (in the context of a dispute with some Scribes from Jerusalem and the fears of οἱ παρ'αὐτοῦ that Jesus is out of his mind) and Matthew's (an exorcism of a dumb demoniac) differ. In such circumstances, when there is a conflict between his sources, Luke often rewrites fairly freely and relocates.[62] Though normally preferring Mark's placement for narrative, Luke may have found Mark's context unacceptable in this present case: we notice that both he and Matthew delete the implicit criticism made by Mark of Jesus' family/friends in 3.21. Matthew's positioning—where it forms part of a discussion concerning an exorcism—was much more congenial to Luke, since the conflict of Christ and Satan is an important theme in his Gospel. Luke indeed takes every opportunity to stress that Jesus' healings represent victories over Satan and his minions, the evil spirits who oppress humanity.[63]

Nevertheless, faced with a Matthaean doublet[64] at this point, Luke simplifies and at Lk. 11.14, he is much closer to Mt. 9.32-33a than to Mt. 12.22-23:

Matthew 9.32-33a	Matthew 12.22-23	Luke 11.14
αὐτῶν δὲ ἐξερχομένων	τότε προσηνέχθη	καὶ ἦν ἐκβάλλων
ἰδοὺ προσήνεγκαν αὐτῷ	αὐτῷ δαιμονιζόμενος	δαιμόνιον καὶ
ἄνθρωπον κωφὸν δαιμονιζόμενον	τυφὸς καὶ κωφός	αὐτὸ ἦν κωφόν
καὶ ἐκβληθέντος τοῦ	καὶ ἐθεράπευσεν	ἐγένετο δὲ τοῦ
δαιμονίου ἐλάλησεν	αὐτόν ὥστε τὸν	δαιμονίου
		ἐχελθόντος
ὁ κωφός καὶ	κωφὸν λαλεῖν καὶ	ἐλάλησεν
ἐθαύμασαν οἱ ὄχλοι	βλέπειν. καὶ	ὁ κωφός καὶ
	ἐξίσταντο πάντες	ἐθαύμασαν οἱ
	οἱ ὄχλοι	ὄχλοι

62. We may compare the pericope of the Mission of the Twelve/Mission of the Seventy (Two) at Lk. 10.1-16. The same is true when there is a conflict between John and the other Gospels, as will be argued below.

63. See, for example, Lk. 8.2; 10.17-20; 13.11-13, and the Lukan summaries at 6.18 (cf. Mt. 12.15) and 7.21 (unparalleled in Matthew's handling of the Baptist's question at Mt. 11.2-6).

64. Mt. 12.22-23; Mt. 9.32-33.

Matthew, however, includes at 9.33b a reference to Israel which Luke, who does not emphasize the Israel theme in the same way (presumably because it may have seemed to limit the scope of Jesus' ministry too explicitly), characteristically omits.[65] The same is true of the reference at Mt. 12.23 to the 'Son of David', which is not an interpretation of Jesus' role which is particularly favoured by Luke.[66]

We notice that whereas in Mark Jesus is disputing with οἱ γραμματεῖς (Mk 3.22) and in Matthew with οἱ Φαρισαῖοι (Mt. 9.34; 12.24), Luke rejects both of these conflicting interpretations. His more general τινὲς δὲ ἐξ αὐτῶν, which is entirely Lukan,[67] is perhaps more to be applied to οἱ ὄχλοι, and it reflects the acceptance/rejection motif in response to Jesus and his message which has been a theme from the first, as is evident from 2.34-35, where there is likewise a combination of inner thoughts being revealed/perceived, and division/separation in relation to a σημεῖον.

Luke links this section with what has preceded it, a consideration of the theme of prayer, by the request of ἕτεροι for a sign from Heaven in 11.16. This may be seen as a too literal response to Jesus' words at 11.10-13, even if it is not as malicious as the Beelzebul accusation. Verse 16 also provides a clear link with the treatment later in the chapter (see 11.29-32) on the theme of looking for signs: Luke is splicing the material together, and showing that both responses to Jesus are wrong.

As far as the actual content of the Beelzebul accusation is concerned, both Luke and Matthew drop the charge[68] that Jesus Βεελζεβοὺλ ἔχει. In the following clause Luke's structure, beginning with a reference to Beelzebul, the prince of demons, is the same as Mark's, but in the addition of ἐν Βεελζεβοὺλ to identify the demon prince, which is necessitated by the omission of the earlier Markan reference to Beelzebul, Luke is in accord with Matthew. Both likewise drop Mark's ἐν παραβολαῖς (see Mk 3.23), the emphasis on the parabolic nature of Jesus' discourse being a

65. He likewise omits Mt. 10.6 and 15.24.
66. Thus he cuts most of the occasions when Jesus is hailed in this way in Matthew, the only exception being Lk. 18.38, 39, where the title is associated with an act of healing. Even in the triumphal entry sequence Luke omits this title (cf. Mk 11.10/Mt. 21.9/Lk. 19.38), perhaps because it carried political implications which Luke is anxious to avoid.
67. See the many Lukan parables which begin τίς ἐξ ὑμῶν, such as Lk. 11.5, 11; 12.25; 14.5, 28.
68. Cf. Jn 7.20; 8.48, 49; 10.20-21.

Markan theme, and they relocate Mk 3.24b, preferring to retain this until a little later in the discourse.[69]

Both Luke and Matthew also begin the 'kingdom divided' illustration in the same way, with πᾶσα βασιλεία, and both use the participle form of the verb μερίζω[70] and the identical ἐρημοῦται. Luke, however, after βασιλεία, inserts Mark's ἐφ'ἑαυτήν, rather than Matthew's καθ'ἑαυτῆς. But Mark's reference to 'Satan casting out Satan' at 3.23b, which Matthew retains and relocates at 12.26a, is dropped by Luke: he prefers to relate the crux of the dispute back to Jesus, since this suits his theme, and he consequently replaces it at Lk. 11.18 with the uniquely Lukan ὅτι λέγετε ἐν Βεελζεβοὺλ ἐκβάλλειν με τὰ δαιμόνια. Matthew and Mark are closer in their 'house divided' image, too, using οἰκία, whereas Luke prefers οἶκος and talks of houses 'falling'.

We observe here that each evangelist displays his own interests and likewise his stylistic preferences: Matthew characteristically 'upscales' the house image, beginning πᾶσα πόλις, and uses the participle μερισθεῖσα, and the form καθ'ἑαυτῆς in v. 25b and v. 25c; Mark in both v. 24 and v. 25 prefers ἐφ'ἑαυτὴν μερισθῇ, and he emphasizes the point in another phrase that picks up the earlier one.[71] Luke's interpretation—and it is to do him a grave injustice to regard οἶκος ἐπὶ οἶκον πίπτει as clumsy and tautological—stresses the catastrophic scale of the disaster, which he views in near-apocalyptic terms.[72] We see an event which not only lays waste kingdoms, but, like an earthquake, causes the wholesale collapse of buildings. The very direct and personal conflict of good and evil which underlies this whole section in Luke, and which is to be evident in his expansion of the Strong Man Bound, is shown in the alteration of Matthew's πνεύματι θεοῦ at 12.28 to a more anthropomorphic δακτύλῳ θεοῦ at Lk. 11.20.[73]

Such, then, is the Beelzebul controversy, which, unless we regard it as a significant Mark/Q overlap, where Matthew has conflated Mark and Q, has been seen to threaten the traditional two-source hypothesis because of the

---

69. Cf. Mt. 12.26b/Lk. 11.18b. Both make this a question beginning πῶς, and link it to a pared-down version of Mk 3.26, which is developed in a similar way, as is evident if we compare Mt. 12.27-28 and Lk. 11.19-20.

70. Luke characteristically uses a compound of this verb, διαμερίζω.

71. The phrase concerning the inability of the kingdom to stand shows only very minor variations of tense.

72. Cf. Rev. 11.13 and perhaps 16.19.

73. Cf. Exod. 8.19 or Deut. 9.10.

number and importance of the agreements between Matthew and Luke. It is not possible to prove whether what we see here is a conflation by Matthew of Mark and the hypothetical Q (which presumably was followed in terms of order by Luke) or a use by Luke of both Mark and Matthew.[74] Griesbachians, who would support the evidence given here of Luke's use and rearrangement of Matthaean material, would say that Mark later abbreviated both—but this is quite uncharacteristic, and does not agree with what we usually see in the text of Mark.[75] Against the Q hypothesis it must be observed that although neither the arguments for, nor those against, Q are conclusive, we do *not* possess any trace of Q, whereas we do have the Synoptic Gospels. Styler's[76] contention that in this sequence Luke would have subtracted from Matthew almost all of the material shared by Matthew and Mark and retained all the rest is not the only explanation for Luke's text. He is seemingly following Matthew, who has expanded Mark, quite closely, though possibly with some awareness of Mark;[77] but in many cases he is reinterpreting material and making minor additions, omissions and alterations to reflect his own concerns. What he has done, in terms of theme, placement of material, and so on, is perfectly comprehensible; and the omissions and other changes he has made are consistent with what we can infer of his redactional practices elsewhere. There is no need to postulate a Q with which Mark overlapped.

Another example is the Parable of the Mustard Seed, where Matthew and Luke are much closer to each other verbally than either is to Mark. Both Matthew and Luke follow the Mustard Seed with the Parable of the Leaven, thus qualifying the contention that Matthew and Luke never agree on the order of Q, and in this case the wording is almost identical. There is also Mt. 12.31-37 and parallels, where Sanders[78] concludes that Matthew seems to be the mid-term, sometimes agreeing with Mark and sometimes with Luke. At this point, one can only suggest either that Q and Luke are very close, and Matthew conflates them with Mark, or that Matthew expanded Mark, and Luke rearranged and used both.

---

74. See the incisive summary of the strengths and weaknesses of the various explanations in Sanders and Davies, *Synoptic Gospels*, p. 78.

75. For example, Mk 3.24-26 is lengthy and repetitive, as was shown above.

76. G.M. Styler, 'The Priority of Mark', in C.F.D. Moule (ed.), *The Birth of the New Testament* (Black's New Testament Commentaries; London: A. & C. Black, 3rd edn, 1981), pp. 285-316 (304).

77. It is perhaps more likely that the echoes of Mark reflect Luke's memory of a source he knew well than that he is attempting to harmonize the two.

78. Sanders and Davies, *Synoptic Gospels*, p. 84.

It should not be assumed that examples of 'doublets' in Matthew's text necessarily represent Mark/Q overlaps: sometimes Matthew seems to have taken a Markan saying or incident relevant to his theme, and perhaps expanded it with a parable or discourse; he will then use it again later in its correct Markan context. (The evangelists seem to have been very reluctant to invent material to demonstrate the points they make; they prefer to reuse episodes.)

There is only one clear sayings doublet in Mark[79] but there are several in Matthew, since he likes to repeat a phrase or citation such as 'I desire mercy and not sacrifice'.[80] An interesting example is the 'sign of Jonah' reference at Mt. 12.39; 16.4. In Mark, *no* sign is to be given to this generation: Matthew, glossing this passage, adds 'except the sign of Jonah', the significance of which he explains to be the resurrection. But Luke sees it differently: he understands it as the preaching of repentance, and, faced with a conflict in his sources, he feels free to offer his own interpretation.[81]

There are twelve verbal doublets in Luke,[82] three of which are shared by Matthew:

Mk 4.25/Lk. 8.18/Mt. 13.12	Mt. 25.29/Lk. 19.26
Mk 8.35/Lk. 9.24/Mt. 16.25	Mt. 10.39/Lk. 17.33
Mk 8.34/Lk. 9.23/Mt. 16.24	Mt. 10.38/Lk. 14.27

There is also what amounts to a doublet at Lk. 11.23, where the wording and context are the same as Mt. 12.30; this logion is, however, very close to the statement at Mk 9.40 (albeit this time expressed in negative terms) which Luke had used in its Markan context at Lk. 9.50. That both forms occur in Luke, in identical words and identical contexts to their Markan and Matthaean parallels, would support the contention that Luke has used them both.[83]

3.2.4. *Conflation of Sources*

Luke seems, in many cases, to be attempting to combine his sources. (This is true whether we regard his second source as Matthew or Q.) A good

---

79. Mk 9.35; 10.43-44.

80. Mt. 9.13; 12.7.

81. So, too, with the 'leaven of the Pharisees' (Lk. 12.1).

82. J.C. Hawkins, *Horae synopticae* (Oxford: Oxford University Press, 2nd edn, 1909), pp. 99ff,, notes 11: Lk. 8.16/11.33; 8.17/12.2; 8.18/19.26; 9.3-5/10.4; 9.23/14.27; 9.24/17.33; 9.26/12.9; 9.46/22.24; 11.43/20.46; 12.11-12/21.14-15; 14.11/18.14. There is also 10.25/18.18.

83. Despite the oft-repeated claim that Luke disliked doublets, he has more narrative ones than any other evangelist.

example of this is the Mission of the Twelve. Here Luke drops Mt. 10.5 'Go into no town of the Samaritans', probably because he is sympathetic to the Samaritan mission (a theme he shares with John), as is evident in both his Gospel and Acts. Likewise, he drops Mt. 10.23, οὐ μὴ τελέσητε τὰς πόλεις τοῦ Ἰσραὴλ ἕως ἂν ἔλθῃ ὁ υἱὸς τοῦ ἀνθρώπου, which was perhaps much too specific about the timing—and location—of the Parousia.[84] Nevertheless, there are also agreements with Matthew against Mark—in both, the disciples are to take no silver (Mark has copper); and not even a staff (in Mark they can *only* take a staff). But Luke agrees with Mark against Matthew that they are to take no bread, nor are they to take gold, which Matthew has characteristically added. Luke seems to be combining the two here. Elsewhere he sometimes seems to be interweaving Johannine material, too, most noticeably in his Passion and Resurrection accounts. F. Lamar Cribbs[85] notes that in at least ten passages Luke's text suggests that he is conflating differing Matthaean, Markan and Johannine elements.[86]

The attempt to combine differing sources, however, created problems for Luke: thus there are numerous occasions when there is what can best be described, in Goulder's term,[87] as a Lukan 'muddle'.[88] For example, in his account of the healing of the paralytic he follows Matthew and does not locate the episode in a house from the outset, which means that when he wants to use Mark's details about the difficulty of penetrating the crowd, which is solved by making a hole in the roof, the result is decidedly awkward. Equally clumsy is the example Sanders[89] cites of the commissioning of the twelve, where Luke's phrase at 9.5, ἐξερχόμενοι ἀπὸ τῆς πόλεως ἐκείνης, has no antecedent, although Matthew mentions a town at 10.11, before the reference to the departure.

---

84. Cf. for instance Lk. 17.20 and also Acts 1.7.

85. F.L. Cribbs, 'A Study of the Contacts Between St Luke and St John', in G.W. MacRae (ed.), *SBLSP*, 12 (Cambridge, MA: Scholars Press, 1973), II, pp. 1-93 (87).

86. Lk. 3.16; 7.37-38; 22.3, 58, 59b, 70; 23.22, 33, 53; 24.1.

87. Goulder, *Luke*, pp. 102-103.

88. Not all Lukan muddles are to be explained in this way, however. In the 'Sign of Jonah' section, the reference in Mt. 12.42 to the Queen of the South makes perfect sense as an example to be pronounced by the men of Nineveh and the queen upon this generation because of its failure to repent. In Luke, the connection between this and the preceding section on the men of Nineveh is obscured because he positions the reference to the queen at 11.31, before the mention of the men of Nineveh.

89. Sanders and Davies, *Synoptic Gospels*, p. 45.

Goulder attributes such lapses to editorial 'fatigue',[90] and Goodacre[91] notes that we do not see the same apparent lapses in Matthew's Double Tradition passages, which argues against their being derived from Q. (We do, however, see the same phenomenon at work in passages where Luke is closer to John than to Mark or Matthew; and it is interesting that we do not find similar evidence in John on these occasions. 'Fatigue', then, which supports Lukan use of Matthew, rather than vice versa, would do the same for Lukan use of John.)

Such inadvertent slips are perhaps to be expected when writers are modifying and reusing existing material, and this was especially so in the ancient world when sources of information were much more cumbersome to handle, and less readily accessible, so that authors relied to a large extent on memory. There are many examples in Josephus; the history of the Hasmonaean dynasty which he narrates in *Jewish War* was probably largely drawn from 1 Maccabees, imperfectly remembered, and it contains many inaccuracies which he later corrected in *Jewish Antiquities*. Similarly, there are tensions in the 2 Maccabees account of the actions of Antiochus IV against Jerusalem, which seem to have resulted from an attempt to uphold the historicity of Dan. 11 and 12 against the facts recorded in 1 Maccabees and Graeco-Roman histories such as that of Polybius. Josephus's somewhat different account here evidences similar inconsistencies.[92]

It has often been suggested that underlying the four Passion accounts there may be a (lost) Passion source,[93] 'Jesus Christ and him crucified' being the heart of the Christian *kerygma*. But non-canonical works such as the *Gospel of Peter* (which is clearly secondary and late) and the *Epistle of Barnabas* suggest another explanation—and the same is true of the writings of Justin Martyr:[94] details of the Passion are in many cases expressed in terms of Old Testament Scripture, and especially of Psalms such as Pss. 22 and 69. We repeatedly find a Christian exegesis of the Old Testament, a practice which began very early, as we can see in Paul. The historical information about Jesus' death which seems to have been most widely

90. See Goulder, *Luke*, p. 110.

91. M. Goodacre, 'Fatigue in the Synoptics', *NTS* 44 (1998), pp. 45-58 (57).

92. See the introduction by J.A. Goldstein to his commentary: 1 Maccabees (AB; Garden City, NY: Doubleday, 1976).

93. Thus, e.g., V. Taylor, *The Passion Narrative of St Luke* (SNTSMS, 19; Cambridge: Cambridge University Press, 1972).

94. See, e.g., *1 Apol.* 38, or *Dial.* 101.3, and compare Ps. 22.7-8.

remembered was that he had been crucified under Pontius Pilate; but since the details recorded in the Passion were validated by Scripture, they must therefore represent what had happened.

Luke's purpose is very different from Matthew's and Mark's; thus in his presentation of the Passion he omits the mockery by the Roman soldiers, although some of its details are transferred to the hearing before Herod, which is uniquely Lukan.[95] Luke emphasizes pathos, rather than lonely humiliation;[96] there is not much evidence of scriptural exegetical tradition shaping his Passion. But it is dangerous to conclude, as does Koester that 'There is little to indicate that he was acquainted with this particular tradition of scriptural interpretation that was used by the other canonical Gospels and by the *Gospel of Peter*.'[97] Elsewhere, as is especially evidenced in the birth narrative, Luke reveals a thorough familiarity with this very tradition.

Luke often seems to take over a basically Markan narrative, but with an awareness of Matthew's more stylish presentation. This would explain why in Triple Tradition passages there are so many verbal agreements between Matthew and Luke. Similarly, he inserts Matthaean teaching material, especially the more detachable apophthegms, into the narrative when an opportunity presents itself. What we often see is a thematic linking of related material in Luke—obvious examples are the collection of sayings on sight at Lk. 6.39-42 or on light at Lk. 11.33-36, where scattered Matthaean sayings are collected together. The same principle is evident elsewhere: the millstone reference seems to have been used by Luke at 17.1-2[98] because this chapter comprises a cluster of sayings, parables etc., dealing with the implications of the advent of the Kingdom, many of which are eschatological. The Matthaean section on seeking for signs, too (see Mt. 12.38-42), is echoed by Luke at 11.29-32; and this is also linked very closely to the saying on good and evil fruit that Matthew places at 12.33. But Luke has already used this in connection with a similar saying of Jesus in the Sermon on the Mount;[99] he therefore transfers Matthew's conclusion on good and bad treasure from Mt. 12.34 to Lk. 6.45, where it rounds off his own section.

---

95. It was probably included to reinforce the Jesus/Paul parallel Luke draws, and may therefore have been based on Paul's later experiences, although it might have been modelled on Ps. 2.

96. See Lk. 22.44-45; 23.27-31, 40-43, 48-49.

97. Koester, *Gospels*, p. 227.

98 Cf. Mk 9.42; Mt. 18.6-7.

99. See Mt. 7.16-20; Lk. 6.43-44.

There are nevertheless occasions when Luke seems perhaps to have missed the point made in his material. Hence the conclusion to the Parable of the Patched Garment/Wineskin makes a point that is in some tension with it (see Lk. 5.39).[100] Similarly, the Parable of the Ten Pounds (Luke characteristically downscales Matthew's talents) seems primarily intended to focus on the actions of the servants in their master's absence, not on the reasons for his delay, and thus the reference to 'kingly power' (so RSV; the Greek is βασιλεία), and the elaboration of this theme at vv. 14, 15a and 27 is unsatisfactory and confusing. The same is true of the House on the Rock/Sand pericope, where the intended point is less how well-built the house is than the nature and strength of its foundations. These, and similar examples, are compatible with Matthew being prior to Luke: it is difficult to imagine how they could work in the other direction.

3.2.5. *Verbal Priority*
Several critics have, however, regarded the many differences in wording between Matthew and Luke in parallel passages as evidence that Luke could not have used Matthew. Some have attributed this to the evangelists' use of differing versions of Q or of sayings (as is arguably the case with the Lord's Prayer), and it is assumed by many that Luke's wording must in most cases be more authentic than Matthew's because it is less polished, and maybe less spiritualized. This is most obviously true of the Beatitudes,[101] where Luke's Jesus blesses οἱ πτωχοί (*not* οἱ πτωχοὶ τῷ πνεύματι), and where those that weep 'shall laugh'. But it is equally possible that Luke is attempting to render Matthew's beautiful but impersonal periods in a pithier, more direct way.[102] In support of this view, it is noticeable that Luke has carefully balanced his four Beatitudes with corresponding Woes,[103] so that the ones he selects are all susceptible of

---

100. Thus Jeremias, *Parables*, p. 29.

101. Thus Creed, *Luke*, p. lxv, concludes, 'on the whole, Luke's version is perhaps closer to the original'. So, too, A. Loisy, *L'Evangile selon Luc* (Paris: Emile Nourry, 1924), p. 29: 'Sans doute a-t-il conservé la forme primitive des béatitudes...' Goulder, *Luke*, p. 16, calls this the 'Lukan priority fallacy'.

102. Matthew himself switches to the second person at 5.11. This variation for greater immediacy was a recognized Greek rhetorical device; see Longinus, *On the Sublime* 27.

103. Structural symmetry of this type is important to Luke, as is evident from the later Woes on the Pharisees and Lawyers. Many critics, even believers in Q such as Fitzmyer (see *Luke*, I, p. 627) think that the Woes are a Lukan editorial feature, a creative elaboration of his source. He could equally have edited the Beatitudes;

straight eschatological reversal—poor/rich; weep/laugh; hungry/filled; persecuted/ rewarded.[104] Eschatological reversal is in any case a favourite Lukan theme, as is evident in the Magnificat, or Simeon's second oracle, or the Parable of the Rich Man and Lazarus. Indeed, Luke uses a logion which states this particular theme on two occasions, at Lk. 14.11 and 18.14: πᾶς ὁ ὑψῶν ἑαυτὸν ταπεινωθήσεται, καὶ ὁ ταπεινῶν ἑαυτὸν ὑψωθήσεται.[105]

The Beatitudes in both Gospels—and hence also Luke's Woes—clearly reflect the editorial concerns of the two evangelists. Luke's is a theology of the poor; the hungry in his Gospel need real food.[106] We cannot, therefore, conclude that Luke's version of the blessing of the poor is any more likely to be authentic than Matthew's,[107] and the same is true of all his Beatitudes.

3.2.6. *The Birth Narrative*

The birth narrative provides another occasion when Luke's text can be explained as a creative rewriting of Matthew. In this sequence, although we need to retain some degree of caution in our assessment of the two evangelists' motives, certain emphases in each case are characteristic. We could therefore reasonably infer that Luke has reinterpreted the material in his own terms to stress particularly Lukan themes. Moreover, despite very obvious differences (no census and no elaborate parallel between John the Baptist and Jesus in Matthew; no Slaughter of the Innocents nor Flight into Egypt in Luke, where shepherds, not Magi, receive the revelation of the birth), there are so many shared points connecting the two accounts that if we deny that Luke used Matthew we must postulate yet another missing common source which both felt free to reinterpret creatively.

Matthew's other Beatitudes on the humble, merciful and spiritually pure represent topics that Luke treats elsewhere, although he often allows the point to be made by the narrative itself.

104. This is a leading Old Testament theme, too, as is evident in Deutero-Isaiah and Trito-Isaiah.

105. Matthew also has the idea expressed twice: but at Mt. 18.4 it is illustrated by a parabolic action.

106. Cf. Jas 2.16. W.E. Pilgrim, *Good News to the Poor* (Minneapolis: Augsburg–Fortress, 1981), pp. 14, 66ff., 72 and elsewhere stresses that Luke's handling of this theme should not be spiritualized, nor its impact dulled.

107. Thus, too, E. Bammel, in his consideration of πτωχός in *TDNT*, pp. 815-915.

Verbal links[108] include the frequent use of the Semitic ἰδού; the use by both[109] of the middle or passive voice of the verb μνηστεύομαι in place of the more usual γαμέω which is used elsewhere by Luke (see Lk. 14.20); the use of the verb γινώσκω in its Old Testament sexual sense;[110] and the term παρθένος applied to Mary (even though only Matthew cites Isa. 7.14 directly). Both speak of God's promises being fulfilled, too, and they echo the Old Testament repeatedly, Matthew's narrative in particular recalling the stories of Moses and Joseph, and Luke's those of Abraham and Sarah, Hannah and Samuel. (The difference here is that Matthew cites; Luke prefers to allude.)[111] In addition, even though Luke does not explain the meaning of the name Jesus in his birth narrative, as Matthew does at Mt. 1.21, he does so later, at Acts 4.12. (Similarly, the reference in Zechariah's canticle at Lk. 1.79 which is based on Isa. 9.2 is cited directly by Matthew in Mt. 4.16.)

The core of material they share[112] includes the names of the parents, Mary and Joseph, who are betrothed, but not yet living together (Mt. 1.18; Lk. 1.27), and the detail that Joseph is of the lineage of David (Mt. 1.16, 20; Lk. 1.27, 32; 2.4). An Angel of the Lord (Gabriel, adds Luke; there are indications here of a postexilic angelology) announces the forthcoming birth (Mt. 1.20-23; Lk. 1.30-35) and instructs that the child is to be called Jesus (Mt. 1.21; Lk. 1.31) because he will be a saviour (Mt. 1.21; Lk. 2.11). It is stressed that Mary's virginal conception (Mt. 1.20, 23, 25; Lk. 1.34) is through the agency of the Holy Spirit (Mt. 1.18, 20; Lk. 1.35). The birth of the child takes place in Bethlehem (Mt. 2.1; Lk. 2.4-6) _after_ Mary and Joseph come together to live there (Mt. 1.24-25; Lk. 2.5) during the reign of Herod the Great (Mt. 2.1; Lk. 1.5), but he is reared in Nazareth (Mt. 2.23; Lk. 2.39).

There are themes common to Matthew and Luke, too, such as the stress from the first on the Gentile mission,[113] which is in Matthew represented by the foreign Magi who come to worship the child, and in Luke by Simeon's beautiful canticle at Lk. 2.32. The evangelist, indeed, clearly

108. These are considered in detail by R.E. Brown, _The Birth of the Messiah_ (New York: Doubleday, 1979).

109. At Mt. 1.18; Lk. 1.27; 2.5.

110. At Mt. 1.25; Lk. 1.34.

111. Thus R.E. Brown, _Messiah_, p. 497; similarly J. Drury, _Tradition and Design in Luke's Gospel_ (London: Darton, Longman & Todd, 1976), p. 62.

112. This is summarized by R.E. Brown, _Messiah_, pp. 34-35.

113. R.E. Brown, _Messiah_, p. 459.

relates the birth of Christ to a wider stage by naming the Roman Emperor in Luke 2[114] as well as the Jewish King. We see thus prefigured a movement from Jerusalem and the Temple (central to both the birth narrative and the Passion) to Rome. Jesus is not just a *Jewish* Messiah: he is, as John 4 puts it, the Saviour of the world (cf. Lk. 3.6; Mt. 28.19).

Structurally, too, we note that both evangelists use *inclusio* to link the beginning and end of their Gospels; in Matthew, we have the Emmanuel prophecy at 1.23, which is picked up in the promise in 28.20; in Luke, the prophecy of Zechariah in 1.77 connects in a similar way with 24.47. Both, too, from the very first point forward to the Passion:[115] the murderous spite of Herod (and the anxiety of the Chief Priests and Scribes) anticipates later action in Matthew, and Simeon's words in Luke at 2.34-35 are similarly ominous.[116]

But despite these numerous links of subject-matter, theme and language, there are also great differences: and here we can perceive Luke's modification of his material in accordance with his own ideas. Hence there is the link he provides with the world stage, and also the very Lukan emphasis on repentance and forgiveness. Also characteristic is Luke's interest in and sympathy for women; we notice that the annunciation is made to Mary, not Joseph. Also entirely Lukan is the sympathy for the down-trodden, the *'ānāwîm*,[117] which informs the Magnificat as it does his version of the Beatitudes. This is a messiah who will exalt the humble and meek, not a glorious political leader who will lead a revolt against Rome. It is utterly typical that Luke 'scales down' Matthew's exotic Magi (Luke had a very low opinion of magicians; we recall Simon Magus in Acts)[118] and replaces them with shepherds who are undoubtedly *'ammê hā'āreṣ* and although not necessarily sinners[119] are certainly of doubtful repute, since they apparently often grazed their flocks on the lands of others. Luke's message is aimed from the first at the poor and flawed.

114. Cf. Lk. 3.1-2.
115. Similarly, R.E. Brown, *Messiah*, pp. 415 n. 18, 461-62.
116. See also Tannehill, *Narrative Unity*, I, pp. 43-44.
117. On the *'ānāwîm*, see R.E. Brown, *Messiah*, pp. 350-55.
118. See the discussion on Luke's attitude to magic in Garrett, *Demise*. This might also explain why Luke omits Matthew's flight into Egypt, which was connected with magic in Jewish sources; for example, there is a reference to 'sorceries from Egypt' in *y. Šab.* 12.4, as is noted by D.R. Catchpole, *The Trial of Jesus* (SBS, 18; Leiden: E.J. Brill, 1971), p. 7; similarly, Justin Martyr, *Dial.* 69 refers to 'Egyptian magicians'.
119. See E.P. Sanders, *Jesus and Judaism* (London: SCM Press, 1985), pp. 188-200.

3.2.7. *Discourses*

We can hence observe that Luke will use his narrative material in a way that suits his own theological purpose. The same is true of the discourses. Thus all Luke's 'omissions' from Matthew's Sermon on the Mount, which scholars who believe in Q regard as proof that Luke cannot have used Matthew,[120] are fully comprehensible, providing we recognize that his emphases differ from Matthew's. In any case, surprisingly few of the supposedly omitted sayings find no echo at all in Luke–Acts,[121] although Luke does drop Mt. 7.6, which is much too Jewish and too hostile to Gentiles in its orientation to be acceptable, and likewise Mt. 5.23-24, which reflects Jewish religious practices that may have seemed irrelevant as instructions for later Christians, especially when the Temple had been destroyed nearly thirty years earlier.[122] He also cuts Mt. 5.19-20, which is too exclusive and Rabbinic (and may have seemed to provide ammunition which could be used against Luke's hero, Paul), and also Mt. 5.21-24, 27-28, 33-39 which make the Torah even stricter, a counsel of perfection, and threaten hell-fire (Luke prefers mercy; see Lk. 6.36).

Instead, we notice that some material, although not included as a saying, is narrated, or forms the basis of a parable, which is Luke's preferred teaching method. Thus, that Jesus fulfils the Law and the Prophets (Mt. 5.17) is emphasized by Luke's overarching prophecy/fulfilment schema; the requirement to love one's neighbour (Mt. 5.43) is quoted at Lk. 10.27, and he expresses the corresponding command to love one's enemies powerfully in the Parable of the Good Samaritan; the core of Mt. 6.1-8, 16-18 is presented dramatically in the Parable of the Pharisee and the Tax-Collector (and perhaps is also reflected in the pericope of Ananias and Sapphira in Acts).

It is therefore entirely plausible that the Sermon on the Plain represents Luke's redaction of Matthew's speech. It is pointed out by Beck[123] that Luke's drastic pruning allows a much greater concentration on the theme of love, with the core of the sermon being located at 6.27-38. *Twelve* of its

---

120. See, e.g., G.H. Stanton, *A Gospel for a New People: Studies in Matthew* (Edinburgh: T. & T. Clark, 1992), p. 288.

121. Thus the warning of Mt. 7.15 forms part of Paul's speech at Miletus (see Acts 20.29-30).

122. We may compare his omission of Mt. 23.16-22, on swearing by the Temple, from the Woes in Luke 11.

123. B. Beck, *Christian Character in the Gospel of Luke* (London: Epworth Press, 1989), pp. 17-20.

thirty verses centre on the theme of ἀγάπη, a word not elsewhere common in Luke or Acts, though love is the message of Luke's finest parables, the Good Samaritan and the Prodigal Son. Indeed, all three parables in Luke 15 show us God's love for us, and invite our response.

The necessity for response is in any case an important part of Luke's pastoral message: his parables are usually imperative, rather than indicative,[124] concluding: Πορεύου καὶ σὺ ποίει ὁμοίως (Lk. 10.37). Doing is essential: love for others must be expressed in consistent actions,[125] and hence the present imperative of δίδωμι is used at 6.30 to show that generosity must be unlimited and repeated. The proper use of wealth is essential—that is the message of both the Rich Fool and the Rich Man and Lazarus. Almsgiving to the needy is shown to be a Christian duty: it is instructive to compare Luke's attack on the Pharisees at Lk. 11.39-42 with Matthew's at Mt. 23.23-36. Only Luke at v.41 contains: πλὴν τὰ ἐνόντα δότε ἐλεημοσύνην, καὶ ἰδοὺ πάντα καθαρὰ ὑμῖν ἐστιν.

3.3. *Conclusion*

To sum up, it is clear that a significant part of the 'synoptic problem' is solved if we accept that Luke knew and used Matthew as well as Mark. This accords with the evidence presented in the text: the Q hypothesis in its full form is unnecessary. We must not, however, rule out any possibility that he also used other material, which may in some cases have been written; in this respect, Goulder's view may be an over-simplification.

Sanders concludes:

> It is our judgment…that Luke knew Matthew. [But] a few examples cannot show that Luke had no other source than Matthew and Mark… We shall briefly mention that the opposite case—that Luke was copied by Matthew —cannot be made out. Luke's priority has been proposed, on the ground that his Greek can often be turned into Hebrew more easily than can that of the other Gospels. That, however, shows little, for the Hebrew which emerges is often classical biblical Hebrew, not first-century Hebrew. Luke… imitated the biblical style, and he appears to have imitated it in Greek. In any case the Hebraisms of parts of his Gospel show nothing about priority… If a simple hypothesis will prevail, it will be that Luke copied Matthew, not the reverse.[126]

124. Jeremias, *Parables*, p. 87, says that Luke's parabolic material has a 'direct hortatory application'. Similarly, Goulder, *Luke*, p. 101.
125. Cf. Beck, *Christian Character*, p. 22.
126. Sanders and Davies, *Synoptic Gospels*, pp. 96-97.

Although neither suggestion can be proven, I shall proceed on the assumption that Matthew was the most likely source for Luke to have used, since a simple theory which involves an extant source in fairly wide circulation at the end of the first century (even in Rome) is to be preferred to one relying on a hypothetical document such as Q. I shall accordingly show reasons for the changes he has made to Matthew's ordering of material in his main 'block' of Matthaean teaching, the central section. It must, however, be stressed that Luke's purpose as revealed by his treatment of his sources, the object of the study, would be the same whether that source were Matthew or the hypothetical 'Q'.

Chapter 4

LUKE'S CENTRAL SECTION (1): LUKE 9.51–14.35

4.1. *Introduction*

The previous chapter has shown that there is evidence which strongly suggests that Luke is using both Mark and Matthew as sources for his Gospel. In the central section, however, there is little indication of the former: indeed, as will be shown in the exegesis below, there is probably more evidence of contact with the Johannine tradition than with Mark. The main source for Luke's travel narrative would appear to be Matthew, but most of the material which the two share is differently placed. It is therefore necessary to examine this section in some detail and try to understand what Luke is doing and how he has arranged the material.

4.2. *Some Proposed Solutions to the Problem*

4.2.1. *Chiasmus*

There have been numerous attempts over the years to detect some kind of order within the seeming chaos of the protracted Lukan journey to Jerusalem. Some critics, such as C.H. Talbert[1] and K.E. Bailey,[2] have proposed a chiastic structure, framing the questions at 10.25 and 18.18 around a centre point which both Talbert and Bailey locate at 13.18-35, with the themes of Sabbath healings, repentance, the cost of discipleship, riches/possessions, conflict with the Pharisees, and prayer occurring on either side in approximately the same sequence. C.L. Blomberg,[3] however,

---

1.   C.H. Talbert, *Literary Patterns, Theological Themes and the Genre of Luke–Acts* (SBLMS, 20; Missoula, MT: Scholars Press, 1974).

2.   K.E. Bailey, *Poet and Peasant: A Literary Cultural Approach to the Parables in Luke* (Grand Rapids: Eerdmans, 1976). Cf. also M.D. Goulder, 'The Chiastic Structure of the Lucan Journey', in F.L. Cross (ed.), *SE II* (TU, 87; Berlin: Akademie Verlag, 1964), pp. 195-202; and, more recently, H. Baarlinck, 'Die zyklische Struktur von Lukas 9.43b–19.28', *NTS* 38 (1992), pp. 481-506.

3.   C.L. Blomberg, 'Midrash, Chiasmus, and the Outline of Luke's Central

notes that repetition of themes, incidents, and so on is common in Luke, so that it may be an oversimplification to apply a scheme such as this too rigidly and regard duplication as indicative of chiasmus. Moreover, not all the material fits this pattern, many of the suggested parallels are dubious,[4] and there are very few of the verbal echoes we might have expected. Blomberg believes, nevertheless, that the evidence of some sort of chiastic structuring (he calculates that Bailey's proposed scheme is an 86 per cent fit) is too strong to be ignored. He instead suggests that Luke has incorporated into his central section a source of chiastically arranged parables which are independent of those recorded by Matthew. But the arguments Blomberg uses against the suggestions of Talbert and others are equally applicable to his own scheme. Thus the verbal echoes between the proposed parallels are often negligible or non-existent. Moreover, there are other parallels, such as that between the Rich Fool and the Dishonest Steward, which extend to both subject-matter and expression and yet are ignored by Blomberg because they do not fit the pattern he perceives. Nor does he account for all Luke's parabolic material; what of the Tower Builders/Warring Kings of 14.28-32, or the Unworthy Servants of Lk. 17.7-10? And what of the parables which have some connections with material in Matthew, like the Lost Sheep, the Fig-tree and the Great Supper, for which Blomberg's explanation seems very forced?

4.2.2. *A Christian Deuteronomy*
Another suggestion, developed most fully by C.F. Evans[5] but also made

Section', in R.T. France and D. Wenham (eds.), *Gospel Perspectives* (Sheffield: JSOT Press, 1983), pp. 217-61.

4.   The same is true of Baarlinck's scheme. His suggestion that we often see the pairing of a 'positive' example (such as the healing of a blind man and the reception by a tax-collector at Jericho as illustrations of the logion 'the Son of Man came to save the lost') with a 'negative' one (the refusal of the Samaritan villagers to receive Jesus) can sometimes be illuminating. But although we may agree that some of the material appears to be arranged chiastically, especially around the proposed centre at 13.31-35, his scheme is open to as many objections as those of Bailey and Talbert. Thus many of the 'parallels' (such as that between the Mission of the Seventy (Two) and the Parable of the Ten Pounds; or between the dialogues at 11.27-28 and 17.20-21) seem very forced. Fitzmyer's criticism of Talbert's scheme (see Fitzmyer, *Luke*, I, p. 97, quoted by Baarlinck on p. 484), that the correspondences are perceived by Talbert rather than by Luke, applies equally to his own.

5.   C.F. Evans, 'The Central Section of Luke's Gospel', in D.E. Nineham (ed.), *Studies in the Gospels: Essays in Memory of R.H. Lightfoot* (Oxford: Basil Blackwell, 1955), pp. 37-53.

by A.M. Farrer,[6] J. Drury[7] and others, is that the central section forms a 'Christian Deuteronomy' and its order accords with the Old Testament text. This suggestion has much to commend it; Deuteronomy is clearly an influence on Luke,[8] and like the Deuteronomist Luke interprets history from a moralist's viewpoint, seeing it as demonstrating God's control over human life. It may be, too—though Evans himself does not make this suggestion—that it was Deuteronomy's restatement, supposedly made by Moses on his deathbed, of what the Book of the Covenant had already presented as the Law given by Yahweh to Moses in Exodus 20–23 which provided Luke with a precedent for his in many respects analogous treatment of the teaching of Jesus as recorded by Matthew: it has often been noted that both Luke and Deuteronomy reflect similar themes and emphases, such as concern for women, the disadvantaged and needy, debtors and so on. One could therefore argue that paraphrasing, restating, re-editing (and occasionally modifying) the words of the Lord in the light of historical experience was very much a part of the Old Testament tradition taken over by Luke.

Evans may be correct, too, to detect an implicit comparison between the situation of Moses, who was not permitted to lead his followers into the Promised Land, and that of Jesus, who will succeed through the ἀνάλημψις he will achieve in Jerusalem; the Moses/Jesus typology is important to Luke, as it is also to John.[9] Moreover, an 'argument from order' can be perceived at some points; thus the consideration of the rights of the first-born and the punishment to be meted out to the disobedient at Deut. 21.15-22 is in close proximity with the instructions on what to do if sheep or oxen go astray, and Luke similarly links the Prodigal Son to the Lost Sheep in ch. 15, even if he reverses the sequence.

It is a little surprising, nevertheless, that there are so few verbal parallels between the two texts, although since it is not being claimed that Deuteronomy is a direct source this perhaps does not matter. It might be thought

6.   Farrer, 'Dispensing with Q', pp. 55-88.
7.   Drury, *Tradition*, pp. 138-64.
8.   There are several allusions to Deuteronomy in Luke–Acts; e.g. Lk. 11.20/Deut. 9.10; Acts 7.51/Deut. 10.16; Acts 3.19/Deut. 11.14; Acts 3,22-23/Deut. 18.15-16; and perhaps Lk. 10.19/Deut. 8.15.
9.   Compare also D.P. Moessner, *The Lord of the Banquet: The Literary and Theological Significance of the Lukan Travel Narrative* (Minneapolis: Augsburg–Fortress, 1989), although he somewhat overstates his case.

a more significant objection that so much of Deuteronomy's material finds no place in Luke, and, similarly, that much of Luke's cannot be matched in Deuteronomy; hence there is no connection between Deut. 21.22-23, on hanging wrong-doers, and the Lukan Parable of the Lost Coin, even if we are prepared to grant that a parallel exists between Deuteronomy and Luke elsewhere in this section with regard to errant sons and missing sheep. Indeed, the connection between the two texts at some points is so tenuous that many would see it as purely coincidental.

A much stronger objection is that Evans overlooks references which clearly connect the central section with Deuteronomy when they do not fit his scheme. Thus he omits any reference to Deut. 16.18-20, on the corruption of justice, when he discusses Lk. 18.1-6; likewise, he does not mention the relevance of Deut. 22.4 to his consideration of Lk. 14.5; nor does he acknowledge that the Fourth Commandment would be far more appropriate in relation to the healing on the Sabbath at Lk. 13.10-17 than is Deut. 15.1-18, where there is not even a verbal link, since Deuteronomy uses ἄφεσις and Luke ἀπολύω and λύω. Further, Evans often ignores synoptic parallels altogether: there are several occasions when the correspondence between Luke's placement and Matthew's is much more evident than any supposed link between Luke and Deuteronomy. (For example, the conjuction of the mission charge and the saying concerning peace is followed in both Matthew and Luke by an injunction to shake from one's feet the dust of hostile villages, which has no apparent Deuteronomic parallel: and this in itself provides a thematic link with the woes on the cities of Chorazin, Bethsaida and Capernaum, which both Matthew and Luke place after it. The connection Evans perceives with the threat of destruction against the enemies of the Israelites in Deuteronomy 2 is much less apparent, even if the two are not necessarily mutually exclusive; it could be a case of both Matthew and Deuteronomy.)

It seems then that Evans, like Blomberg and Talbert, has sought to impose his scheme in an over-rigid way upon the text. The connection with Deuteronomy must not be minimized, but it cannot provide the key to unlock the mystery of Luke's order without a great deal of force. We may conclude that the principle governing the selection and ordering of the material in this section remains a puzzle, although I hope to show by a detailed analysis that even if we reject the suggestions of Lummis and Goulder[10] as to Luke's method, or those of Talbert, Blomberg and Evans

---

10. Lummis, *Luke*, pp. 9-10; Goulder, *Luke*, pp. 581-83.

concerning the structuring of his material, it is still possible to perceive a consistent and coherent purpose in Luke's redaction of the other Gospels.[11]

4.2.3. *Other Suggestions*

It is apparent, however, that any explanation which attempts to impose a fixed scheme, consistently applied, is unsatisfactory to a greater or lesser degree. For this reason, Maddox's[12] suggestion, which is much more flexible, is less open to objection. He proposes that Luke is here trying to reconcile the predominantly Galilaean ministry of Jesus in Mark and Matthew (and as is evident in Acts, Galilee was not significant in any way to the later spread of the Church as far as Luke was concerned) with the greater emphasis on Judaea/Samaria in John.[13] In this connection, Conzelmann[14] notes that Luke omits the reference to Judaea in connection with John the Baptist (cf. Mt. 3.1; Mk 1.5; Lk. 3.2) and infers that this is because he wishes to present Judaea as Jesus' field of operations. It is observable elsewhere that, whereas at Mk 1.39 there is a reference to Jesus preaching throughout all the synagogues of Galilee, Luke says that he preaches in the synagogues of *Judaea* at 4.44 (cf. 7.17).[15] The section of Luke's Gospel beginning at 9.51 with the rejection by the Samaritan cities and continuing with the Good Samaritan parable and the story of Mary and Martha seems, like John's Gospel, to have connections with Samaria and also with Judaean traditions.

Like the other evangelists, to a greater or lesser degree, Luke's technique is to group thematically-related sayings, parables, and actions, and he often wishes to stress particular items differently and to offer a different interpretation from those found in his sources. Thus, since Matthew's five major discourses clearly do not represent actual sermons, Luke quarries

11. That a coherent purpose is observable in Luke's redaction of the other Gospels provides an answer to the objection made by Chilton, *Profiles*, pp. 42-43, that source criticism 'fails to treat the Gospels as coherent documents in themselves. The meaning of each Gospel is ignored in order to explain it as a collation of sources'.

12. Maddox, *Purpose*, p. 169.

13. Cf. P. Parker, 'Luke and the Fourth Evangelist', *NTS* 9 (1963), pp. 317-36, especially pp. 318-19.

14. Conzelmann, *Theology*, p. 19.

15. Contra M.D. Goulder, 'John 1:1-2:12 and the Synoptics', in A. Denaux (ed.), *John and the Synoptics* (Proceedings of the 1990 Leuven Colloquium; BETL, 101; Leuven: Leuven University Press, 1992), pp. 201-37 (229), there is no reason why Judaea in Lk. 7.17 should instead be considered synonymous with 'Jewry'. In Luke Jesus is active in Judaea as well as Galilee.

their sayings and relocates the material elsewhere to suit his own purposes. The narrative material included in Luke's central section does not seem to be treated with the same freedom; it is either Judaea-based (such as the third prediction of the passion, the healing of the blind man at Jericho, and the story of Mary and Martha) or it occurs only in Luke (such as the healings of the crippled woman and dropsical man, the story of Zacchaeus, the reaction of the Samaritan villages to Jesus, and the sending out of the seventy [two] emissaries). No narrative material is relocated: we must therefore assume that Luke did not feel at liberty to do so.

4.3. *Exegesis of Luke 9.51–14.35*

4.3.1. *Ch. 9.51-56*

The central section/travel narrative proper begins at 9.51. Luke draws attention to the fact that Jesus is travelling south towards Judaea—and destiny—by referring to Samaria in v. 52. (Other geographical indications[16] also tend to occur near the beginning or end of Luke's central section, as he tries to fit his material into an already given narrative structure and scheme.) Contra W. Gasse,[17] the references at vv. 52 and 56 suggest some kind of Samaritan ministry (cf. Jn 4.4-42),[18] of which the Synoptics otherwise give no indication.

16. See Lk. 10.38; 13.22, 33; 17.11; 18.31-35; 19.1, 11, 28. D. Gill, 'Observations on the Lucan Travel Narrative and Some Related Passages', *HTR* 63 (1970), pp. 199-221, observes that these references occur in connection with either the Gentile mission or mistaken ideas about Jesus' role; see 9.51-56/9.57-62; 10.38/10.41-42; 13.22/13.28-29; 13.33/13.34; 14.25-35; 17.11/17.18-19, 21; 18.31/18.32-34; 18.35/18.38-42; 19.1, 11, 28/19.9, 12-27, 44. Many other critics see a theological significance in the journey motif: it is not just a framework, like Chaucer's *Canterbury Tales*. See F.V. Filson, 'The Journey Motif in Luke–Acts', in W. Ward Gasque and R.P. Martin (eds.), *Apostolic History and the Gospel* (Exeter: Paternoster Press, 1970), pp. 68-77; Tannehill, *Narrative Unity*, I, *passim*; W.C. Robinson, 'The Theological Context for Interpreting Luke's Travel Narrative', *JBL* 79 (1960), pp. 20-31; J.H. Davies, 'The Purpose of the Central Section of Luke's Gospel', in F.L. Cross (ed.), *SE II* (TU, 87; Berlin: Akademie Verlag, 1964), pp. 164-69.
17. W. Gasse, 'Zum Reisebericht des Lukas', *ZNW* 34 (1935), pp. 293-98.
18. See Creed, *Luke*, p. 140. Creed sees the geographical difficulties involved in a journey from Galilee to Jerusalem via Samaria and Jericho as arising from a literary cause; the desire to include a Samaritan mission (as in John) and yet to adhere to the Markan Jericho/Jerusalem account. Luke is, by implication, trying to splice the two together.

4.3.2. *Ch. 9.57-62*

Verses 57-59 reflect the experience of itinerant prophets,[19] and Matthew's parallel at 8.18-22 is imprecise (εἰς τὸ πέραν) in its location. Luke therefore feels able to transfer it to this context, since it links with a theme he wishes to develop in the next section—the cost of discipleship. It is noticeable that Luke's modification at Lk. 9.60 (cf. Mt. 8.22) turns the demand of Jesus into a pastoral imperative; the duty to proclaim the Kingdom of God, entrusted to the disciples, as we see in Acts (Acts 8.12; 14.22; 19.8; 20.25; 28.23, 31), takes precedence over all else. Luke adds a 'domestic' reference at 9.61, which calls forth Jesus' very stringent saying in v. 62. All these sayings about the implications and demands of discipleship[20] are thematically connected and will be elaborated later. The references in vv. 60 and 62 to the Kingdom are both peculiar to Luke, since the first is a Lukan addition to Mt. 8.22 and the second occurs in two verses which are unparalleled in Matthew. They, too, are to be elaborated throughout the teaching of the central section, where 'the Kingdom' is a major unifying theme.

4.3.3. *Ch. 10.1-12*

At the beginning of the real 'teaching' of the central section, Luke places the pericope of the Mission of the Seventy (Two), which is peculiar to his Gospel. Its position demonstrates its importance: so does the fact that it is an elaboration of the earlier Mission of the Twelve (see 9.1-6), since what Luke regards as significant he repeats, as we see throughout the whole of Luke–Acts. This pericope may illustrate a Jesus/Moses typology relating to the appointment of seventy (two) elders: but it is more probably[21] to be

19. Cf. Beck, *Christian Character,* pp. 95ff.; Esler, *Community and Gospel*, p. 118; G. Theissen, *The First Followers of Jesus* (London: SCM Press, 1978 [= *The Sociology of Early Palestinian Christianity*, Philadelphia: Fortress Press, 1978]).

20. The Greek term μαθητής is common to the Gospels and Acts, but it does not occur elsewhere in the New Testament, and it is only found in the Septuagint in three places where there are variant readings in some major manuscripts. It is part of the normal vocabulary of Hellenistic Judaism (there are several examples in Philo), and it seems to reflect the influence of the Greek philosophical schools. It is characteristic that of the canonical writers only Luke has the feminine form μαθήτρια at Acts 9.36. The cost of discipleship is a leading Lukan theme, as many have recognized. See, e.g., N. Richardson, *The Panorama of Luke* (London: Epworth Press, 1982), pp. 27-38; C.H. Talbert, *Reading Luke* (London: SPCK, 1990), pp. 114-19; Beck, *Christian Character*, pp. 100, 109.

21. Contra C.F. Evans, *St Luke* (London: SCM Press; Philadelphia: Trinity Press

seen as prefiguring the Gentile mission (Genesis 10 probably refers to seventy [two] Gentile nations).[22] This would be appropriate at this point, when Jesus is en route to Jerusalem: the Church spreads out from Jerusalem in Acts until it reaches the Gentile capital, Rome. The two are not, in any case, mutually exclusive; both may be true.

Luke seems to have split the material into two commissionings (or he may have been using two sources). Thus:

- at Lk. 9.3 he puts the instruction not to take anything for the way (cf. Mk 6.8), and likewise the reference to a ῥάβδον (Mk 6.8; Mt. 10.10—and here Luke follows Matthew), to ἄρτον (cf. Mk 6.8), to ἀργύριον (cf. Mt. 10.9) and to δύο χιτῶνας (Mk. 6.9; Mt. 10.10: again, Luke is closer to Matthew). Thus:

Mt. 10.10	Lk. 9.3	Mk 6.8-9
μηδὲ δύο χιτῶνας ...μηδὲ ῥάβδον	μήτε ῥάβδον... μήτε ἀνὰ δύο χιτῶνας	εἰ μὴ ῥάβδον μὴ ἐνδύσησθε δύο χιτῶνας

- at Lk. 10.4 sandals are forbidden (cf. Mt. 10.10: we may compare Mk 6.9, where they are told to wear sandals). Luke also adds a prohibition on 'greeting anyone on the way', which perhaps serves to remind us that a journey is in progress (cf. 9.57); this may have been suggested by Mt. 10.12, since ἀσπάσησθε is common to both evangelists.

Luke's prohibition on taking a πήραν (as in Mk 6.8; Mt. 10.10) occurs in both his mission charges. (It is interesting that whereas Luke at 6.13, like Matthew at 10.2, refers to the 'Twelve Apostles' [cf. Rev. 21.14], this is not a title accorded to the seventy [two], despite the fact that the term 'apostle' simply means 'one who is sent', and it seems to have been used in this way in the early days of the Church.[23] It soon acquired great significance, as we can see from Paul's Epistles, and despite his frequent

International, 1990), p. 445, the context here, especially v. 8, and the clear links with Acts, suggest that the Gentile mission was in Luke's mind at this point.

22. There are variations between the Masoretic text of the Old Testament and the Septuagint at both these points, too, so that it is a matter of dispute whether there were 70 or 72 elders appointed by Moses in Exod. 24.1; Num. 11.16, or 70 or 72 Gentile nations in Genesis 10.

23. Creed, *Luke*, p. 88, suggests that this usage may be reflected in Lk. 11.49, which is a Lukan addition to the Matthaean parallel at Mt. 23.34. Cf. Rev. 2.2; 18.20; and also many examples throughout Paul's letters, such as Rom. 16.7; 1 Cor. 4.9; 12.28, 29.

claim to the title,[24] Luke normally limits its use to the Twelve. The only exceptions are at Acts 14.4 and Acts 14.14, where the handing on of the apostolic tradition is at stake in the appointment of elders for new churches [see Acts 14.23]; on these occasions Paul and Barnabas, too, are thus styled.)

The 'Lord of the harvest' motif was connected to the Mission of the Twelve in Matthew: Luke avoids a doublet by retaining it until now. Matthew places before it the 'sheep without a shepherd' saying which Luke does not include, although in its place he uses Matthew's later 'sheep in the midst of wolves' saying (see Mt. 10.16). This particular saying was presumably chosen because it relates to the theme Luke wishes to develop: the dangers facing missionaries. (The greater importance of this to Luke is emphasized by the fact that this whole section is much fuller than the Mission of the Twelve.) Connected with this are the details about entering houses, how to behave if one is refused entry, and so on; once more, Luke's account is fuller than Matthew's and relates to the later situation of Christian missionaries, as reflected in Acts. It is nevertheless interesting that he replaces Matthew's πρόβατα with ἄρνας. One wonders if this Lukan modification could have some connection with the injunction by John's Jesus to Peter, βόσκε τὰ ἀρνία μου (Jn 21.15). Although the 'flock' image is a traditional one, Luke elsewhere uses ποίμνιον (see Lk. 12.32; Acts 20.28, 29), and it is difficult otherwise to account for the change. It could, perhaps, be an example of a 'verbal reminiscence'[25] connecting the Gospels of Luke and John.

Luke's omission of Mt. 10.16, the injunction to be 'as wise (φρόνιμοι) as serpents', is explicable because serpents, like scorpions, are tradition-ally associated with evil,[26] as is evident from Revelation. Luke presumably does not wish to present Christian disciples in these terms at all, just as later he does not wish to present Christianity as a yoke. In both cases Luke

24. See, e.g., 1 Cor. 9.1, 2.

25. Verbal reminiscences provide many of the points of contact between the Gospels, as H. Schürmann observes, although he uses the phrase in a different sense and context. (See H. Schürmann, 'Sprachliche Reminiszenzen an Abgeänderte oder Ausgelassene Bestandteile der Spruchsammlung im Lukas- und Matthäusevangelium', *NTS* 6 [1959], pp. 193-210.)

26. Another possibility is that the quality recommended here, prudence, and the adjective used, φρόνιμος, are picked up by Luke later in the problematic Parable of the Dishonest Steward, where it is precisely this quality which is praised by ὁ κύριος, and where the steward's actions certainly display a serpentine cunning. (See Creed, *Luke*, p. 202.)

alludes to the omitted verse in his own text; allusion, rather than citation, is a Lukan characteristic.

If we see this whole section as prefiguring the Gentile mission, then Luke's Jesus by implication rejects Jewish food laws for later disciples (see 10.8; it is interesting that this verse, which clearly reflects the experience of missionaries, is very close to the words of Paul in 1 Cor. 10.27). In this context we recall that Paul in Acts does indeed 'heal the sick' and preach the Kingdom of God (see Acts 20.25). There is also, perhaps, a connection with Matthew's charge at 10.8b to 'raise the dead'; Luke does not include this in his instructions, but he presents it in the actions of both Peter and Paul in Acts. In addition, we see Paul and Barnabas 'shaking the dust' of Pisidian Antioch from their feet in Acts 13.51; there is a very clear link here with Acts,[27] and it is for that reason that the Mission of the Seventy (Two) probably relates to the Gentile mission. Luke stresses at Lk. 10.11 the point that is also made by the signs wrought by Peter and Paul in Acts; disciples (and hence later Christian leaders, too) can bring the Kingdom closer by their actions.[28] It is a characteristically ecclesiological emphasis.[29] And the consequences of rejecting that message are, by implication, grave; the context is very threatening, and this provides a transition to the next section.

4.3.4. *Ch. 10.13-20*

The proclamation of doom over the town which rejects Jesus in Lk. 10.12 (cf. Mt. 10.15) can clearly be related thematically to the Woes over Chorazin and Bethsaida which Matthew places later, at 11.20-24, the two being connected in Matthew by the reference to Sodom at Mt. 10.15 and 11.23, 24. Luke uses these Woes to round off his own section, and they may perhaps express his verdict on Judaism. The theme is encapsulated in the logion at 10.16, Ὁ ἀκούων ὑμῶν ἐμοῦ ἀκούει, καὶ ὁ ἀθετῶν ὑμᾶς ἐμὲ ἀθετεῖ ὁ δὲ ἐμὲ ἀθετῶν ἀθετεῖ τὸν ἀποστείλαντά με, which is similar to the saying that Matthew has used at 10.40 to end his second discourse—and there are slight connections here with Johannine material, too (see Jn 5.23-24; 12.44-45,[30] and 13.20).

---

27. See Talbert, *Reading Luke*, pp. 116-17.
28. Cf. Acts 14.22.
29. Similarly, Conzelmann, *Theology*, p. 107.
30. M.D. Goulder, 'From Ministry to Passion in John and Luke', *NTS* 29 (1983), pp. 561-68, regards Jn 12.44 as dependent on Lk. 10.16, since John does not elsewhere use the verb ἀθετέω, and the motif of acceptance/refusal is a leading Lukan theme.

The ordering of Luke's material in this section is not the same as Matthew's, since Luke focuses much more explicitly on the situation facing itinerant missionaries, whereas Matthew chooses to emphasize that Jesus' mission is to Israelites, not to Samaritans or Gentiles. Although this is, in effect, borne out by Luke's presentation more than it is by Matthew's, Luke finds such an exclusive statement unacceptable, and he therefore omits it. It remains true, nevertheless, that Luke's treatment of Matthaean material makes perfect sense in its new context. Thus he begins with the material which parallels the commissioning of the seventy (two) to that of the Twelve, since this by inference links the Gentile mission to Jesus;[31] he proceeds by a consideration of the situation facing missionaries which links with the events narrated in Acts and reflects on their implications for Judaism; and he concludes with an account of the conflict of Jesus' followers with Satan and an assurance of their victory over evil which seems to have its closest links with Johannine material.[32] This follows the narration of the Return of the Seventy (Two), which was clearly modelled on that of the Twelve, albeit in a much abbreviated form. Verses 17-19 are linked thematically to what has preceded;[33] they set Luke's understanding of the implications of Jesus' ministry and that of his disciples in a wider apocalyptic context which involves the defeat of Satan.[34] It is entirely appropriate that this is placed here, at the conclusion to what is a prefiguration of the Gentile mission, since the point is ecclesiological: the

---

But it must be stressed that Luke himself outside this verse has only one other use of the verb, at Lk. 7.30, so it can hardly be termed Lukan. Acceptance/rejection is a Johannine theme, too; in the context of a reaction to Jesus it occurs at Jn 5.43; 6.29. and elsewhere. 'Him who sent me', although it occurs in all four Gospels, is a characteristically Johannine idiom; indeed, John uses numerous forms of this logion throughout his Gospel, on each occasion slightly differing in vocabulary (see, e.g., 5.23, 37; 6.29; 7.28-29; 12.44; 13.20; 14.24) so one could argue that at this point Luke is more likely to have borrowed the form that most suited his theme from John, rather than the reverse, and then added vv. 29-30 (which seems extraneous in their context) as a link forwards to it.

31. Cf. Talbert, *Reading Luke*, p. 116.

32. There is also an allusion to Isa. 14.12 at Lk. 10.18.

33. Contra Evans, *Luke*, p. 453, who regards v. 19 as breaking the connection between vv. 18 and 20, it is integral to the apocalyptic schema which dominates this whole speech. It also seems to have some connection with Acts 28.3-6; Luke is carefully linking his two narratives throughout this section.

34. Contra Conzelmann, *Theology*, p. 188, who sees Jesus' ministry as Satan-free until the Passion, and regards this passage as supporting his interpretation.

authority granted to Christians. This is of crucial importance to Luke, and
it is repeatedly demonstrated by the narrative of Acts (Paul, for example,
does not exactly trample on a serpent, but he is certainly unharmed by
one!). Luke retains the section in Matthew's discourse about 'having
authority over unclean spirits' (Mt. 10.1) and uses it here to form a climax;
and he underlines the significance of this in v. 20, by subordinating this
authority to the fact that Christian missionaries have by their actions won
heavenly approval.[35] In a sense, then, Luke is playing down the significance of the miraculous, even while acknowledging it.[36]

4.3.5. Ch. 10.21-24.

The connection to the next section is provided by the word 'rejoice',
although the term used in v. 20 (the verb χαίρω) is different from that in
v. 21 (ἀγαλλιάω). The linkage is once more thematic: Jesus has been
talking of the joy of the disciples, and this leads naturally to a consideration of his own joy, in a passage Luke mainly derives from Mt. 11.25-27,
although the stress on joy[37] perhaps has closer links with John (see Jn
15.11; 16.20-24; 17.13: we should note that Jn 17.13 is concerned with the
joy felt by Jesus, as in Luke). The reference to the Holy Spirit in Lk. 10.21
is a Lukan insertion which is probably intended to provide a link forward
to Acts, where the disciples receive the Spirit and the initiative of the
Spirit guides events. Matthew's reference to revelation at 11.26, which is
followed by an observation about the mutual knowledge of Father and Son
and the imparting of that knowledge to those with whom the Son chooses
to share it, is combined in Luke with a blessing of the disciples in the
knowledge they have been granted (see 10.22-24); the emphasis on
personal witness is a repeated Lukan theme, which also has links with
John.

Luke does not wish to present Christianity as a yoke,[38] although on one
occasion (Acts 15.10) he refers to the Torah in these terms, and in consequence he drops Mt. 11.29-30. His omission of Mt. 11.28 is less easy to
explain, since one would have expected it to have been congenial to the
evangelist. Goulder's suggestion here is that he has already alluded to this

---

35. This reflects a theme also found in Revelation (see Rev. 13.8; 17.8; 20.12, 15);
see also Dan. 12.1; *1 Enoch* 96.1-4, 97.1-2.

36. Similarly Talbert, *Reading Luke*, p. 117.

37. See R.F. O'Toole, *The Unity of Luke's Theology* (GNS, 9; Wilmington, DE:
Michael Glazier, 1984), pp. 225-60.

38. Thus M.D. Goulder, *Luke*, pp. 483ff.

Matthaean verse, with its promise of Messianic rest, at Lk. 10.5-6, where he has transferred the Matthaean blessing (εἰρήνη) on the house at Mt. 10.13 to the owner of that house. Matthew's Jesus at 11.28 promises to give rest (ἀναπαύω) to those who come to him; Luke, as is frequently his practice, uses a compound of the same verb (ἐπαναπαύομαι) in conjunction with εἰρήνη at 10.5, where the context clearly relates to continuing, eschatological (i.e. Messianic) peace and rest.

Luke has thus placed the implication and promise of this verse in an appropriate context which relates to the later mission of the Church, and this is typical. Moreover, he may have wished to avoid Matthew's connection here of Jesus to the Wisdom tradition,[39] which may have had links with developing Gnostic speculations;[40] he consistently refuses to identify Jesus with Wisdom, as is also evident at Lk. 7.35. (Luke's interpretation seems closer to apocalyptic texts such as *1 En.* 42, where Wisdom is located in Heaven in the presence of God, and is available to humans only through angelic mediation and revelation.)

The material Luke has retained in close verbal parallel from this Matthaean section thus includes only Mt. 11.27/Lk. 10.22 (which also has connections with Jn 10.15; 17.25, so that by the Jewish rule of 'double testimony' it may have seemed confirmed); Mt. 11.26, which is a Jewish prayer formula; and Mt. 11.25/Lk. 10.21, which is quite close to 1 Cor. 1.26-28. (Even if Luke did *not* know 1 Corinthians, which is a matter of dispute, this particular saying, with its championing of the 'little ones', and its opposition to the elitism of those who felt that their wisdom exalted them above others—a feature of much later Gnostic thought, which was already a problem in Corinth during the Pauline mission—would presumably have been congenial to Luke.) The other Matthaean verses are unparalleled except in Wisdom literature, and although Luke may use them elsewhere, he only does so allusively.

---

39. Matthew is very close in some places to Sir. 51.23-27: 'Draw near to me, you who are untaught…put your neck under the yoke (of wisdom) and let your souls receive instruction… I have found for myself much rest'. There is a dense web of Old Testament allusions here ('Thou hast hidden' [cf. Isa. 29.14], 'from the wise' [Isa. 29.11], 'rest for your souls' [Jer. 6.16]). J.C. Fenton, *St Matthew* (Pelican Gospel Commentaries; Harmondsworth: Penguin, 1963), p. 186 concludes, 'The passage reads more like a piece of Church writing based on a number of O.T. quotations and put into the Lord's mouth (such as we have in the discourses of John's Gospel) than a tradition of Jesus' words spoken during the ministry.'

40. See R.M. Grant, *Gnosticism and Early Christianity* (New York: Harper & Row, 2nd edn, 1966), pp. 153ff.

4.3.6. *Ch. 10.25-37*

The next section concerns the true purpose of the Torah, and Luke is characteristically not concerned with what is the greatest commandment—a Rabbinic question—but with its salvific force: how to attain eternal life. This pericope is placed by Mark and Matthew when Jesus leaves Galilee and enters Judaea (see Mk 10.17-22; Mt. 19.16-22); Luke also places it near the beginning of *his* Judaean section, even though this is considerably longer in his Gospel. He also uses it later—a notable Lukan narrative doublet—at 18.18-27; the question is crucial, and Luke wishes to underline its importance. At 10.25 Luke uses the exchange with the Lawyer[41] to lead into the Parable of the Good Samaritan at 10.29-37, after a very good example of what Goulder terms a 'guillotine question'[42] at 10.29, which places the head of Jesus' self-righteous victim very neatly on the chopping-block. This parable, which in many respects echoes 2 Chron. 28.15, is clearly an interpretation of Leviticus 19, which is summarized by Luke at 10.27. The connection is again thematic; Luke, as so often in this section, is expressing a teaching point by means of a vivid and memorable story.

4.3.7. *Ch. 10.38-42*

The characterization of Mary and Martha[43] in this pericope has clear points of contact with John's Gospel. Luke seems to have simplified the

41. Lawyers (Lk. 7.30; 11.45, 52; 14.3) as well as Pharisees are Jesus' main opponents in Luke. This may reflect the later situation when legal proceedings against Christians were usually initiated by informers—who were perhaps frequently Pharisees—and prosecutions depended on individual legal action.

42. Goulder, *Luke*, p. 96. The same is true elsewhere, for example, at Lk. 14.3.

43. Luke's attitude to women is patently very different from that shown in other early Christian documents like the Pastoral Epistles. To Luke (see Lk. 11.27-28), women are not saved by bearing children (cf. 1 Tim. 2.15), but by responding to the word of God. Thus when E. Tetlow, *Women and Ministry in the New Testament* (New York: Paulist Press, 1980), pp. 108-109, regards Priscilla (who instructs a male disciple in Acts 18.26) as part of the 'tradition' that the evangelist took over—with the implication that he would otherwise have changed it—we should compare 1 Tim. 2.11-12, where women are expressly forbidden to teach, and also 1 Cor. 14.33b-35. Tetlow's interpretation of Luke also plays downs his deliberate pairing of female with male throughout his whole work, from the birth narrative onwards, where (contra Matthew) the angelic message is given to Mary, rather than Joseph, as well as to Zechariah. Indeed, it is typical that the first Christian confession in Luke's Gospel is made by a woman—Elizabeth—at Lk. 1.43. Examples such as these demonstrate a very positive attitude to women, not an obligation to cater for the needs of the catechetical instruction of females, which Luke would have preferred if possible to avoid.

material included by John about Mary of Bethany by splitting it and placing some much earlier, in ch. 7. He does not name the village as Bethany at 10.38, perhaps because its proximity to Jerusalem would have proved difficult to reconcile with the amount of Judaean material he has yet to cover, but its location can only be in Judaea or Samaria since the implication of the text is that Jesus has by now left Galilee. The Lawyer's question is therefore presumably to be seen as Judaea-based, as was the case in Mark and Matthew. Luke seems to have regarded Jesus as being in Judaea after the rejection by the Samaritan villagers.[44]

Verse 38 reminds us that a journey is still in progress. Such 'travel notices' are consistently followed by either a reference to the Gentile mission, or a correction of some erroneous idea about Jesus and his role. The two themes of mission and discipleship are closely linked by Luke, and they are of central importance in this travel narrative, which instructs later disciples in both. Here Mary is seeking 'eternal life', thus picking up the Lawyer's question at 10.25, by listening to the words of Jesus, unlike her sister who is distracted by less important concerns. Mary thus embodies the theme of discipleship which is to dominate the whole section, as she is the ideal disciple who gets her priorities right—and this is in itself a repeated theme, as we see in the parables of the Rich Fool and Lazarus (negative examples) and the pericope of Zacchaeus (like Mary, a positive one).[45]

This portion of Luke's travel narrative has therefore revolved around a consideration of the later mission of the Church, with clear links forward to Acts. It has also been concerned with Christian behaviour and the nature and consequences of discipleship, which is a theme uniting the whole. Luke is opening up themes for further development within both his Gospel and its sequel.

44. Gasse, 'Reisebericht', pp. 294ff., maintains that 'another village' (Lk. 9.56) is Galilaean rather than Samaritan, and he sees Jesus as remaining in Galilee until 18.34. This is not the impression given by the text, however, and Gasse's argument, especially regarding Lk. 17.11, is not convincing. Conzelmann, *Theology*, p. 69, notes that in Acts 9.31 we seem to have the same sequence of Judaea and Galilee, although in reverse order, with Samaria conceived as bordering both: 'This idea is not inconceivable for a man who knows that the inhabitants of Galilee and Judaea are Jews, and that the Samaritans are distinct from them.' Conzelmann further notes that Pliny the Elder (*Natural History* 5.14.68) also seems to have believed that Judaea adjoined Galilee directly, with Samaria bordering them both.

45. Cf. the suggestion of Baarlinck, 'Die zyklische Struktur', where there is a chiastic pairing in Luke of positive and negative examples.

4.3.8. Ch. 11.1-13

The next section of material clusters around the topic of prayer, which is a major Lukan interest; and it no doubt seemed appropriate to begin it with Jesus' best-known one. (This has its Matthaean parallel in the Sermon on the Mount, at Mt. 6.9-13; Luke, who disliked long uninterrupted blocks of teaching, relocates most of Mt. 6 and 7 elsewhere in suitable contexts.) The Lord's Prayer exhibits the correct way to pray, the right way to relate to God, thus having a thematic connection with the Parable of the Unworthy Servants at 17.7-10. It is clearly crucial to the theme of discipleship which dominates the travel narrative.

Luke follows Jesus' prayer with the Parable of the Friend at Midnight (11.5-8), which stresses the importance of prayer; and there is a further link in that the bread for which we are exhorted to pray at 11.3 (and which we receive, since the implication of the parable is that God answers our prayers) is what we must be prepared to give to those in need (see v. 5). The requirement to give to those in need is also closely related topically to the plea in v. 4 to forgive us our sins as we forgive our debtors: Luke does not wish the ethical implications of the prayer to be overlooked, and he reinforces the point dramatically and concretely in a parable.

The word ἀναίδειαν in v. 8 should probably be translated 'shameless-ness' (thus NEB), which is the usual meaning, not 'importunity' (so RSV).[46] It may therefore relate not to the visitor but to the sleeper, who would have been dishonoured if he failed to help a friend. The content of this parable thus connects logically with vv. 11-13, where the message is similarly directed at the donor, not the recipient (see v. 11). The motif of answered prayer, which is common to both, is derived from the Sermon on the Mount (cf. Lk. 11.9-13 and Mt. 7.7-11), although it is interesting that the same sequence of asking—in prayer, obviously—and receiving the Holy Spirit also occurs in Jn 14.13-17 (contra Matthew, where we only receive 'good gifts').[47] This seems to be another link forward to Acts, where the reception of the Holy Spirit by Christ's followers is a leading theme.

The reference at Mt. 7.10 to a serpent and to evil seems to have struck a chord in Luke, and he follows Matthew's serpent/fish pairing with scor-pion/egg; serpents and scorpions are linked as symbolic of evil in Revela-tion, too. There is an evident connection between this and the preceding material at 10.18-19, and an even clearer one with that which follows, the

---

46.　See K.E. Bailey, *Poet and Peasant*, pp. 127ff.
47.　See Mt. 7.11. It is interesting that Luke uses both in v. 13.

victory over Beelzebul, the prince of demons, which is introduced by an exorcism at 11.14.

4.3.9. *Ch. 11.14-23*

The Beelzebul controversy, where Luke is quite close contextually and verbally to Mt. 12.22-30 (though he writes seemingly with some recollection of Matthew's earlier treatment at 9.32-33 and Mark's at Mk 3.22-27), was examined above. As noted there, Luke develops the Strong Man Bound parable at 11.21-22 (cf. Mt. 12.29) to emphasize the struggle between Christ and Satan and Christ's ultimate victory, an apocalyptic theme that is very important to him and which has many affinities with Johannine material and treatment that will be considered in a later chapter.

Lk. 11.23 is identical in wording and context to Mt. 12.30. It does not seem to connect logically with the material which Luke places next, although it reflects the 'divided response' theme which is a recurring motif.[48] The verse is a Lukan doublet, being very close to the saying at Lk. 9.50 which Luke had used in its Markan form and in its Markan context; this would support the contention that Luke used both Mark and Matthew.

4.3.10. *Ch. 11.24-26*

The topical link between 11.22 and 24-26 (the unclean spirit seeking rest) is obvious. Luke omits the next section of Matthew (Mt. 12.33-35), on good and evil fruit, since he has already used this, a Matthaean doublet, earlier (cf. Mt. 7.16-20 and Lk. 6.43-45; we notice that he has transferred the conclusion to this image, concerning good and bad treasure, from its context in Mt. 12.35 to form the climax to his own earlier section).

4.3.11. *Ch. 11.27-28*

These two verses[49] are not directly related to the preceding or the following material. Evans calls them 'puzzling';[50] we may compare other

---

48. See 2.34-35; and also for instance 12.49-53.

49. There is a very close verbal parallel to these verses in *The Gospel of Thomas* 79, which ends with an equally close parallel to Lk. 23.29: 'A woman from the crowd said to him, "Blessed are the womb which bore you and the breasts which nourished you". He said to her, "Blessed are those who have heard the word of the Father and have truly kept it. For there will be days when you will say, 'Blessed are the womb which has not conceived, and the breasts which have not given milk'".' There is also a saying similar to Lk. 11.27-28, similarly expressed, in Rev. 1.3, and there is some affinity to that found in Josephus, *Apion* 2.210. The idea may have been a conventional one.

50. Evans, *Luke*, p. 495.

examples at 12.48b or 16.16-18 of 'detached' and isolated sayings in this
section which are similarly difficult to explain, except in a very tentative
way. As far as 11.27-28 is concerned, we can only suggest that like the
Lawyer's question at 10.25 and the Mary/Martha pericope at 10.38-42,
these verses are intended to keep the focus on the true function of all this
teaching. Disciples are being taught where their true priorities should lie.

4.3.12. *Ch. 11.29-36*

The connection between these verses and vv. 24-26 is admittedly tenuous;
it seems to be the word πονηρότερα (11.26)/πονηρά (11.29). The two
are, however, also linked by Matthew, and Luke may have been unable to
find a more appropriate context. The interpretation of 'the sign of Jonah'
as repentance goes against that of Mark (Mk 8.12), who says that no sign
will be given, and Matthew (Mt. 12.40-41), who sees this as a reference to
the Passion/Resurrection; where there is a conflict in his sources, Luke
feels free to offer his own interpretation, as is also the case with the
'leaven of the Pharisees' saying at 12.1. Luke's interpretation nevertheless
suits the 'instruction in discipleship' theme and is to be developed in more
detail elsewhere, especially in the three parables of ch. 15. Verses 29 and
31-32 express a critique of Judaism, which is also a strong undercurrent
throughout.

The following verses (vv. 33-36) are evidently related only by theme,
and link with the previous section on looking for signs. Luke has collected
two scattered Matthaean sayings on light: Mt. 5.15, where Luke's modification reflects his interest in the Gentile mission, and Mt. 6.22-23. Verse
36 seems to represent Luke's reflection on his material; it is tautological
and clumsy, but he is anxious that his audience should not miss the point.

4.3.13. *Ch. 11.37-54*

It is possible that Luke wanted to give an actual example of what he meant
by people who are 'full of darkness' (see 11.34). He often dramatizes
teaching material in this way; thus, Zacchaeus and the sinful woman of ch.
7 both illustrate repentance; the blind man in 18.35-43 embodies persistence in supplication; the rich ruler of 18.18-30 represents the point made
by the Parable of the Rich Fool. Luke therefore transfers some of Matthew's Woes against the Pharisees from their Jerusalem context into the
perhaps, to us, surprising[51] setting of a meal with a Pharisee. An additional

---

51. The *symposium*, however, where the virtuous sage/philosopher boldly argued

motive here may be that he does not want to lessen the impact of that final week in Jerusalem; to avoid this, he relocates much of the teaching material from Matthew 22 and 24 into his central section.

We are aware that Luke has extensively recast Matthew's section, condensing it considerably and replacing Matthew's seven Woes against the Scribes and Pharisees with six,[52] which are evenly divided between the Lawyers (major enemies of Jesus in Luke, we recall) and the Pharisees, whose 'hypocrisy' was a favourite target for rebuke in both Luke and Matthew. Luke omits Matthew's second Woe, on swearing by the Temple, which had lost much of its impact once the Temple had been destroyed, and would have been of little relevance in a Gentile society. In place of this, he uses the 'loading men with burdens' section of Matthew's lead-in at 23.4 for the first of his Woes against the Lawyers at 11.46; Luke characteristically prefers to begin by attacking extortion and lack of charity. The point in Matthew's first Woe condemning missionary activity —the theme of Acts—is also omitted by Luke, presumably because he regards it as too important to censure.

The hypocrisy of the Pharisees, the contrast between the appearance and the reality, unites Matthew's whole section; it is powerfully expressed in the image of the 'whitewashed tombs' at 23.27. The 'tomb' reference occurs in Luke, too, at 11.44: but there is a significant difference of emphasis. In both cases, the reference seems to be to the Palestinian custom of whitewashing the tombs before Passover to prevent anyone being inadvertently defiled; but in Matthew the contrast is between exterior fairness and internal corruption, which is perhaps in some tension with this practice, since the white of the tombs was intended to make them noticeable. Luke instead stresses that the tombs are defiling because they are hidden ($\check{\alpha}\delta\eta\lambda\alpha$), which would not be the case if they were white-washed, a custom he does not mention. The Pharisees are also accused of ostentation in v. 43 and the over-rigorous application of what seemed trivial points of Torah-observance[53] in v. 42, although Luke typically omits Matthew's reference to 'weightier matters of the Law', which is

with his opponents, was a recognized genre in antiquity, as is argued by E.S. Steele, 'Luke 11:37-54: A Modified Hellenistic Symposium', *JBL* 103 (1984), pp. 379-94.

52. We may compare the Sermon on the Plain, where the nine Beatitudes of Matthew are replaced by four, and Luke constructs four corresponding Woes to balance them. Structural symmetry of this sort seems to have been important to Luke.

53. We cannot tell whether Luke was aware that at this time rue, and probably mint, were not tithed.

essentially Rabbinic terminology. He nevertheless interprets these 'weight-ier matters';[54] they are justice (right action to others) and the love of God (that is, love for him, which is exhibited by showing love for one's fellows, a central emphasis of the Sermon on the Plain, as had been made clear in the Parable of the Good Samaritan). Their neglect of these two in their concern for trifling legalistic details is to Luke the gravest of the charges against the Pharisees, and he in consequence places it first.

The charges against the lawyers are also derived, albeit in an abbreviated way, from Matthew. The first Woe against the Lawyers is perhaps as appropriately directed at them as at Pharisees, but the second and third Woes (11.47, 52) do not seem especially applicable to lawyers. Moreover, the charge of ostentation levelled at the Pharisees in v. 43 is at 20.45-47 aimed at Scribes (Mt. 23.5-10 addresses Scribes and Pharisees; Luke splits them, although he still condemns both groups). This too would support the view that the structure has been imposed by the author on the material and is a secondary feature; it does not reflect his source.

There is nothing in this section which requires us to postulate either a Lukan abbreviation or a Matthaean expansion of Q to explain the differences between the two evangelists. Although the phrase 'the wisdom of God' (cf. 1 Cor. 1.21, 24) at Lk. 11.49 is peculiar to Luke, in Mt. 23.24 Jesus sends prophets, wise men and Scribes, and the context reflects the experiences of the later Church; and while Luke knows of Christian prophets (see Acts 21.9, 10), he clearly interprets the prophets in Old Testament terms here (see Lk. 11.51), and—as elsewhere (cf. Lk. 7.35; Mt. 11.19)—he reserves wisdom for God. The idea that wisdom was responsible for inspiring the words and actions of the prophets can be paralleled in Jewish sources.[55] There is therefore no reason why Luke's source at this point need have been Q: what we see may be echoes of Luke's other reading woven into Matthew. Luke's practice here accords with what we observe elsewhere in his redaction of Matthew; the evidence which Evans notes[56] as indicative of the abbreviation of a source could as well apply to Luke's abbreviation of Matthew as to Q. Matthew's order is, however, clear and coherent, reaching a fitting and impressive climax in the apostrophe to Jerusalem, whereas there is no central unifying theme to

54. See Beck, *Christian Character*, p. 26.
55. See, e.g., Wis. 7.27, 10.15-16, 11.1-3.
56. Evans, *Luke*, p. 502.

Luke's Woes, and his conclusion, far from forming a climax, is limp and abrupt.[57]

Shared meals are very important in Luke, and there are several where Pharisees are present (see 5.30; 7.36; 11.37; 14.1). Table-fellowship was a major issue in the early Church, and Luke emphasizes at 5.30; 15.2; 19.7 that Jesus displays his acceptance of outcasts and sinners by eating with them. Verse 38 seems to have some connections with the section on Jewish traditions (see Mt. 15.2-20; Mk 7.5-15) which Luke omits, since he is careful not to depict Jesus as directly opposing the Torah: clashes are postponed until Acts.[58]

Luke avoids a monologue by the insertion of v. 45, perhaps to prevent monotony and provide variety, in the same way that at 17.37 he introduces a question to preserve a dialogue framework. Verses 53 and 54 remind us of the wider context in which Luke has placed this dialogue and give the whole a very ominous undertone.

4.3.14. *Ch. 12.1-12*

The Pharisees provide the connection with the next verse, 12.1. Luke here takes a logion of Jesus concerning the 'leaven of the Pharisees', which Mark and Matthew had both interpreted in different ways (and this may be why Luke feels free to offer his own interpretation), and describes it as hypocrisy. He links this with the previous Woes and the charges made against the Pharisees (see 11.46, 47) and with the next verse, on things hidden coming to light (that is, 'truth will out'), which serves as a warning. The material is derived from Mt. 10.20-32, where it forms part of a discourse exhorting disciples to trust in God's protection and fearlessly confess their faith—that is, to resist apostasy, a serious danger facing the early Church.[59]

This section therefore has some connection with the instructions on discipleship which has been a constant theme since the Mission of the Seventy (Two), and it relates to the later situation of the Church. There is yet another link with Acts, since Luke replaces Matthew's 'Spirit of your Father' (Mt. 10.20)[60] with a reference at 12.12 to the Holy Spirit. The idea

57. Similarly, Creed, *Luke*, p. 165.

58. Ritual washing was not enjoined in the Torah, as such: it was part of the later traditions which were incorporated into the Talmud.

59. There is thus the significant addition of ἐν ὑπομονῇ to Mk 4.20/Mt. 13.23 at Lk. 8.15. We may compare the attitude in Hebrews 6.

60. See Evans, *Luke*, p. 513. Evans sees the order in this section as Lukan, rather than as reflecting Q.

New Light on Luke

that the Spirit teaches the disciples what to say, which Luke shares with John (see Jn 14.26), is peculiar to Luke among the Synoptics, since in Mk 13.11 and Mt. 10.20 the Spirit speaks through them in their place.[61] The Spirit provides the connection which Luke uses to group two related sayings (see Mt. 12.31-32; Mt. 10.19-20).

Although the wording of some verses of this section is very close to Matthew,[62] there are also a great many differences. We can only assume that at this point Luke has rewritten very freely, if his source was indeed Matthew and not Q. Some of his modifications are perhaps stylistic, such as the replacement of Matthew's εἴπατε (Mt. 10.27) with ἀκουσθήσεται at Lk. 12.3, or the insertion of ταμείοις[63] in the same verse to balance the δωμάτων he shares with Matthew. The same is perhaps true of the 'downvaluing' of Matthew's two sparrows for an ἀσσαρίον to five for two ἀσσαρία: this is extremely unlikely to reflect a Lukan experience of inflation, and Evans[64] sees it as an attempt to improve the rhythm of the Greek.

Other changes perhaps are more illustrative of Lukan redactional emphases; that Jesus addresses his disciples as 'friends' at 12.4 is a touch of typical Lukan sentiment, which is related to his whole presentation of the Passion, since the betrayal of trust there by one of the Twelve is a major Lukan theme. (We may note in passing that John, too, at 15.14-15 also uses φίλοι μου; this is one of many connections between Luke and John which are especially evident in the Passion but extend elsewhere, too, and which frequently sound like verbal echoes.)

It is noticeable that Luke does not separate body and soul, as does Matthew in Mt. 10.28; he stresses, instead, the question of authority, ἐξουσία, at Lk. 12.5. This relates to the important Lukan theme of the conflict between Christ and Satan,[65] which is also a Johannine emphasis. Luke, indeed, underlines this even more by the repetitious ναὶ, λέγω ὑμῖν, τοῦτον φοβήθητε.

The phrase 'my Father in Heaven' at Mt. 10.32 is typically Matthaean, and Luke consistently avoids it; its replacement in Lk. 12.8, 9 by a reference to the angels who witness both confession and denial is rather more

61. See Johnson, *Gospel of Luke*, p. 196.
62. Cf. Mt. 10.26/Lk. 12.2; Mt. 10.27a/Lk. 12.3a; Mt. 10.31/Lk. 12.7b.
63. See Creed, *Luke*, p. 171.
64. Evans, *Luke*, p. 516.
65. Cf. Conzelmann, *Theology*, pp. 181ff.

difficult to explain. Evans suggests[66] that Luke may have wanted to match the (plural) men with (equally plural) angels, since he seems concerned with stylistic balance in this section; or, alternatively, it could be a periphrasis to avoid repetition. Neither of these suggestions is particularly convincing, and the link with Rev. 3.5 which Evans also notes is perhaps more suggestive. We may observe that the eschatological Son of Man with the function of a prosecuting attorney or a defence counsel, which we see here, links with the theme of judgment which was heavily emphasized in ch. 11, and which is touched upon again—albeit briefly—at 12.2, and also at 12.11 where the verb ἀπολογέομαι means to conduct a defence at law.[67] It is to be important in ch. 13, too.

There remains Luke's repositioning of 12.10, which in Matthew and Mark had formed part of the Beelzebul controversy, the unforgivable sin against the Holy Spirit being to see Jesus' power as demonic (Mk 3.30). Luke has removed the saying from this context, and it sits rather uneasily in its new one; nevertheless, from the surrounding context it seems to be interpreted as apostasy,[68] which is a Lukan preoccupation. The connection is presumably the Son of Man reference which Luke adds to Mt. 10.32, and the exhortation to confess and not deny him.[69] Luke integrates the whole section into his existing material by picking up the reference to the Holy Spirit again at 12.11-12, which clearly relates to the later situation facing Christians. (It should be noted that the promise of aid in speech by the Spirit is borne out at Acts 4.13; once again, Luke is linking forward to his sequel.)

4.3.15. *Ch. 12.13-34*
Discipleship is closely connected with Luke's views on possessions/ property and the importance of this theme to Luke is obvious from the full treatment he affords it. Verses 13-15, on sharing one's possessions, are Torah-based (see Deut. 15.7-11).[70]

66. Evans, *Luke*, p. 517.

67. Cf. Lk. 21.14. Evans, *Luke*, p. 519, notes that this usage occurs only in Luke–Acts in the New Testament.

68. G. Bornkamm (cited in Conzelmann, *Theology*, p. 179) suggested that blasphemy against the Son of Man is forgivable because it is not until after Pentecost, and the reception of the Spirit, that it is plainly revealed who Jesus is.

69. Tannchill, *Narrative Unity*, I, p. 245, observes that in Acts 7.55-56 Stephen does indeed 'confess the Son of Man'. This is another of the links between Luke's Gospel and its sequel.

70. Luke and Josephus both stress the importance of κοινωνία; cf. *Apion* 2.196; Acts 2.44-46; 4.32-37.

There are analogues to some of the material in the Rich Fool in both Jewish and non-Jewish sources.[71] The parable clearly owes its position here to the theme it exemplifies, which unites this section of material: the folly of relying on oneself and one's possessions in view of the certainty of death which comes to all, often unexpectedly. The (related) topic raised in 12.4-7, the stupidity of relying on oneself when God's providential care for all is assured, is picked up again in vv. 22-30. But Luke develops this further, using a section of the Sermon on the Mount (Mt. 6.25-33) which is also closely related, topically, although there are some typically Lukan modifications—such as the omission of Matthew's πρῶτον at Lk. 12.31 (cf. Mt. 6.33)—which clearly reflect the discipleship theme so important to this whole section: followers of Jesus in Luke's Gospel are never to seek anything but the Kingdom.[72] The evangelist, who directs the passage firmly at the later Church by the 'little flock' reference at 12.32, characteristically exhorts followers of Christ to sell their possessions and give alms, both of which commands are unparalleled in Matthew; this, to Luke, is conduct representative of the Kingdom. ('Sell what you have and give alms', may also have been the implication of 12.21;[73] almsgiving is very important throughout the whole of Luke–Acts.)[74] Luke in these verses reverses Matthew's order (cf. Mt. 6.19-34), but provides a better introduction to the following material, and he has utilized both of the motifs which had informed the Parable of the Rich Fool, possessions and the inevitability of divine judgment. The whole is very tightly linked, thematically.

4.3.16. *Ch. 12.35-48*

The reference in v. 33 to the coming of the κλέπτης may explain why Luke places the Parable of the Thief at Midnight at 12.39, as the climax to a collection of brief parables which he presumably saw as illustrating the same point. In Matthew they are placed much later, in the context of the eschatological parables of the final week's teaching; Luke has summarized and combined two of them here, the Bridegroom and the Marriage Feast (Mt. 25.1-13/Lk. 12.35-36) and the Thief at Midnight (Mt. 24.43-44/Lk.

---

71. See, e.g., *1 En.* 97.8-10; or Sir. 11.18-19; and also Horace, *Odes*, 2.3; 2.14; and 2.13 (sudden death).

72. Similarly, Beck, *Christian Character*, pp. 32-33.

73. See G.W.E. Nickelsburg, 'Riches, the Rich, and God's Judgment in 1 Enoch 92-105 and the Gospel According to Luke', *NTS* 25 (1978), pp. 324-44 (337).

74. See Lk. 11.41: Acts 10.2, 4, 31. Prayer and almsgiving are two features of Jewish piety which Luke emphasizes.

12.39-40). The Parable of the Watchful Servants at Lk. 12.37-38 is pecu-liar to Luke, although it seems to have links with both the Lukan and the Johannine Passion (see Lk. 22.27; Jn 13.4-5).[75]

The relevance of this teaching to Christians is underlined at 12.40; the Parousia may not necessarily be imminent, but it is nevertheless inevita-ble, and one must be prepared for it (cf. 12.21). Peter himself draws attention at 12.41 to the intended recipients of Jesus' message here; although what is said is of general relevance, the teaching at this point is primarily aimed at the disciples.[76] This is made explicit in Jesus' reply, where Luke changes Matthew's δοῦλος to οἰκόνομος, since the steward is in a position of authority over other servants, as the disciples are to be over the infant Church in Acts.

Luke's wording is nevertheless very close to Matthew's in many places[77] in this section, although we notice that he alters the punishment Jesus metes out to the ὑποκριταί in Matthew and instead awards it to the ἄπιστοι. This links with the earlier treatment of apostasy, perseverance in faith being a Lukan emphasis[78] which is also important throughout the Johannine tradition. Here, Luke wishes to distinguish between the punishment of the apostates who are aware of what they are doing (and the future relevance of this teaching is again apparent) and that of those who do not know: presumably, unconverted pagans. He therefore adds vv. 47-48, which reflect Jewish thought concerning the difference between unintended sins and deliberate ones.[79]

The saying at 12.48b does not seem to relate very closely either to the preceding or following material: the connection may be simply the catch-word πολλάς at 12.47, πολύ at 12.48b,c. The reference to much being required of those to whom much is given may conceivably provide a

75. There are also connections with the Parable of the Unworthy Servants of Lk. 17.7-10.
76. Similarly, Creed, *Luke*, p. 177.
77. Cf. Mt. 24.46/Lk. 12.43; Mt. 24.47/Lk. 12.44; Mt. 24.50-51c/Lk. 12.46 a,b,c.
78. Cf. S. Brown, *Apology and Perseverance in the Theology of Luke* (AnBib, 36; Rome: Pontifical Biblical Institute, 1969). Brown suggests that it is because Luke wishes to present the disciples as models of 'faith under fire', who persevere in the face of trial, that he does not show them as fleeing and leaving Jesus to die alone. The 'exemplary' nature of Christ's death would thus extend to the treatment of the disciples, too, who are also to serve as examples to the later Church. Brown's inter-pretation, however—though attractive—runs counter to the text at points such as Lk. 22.31-32.
79. Cf. Num. 15.27-31; Lev. 4.2, 13, 22, 27; Ps. 19.12-13; *b. B. Bat.* 60b.

connection with Lk. 12.49-50, which reminds us of the goal of the journey
—the Passion.

4.3.17. *Ch. 12.49-59*

Since the theme of suffering has been touched on, Luke applies this to
Jesus' followers, the later Church, using Matthew's section on division in
households, which Matthew, too, had related to the theme of discipleship.
Lk. 12.49, which may balance 12.50 structurally, is without parallel. It
perhaps points forward to the fire of the Holy Spirit at the Lukan Pentecost
(Acts 2.3), reinforcing the connection between Jesus and the Spirit (cf. Lk.
24.49; Acts 16.6-7), and it may also pick up the image of refining fire
inferred in Luke's presentation of the Baptism at 3.16, which gains support
from the reference to baptism in the following verse. Luke 12.50 may
conceivably have some relation to Mk 10.35-41, in the request of the sons
of Zebedee, which Luke omits.[80] If we regard Lk. 22.43-44, which are
omitted from many of the best Lukan manuscripts (including Codex
Sinaiticus and papyrus 75), as an early insertion into Luke's text, [81] then
Lk. 12.50 and 22.42 are all that remains of the agony in the garden, which
Luke, like John, prefers to downplay.

Luke next turns the focus of the teaching on all, not just on the later
disciples, which explains the significant and judgmental term ὑποκριταί
at 12.56.[82] This is perhaps a piece of anti-Jewish polemic; to Luke, it is
culpable stupidity, deliberate blindness, not to be able to read the 'signs of
the times'.[83] The themes of judgment and perception informing vv. 54-56
are combined in v. 57, which Luke appends to them, probably to provide
the transition to vv. 58-59. These two verses are an expansion of Mt. 5.25-
26, and they may reflect Luke's greater familiarity with Roman legal prac-

---

80. In consequence he doubles (a narrative doublet; compare Lk. 9.46; 22.24) the
'dispute about greatness', leaving it unspecified who is engaged in the argument.
Matthew was clearly embarrassed by the story, too; he transferred the request to the
mother of James and John, and we are all familiar with maternal pride and ambition.

81. This is the opinion of many critics, including Evans and Tiede. Creed observes
(*Luke*, p. 273), 'It might have been expected that the appearance of the strengthening
angels would be recorded after, rather than before, the earnest prayer and the bloody
sweat…'

82. Though not especially enamoured of this Matthaean term, Luke uses it twice in
the central section: here, and at 13.15. (There is also the related ὑπόκρισις at 12.1.)

83. We may note that Luke's meteorological reference at 12.54-55 is completely in
accordance with the situation we would expect in the eastern Mediterranean.

tice. (We may note that he characteristically scales down the financial reference; a *lepton* was worth half a *quadrans*.)

To sum up, it is evident that once more theme has been the deciding factor throughout this whole chapter; the themes raised here include possessions and their proper use, God's care for all, the Kingdom, the inevitability of judgment,[84] and the cost of discipleship. Luke is carefully instructing the later Church in principles of conduct and indicating the consequences of rejecting Jesus' message.

4.3.18. *Ch. 13.1-9*

The grim caution which closes the previous section (see 12.59) provides a bridge to the next section, which is concerned with the need for repentance. This is a favourite Lukan emphasis, and it is combined at this point with a warning of destruction, which in addition links back to the Rich Fool. Verses 1-5 also relate to the theme of discipleship; Luke wishes to stress that so-called 'poetic justice' is a fallacy; good conduct does not necessarily guarantee success and prosperity. (There are interesting connections here with Jn 9, where a healing linked to Siloam[85] raises a similar issue; compare Jn 9.2 and Lk. Luke's contacts here would therefore be with John's Gospel, not his source at 13.2. This is another example of what seems to be a verbal reminiscence linking the two Gospels.) Luke emphasizes that a total transformation of one's life, priorities and values is needed: this is an undercurrent throughout Luke's entire course in discipleship. The reference to Pilate in v. 1 (and this incident is not recorded in any extra-canonical source, even one as hostile to Pilate as Josephus) is somewhat at variance with Luke's later presentation of the Roman governor. It is perhaps to keep us in mind of the end of this particular journey; Luke inserts such reminders at intervals.[86]

Repentance is also the theme of Luke's version of the Parable of the Fig-tree. Mark, at 11.20-24, and Matthew, at 21.18-22, had interpreted this parable as a (negative) example of the power of faith. Luke prefers to present it as an illustration of 'one last chance', which is enacted historically in Acts, where the preaching of the gospel to the Jews by Peter and

---

84. Goulder, *Luke*, pp. 549-70, sees Luke as presenting the effect of Jesus' coming in a three-fold model of judgment: at 12.41-53 for the Church, at 12.54–13.9 for the world, and at 13.10-21 for the Jews.

85. R.T. Fortna, *The Gospel of Signs* (SNTSMS, 11; Cambridge: Cambridge University Press, 1970), pp. 110ff., regards Jn 9.2 as a feature of John's redaction of his 'Signs' source.

86. See Lk. 11.53-54; 12.49-50; 13.31-35 and perhaps 16.16.

Paul represents this final opportunity, after which we are to assume that the prospect is destruction. This is especially evident in Lk. 13.9, and it was how the fall of Jerusalem was seen by many, including Matthew (see Mt. 22.1-10). In this case, we notice that not only has Luke recast and reinterpreted the parable; he has also relocated it, since Mark and Matthew refer to an actual fig-tree which Jesus sees outside the city. Luke presents the story as a parable, pure and simple, and he gives no precise location for its telling. His reference to 'three years', which seems to relate to the Jews' response to Jesus, may perhaps reflect some knowledge of John's chronology, even though Luke's Gospel follows Mark over the length of the ministry.

4.3.19. *Ch. 13.10-17*
The story of a crippled woman continues Luke's implicit critique of Judaism. Verse 15 is unparalleled in Mark and Matthew, and the term ὑποκριταί directs the attack squarely at those who put concern for the Law before human need. The word itself provides a link back to the earlier criticism of the Pharisees, since this attitude is at 12.1 presented as especially characteristic of them; it forms part of Luke's ongoing polemic which is evident throughout his Gospel. The point made here is very closely related to that concerning the ox/ass in a pit[87] which Matthew adds to Mark's pericope of the Man with the Withered Arm at Mt. 12.11-12. Luke severs it from its context there (see Lk. 6.6-11) and places it instead in the unparalleled Lukan story of the Healing of the Man with Dropsy (Lk. 14.1-6). It should be noted that at 6.9 Luke has already used the logion of Mk 3.4, which makes the point he intends all the Sabbath healings to illustrate: εἰ ἔξεστιν τῷ σαββάτῳ ἀγαθοποιῆσαι ἢ κακοποιῆσαι, ψυχὴν σῶσαι ἢ ἀπολέσαι. The relevance of this to the later Church is apparent, and the placement here clearly polemical. We may note that the 'rejoicing' of the people at his action is a typically Lukan feature.[88]

4.3.20. *Ch. 13-18-35*
The next four verses (vv. 18-21) connect with Matthew's parable collection in ch. 13 (see Mt. 13.31-33), although there is also a parallel to the

---

87. Saving life was accepted as a reason for breaking the Sabbath regulations even by many of the very orthodox, so the example given at Mt. 12.11/Lk. 14.5 would not have posed a problem, although the situation was different among sectarian Jews, as the *Damascus Document* makes clear (see *CD-A*. 10-11).

88. See Lk. 10.17; Acts 8.8; 12.14; 15.3.

Mustard Seed at Mk 4.30-32. The juxtaposition in both Matthew and Luke of the parables of the Mustard Seed and the Leaven is always used to qualify the statement that Matthew and Luke never agree in the order of Q material. We should notice that apart from the use by both Mark and Luke of the phrase βασιλεία τοῦ θεοῦ instead of Matthew's βασιλεία τῶν οὐρανῶν, a change which is characteristic of Luke,[89] there is no evidence of Mark in Luke's version of the Mustard Seed; it seems, rather, to be a somewhat condensed version of Mt. 13.31-33.

The link here seems to be with the following material, since these two brief parables concern the Kingdom, which is the theme of the next section. Entry into the Kingdom has indeed been an implicit theme of the Kingdom parables of ch. 12, and this is the aspect Luke concentrates on in 13.22-30, uniting it with the grim threats that have also been a recurring motif in this chapter (see 13.1-5, 9; the words αἷμα and ἀπολεῖσθε set the tone for the whole). Verses 23-27 seem to be a somewhat clumsy combination of two Matthaean parables, the Narrow Gate (Mt. 7.13-14) and the Shut Door (Mt. 25.10-12).[90] Luke attempts to link the two by substituting θύρα for πύλης in the first one, but the result is not entirely satisfactory.[91]

The topic obviously has points of contact with much of ch. 12, but Luke is even more critical of the consequences of rejecting Jesus and his message here.[92] Thus in vv. 26-27, which have a thematic connection with much of the preceding material including 13.3, 4, Luke links the criticism of those who think that paying lip-service to belief is enough to that of the exclusion of the Jews from the Kingdom of God. If we compare Lk. 13.28-30 and Mt. 8.11-12, we notice that Luke makes an implicit reference here to the extension of the gospel message to the Gentiles—a major theme made evident at the very beginning of this whole central section in the Mission of the Seventy (Two)—even more emphatic by adding βορρᾶ and νότου to Matthew's ἀνατολῶν and δυσμῶν. Luke underlines the implications for Judaism in v. 30, which picks up a saying repeated in

89. Cf., e.g., Mt. 5.3/Lk. 6.20; Mt. 8.11/Lk. 13.28; Mt. 10.7/Lk. 9.2; Mt. 11.11/Lk. 7.28.

90. This is the conclusion of the parable of the Foolish Virgins which Luke had already used at 12.36.

91. Evans, *Luke*, p. 556, calls Luke's version 'barely intelligible'.

92. The threat of impending retribution is a major emphasis in Matthew, and as a result there is plenty of material which can be utilized for Luke's purpose.

Matthew, albeit with some modification;[93] Luke typically begins with the underdogs. Those who are now last will be first. Luke's interpretation here seems to be that the 'last who will be first' are the Gentiles, and he accordingly reverses the order of Matthew, who begins by condemning the 'first' (in Luke, the Jews).

Verses 31-35 tie together many themes: there is a critique of Judaism[94] (see vv. 31-32); the terrible consequences for Judaism of the rejection of Jesus' message; and Jesus' own grief at the tragedy this involves (vv. 34-35),[95] which is connected with his awareness of what it implies for him, too (vv. 32-33).[96] It is interesting that the clear allusion to the Passion in v. 32 (τῇ τρίτῃ, coupled with a reference to Jerusalem in v. 33) is expressed in the verb τελειόω, which is closely related to that which John's Jesus uses on the cross—τελέω[97]—and in both cases there is the same sense of having accomplished and completed a task. Once again, there could be an echo of one Gospel in the other.

4.3.21. *Ch. 14.1-6*

The reference to the ubiquitous Pharisees at 13.31 connects this material to the succeeding pericope at 14.1-6, which is in many respects a narrative doublet of 13.10-17, though Luke also links it to the following section by the use of the verb φαγεῖν at 14.1.

---

93. See Mt. 19.30; and cf. also Mt. 20.16 (and Mk 10.31).

94. Conzelmann, *Theology*, p. 133, says, 'The prophets do not perish merely in, but by means of, Jerusalem…the journey, the Passion, the guilt of the Jews, and the resulting fate of the city form a closely linked chain.'

95. Contra J.T. Sanders, *Jews*, the anguish in Jesus' tone here, and later, the beating of their breasts by the multitude who watch the crucifixion, suggest that Luke perceives Jerusalem's fate, and that of the Jews, as a tragedy. (Similarly D.L. Tiede, *Prophecy*, pp. 103ff.)

96. Conzelmann, *Theology*, p. 110, observes that vv. 34-35 pose a problem in the context in which Luke has placed them, since they imply some kind of a ministry in Jerusalem (such as is recorded in, for instance, Jn 2.23–3.22; 5.1-47; 7.14–10.40; etc.). Matthew avoids this problem by placing the saying in a Jerusalem context.

97. Compare Lk. 13.32 τελειοῦμαι; Jn 19.30 τετέλεσται. The use of the verbs τελέω and τελειόω with this connotation is characteristic of both John and Luke. We may compare Luke's use of τελέω at 12.50 and 18.31, in clear allusions to the Passion, and also in 22.37, where the reference to the fulfilment of prophecy also clearly relates to it; and John's use of τελειόω in connection with the accomplishment of Christ's work (supremely, in John's presentation, by his Passion) at 4.34; 5.36; 17.4. The verbs are not used in precisely this sense and context elsewhere in the New Testament, although the implication of Acts 20.24 and 2 Tim. 4.7, as applied to Paul, is similar.

If those critics are correct who detect a chiastic structuring in much of Luke's travel narrative, then the preceding section, namely 13.18-35, would form the centre of a chiasmus, framed by the two Sabbath healings at 13.10-17 and 14.1-6. It is in any case an *inclusio*, whether or not we see it as the centre of a chiasmus. We can well understand why Luke might have wished to emphasize its importance by structuring it in this way, since the theme of this entire section is the Kingdom of God, as proclaimed by Jesus (hence, the 'growth' parables of Lk. 13.18-20), and a consideration of the significance of this for Israel and for other nations, which culminates in the apostrophe to Jerusalem at 13.34-35.

4.3.22. *Ch. 14.7-24*

As was noted above, the verb φαγεῖν provides the link with the preceding material; the dining motif picks up an element in 13.29, 11.37-52, and elsewhere. The Parable of the Places at Dinner dramatizes the point made in Mt. 23.6b, which Luke has omitted from his parallel to Mt. 23.5-6 at Lk. 11.43, presumably because he intended to develop it later and link it to related material. The parable is Luke's preferred teaching method, and here as elsewhere (cf. Mt. 5.43-46, Lk. 10.27-37) he chooses to present ethical instruction in this way. The Places at Dinner reflects the theme of humility, which will be picked up later in the Parable of the Pharisee and the Tax-collector, and there are also connections with the 'reversal' motif evident throughout Luke's Gospel, from the Magnificat onwards, and which has been broached at 13.30. The whole of this section—and the same is true of most of the material in chs. 13 and 14 and much of ch. 12—seems to represent 'variations on several themes', with frequent repetition, amplification and modification.[98] The principal theme of ch. 14, however, concerns feasting and dining, which once again has implications both for a consideration of discipleship and for the conduct of later Christians (see vv. 12-14).

The implicit critique of the Cult is continued at v. 13, since these categories of people were specifically excluded from Temple worship by Judaism, and Jesus commands in vv. 13 and 21 that it is they who must be invited to his banquet. Jesus sets these instructions respecting the dispossessed, a major Lukan concern, in the context of eternal life at v. 14, which is itself a constant theme.[99]

---

98. Similarly, Tannehill, *Narrative Unity*, I, p. 243.

99. See Lk. 10.25-28; much of Luke 12, including the Rich Fool; the Parousia parables; Lk. 13.1-9, 22-30; 16.9; 18.9-14; 19.8-9.

At 14.15, a faint echo of the sentimental exclamation at 11.27-28 calls forth the Parable of the Great Supper. This is quite close to that recorded in Mt. 22.1-10, although there are some typical modifications; the excuses, for example, seem to be derived from Deuteronomy, and they are inserted to enliven the narrative, since Luke likes dialogue. We note that Luke—contra Matthew—has two instructions to 'go out' (see 14.21, 23). The first is confined to the streets and lanes of the city (τῆς πόλεως); the second is more general (τὰς ὁδοὺς καὶ φραγμούς). The 'repetition with variation' could be a form of Lukan tautology; but it may be that the second injunction is deliberately unqualified, the reference being to those outside Judaism[100]—i.e. the Gentile mission, which is a recurring theme (see, for example, 13.29-30). This is supported by the explicit reference to the experiences of the later Church in v. 27. Luke connects the parable back to the previous section warning the Jews of the consequences of their actions by the ominous statement at 14.24. He also emphasizes the thrust of this teaching, underlining its relevance to the overarching theme of discipleship, by inserting vv. 26-27 after a 'bridging' verse (v. 25) and aiming it at them all (ὄχλοι πολλοί).

In this context, we notice that whereas the warning at 12.40 was specifically only addressed to Peter and the disciples, as in Matthew—although its relevance to later followers is obvious—Luke repeats it[101] but addresses it to the multitudes here. Indeed, this seems to be a part of the reason for the repetition of material. Luke wants there to be no possible misunderstanding; what is said applies to all. Thus, the 'exhortation to fearless confession' is at 12.8-12 aimed only at the disciples (see 12.1), as is the teaching on trusting in God's providence and the inevitability of judgment (see 12.22); at 12.54, however, it is extended to the multitudes. The same is true of the injunction to sell one's possessions: at 12.33 it is aimed at the disciples, but at 14.33 it is directed at all. Luke differentiates[102] very carefully between the two audiences for Jesus' teaching, stressing which material is aimed at disciples and which has a wider reference, as is evident in 12.13, 54; 14.25.[103]

100. See T.W. Manson, *The Sayings of Jesus* (London: SCM Press, 1949), p. 130.
101. Cf. Lk. 12.51-53 and Lk. 14.26.
102. See Tannehill, *Narrative Unity*, 1, pp. 241-43; P.S. Minear, 'Jesus's Audiences, According to Luke', *NovT* 16 (1974), pp. 81-109; Moessner, *Lord of the Banquet*, pp. 213-16.
103. None of the material in chs. 13 and 14 is aimed solely at the disciples—and we have seen how often Jesus is restating here themes Luke has initiated earlier.

4.3.23. *Ch. 14.25-35*

The theme of the final verses of this chapter, the likelihood of separation, persecution and death, is the same as that found at 12.51-53. In Matthew, the material is joined; Luke separates it, perhaps for especial emphasis, and, as Goulder points out, Luke's repeated phrase οὐ δύναται εἶναί μου μαθητής in vv. 26, 27 and 33 is stronger than οὐκ ἔστιν μου ἄξιος at Mt. 10.37, 38. It may be because he does not want anyone to miss the point—inevitable destruction—if they disregard what Jesus has said that he ends with the very threatening 'salt' logion, drawn from the Sermon on the Mount (see Mt. 5.13). Luke's introduction, καλὸν οὖν τὸ ἅλας, is nevertheless very close to Mk 9.49-50, even though the rest seems to be his rewriting of Matthew; the most likely explanation for the Markan echo is that Luke has remembered Mark's wording when using Matthew. Alternatively, he may conceivably be combining his two sources here; we may note that there could equally be an echo of the preceding section of Jesus' speech in Mk 9.42-48 at Lk. 17.1-2. Matthew, although retaining much more of this very threatening speech than Luke, had recast it and used part in the Sermon on the Mount and part in the discourse in ch. 18; Luke may perhaps likewise have felt free to use the material at appropriate points in his narrative to suit his own context, just as he does with the Jesus sayings in Matthew.

Chapter 5

LUKE'S CENTRAL SECTION (2): LUKE 15.1–19.27

5.1. *Introduction*

From the preceding analysis of Lk. 9.51–14.35 it has been shown that Luke's examination of what it means to follow the path of discipleship—the true focus of his travel narrative—is dominated by certain recurring themes such as mission (particularly the Gentile mission), repentance, prayer, the proper use of possessions, the Kingdom and the behaviour required so that one is ready for its coming. The same themes are repeated in the later chapters, too, albeit sometimes with some variation in treatment, as will be shown below.

5.2. *Exegesis of Luke 15.1-19.27*

5.2.1. *Ch. 15.1-32*

Chapter 14 had closed on an ominous note, with a threat of judgment for those whose discipleship is not wholehearted. Chapter 15 offers us an alternative to destruction—penitence: and since this is relevant to all, Luke therefore emphasizes that the parables of this chapter are addressed to the tax-collectors and sinners (15.1), as well as to the Pharisees and Scribes (15.2). The theme of repentance is so important to Luke that he devotes three parables in succession to it, the third particularly being fully developed. But whereas Luke's earlier treatment of it had been set in a threatening 'or else' context (see 13.9), the parables in ch. 15 are very different, centring instead on forgiveness, God's gracious action to save the lost.

The Parable of the Lost Sheep has a parallel in Mt. 18.12-14, although Luke's version, with the theme stated in v. 7 as repentance (a word that does not occur here in Matthew), is different from that of the first evangelist, whose parable is closer in some respects to Deut. 22.1-2 (the verb πλανάω, for example, is common to both). In Luke's parable, which has affinities with Ezekiel 34 in its presentation, the shepherd seeks the sheep until (ἕως) he finds it, and we have the very vivid picture of his tender care of the animal and the rejoicing of his friends over its recovery; in Matthew, there is only the possibility (ἐάν) of finding it, and the joy is confined to him.

Many would regard Luke's version of the parable as the more primitive;[1] indeed, most (unconsciously influenced, perhaps, by Psalm 23 and also the powerful Johannine image of Christ, the Good Shepherd) would probably prefer it to be dominical. The difficulty here is that Luke has used the same theme, which he obviously liked, in the adjacent parables of the Lost Coin and the Prodigal Son. The Lost Coin is clearly the female equivalent of the Lost Sheep, transposed into a domestic sphere but making the same point. It is a good example of the male/female pairing characteristic of the evangelist and it seems to have no parallels elsewhere, which would support the contention that it is Lukan. It would therefore be equally possible to argue that Luke has rewritten the Matthaean parable to reflect his own concerns, and has cast it into a suitable context. The Parable of the Lost Sheep as told by Matthew is thoroughly Matthaean in its concerns and in its present form is very unlikely to be authentic; but we cannot conclude that Luke's much more congenial parable is necessarily closer to any version told by Jesus.

There is, of course, no evidence of repentance as such in these two parables, except the use of the verb μετανοέω at 15.7, 10; neither sheep nor coins can repent. The situation regarding the Prodigal Son,[2] which is very detailed, is slightly different, since the son does confess his error and repent (see vv. 18-19), though even here we are more aware of the father's compassion and forgiveness, which in any case precedes the son's carefully rehearsed acknowledgment of culpability.[3] Luke uses the parable to

---

1.   E.g. J. Jeremias, *Parables*, p. 40, 'There can be no doubt that Luke has preserved the original situation'.

2.   There is a Deuteronomic parallel to The Prodigal Son at Deut. 21.18-21. Drury, *Tradition*, pp. 75-77, additionally sees Matthew's Parable of the Two Brothers (Mt. 21.28-32) as providing some suggestions for amplification. Evans, *Luke*, p. 588, adds that there are points of contact between the words of the returning Prodigal to his father at vv. 18-19 and those in the Syriac and the Armenian recensions of the *Story of Ahiqar* (see *Ahiqar* [Arm. 8.24b; Syr. 8.34]; they are not in the Aramaic version, which may date back to the fifth century BCE), although since these recensions are late, we cannot tell in which direction any dependence may have operated. It remains possible, nevertheless, that Luke used all of these to create a new and effective whole.

3.   Luke leaves it unclear whether we are to construe his motive chiefly as a self-interested desire to avoid starving to death. It was pointed out to me by J.C. Fenton that

contrast the attitude of the two sons, the self-righteousness and pride of the elder and the penitent humility of the younger—which in itself links with the censure of the Pharisees throughout, and also the sympathetic treatment of repentant sinners, such as the woman of Luke 7 or Zacchaeus. We may compare, too, the Parable of the Pharisee and the Tax-collector. Once again, Christians are being instructed in discipleship, the theme which unites the whole central section.

5.2.2. Ch. 16.1-15

Luke now reverts to the theme of possessions, which had been a secondary motif in the Prodigal Son, too (see vv. 12, 13, 30, 31; the verb διασ-κορπίζω occurs in both 15.13 and 16.1, providing a verbal link, as Evans points out).[4] The connections between the Parable of the Rich Fool and that of the Dishonest Steward have often been noticed. We may compare 12.16b ἀνθρώπου τινὸς πλουσίου, 16.1b ἄνθρωπός τις πλούσιος, and in both, the chief character says τί ποιήσω (12.17; 16.3)[5] and then resolves on a course of action, which invites a comment relating to the next world (12.20: 16.9). It is perhaps noteworthy that whereas the Parable of the Rich Fool was addressed to the multitude (12.13), that of the Dishonest Steward is aimed at the disciples, as 16.1 makes clear.

The parable itself defies easy interpretation; Derrett[6] argues that what we see here is an implicit condemnation by Luke of the usurious actions of the master and the steward;[7] the steward, by forgoing his 'commission' on loans, in practice acts generously to the debtors, even if his motives are questionable, and we may compare the Prodigal, whose repentance is the result of semi-starvation.

It may be, however, that Luke is using the steward as an *anti*-model, rather than as a model;[8] it is emphasized that he expects a reward for his

---

all the characters who soliloquize in parables unique to Luke are self-interested; we may compare the unjust judge, the dishonest steward and the self-righteous Pharisee.

4.   Evans, *Luke*, p. 595.

5.   This was, however, a very common idiom, and one of which Luke was particularly fond: see Lk. 3.10, 12, 14; 10.25; 18.18; 20.13.

6.   J.D.M. Derrett, 'Fresh Light on St Luke 16: The Parable of the Unjust Steward', *NTS* 7 (1961), pp. 198-219.

7.   Usury was against the Torah when applied to fellow-Jews; see Deut. 23.20.

8.   J.D. Crossan, *In Parables: The Challenge of the Historical Jesus* (New York: Harper & Row, 1973), sees it as deliberately shattering our expectations; we may compare the Good Samaritan or the Prodigal Son. Luke has a fondness for rogues as heroes, as is evident in parables such as the Unjust Judge.

actions, in the shape of a reception by his ex-master's grateful debtors, and Luke's Jesus has already made it clear that generous actions should be performed without any such expectation.[9] In the parable this reward is significantly expressed in v. 4 as reception into the houses (τοὺς οἴκους) of his ex-master's debtors. The 'sons of light' who in v. 8 act generously without expecting a reward will receive one in any case: reception into eternal habitations (αἰωνίους σκηνάς). There is thus an implicit contrast here, which reinforces the explicit one in v. 8, where the sons of this age (οἱ υἱοὶ τοῦ αἰῶνος τούτου) are set against the sons of light (τοὺς υἱοὺς τοῦ φωτός); the contrast between the present age and the eternal recurs throughout this entire section.

The whole of v. 8 may perhaps therefore be Jesus' comment on the parable; κύριος would therefore refer to Jesus.[10] His commendation of the steward's 'prudence' is perhaps to be compared with the behaviour of the father in the Prodigal Son; the good action of returning home by the son is accepted there at face value, with maybe some implication that there is nothing actually wrong with responding to need. The steward's behaviour is certainly wise by worldly standards, but v. 9 shows that these are not those that matter, ultimately—and Luke perhaps expects us to be aware of both levels of truth. Nevertheless, acting generously (which may be construed as 'making friends by means of unrighteous Mammon', the obvious example being Zacchaeus) does bring reward in Heaven, as is made clear in 6.35; 12.33; 14.14; it is therefore to be enjoined on all. Again, the relevance of this teaching to the discipleship theme is apparent.

Luke is here condemning not wealth as such—although in the following verses he comes very close to it—but its abuse: he is leaving an opening for the rich to act generously, like Zacchaeus, and hence to be saved (see 19.9). The verb ἐκλίπη in 16.9, which the RSV translates as the 'failure' of

---

9. See Lk. 6.34-35 and 14.12-14, both of which are peculiar to his Gospel.

10. This interpretation of ὁ κύριος, which was suggested by J. Wellhausen, is considered with some sympathy by Creed, who refers to it in *Luke*, p. 202, although he points out that even while it solves some of the problems posed by this difficult parable, not the least of which is 'the very awkward transition [that is] involved in the remaining half of the verse, which cannot possibly represent the sentiment of the Steward's master, but must be intended for a comment of Jesus', it nevertheless leaves unexplained the sudden transition to the first person in v. 9. No attempt to explain this parable so far proposed seems able to resolve all the problems raised by the text. An interpretation similar to mine is that of Bailey, *Poet and Peasant*, pp. 96ff., although Bailey regards ὁ κύριος in v. 8 as applying to the lord in the parable.

Mammon is perhaps better rendered 'comes to an end',[11] since it refers to death, when worldly possessions are left behind. It thus picks up the theme of the Rich Fool. Luke is, however, in no way commending[12] the steward, who is explicitly called ἀδικίας in 16.8, the same word that is applied to Mammon at 16.9.[13] Jesus' praise here is therefore to be seen as tongue-in-cheek; we notice that the steward is termed 'wicked' after he has performed the actions which Derrett thinks are commendable. The actions may be good, but the steward remains wicked; and it is the actions which the 'sons of light' should emulate. We should perhaps point out that vv. 10-13 (which seem to be a Lukan expansion of Mt. 6.24) are in some tension with this parable if we interpret it as Derrett proposes, since the steward has hardly been 'faithful' in unrighteous Mammon. It is not fortuitous that we are reminded at 16.10 that ὁ ἐν ἐλαχίστῳ ἄδικος καὶ ἐν πολλῷ ἄδικός ἐστιν. The connection between 16.9 and 16.11 is therefore more[14] than just the catchword 'Mammon':[15] it is the clear contrast which is drawn between the values of the present age and eternal ones, which is made explicit not just at 16.8 and 16.9 but at 16.15, too, where the Pharisees, who are honoured by men, are an abomination to God.[16] The

---

11, See *1 En.* 100.5; Heb. 1.12.

12. Contra the interpretation of Beck, *Christian Character*, pp. 28-30. Beck sees ἀδικίας in v. 8 as perhaps implying 'worldly' (cf. v. 9); alternatively, it may be a contrast between the steward's earlier, wicked behaviour and his later 'prudence'. But this does not explain why he is still termed 'wicked' after the prudent action. There is no evidence of the change of heart Beck proposes; the steward's motives are a combination of pride, self-pity and weakness, as v. 3 has already made clear.

13. It is possible, however, that τὸν οἰκονόμον τῆς ἀδικίας is not just a Semitism, to be rendered as 'the wicked steward'. Although this construction is used by Luke at 18.6, as well as being frequent in the Septuagint, the meaning of the phrase may instead be 'the steward of wicked Mammon', the ἀδικίας referring to the μαμωνᾶ, not the οἰκονόμον. We cannot be sure; but the Lukan parallel construction at 18.6 tips the balance in favour of the first interpretation.

14. Contra Creed, *Luke*, p. 202, and Evans, *Luke*, p. 597.

15. Luke's use of this Aramaic word may suggest a Jewish source for the parable. Luke is an excellent imitator of style, with a chameleon-like quality about his Greek, so that it is dangerous to refine too much upon it, but it would be fair to say that his Greek is at its most Semitic when it is influenced by the Septuagint, as in his birth narrative, or—perhaps—a Judaean source and/or provenance, as is the case at the beginning of Acts. (We may contrast the obsequious phrases of Tertullus the lawyer, or the correct and elegant Greek of Luke's Prologue.)

16. The theme of justifying oneself is a motif repeated elsewhere in Luke; see Lk. 10.29. (In the Parable of the Pharisee and the Tax-collector the 'justification' refers, instead, to the action of God.)

criticism of the Pharisees is thus set here into a context concerning the eternal significance of one's actions.

The terminology τοὺς υἱοὺς τοῦ φωτός which is used at 16.8 is not typically Lukan: it has more affinities with John's Gospel (see Jn 1.4, 5, 7, 8, 9; 3.19, 20, 21; 5.35; 8.12; 9.5; 11.9, 10; 12.35, and especially 12.36, υἱοὶ φωτός). Its usage here suggests the light/dark antithesis commonly encountered in apocalyptic texts: we may compare Qumran,[17] where there is a contrast between the sons of light who abhor wealth and those of darkness who are by implication connected with it, as Moxnes[18] points out. This inherent dualism is reflected in the 'two masters' image of Lk. 16.13, where Mammon is an enslaving power (like ἁμαρτία in Paul) which is opposed to God. What is at issue here is hence a form of idolatry, and this may explain the apocalyptic language of βδέλυγμα at 16.15.[19] It is significant that this profoundly evocative word seems to be aimed at the Pharisees in Luke; they have chosen the wrong master.

5.2.3. *Ch. 16.16-18*

Verses 16-18 do not fit the theme of possessions/judgment, and they seem difficult to fit into any scheme, although vv. 17-18 are connected in Matthew, too, where the Matthaean parallel to v. 17 at Mt. 5.18, concerning the continuing validity of the Torah, provides the introduction to the antitheses, of which divorce (cf. Lk. 16.18)[20] is one. Lk. 16.16 perhaps serves to point out that the message of Jesus involves both continuity with Judaism and discontinuity (and we may compare 13.28-29). It also reminds us of the forthcoming Passion; as Christians will all too often discover, entry into the Kingdom may be the result of violence. The violence would thus refer to persecution and would link forward to Acts.[21]

We note that Matthew's treatment of John the Baptist, who at Mt. 11.12 is linked to the new present in Christ and is greater than any born of woman, is recast by Luke so that John the Baptist is instead linked, albeit

---

17. For example, 1QS 3.13–4.36.

18. H. Moxnes, *The Economy of the Kingdom* (Philadelphia: Fortress Press, 1988), p. 144.

19. See Moxnes, *Economy*, p. 148. Cf. Rev. 17.4, 5.

20. The grouping of these three very tenuously connected sayings could possibly reflect the hypothetical Q, though Evans (*Luke*, p. 605), despite accepting the Q hypothesis, thinks it is Lukan.

21. For example, the death of Stephen in Acts 7.

as the final example, to the past history of Israel,[22] which is firmly separated (ἀπὸ τότε) from the present-day preaching of the Kingdom, which
stretches forwards.[23]

Luke seems also to have been anxious to remove any dangerous political implications from Matthew's word βιασταὶ; his version may still be
obscure, but no threat is any longer even remotely to be feared, except
perhaps by those struggling to enter the Kingdom. The retention of the
Matthaean statement affirming the eternal validity of the Torah may
surprise us, even while we are aware that Luke goes out of his way to
present both Jesus and Paul as devout, Torah-observant Jews; but at 11.42
Luke has already indicated what is really important in the Law—justice to
one's neighbour and love of God—and these are of continuing relevance.[24]
It is no coincidence that Luke places this statement close to the Parable of
the Rich Man and Lazarus, which powerfully demonstrates the eternal
consequences of ignoring the needs of one's fellows. Evans points out[25]
that, in contrast to Matthew's version, Luke's comparative εὐκοπώτερον
does not rule out any change ever; the implication is that it is very difficult
for it to happen.[26]

On the issue of divorce, there were clearly differing memories[27] of what
precisely Jesus had said concerning it. Luke may here be resisting an
interpretation which could be drawn from Mt. 5.32; 18.9, that if a man[28]
divorces his wife—for adultery, probably—and marries another, this is

22. The implicit downvaluing of John the Baptist and his influence is an important
motif connecting Luke and John.

23. The deliberate temporal structuring here formed the basis of Conzelmann's
thesis (*Theology*, pp. 16, 20ff., 25ff. and elsewhere) that history in Luke–Acts is
periodized into the (past) age of the Prophets, which ended with John the Baptist, the
(present) age of Jesus, and the (future) age of the Church. Many later critics, however,
have seen this model as greatly oversimplified or wrong.

24 Cf. Talbert, *Reading Luke*, p. 158. But Conzelmann, *Theology*, p. 185,
interprets this statement as meaning the call to repentance. Both may be true.

25. Evans, *Luke*, p. 608.

26. Fitzmyer, *Luke*, II, p. 1116, observes that the conclusion of the Lazarus parable
of 16.19-30 also asserts the continuing relevance of the Law and the Prophets—in
Luke's interpretation, their function remains as a witness to the death and resurrection
of Christ. Conzelmann, too (*Theology*, p. 159), notes the continuing relevance of the
Law in a prophetic function.

27. Cf. Mt. 5.31-32; Mk 10.11-12; 1 Cor. 7.10-13.

28. In Jewish law, only a man could secure a divorce; see Deut. 24.1-4. In Roman
law, women were allowed to divorce their husbands, and this is clearly reflected in
both Mark and Paul.

acceptable, although for a divorced woman to remarry is adultery. Luke applies the same standards to both partners, condemning remarriage for either sex, in which respect he resembles Mark, although his primary target is remarriage, not divorce. Luke's emphasis here is characteristically rigorous;[29] we recall that only Luke at 14.26 and 18.29 includes wives among the close family members whom disciples must be prepared to leave for the Kingdom. This is the cost of discipleship.

5.2.4. *Ch. 16.19-31*

The Lazarus parable picks up the themes of possessions and of judgment which had dominated the Dishonest Steward and the succeeding related material, and also the critique of Jewish exclusivity which is an undercurrent throughout, since it seemed to exalt the Torah above human need.[30] Thus Luke refers here to Lazarus's sores being licked by dogs which would have made the man unclean (like the seemingly mortally wounded or dead traveller at 10.30), and therefore to be avoided by respectable and orthodox Jews. There are interesting points of contact between this parable and the Johannine tradition; links include not only the name of the central character (a unique feature of this parable being the naming of any of the characters)[31] but also the description of Hell in vv. 23-28, which is quite close to Revelation in its portrayal of the sufferings of the damned. The point Luke is making here is very clear, and like much of this chapter, it is polemical:[32] Εἰ Μωϋσέως καὶ τῶν προφητῶν οὐκ ἀκούουσιν, οὐδ᾽ ἐάν τις ἐκ νεκρῶν ἀναστῇ πεισθήσονται.

5.2.5. *Ch. 17.1-10*

Luke has already used part of Jesus' discourse to the disciples in Matthew 18, the Parable of the Lost Sheep (Mt. 18.12-14/Lk. 15.3-7); and the injunction to humility (Mt. 18.1-4) Luke has treated in the parallel to Mk

29. Contra Esler, *Community and Gospel*, p. 123, making the Torah more stringent did not reveal a 'shocking disregard' for the Law by Jesus; see E.P. Sanders, *Jesus and Judaism*, p. 5.

30. We may compare the implication of The Good Samaritan; likewise, Zacchaeus, and the sinful woman of Luke 7.

31. Creed (*Luke*, p. 211) inclines to think that the story of Lazarus was already in circulation at the time of the composition of Luke's Gospel, and that 'the conclusion of the parable may have been composed and added and the name Lazarus incorporated under the influence of that story'. Some connection between Luke and John here, at least of the order of a verbal reminiscence, seems very likely.

32. See Esler, *Community and Gospel*, p. 119.

9.33-37 at Lk. 9.46-48, although there is also a thematic link to Lk. 14.7-11. After he has dropped uncongenial material such as vv. 17-18, and vv. 8-9 (to him, the Kingdom represents healing and wholeness), Luke summarizes what is left, the connection perhaps being provided by the reference in 17.3 to ὁ ἀδελφός, sinning (cf. 16.28), and to repentance (cf. 16.30).

The structure of the speech nevertheless remains basically Matthaean. Thus Mt. 18.6-7 provides the basis for Lk. 17.1-2.[33] Mt. 18.15-20, with its criticism of Gentiles and its references to late church practice,[34] is abbreviated in Lk. 17.3, where the censure of Gentiles disappears altogether. Mt. 18.21-22 is paralleled in Lk. 17.4, although Luke characteristically renders these Matthaean verses on forgiveness in a positive context, and omits what may perhaps have seemed an implicit rebuke of Peter. The seeming failure in Matthew of the disciples, as represented by Peter, to understand the full implications of Jesus' message may explain why Luke takes next, from Matthew's preceding material (Mt. 17.20-21), a thematically related section on the disciples' need for faith, although Luke typically softens the Matthaean criticism and omits the reference to their ὀλιγοπιστία. It is equally typical that he replaces Matthew's Parable of the Unmerciful Servant and its chilling conclusion at Mt. 18.35 with his own Parable of the Unworthy Servants at vv. 7-10, which once more touches on the theme of reward, and which seems to have some connections with an earlier Lukan parable, the Watchful Servants (Lk. 12.35-38). What is taught here is one's duty towards God; this is clearly a crucial part of the instruction in discipleship which is Luke's main concern in the central section of his Gospel.

5.2.6. *Ch. 17.11-19*
Verse 11 reminds us once more that a journey is in progress, and that Jesus has left Galilaean territory. There follows the pericope of the Ten Lepers which is peculiar to Luke, where the treatment of Samaritans calls to mind Luke's parable in ch. 10, and makes a similar implicit critique of Judaism. The concluding comments (vv. 18-19) relate the pericope more closely to

33. There may also be an echo here of Mk 9.42 in the words περίκειται...εἰς τὴν θάλασσαν at Lk. 17.2. Mt. 18.6-9 is quite close, verbally, to Mk 9.42-48, and Luke seems to combine elements of both.

34. Although Luke is interested in the spread of the Church, which forms the subject-matter of Acts, he probably felt that the term was anachronistic here. Hence he omits it.

the immediately preceding material, so that the need to give praise to God links with v. 10 (duty to God) and the power of faith with vv. 5-6. Once more, Luke presents teaching material dramatically, for extra emphasis.

5.2.7. *Ch. 17.20-37*

Luke then returns to the theme of the Kingdom, which has been important throughout: entry into the Kingdom is the goal of discipleship. Here Luke emphasizes that it is in some senses already present (see 17.20-21), and this provides a de-eschatologized introduction which modifies how we respond to what follows. This section is mainly derived from Matthew 24, and the order, too, owes much to Matthew, albeit with numerous modifications. I shall analyse it in some detail, since there are many differing opinions as to Luke's source and purpose.[35]

5.2.7.1. *vv. 20-21*. As was noted above, at 17.11 Luke had inserted another 'travel notice', and these are consistently followed by examples of the correction of false notions relating to the role of Jesus and his disciples or by references to the Gentile mission. The preceding pericope concerned the cleansing of a Samaritan leper, which prefigures the wider mission of the Church;[36] here, we see the correction of erroneous ideas about the coming of the 'Kingdom of God'. This is not to be equated with the Eschaton (which some have assumed is about to happen); its coming, indeed, is not to be construed in a spatial or temporal sense at all at this point, since it is in important respects already present in Jesus' ministry.[37] Nevertheless, as the succeeding discourse (vv. 22-37) makes clear, this is not to be interpreted to mean that no final consummation is envisaged; Luke also wishes to refute any idea of an already realized eschatology which could be derived from vv. 20-21.[38]

The only possible indication of Mark 13 here is the word ἐκεῖ in Lk.

---

35. Thus Creed and others such as Evans see possible echoes of Mark at various points: Creed (*Luke*, p. 221), for example, suggests that Lk. 17.31 may have been derived from Mk 13.15 rather than Mt. 24.17/Q, as Lk. 17.33 may be from Mk 8.35 rather than from Mt. 16.25/Q. But this must remain an open question.

36. Thus Conzelmann, *Theology*, p. 72.

37. This point is made by O. Merk, 'Das Reich Gottes in den lukanischen Schriften', in E.E. Ellis and F. Grässer (eds.), *Jesus und Paulus: Festschrift für W.G. Kümmel zum 70 Geburtstag* (Göttingen: Vandenhoeck & Ruprecht, 1975), pp. 201-20, contra Conzelmann, *Theology*, p. 121ff.

38. Cf. Talbert, *Reading Luke*, pp. 164, 166ff.; see also his earlier study: C.H. Talbert, *Luke and the Gnostics* (Nashville: Abingdon Press, 1966), pp. 44ff.

17.21 (cf. Mk 13.21), and this could very easily be a coincidence, since ἰδού, ἐκεῖ is a very common comparison. Lk. 17.20 is redactional; Luke is fitting the section into his own frame, and adapting it to suit his own interpretation—that the 'today' of salvation (see 19.9), though not the Eschaton, is a present reality.

5.2.7.2. *vv. 22-23*. Verse 22 is also redactional, and introduces the theme, albeit with a particular nuance (see below), which is to dominate the whole section—the 'Day of the Son of Man'. To this end, Luke collects separated material, and paraphrases freely, creating a new whole which accords with his own ideas. The first reference, in v. 22, to 'one of the days of the Son of Man'[39] seems nevertheless to have a slightly different implication from the rest, and to refer in this context to the earthly life of Jesus, Son of Man, which is not what the Eschaton, the future day of the Son of Man, implies and should not be construed as such. However much they long for Jesus to be with them again after his Passion and Resurrection, his followers are firmly told, καὶ οὐκ ὄψεσθε. Nor are the disciples to believe claims that the 'New Age' is already here, as is made clear in v. 23b. Even though many of the words used in this verse differ from Mt. 24.26, there are evident points of contact in idea and structure: the Lukan verse is a free paraphrase of the Matthaean, wherein Luke also picks up again the 'here' and 'there' comparison of v. 21, which was a modification of Mt. 24.23.

5.2.7.3. *vv. 24-26*. The link between Mt. 24.27 and Lk. 17.24 is readily apparent, especially at the beginning of Lk. 17.24, but whereas Matthew follows the reference to lightning with a description of it 'coming from the East and shining out to the West', Luke rewrites the simile; it simply lights up the sky from one side to the other. (The repetition of οὐρανὸν is typically Lukan.)[40] He omits the Parousia reference of Mt. 24.27c, and this could be, as Conzelmann[41] proposes, to accommodate the fact that the Parousia had apparently been delayed; or Luke may have wished to avoid any dangerous political implications which could be derived from the term. The import of the phrase Luke uses instead at 17.24, 26 and 30—'the

39. This is a phrase peculiar to Luke. My interpretation of this verse is similar to that of Evans, *Luke*, pp. 630-31.

40. Goulder, *Luke*, p. 111, observes that repetition is a Lukan characteristic (e.g. Lk. 4.18; 9.25).

41. Conzelmann, *Theology*, pp. 121ff.

day(s)[42] of the Son of Man'—is nevertheless very similar to Matthew's 'Parousia', and this may support Talbert's[43] alternative proposal; the omission reflects an implicit Lukan critique of a realized eschatology. Luke prefers to concentrate on Jesus' exaltation, rather than his return or his future presence, as is evident in the Lukan modification to Mk 14.62 at Lk. 22.69. In any case, the word Parousia in Mt. 24.27 and 24.37, which Luke consistently avoids, provides the connection between Lk. 17.24 and 17.26; Luke groups together topically two separated Matthaean sections, and uses them as part of his interpretation of the discourse.

5.2.7.4. *vv. 27-30*. These verses are a free paraphrase of Mt. 24.38-39, which were clearly suggested by the Noah reference in Mt. 24.37 (we may compare, especially, Mt. 24.38-39a and Lk. 17.27). Luke has added another biblical image of destruction—Sodom. This is not in Matthew at this point, but it had been used earlier by Luke as an example of God's vengeance in a passage which has a clear Matthaean parallel (cf. Lk. 10.12 and Mt. 10.15). Once again, Luke excises the word Parousia at 24.39b and restates this in his own terms at v. 30: κατὰ τὰ αὐτὰ ἔσται ᾗ ἡμέρᾳ ὁ υἱὸς τοῦ ἀνθρώπου ἀποκαλύπτεται (v. 30).

5.2.7.5. *vv. 31-33*. The 'fire and brimstone' destruction in the Sodom image, as the unparalleled v. 32 makes clear, is continued in Luke's paraphrase of Matthew's vv. 17 and 18, which he places next;[44] once more, the link between the material is a topical one. What Luke has done in this section is to utilize a (modified) earlier section of Matthew's discourse. Thus Luke's v. 31, which he connects with the preceding verse by stressing the thematic link in the words ἐν ἐκείνῃ τῇ ἡμέρᾳ is akin to Matthew's 24.17:[45]

42. The plural form in v. 26 is to balance stylistically the preceding reference to the days of Noah.

43. Talbert, *Reading Luke*, pp. 164, 166; *Luke and the Gnostics*, pp. 44ff.

44. He reuses this saying, again paraphrased, in its Markan context at Lk. 21.21 (cf. Mk 13.15-16). This also suggests that he could be using Mark and Matthew.

45. Contra Creed, *Luke*, p. 221, who sees the connection with Mk 13.15-16 here, not Q/Matthew. Matthew and Mark are very close, but Matthew does not contain Mark's μηδὲ εἰσελθάτω τι and neither does Luke; similarly, both agree against Mark in the phrase ἐν ἀγρῷ (Mark has εἰς τὸν ἀγρὸν). The connection with Matthew is therefore closer, and no use of Mark need be assumed.

Mt. 24.17	ὁ ἐπὶ τοῦ δώματος μὴ καταβάτω ἆραι τὰ ἐκ τῆς οἰκίας αὐτοῦ
Lk. 17.31	ὅς ἔσται ἐπὶ τοῦ δώματος καὶ τὰ σκεύη αὐτοῦ ἐν τῇ οἰκίᾳ, μὴ καταβάτω ἆραι αὐτά...

The reference to τὰ σκεύη has no parallel in Matthew (nor, indeed, Mark), but it is perhaps the sort of naturalistic touch we often find in Luke—people in a crisis often do try to save their possessions.[46] Lk. 17.31c seems to be a paraphrase of Mt. 24.18, and since Luke has already made the point about not leaving possessions behind, he drops Matthew's very specific mention of a cloak.

Lk. 17.33 is a logion which Matthew uses twice, albeit with variations (see Mt. 10.39; 16.25). Mark has it, too, at 8.35, and Luke has already used it in his parallel to that at Lk. 9.24. This was obviously a saying of Jesus' which was widely known, its paradoxical nature and antithetic parallelism facilitating memory, but it was freely adapted by the evangelists to suit different contexts. The form Luke uses here is unique in many respects, the verbs ζητέω, περιποιέομαι and ζωογονέω having no parallels elsewhere; the verb περιποιέομαι perhaps picks up a thought suggested by τὰ σκεύη, and refers to the wrong sort of gain. Luke is reminding his audience that the whole discourse is to be seen as a lesson in discipleship; hence its inclusion.

5.2.7.6. *vv. 34-36.* Luke now returns to Matthew 24, and he amplifies to some extent the image of Mt. 24.40-41 in his own verses 34-35, adding ὁ ἕτερος to balance the εἷς, and replacing Matthew's ἀγρός with a more domestic (and urban) κλίνης,[47] and Matthew's μύλος with ἐπὶ τὸ αὐτό, perhaps because its sense was already incorporated in the verb ἀλήθω.[48]

5.2.7.7. *v. 37.* Luke rounds off his discourse by inserting a question which adds variety of tone, and also reminds us that this is addressed to an

---

46. The correct attitude to worldly goods—and this behaviour is very clearly the reverse—is a Lukan theme. Similarly, I.H. Marshall, *The Gospel of Luke* (Exeter: Paternoster Press, 1978), p. 664.

47. The 'urban' emphasis of Lukan redaction has often been noticed; see Cadbury, *Making of Luke–Acts*, pp. 245-49. Both these features are therefore to be considered characteristic of Luke.

48. Verse 36 is poorly attested, and it was presumably an assimilation of Luke's text to Matthew's, since it, too, talks of two being in a field.

audience; the instruction in discipleship that is being given is to be heeded and acted upon. The word ποῦ seems to provide a catch-word link with the concluding portion of the verse, ὅπου τὸ σῶμα, ἐκεῖ καὶ οἱ ἀετοὶ ἐπισυναχθήσονται. This is very close to Mt. 24.28, which Luke has obviously reserved until now to provide the conclusion to his whole discourse. The 'carcase' is maybe to be construed as Judaism here, and the context is very threatening;[49] Luke is reminding his audience of the consequences of rejecting the Son of Man and of misinterpreting his message (see v. 20) as to what the Kingdom involves.

We may conclude that this entire section is not only completely coherent; it reflects Lukan themes and emphases which have been made apparent all along, and it is well integrated into its context. There is no need to postulate any use of Mark or Q here at all: what we see is a paraphrase and reordering of Matthew.

5.2.8. *Ch. 18.1-8*

The beginning of this chapter again raises the topic of prayer, which had been placed near the start of the teaching in ch. 11. There is a very definite parallel between 11.5-8 and 18.1-5 on persistence in prayer; we note that the idiom παρέχω κόπον occurs in both. The same is true of 11.9-10 and 18.6-8a, which points the moral and assures Luke's audience that God indeed hears and answers prayers. But there is no parallel in the earlier parable for the conclusion at 18.8b: 'When the Son of Man comes, will he find faith[50] on the earth?' It does, however, pick up the theme of faith which is important throughout to Luke (see, for example, 17.5-6, 19) and also that of the Son of Man, which had been a major topic in the previous section (see 17.22-37); the day of the Son of Man will one day come, even

---

49. Evans, *Luke*, p. 664, believes that the Greek word ἀετοὶ, translated 'eagles' in the RSV, probably means vultures here, since the eagle is not a carrion bird. The saying in this case would be a proverbial one, not an allusion to the destruction of Jerusalem by Rome.

50. τὴν πίστιν could in this context mean 'The Faith', i.e. Christianity, and refer to the threat posed by false teaching; it is so taken by Creed, *Luke*, p. 224, and cf. also S. Brown, *Apology*. The ecclesiological emphasis would be characteristic; it would also lend support to Talbert's suggestion (Talbert, *Reading Luke*, p. 164ff.) that the evangelist in this section is concerned to combat heretical ideas.

if it does not arrive speedily, as in v. 8a,[51] and disciples are not to lose heart.[52] Luke seems to be drawing the threads together here.

5.2.9. *Ch. 18.9-14*

The Parable of the Pharisee and the Tax-Collector expresses dramatically, in a way that would catch the audience's attention, many ideas relating to the dominating theme of discipleship which have already been developed by Luke. (Indeed, the purpose of all the repetition, the parallelisms, the use of *inclusio* and chiasmus, is presumably to ensure that the important points are remembered; like any good pastor, Luke knows the value of constant reinforcement.) Motifs found in this parable include the castigation of Pharisaic hypocrisy, the stress on the need for repentance and prayer, the assurance of God's mercy and forgiveness and the intimation of the eternal significance of one's actions. If the Good Samaritan is to be seen as an example of the correct way to behave to others, this one centres on the correct way to relate to God.[53]

The parable is topically connected to the previous one, since both concern prayer; but as we have seen they are also linked to much of the rest of the teaching material in this section. The necessity for humility, for example, which is the conclusion drawn at 18.14, is another theme broached earlier; v. 14 itself is, indeed, a doublet of 14.11, and it provides the transition to the next section, vv. 15-17.

5.2.10. *Ch. 18.15-30*

Luke has now completed his very free and creative reinterpretation of Matthew's teaching material,[54] and from this point on, at 18.15 (cf. Mk

---

51. Evans (*Luke*, p. 640) says that the force of the particle ἆρα in 18.8 is 'to express considerable anxiety or doubt'. It may therefore be seen as qualifying the preceding ἐν τάχει.

52. There may be some connection, a similarity of concept and—to a very limited degree—of language, between this Lukan parable and Rev. 6.10-11, where God assures the martyrs that if they wait a little longer until his plan is carried out, they will be avenged; see U. Vanni, 'The Apocalypse and the Gospel of Luke', in G. O'Collins (ed.), *Luke and Acts* (New York: Paulist Press, 1993), pp. 9-25. The conception of God as judge is a traditional one, however, so we cannot assume that Revelation drew it from Luke's parable. Vanni's assumption that Revelation expands Luke is reversible; if there is a literary connection between the two texts, Luke could equally have abbreviated Revelation, as he abbreviates the Sermon on the Mount.

53. Similarly, Talbert, *Reading Luke*, p. 165.

54. H.B. Green, 'The Credibility of Luke's Transformation of Matthew', in C.M.

10.13), he once more rejoins Mark's narrative, deftly weaving his two sources together. He omits Mark's section on divorce since he has already covered this topic—albeit briefly—in a context closer to its Matthaean placement. The 'suffer the little children' pericope (vv. 15-17) is very close to Mk 10.13-15; much closer than it is to Mt. 19.13-14 or Mt. 18.3. Here, too, entry into the Kingdom, the theme of so much of the central section, is the real issue.

In Luke's treatment of the Rich Ruler we find evidence which could suggest a harmonization of Mark and Matthew.[55] Although in the main[56] he is much closer to Mark than to Matthew in this pericope, and contacts with Matthew amount to the occasional word (ἐν οὐρανοῖς in Lk. 18.22, Mt. 19.21, contra Mk 10.21 ἐν οὐρανῳ; ἀκούσας in Lk. 18.23, Mt. 19.22, contra Mk 10.22 στυγνάσας; τρήματος in Lk. 18.25, cf. Mt. 19.24 τρυπήγατος contra Mk 10.25 τρυμαλιᾶς; εἰσελθεῖν at Lk. 18.25, Mt. 19.24 contra διελθεῖν in Mk 10.25; ἀκούσαντες at Lk. 18.26, and Mt. 19.25),[57] there are several significant omissions which Matthew and Luke share. Thus neither mentions the affection Jesus feels for the young man, and both omit the references to the gospel[58] and to the coming persecutions. One might have expected this would have suited Luke's theme of discipleship and the way he repeatedly links forward to Acts; Creed calls his omission of Mark's μετὰ διωγμῶν 'remarkable',[59] but his motive may have been to avoid exacerbating tension with regard to Rome. In addition, both drop Mark's μὴ ἀποστερήσῃς, which seems to be derived

Tuckett (ed.), *Synoptic Studies* (Sheffield: Sheffield Academic Press, 1984), pp. 131-55 (134), says, 'It is clear enough that Luke prefers to follow one primary source at a time, using the second, when they overlap, chiefly as a source of minor verbal variations.'

55. We should notice that here, too, Luke feels free to relocate 'Jesus sayings' in Matthew which are not paralleled in Mark. Thus Mt. 19.28 is retained by Luke for use, albeit with some modification, in the farewell discourse at Lk. 22.28-30.

56. Cf. Lk. 18.18/Mk 10.17b; Lk. 18.19/Mk 10.18; Lk. 18.24/Mk 10.23b.

57. Some of these are disputed in some Matthaean manuscripts.

58. There is a similar omission at Mt. 16.25/Lk. 9.24 (cf. Mk 8.35). Luke perhaps felt that it was anachronistic at this point; we recall that he similarly drops Matthew's reference at 18.17 to the Church (cf. Mt. 18.15-17/Lk. 17.3). Because Luke continues his story into Acts, he can afford to omit such references in his Gospel.

59. Creed, *Luke*, p. 227. However, Tannehill, *Narrative Unity*, I, pp. 121-22, sees Markan irony in this juxtaposition of extravagant rewards and persecutions, which Luke chooses to omit, since it seems to be aimed at the disciples. As usual, Luke softens any censure of the Twelve: we notice that when he uses Mk 10.35-45 at Lk. 22.24-27, he modifies it to remove the direct criticism of James and John.

from Deut. 24.14, from the summary of the Law found in Exod. 20.12-16 and cited by all three evangelists.

There are nevertheless some characteristic Lukan touches here, such as the addition of πάντα at 18.22 to the instruction to sell what one has and give it to the poor, and the injunction to leave even one's wife to follow Jesus (we may compare 14.26, where the addition of γυναῖκα is again peculiar to Luke). It may also be significant, perhaps, that only Luke calls the man an ἄρχων, especially in view of the hostility he consistently shows to rulers throughout Luke–Acts,[60] and the equivocal attitude to worldly power that may be evidenced in Lk. 22.25:[61] we recall the identi-fication of ὁ ἄρχων τοῦ κόσμου τούτου in Jn 12.31; 14.30; 16.11.[62]

Picking up the implication of the reference at 18.16-17, v. 18 takes us back explicitly, and in identical words, to the topic of inheriting eternal life which was raised by the Lawyer at 10.25. It is possible that the whole central section is to be seen as bearing on this topic, so that it forms a huge *inclusio*. In this context, we notice that there is a reference to the Law at both beginning (10.26) and end (18.20). On the other hand, the answers to the questions are somewhat different, and the material in 18.18 is con-tinued into the succeeding section, so that it does not form a conclusion as such. Luke is seemingly again gathering the threads together here: we note an illustration of self-satisfaction (v. 21); the true purpose of the Torah— namely, doing good to others (v. 22); reward in Heaven (v. 22); posses-sions and their proper use (v. 22); divided loyalties and the difficulties posed by wealth (v. 24); following Jesus (v. 28); division in families (v. 27) and the cost of discipleship (v. 29).

5.2.11. Ch. 18.31-43

At 18.31, Jesus warns that they are approaching Jerusalem; once more, we are reminded of the goal of this journey. The Son of Man reference under-lines the point further, precipitating another Passion prediction at vv. 31-33; the link, as in Mark and Matthew, is thematic. Here, too, Luke's version is very close to Mark; indeed, in some respects, it is closer to Mark than Matthew is (παραλαβὼν at Mk 10.32/Lk. 18.31, and the verbs ἐμπτύω at Mk 10.34/Lk. 18.32, ἀποκτείνω at Mk 10.34/Lk. 18.33, and ἀνίστημι at Mk 10.34/Lk. 18.33). Agreements with Matthew are mainly

60. Cf. Lk. 14.1; 23.13, 35; 24.20; Acts 4.5, 8; 13.27; 14.5.
61. See Evans, *Luke*, p. 649.
62. The only human 'ruler' referred to explicitly by John is Nicodemus, and he is treated equivocally.

small-scale and stylistic; both omit Mark's favourite πάλιν and replace ἤξατο λέγειν with εἶπεν. In addition, as is consistently the case, both replace Mark's μετὰ τρεῖς ἡμέρας with a more historically accurate 'on the third day' (Mt. 20.19 τῇ τρίτῃ ἡμέρᾳ Lk. 18.33 τῇ ἡμέρᾳ τῇ τρίτῃ).

We are nevertheless aware that some details, most notably v. 34 with its emphasis on the disciples' failure to understand, are entirely Lukan: we recall that ignorance only merits a 'light beating' at Lk. 12.48. Lukan, too, is the stress at 18.31 on the fulfilment of prophecy. In addition, Fitzmyer[63] notes that Luke, who had omitted the reference to 'the way' at 9.46 (cf. Mk 9.33-34), also omits ἐν τῇ ὁδῷ in his parallel at 18.31 to Mk 10.32. We may compare, too, Mk 8.27 and Lk. 9.18. To Luke, 'The Way' is Christianity, and its time is after the Ascension.[64]

The incident of the blind beggar, whom only Mark names as Bartimaeus, again shows Luke closer to Mark[65] than he is to Matthew, although here too each evangelist has items that are peculiar to his own account. Thus in Matthew there are, characteristically, two blind men, and vv. 33 and 34a are effectively unparalleled; in Mark, there are the likewise unparalleled 20.49b, 50; and in Luke, 18.36b, 40b, 43b. (The place—Jericho—provides a link forwards to the next pericope which is only in Luke.) Once more, many of the themes Luke has been developing are dramatized in this story, such as mercy (vv. 38, 39); faith (v. 42); rejoicing and glorifying God (v. 43), which is the purpose of healing, as has been clear from the start (see 10.20); and indeed persistence (compare 18.39 and 18.5-8: the healing is almost a direct illustration of the parable, although the implication may well be christological, since God vindicates the elect who cry out to him in v. 7, whereas in 18.40-42 it is Jesus who responds).

5.2.12. *Ch. 19.1-10*

As was noted above, Jericho provides the connection between the previous healing and the final section of this very lengthy journey—the call of Zacchaeus.[66] This has affinities with the call of Levi in ch. 5: it is one of

---

63. Fitzmyer, *Luke*, II, p. 1207.
64. See Acts 9.2; 19.9, 23; 22.4; 24.22.
65. See Lk. 18.35b/Mk 10.46e; Lk. 18.39b,c/Mk 10.48b,c; Lk. 18.42/Mk 10.52.
66. On the ideas expressed in this pericope and their importance to Luke, see especially J. O'Hanlon, 'Zacchaeus and the Lukan Ethic', *JSNT* 12 (1981), pp. 2-26. O'Hanlon points out the typically Lukan vocabulary of this pericope: for example, σήμερον, χαίρων, σωτηρία, σπεύσας, ὑπαρχόντων, καθότι. In sentiment, too, it is entirely Lukan.

the many parallels which occur throughout the entire Gospel and Acts. It is noticeable that this incident, which relates to Luke's favourite theme of repentance, has been placed at the close of the travel narrative for especial emphasis. In order to make room for it, Luke has altered the timing of the healing of the blind man, whom the evangelist does not name, so that it now precedes the entry into Jericho (cf. Lk. 18.35 and Mk 10.46/Mt. 20.29). Here, too, Luke dramatizes themes—riches (v. 2) and their proper use (v. 8); forgiveness, manifested in dining with outcasts and sinners (v. 7); repentance and restitution (v. 8); and the reward of this in Heaven— that is, salvation (v. 9). There may also be a critique of Judaism, since the implication is that Zacchaeus, though a Jew, is one of the lost (v. 10) who needs to be saved: clearly, then, the Law does not effect salvation (a somewhat Pauline conclusion!). The inference here is that Judaism, by stigmatizing Zacchaeus because of his profession, has failed in this respect; he is simply excluded by the devout[67] as akin to the sinners.

5.2.13. *Ch. 19.11-27*

If we include this parable in the central section, as Conzelmannn thinks[68] we should, then it once more serves to emphasize the proximity, significance and forthcoming judgment on Jerusalem (see v. 27). Jesus' arrival there is carefully and explicitly separated from the expectation of the Parousia, which is inevitable, but not necessarily imminent, as the parables of ch. 12 have already made clear. The Kingdom, although the focus of all the teaching material that has preceded it, is not to appear immediately, as v. 11 emphasizes. Salvation may have come in Jesus (v. 9), but not the Kingdom in the form his followers seem to have expected.

In many respects Luke's parable poses as many problems as that of the Dishonest Steward. In both (and we may compare, too, the Unjust Judge) the nominal 'hero', who according to almost any interpretation is guilty of sharp practice (indeed, in Luke's version, he admits to extortion at 19.22, just as the unjust judge admits to his own contempt for others at 18.4), is seemingly presented as a role model who serves to illustrate some aspect of the interrelationship of God and humanity.[69]

Luke's Parable of the Ten Pounds nevertheless has clear affinities with

---

67. Cf. Tannehill, *Narrative Unity*, 1, pp. 124-25.

68. Conzelmann observes (*Theology*, p. 73) that the entry into Jerusalem does not occur until 19.28-44. So, too, Baarlinck, 'Die zyklische Struktur', although Baarlinck sees the central section as beginning with the second Passion prediction at 9.43b.

69. See Lk. 16.8-13; 18.6-8; 19.26.

Matthew's Parable of the Talents: cf. Mt. 25.26-27/Lk. 19.22-23; Mt. 25.28/Lk. 19.24 (where the only real difference is the amount of money in question) and Mt. 25.29/Lk. 19.26. Creed comments, 'The verbal resemblances between the Matthaean and the Lukan parables, especially towards the close, make it almost certain that there is a literary relationship.'[70]

However, despite an underlying structural similarity, and some definite verbal correspondences, we are aware that Luke has not only paraphrased very freely (cf. Mt. 25.21 and Lk. 19.17; or Mt. 25.24-25 and Lk. 19.20-21) but has also made changes for which the reason is not always immediately apparent, assuming that his source was Matthew, or indeed Q. This is not true of all the changes he makes; the downscaling of Matthew's fantastically large sums is to some extent typical.[71] We can well understand, too, why Luke preferred a μνᾶ, since a modest amount like this, given equally to all, makes the parable more relevant to the experience of the audience and to the theme of discipleship. The parable in this respect is clearly directed at Christians and the way they should behave as they await their Lord's return. We can understand, too, why Luke omits Matthew's reference at 25.30 to 'outer darkness' where 'there will be a wailing and a gnashing of teeth'. This is not a location to which Luke readily consigns anyone; he may have felt that death in this world (see Lk. 19.27) was quite sufficient.

It is perhaps less easy to decide why Luke replaced Matthew's three servants with ten at Lk. 19.13, especially when this alteration is not sustained throughout. In this case, the explanation could possibly be, as Creed[72] suggests, that the change was made to accord with the fact that the man of Mt. 25.14 has become a nobleman in Lk. 19.12, even if we might therefore have expected the number of servants to be even greater.

Almost all would concede that Luke has been clumsy in his handling of this parable. The incongruity of the reward of five or ten cities for being 'faithful' over a trifling sum (and here the reward is much more consistent with the scale of Matthew's account), and the equally strange protest of the bystanders at v. 25, who seem to feel that the possession of ten pounds is of more significance than that of ten cities, is especially glaring.

70. Creed, *Luke*, p. 231.

71. Thus missionaries in Luke are not expected to take gold with them; cf. Lk. 9.3/Mt. 10.9. Likewise, the *quadrans* of Mt. 5.26 is reduced still further to a *lepton* at Lk. 12.59.

72. Creed, *Luke*, p. 234. Luke is fond of tens: there are ten coins in Luke 15, and ten lepers in Luke 17.

Some critics, who are presumably anxious to defend Luke against what Evans[73] terms 'slovenliness' here, have suggested that he has used another source at this point, rather than Matthew/Q.[74] But a source which accounts for all the peculiarities of Luke's version remains a hypothesis only. Can any other explanation be offered on the basis of the text we have as to why Luke's parable is so unsatisfactory? It could fairly be contended that what Goulder terms 'muddles' of this sort are frequent features of Luke's redactional activity when he is adapting sources. He often makes changes at the beginning of a pericope which he fails to maintain consistently; we may compare the peculiarly Lukan setting of the Feeding of the Five Thousand near Bethsaida at Lk. 9.10 which conflicts with the reference at 9.12 to being in a 'lonely place': or the excision of the 'Beloved Disciple' at Lk. 24.12 which seems to have been forgotten by 24.24. In the case of the Parable of the Ten Pounds, Luke is reinterpreting his source, and combining it with a fresh motif; the nobleman who goes away to receive a kingdom and his actions on his return to his rebellious subjects (see 19.12, 14-15a, 27). Under such circumstances, when Luke is attempting to reconcile conflicting material, lapses like this are not surprising.

'The nobleman who receives a kingdom' seems to be a topical allusion to the events of 4 BCE concerning Archelaus,[75] which Josephus narrates (see *War* 2.1-11 and *Ant.* 17.228-239). In this instance, it is difficult to understand why the story should have lodged in Luke's mind unless he had read about it recently, since the incident itself took place at least 65 years before the earliest suggested date for the composition of his Gospel. The most likely explanation would therefore seem to be that Luke drew his information from Josephus.[76]

As to why Luke has combined the two motifs, we would perhaps expect the answer to be provided by the introduction to the parable at v. 11,

73. Evans, *Luke*, p. 666.

74. Another version of the parable is recorded in the *Gospel of the Nazareans*, p. 18. See E. Hennecke and W. Schneemelcher (eds.), *New Testament Apocrypha* (trans. R.M. Wilson; 2 vols.; Philadelphia: Westminster Press, 1963), I, p. 149, in a form which seems to be midway between Matthew and Luke and contains elements of both. (Thus, the three servants [cf. Matthew] are each [cf. Luke] given one [Luke] talent [Matthew]). But this version also appears to reflect Luke's Prodigal Son; it therefore was presumably a later conflation.

75. Cf. Talbert, *Reading Luke*, p. 178; and Evans, *Luke*, pp. 668-69, contra B.B. Scott, *Hear, then, the Parable* (Philadelphia: Fortress Press, 1989).

76. This does not, however, help us to date Luke's account, since Josephus refers to it in both *Jewish War* (c. 80 CE) and *Jewish Antiquities* (93–94 CE).

which is redactional (εἶπεν παραβολήν is a Lukan expression, as are προσθεὶς and παραχρῆμα; and the use of διὰ before an articular infinitive is also frequent in Luke, although it is rare elsewhere in the New Testament). According to this introduction, the aim is to refute the idea that the Kingdom of God is to appear immediately.[77] The reason for this emphasis may be that Luke, who prefers for apologetic reasons to downplay Messianic fervour, wishes to cool any speculations which the recent ferment in Judaea had tended to feed. Alternatively, it may be to refute an over-realized eschatology, which seems to have been a problem to the Church from the early days, since Christ's Resurrection was seen as the 'first fruits' of the Last Things, an eschatological act, like the gift of the Holy Spirit. This apparently led some (as we infer from 1 Cor. 15; cf. 2 Tim. 2.18) to assume that they were already living the resurrection life, and it was a feature of one stream of the ideas which seems to have provided a source for second century Gnosticism.[78]

In Matthew's parable, which is concerned primarily with how the Christian acts in the meantime, and also the resulting final judgment, the length of time the master is away (see Mt. 25.19) is a subordinate point. Luke, however, focuses on it and amplifies it in such a way that it imposes severe tensions on the underlying story. Evans[79] observes that the topical allusion Luke adds cannot be regarded as a parable in its own right, so that it is a mistake to talk about a 'combination of parables' as does Jeremias.[80] It is, rather, a gloss—but one which seems to bear little relation to the situation presented in the original parable. Nevertheless, the intention of the ominous and uniquely Lukan v. 27 is unmistakable; the judgment of God on Israel still stands. Evans sees this as perhaps the explanation for the Archelaus allusion, since the episode culminated in the punishment by Rome of rebellious Jews. The Romans are thus by implication God's agents here, just as in Isa. 10.5 the Assyrians are 'the rod for [his] anger'. The central section opens at 9.51-56 with Jesus' refusal to allow his disciples to call down fire on the Samaritans who have rejected him: it closes

77. Cf. Acts 1.6-8, where it is likewise emphasized that the Kingdom is not necessarily imminent, although it is prefigured by the gift of the Spirit at Pentecost which Luke interprets in eschatological terms via the Joel prophecy.

78. Talbert, *Luke and the Gnostics*, pp. 44ff., points out how many of the ideas which were to be developed more fully in second-century Gnosticism are refuted in Luke–Acts.

79. Evans, *Luke*, p. 669.

80. Jeremias, *Parables*, p. 59.

with this awful warning of the consequence of Jewish unbelief, which leads naturally and inevitably into the lament over Jerusalem in 19.41-42.[81] Just as the denial that the Kingdom was necessarily about to appear is developed in Acts, so, too, this second theme links forward to Acts, where the motif of Jewish rejection and Gentile acceptance dominates the whole narrative.

To sum up, in his redaction of Matthew's parable Luke has separated the historical details he has introduced from the eschatological ones he has inherited,[82] so that the concern is no longer the delay of the Parousia and the Last Judgment, nor a misconception of their significance, but the forthcoming doom facing Jerusalem. In Luke's version we have a two-edged message, with the underlying Parable of the Ten Pounds giving instruction in Christian discipleship and reminding believers that their response must be active, and the grim historical allusion Luke has constructed over this being aimed at the Jews who have failed to recognize the 'time of their visitation'. If rebellion against the king approved by the Romans has resulted in death for the rebels, what will be the consequence of rejection of the king appointed by God?[83] (It is noteworthy that one of the very few Lukan acclamations of Jesus as βασιλεὺς occurs in the pericope immediately following this parable, and in this instance Luke uncharacteristically prefers βασιλεὺς, as in Mt. 21.5 and Jn 12.15, to the βασιλεία of Mk 12.10.) There is nothing in Luke's redaction which requires us to assume that the source he used was not Matthew, even if we are aware that he has modified it considerably to suit his own purpose, and to provide yet another link with the second volume of his work.

5.3. *Some Conclusions*

5.3.1. *Luke's Use of Matthew in this Section: Purpose and Technique*
We may conclude that in Luke's central section the material is consistently grouped according to theme and placed wherever seems most appropriate. Many have found the result far from satisfactory, and have been baffled by the way Luke has destroyed the very clear and logical order of Matthew's five major discourses, and interwoven short sections of teaching drawn from them with narrative and parable in an order which often appears far

81. Similarly, Tiede, *Prophecy*, pp. 79ff.
82. Conzelmann, *Luke*, p. 128, shows that the same is true in Luke 21 in his redaction of Mark's 'Little Apocalypse'.
83. Cf. Tiede, *Prophecy*, p. 79.

from logical.[84] The whole section, however, can be seen to provide a course in discipleship; Luke's concerns are pastoral throughout.[85] Thus, the cost of discipleship is emphasized at 9.57-62, before the Mission of the Seventy (Two), which is programmatic for the wider mission of the Church, as depicted in Acts. At the end, too, Luke emphasizes that salvation (19.9)—the purpose of discipleship, and evident throughout in the stress on the eternal consequences of one's actions—involves considerable personal sacrifice (see 18.24-30; 19.8). Following Jesus (the verb ἀκολ-ουθέω is, significantly, repeated at 9.57, 61 and again at 18.22, 28) is no easy option.

Luke expresses the purpose of the teaching in dramatic terms in the pericope of Mary and Martha at 10.38-42, having already drawn attention to its significance for Christians present and future in the section which culminates in the Parable of the Good Samaritan. It is thus entirely fitting that the theme of a person's relation to God, which is the point of Christian discipleship, is used to introduce the teaching proper after this pericope, and the starting-point is Jesus' best-known prayer. The themes which Luke wishes to emphasize are so important that they are repeated over and over again, and they are expressed in teaching, parable and narrative. They inform the structure he has utilized, too, and he skilfully weaves his various sources together, with an eye constantly to the situation facing the later Church,[86] noticeably gathering the threads together at the end.

The message is paraenetic throughout, and Luke may have set it in the form of a journey to Jerusalem, the significance of which is stressed more than once, because the spiritual journey to be undertaken by later disciples as they follow their Lord may conceivably lead to a death like his. (Jesus' death in Luke's Gospel is presented as a supreme example to later Christians of the correct way to die; Jesus is the perfect martyr.) What we see in the central section thus amounts in some respects to a 'pilgrimage'.[87]

Luke nevertheless takes care to show that Jesus' death is no defeat; it involves his final and conclusive victory over Satan, his ἀνάλημψις, just as for believers the reward is ζωή αἰώνιος (see Lk. 10.25). Luke's presentation is thus perfectly consistent; in no way is his rearrangement of

84. They have therefore attempted to impose a structure on the journey.

85. This is also the conclusion of Goulder, *Luke*, I; Baarlinck, 'Die zyklische Struktur', p. 603; and many others.

86. See, e.g., 10.8; 12.8-12, 13-15, 46, 47-48a.

87. Cf. B. Reicke, 'Instruction and Discussion in the Travel Narrative', in K. Aland (ed.), *SE I* (TU, 73; Berlin: Akademie Verlag, 1959), pp. 206-16.

Matthew's material to be seen as the action of 'a crank'.[88] On the contrary, it makes perfect sense, providing we judge him according to what he is seeking to achieve with the material, and not according to Matthew's very different purposes.

We see in the central section Luke's use of basically Matthaean teaching material adapted to new contexts and inserted into the narrative at appropriate times, fleshed out with some distinctively Lukan material—most obviously the parables—which are similarly placed to illustrate particular themes. Luke has therefore recast much of the discourse material he has derived from Matthew in line with his own interpretation, as is especially evident in the Woes of ch. 11 and the eschatological discourse of ch. 17.

He often groups topically items which are separated in Matthew; the sayings on light/sight at 11.33-36 are an obvious example, but the same is true at Lk. 10.12-15, which combines Mt. 11.20-24 and Mt. 10.15, the connection being the word Sodom; at Lk. 12.12, where he replaces Matthew's 'Spirit of your Father' (Mt. 10.20) with a reference to the Holy Spirit, which provides the necessary link between Mt. 12.31-32 and Mt. 10.19-20; and also at Lk. 11.14-26, which groups material relating to the Christ/Satan conflict with the Beelzebul controversy.

But Luke will just as readily separate items joined in Matthew for special emphasis, as is evident in the section on the costs of discipleship in Lk. 14.26-27, which is closely related, topically, to Lk. 12.51-53, the two being placed together in Mt. 10.34-38. It is also noticeable that Luke often reserves a statement occurring during a Matthaean discourse to form a climax. Thus he transfers the conclusion to the section in Mt. 12.33-35 on good and evil fruit to his own use of the image, a Matthaean doublet, in the parallel to Matthew's earlier use of it.[89] Likewise, he avoids another verbal doublet by appending the 'Lord of the harvest' motif to the Mission of the Seventy (Two), not the Twelve, although he is quite prepared to double incidents and sayings if necessary.

The 'bridges' connecting differing sections of material, which are important because they preserve a connected sequence to the narrative, are usually Lukan constructions; Lk. 12.13-15, for example, provides a transition which leads into the topic (namely, possessions) of the Rich Fool, and yet, since Jesus is asked to arbitrate between two squabbling brothers, it also has points of contact with the preceding pericope, where there is judgment

88. Thus, Streeter, *Four Gospels*, p. 183.
89. Cf. Mt. 7.16-20/Lk. 6.43-45.

depending on whether one has acknowledged or denied the Son of Man. Similarly, Luke uses the sentimental exclamation at 14.15 to provide the stimulus for the ominous parable of the Great Supper, which picks up and illustrates the point of the saying at 14.11. Luke deliberately juxtaposes differing material in this way to allow reciprocal interpretation and comment, and sometimes, an introduction modifies the way the succeeding material is read, as seems to be the intention of Lk. 17.20-21.

We may conclude that Luke does not seem to feel in any way bound by the order or location of the sayings material he derives from Matthew, any more than Matthew is usually supposed to have felt bound by the order of the hypothetical Q, although the actual words spoken by Jesus are another matter entirely. Even when Luke seems to have disliked some of Matthew's most characteristic expressions, such as 'howls of lamentation and gnashing of teeth', 'men of little faith' and 'hypocrites', these are nevertheless included at least once by Luke; as we have seen, he usually alludes to those few which he does not include.

Luke nevertheless places the shared teaching material in different contexts which accord with his own emphases, a clear example being the interpretation of the 'sin against the Holy Spirit' as apostasy rather than as seeing Jesus' power as diabolical. Indeed, very often it is the material peculiar to Luke which governs the placement of the Matthaean sayings he includes, so that it provides a new context for them. The warning by the Pharisees at 13.31 of Herod's wish to kill Jesus thus leads naturally into the apostrophe to Jerusalem which Luke derives from Mt. 23.37-39, just as the parable of the Rich Fool provides the context for the consideration of worldly cares. In this case, Luke has recast Matthew's section, reversing his order but providing a much better introduction to the following material. Similarly, the Friend at Midnight parable concerning answered prayer provides the setting for a Lukan parallel to Mt. 7.7-11, just as the Pharisee and the Tax-Collector illustrates the logion at the end (Lk. 18.14/ Mt. 18.4). But equally, sometimes the framework for a Lukan section seems to be provided by Mark/Matthew, such as the Lawyer's question, which calls forth the Good Samaritan parable as an example of love of neighbour, with the Mary and Martha pericope which follows being an illustration of love for God. Luke has certain key themes relating to his overarching concern—discipleship—which he wishes to illustrate, and these themes seem to be the most important elements in the structuring of his narrative.

In this connection, we note that although Luke usually adheres to the Markan order for narrative, albeit with some exceptions, especially in the

Passion sequence, this is not the case with the Markan sayings material which is shared with Matthew, such as the 'salt' logion, or the consideration of divorce, or causes of offence, or leaven. In the Lukan version of some of these, and also, perhaps, in the Beelzebul controversy, there are features which might suggest an attempted harmonization of Mark and Matthew, although it is probably more likely that the faint echoes of Mark may be unconscious, reflecting Luke's memory of a text he knew well, since throughout this section (at least until 18.15) Matthew is clearly his main source.

5.3.2. *Contacts with Johannine Material*

At the same time, however, Luke's often very creative readaptation of Matthew's Jesus sayings into new contexts, joined with new material which sometimes itself seems to control the ordering of these sayings, is also combined with allusions (whether conscious or otherwise we cannot be sure) to Johannine material. The whole section is not so much a reconciliation of Matthew and Mark, since there seems to have been very little use of Mark at all, except at beginning and end, but more a free adaptation of Matthew, interspersed at many points with items which have clear connections with the Johannine writings; any 'combining' in the main body of the travel narrative is more evidently of Matthew and John than of Matthew and Mark.[90]

It must be appreciated that the connections between John and Luke are not all of the same type. In some cases, points of contact between them could be regarded as linked traditions (for example, the Christ/Satan conflict and the stress on the authority of Christ in Luke 10 and 11, a leading theme in both John's Gospel and Revelation). At other times, they rather involve the employment of similar themes, such as the joy of the disciples which is linked to the gift of the Spirit, or the importance of witnessing and of personal revelation; all of these will be examined in more detail in the following chapter.

---

90. The synthesis of material, which involved fusing the best elements of various texts into a new whole, was recommended to ancient writers; see Quintilian, *Institutio Oratoria* 10.1.108ff.; 10.2.25, and also Longinus, *On the Sublime* 13.2–14.1. Transformation, which involved the inventive imitation of a text, was encouraged. The way ancient writers imitated texts, which is important to any source criticism of the Gospels, is considered by T.L. Brodie, 'Greco-Roman Imitation of Texts as a Partial Guide to Luke's Use of Sources', in C.H. Talbert (ed.), *Luke–Acts: New Perspectives from the SBL* (New York: Crossroad, 1984), pp. 17-46.

But there are also occasions when the verbal links between Luke and the Johannine tradition are more apparent. As was the case with Luke's use of Mark in this section, many of these are on a small scale, such as the use of φίλοις μου at 12.4 (cf. Jn 15.14); or υἱοὺς τοῦ φωτὸς at 16.8 (cf. Jn 12.36); or ἀποκαλύπτω with the meaning 'revealed heavenly secrets' in 17.30 (cf. the title of Revelation itself); or perhaps ἄρνας at 10.3 (cf. ἀρνία in Jn 21.15), τελειοῦμαι at 13.32 in a Passion reference (cf. τετέλεσται in Jn 19.30), and the reference to σκορπίοι at 11.12 which may have affinities with Revelation 9. Some, however, are much more significant, such as confessing Christ before the angels of God at Lk. 12.8-9 (cf. Rev. 3.5); or the linking of 'ask and you will receive' not to the gift of 'good things' (as in Matthew) but to that of the Spirit (cf. Lk. 11.9-13 and Jn 14.13-17); or the conceptual link between Jn 9.2-3 and Lk. 13.2 and the fact that both are connected with a reference to Siloam, which it is difficult to dismiss as mere coincidence.

In some cases, the events in the narratives themselves are connected. The case of the Lazarus parable, and especially the comment at Lk. 16.31 (which is borne out by the events succeeding the Lazarus incident in John) is contentious, but the presentation of Mary and Martha in Lk. 10.38-42 (cf. Jn 11; 12.1-8) is surely related: the only other possible explanation is a very closely linked tradition/lost source, of which we have no actual evidence. The same is true in the final section of Luke's Gospel, the Passion and Resurrection accounts, where the connections of theme, treatment and wording between Luke and John are often so close that they are quite impossible to dismiss, even if their significance has been consistently misinterpreted. These connections, too, will be investigated in the following pages.

5.3.3. *Use of Sources by Ancient Writers*
Some critics reject the notion that Luke could have been working with more than one source at a time because of the practical difficulties involved in using scrolls with no chapter divisions in this way.[91] While it must be conceded that the problems were acute, they were not insurmountable. 'Gospel harmonies' were written, as we know, from the second century onwards, the best-known example being Tatian's *Diatessaron*; and Luke in his prologue (1.1) refers to many sources. R.A. Burridge[92] has examined

---

91. E.g. Wenham, *Redating*, pp. 204-207; F.G. Downing, 'Compositional Conventions and the Synoptic Problem', *JBL* 107 (1988), pp. 69-85; Chilton, *Profiles*, pp. 38-39.
92. Burridge, *What Are the Gospels?*, p. 174.

the way ancient writers used their sources, and describes how, as we are told by Pliny the Younger in *Epistles* 3.5, the Elder Pliny would begin by reading very widely. The same is true of Plutarch, who cites over one 150 sources; he refers to more than 25 in the later *Roman Lives*.[93] Writers would usually, it seems, take some notes[94] from a scroll as they were using it, and this explains the verbal echoes we often find, since sometimes these notes might be almost verbatim, whereas at other times the source might be extensively paraphrased. For practical reasons authors normally followed one main source at a time, supplementing this by their own notes and their memory[95] of what they had read elsewhere. They also felt free to construct incidents illustrating what they thought must have happened even if they had no actual evidence of it, just as they composed speeches in accordance with what seemed fitting and appropriate for the circumstances and character.

The relevance of all this to a consideration of Luke is clear. As we have seen, he does normally follow one main source at a time. In the central section this is usually Matthew, although it would matter little to this analysis of Luke's treatment of his source if he had instead used some of the traditions lying behind Matthew (i.e. Q). He supplements this, however, not just from his own material, but also from Mark, and in this case we cannot be sure whether he is relying on memory, his own notes, or the text itself. The practical difficulties pointed out by Wenham and others would perhaps suggest that the last is the least likely; but there are nevertheless occasions throughout his Gospel where Luke does seem to be conflating Markan, Matthaean and also Johannine material, so this cannot be ruled out altogether.

In addition, we cannot be sure that Luke's source material was necessarily in scroll form. Metzger says, 'Early in the second century (or perhaps even at the close of the first century) the codex...began to come into extensive use in the Church'.[96] He suggests that the use of codices was

93. See Pelling, 'Roman Lives', p. 74; 'Adaptation', pp. 131ff.
94. See Lucian, *How to Write History* 48. The same was often true when they listened to speeches, which some would record in a sort of shorthand (see Quintilian, *Institutio Oratoria* 11.2.25) although Quintilian himself recommends careful memory at 11.2.2.
95. For this reason, minor verbal agreements are to be expected and do not constitute a problem for the suggestion that Luke used Matthew, contra Tuckett, 'Existence of Q', p. 42.
96. B.M. Metzger, *The Text of the New Testament* (Oxford: Clarendon Press, 1964), p. 6.

adopted very rapidly by Gentile Christians,[97] perhaps as a way of differentiating their sacred Scriptures from those of the Jews, who used scrolls. If Luke is indeed to be dated late (that is, c. 100 CE), as has been argued above, then this increases the possibility that he worked from codices rather than scrolls, which would certainly have facilitated a much freer use of sources like Matthew.

97. See P. Katz, 'The Early Christians' Use of Codices Instead of Rolls', *JTS* 46 (1945), pp. 63-65.

Chapter 6

LUKE AND THE JOHANNINE TRADITION:
COMMON IDEAS AND THEMES

6.1. *Introduction*

Luke's closeness to the other Synoptic Gospels, which has been considered in the preceding chapters, is such that few would deny some direct literary relationship between them. But as is evident from the exegesis above of Luke's central section, there are also many conceptual links between Luke and the Johannine tradition, and it is interesting to note that in his treatment of themes such as wealth and the Christ/Satan conflict Luke seems closer to the book of Revelation than John's Gospel is, as will be shown below. Many of the points of contact seem to derive from a matrix in intertestamental Judaism, and they provide us with a literary context that is important to our understanding of Luke, since ideas that were current at the time and that an author reflects are in some respects also to be counted as a source on which he drew. Biblical scholars need, perhaps, to have a more flexible understanding of the nature of literary dependence, which may extend beyond direct and easily identifiable verbal borrowing (such as we see in Luke's use of Mark and Matthew/Q) and involve instead the use of common ideas and themes. The connections between Luke and the Johannine tradition that fall into this category are numerous and striking, as not a few critics have pointed out. Indeed, I would suggest that it may be the presence in Luke of ideas that can be paralleled in the Johannine literature and are different in many respects from those found in the other Synoptics that produce some of the tensions that scholars have detected in Luke's treatment of topics such as eschatology and wealth.

As a preliminary to a consideration of these shared ideas, it seems necessary to say a little about their cultural background. It must firstly be appreciated that first-century Judaism was thoroughly diverse, as archaeological evidence, especially the finds at Qumran, has confirmed; here were numerous sects, many (maybe most) of which believed that they alone had contact with the real purpose of Yahweh for his people, even if to outsiders such as Rome a Jew was a Jew, and one Jewish group was very much like any other. The situation was fundamentally changed by the Romano-Jewish war of 66–73 CE, and especially the (to Jews) catastrophic fall of Jerusalem in 70 CE, the effects of which were reinforced by more tough Roman action after the Bar-Kochba revolt in 132–135 CE. In order to preserve the Jewish identity, and to survive once the cultic centre had been destroyed, the post-Jamnia Rabbinate needed to emphasize the features which separated Judaism from surrounding cultures. Erecting barriers of this kind is characteristic of a society or a group which feels threatened, as studies by anthropologists such as Mary Douglas have shown.[1] The result is a fierce exclusivity, which is especially evident in the literature of sectarian groups, as the Dead Sea Scrolls demonstrate (see, in particular, the *Damascus Document*).

There is much variety in the writings of the 'intertestamental' period, when Judaism was far less homogeneous than it later became. This is especially evident in those that are usually classified as 'apocalyptic', such as *1 Enoch, Jubilees, The Testament of the Twelve Patriarchs, 4 Ezra, Baruch, The Testament of Abraham, The Ascension of Isaiah*, and also the canonical Daniel. The dating of most of these is problematic, and some, such as *1 Enoch*, may have evolved over a long period; but some of their differing ideas seem to be reflected—indeed, presupposed—in many early Christian texts. (This includes the Gospels, not just Christian Apocalypses such as Revelation, or the visions in *Hermas*.) They are, in fact, far more significant in Luke than many have supposed. Thus when Esler talks of Luke's, 'firm rejection of the apocalyptic strand in the early Christian tradition',[2] this can only be seen as true if we limit our understanding of the word 'apocalyptic' to a type of super-heated eschatology dealing with the imminent End, and Rowland[3] shows that this is actually a common misunderstanding of the genre. Susan Garrett, in her fascinating study of the importance of magic and the demonic in Luke, reaches a very different conclusion from Esler's: 'The message [of Christ's authority over the Devil] is interwoven with an overarching and surprisingly apocalyptic myth about Satan's struggle and fall.'[4]

---

1. Mary Douglas, *Purity and Danger* (London: Routledge & Kegan Paul, 1966).
2. Esler, *Community and Gospel*, p. 65.
3. C. Rowland, *The Open Heaven* (New York: Crossroad, 1982). See especially pp. 23ff.
4. Garrett, *Demise*, p. 102.

It is in the wider sense of 'apocalyptic' that there are so many connections between Luke–Acts and the Johannine tradition.[5] (This includes John's Gospel and the Johannine Epistles as well as Revelation, all of which seem to reflect a similar intellectual *milieu*, even if they were written by different people.)[6] I shall investigate in detail some of the ideas Luke shares with the Johannine tradition that fall into the very broad category of 'apocalyptic' envisaged by scholars such as Rowland,[7] since they are a source which has as yet received far less critical attention than seems warranted.

6.2. *Themes*

6.2.1. *Treatment of History*

We should note, first, that an apocalypticist does not usually seek to portray the specific course of historical events. References tend instead to be general, expressed via frequently ambiguous symbols that are problematic to interpret with any precision.[8] This makes most texts difficult to date, especially since the very ambiguity of many of the references invites, as was surely intended, successive reinterpretation in accordance with changing circumstances. This is evident in Daniel, which is intended to be read on two levels, that of the historical narrative and that of the (related) present historical situation. The same—as many critics such as J.L. Martyn[9] and R.E. Brown[10] maintain—is true of the Johannine literature.

---

5. The connections between Revelation, Luke–Acts and *1 En.* 92–105 are nevertheless particularly close, and these are considered in more detail in the Excursus at the end of this chapter.

6. Like most scholars, I am assuming that the author of Revelation, called John at Rev. 1.1, was not the unnamed author of either the Gospel or the Epistles. Although there are close verbal links between John's Gospel, the Johannine Epistles and Revelation, this only demonstrates a common understanding and interpretation.

7. Rowland, *Open Heaven*, pp. 70-72.

8. E.g. it is difficult to know what is the significance of the various heads and horns of the Beast in Rev. 13 and 17.

9. J.L. Martyn, *The Gospel of John in Christian History* (New York: Paulist Press, 1978); *History and Theology in the Fourth Gospel* (Nashville: Abingdon Press, 2nd edn, 1979). The first level is that of the story, but the evangelist's real concern is the second level, which relates to the problems faced in his own day.

10. R.E. Brown, *Beloved Disciple.* It is an approach which John Ashton (*Understanding the Fourth Gospel* [Oxford: Oxford University Press, 1991], pp. 5-7) finds fruitful.

Although the narratives do not function in precisely this way, there are also occasions in the Synoptic Gospels when the future significance of what is described as past history is inherent in it. This is especially evident in Luke, whose modifications are often ecclesiological; Lk. 12.32, for example, although having some affinities with Jn 21.15-17, is effectively unparalleled elsewhere and was obviously aimed directly at the Church of Luke's day. The use of the future tense of εἰμὶ at 19.46, too, relates what is said to the later situation of the Church, and the same is true of much of Acts, most obviously the words of Paul at Miletus.

Many apocalyptic texts perceive a relationship between events in the human sphere and those in the realm above, so that what is revealed is significant on two levels, in the same way that 'historical' events function on two levels; an obvious example is the Ascension itself, a motif limited to Luke and John among the evangelists, although only Luke attempts to narrate it. Often things which the seer observes in Heaven are related to those yet to come on earth, as is presumably the case at Lk. 10.18. Thus in the war between Michael and Satan in Revelation, Satan's defeat and ejection mean that man no longer has an accuser in Heaven (Rev. 12.10), and judgment, which is intended eschatologically on earth, is already a fact there: the triumph of Good over Evil and Death is already realized. The guarantee of this to us is the Resurrection.

The cosmic calamities leading up to the Eschaton, too, demonstrate the connection between the world above and that below. Events like Caesar's death and the fall of Jerusalem in 70 CE.[11] seem to have been accompanied by startling portents; we may compare the unnatural darkness at the crucifixion (and the other details that Matthew adds of earthquakes, gaping graves, and so on). In this context, Luke's comment on the absence of sunlight at Lk. 23.45, τοῦ ἡλίου ἐκλιπόντος, should not be regarded as an attempt at finding a natural explanation that was provided by the incurably prosaic Luke, who needed to 'de-mythologize' it. Luke, like his contemporaries, would have seen such an eclipse as being an example of divine action expressed through a natural event: he would not have regarded the two as mutually exclusive.

The focus is on history seen as evidencing God's overarching control; in this respect, apocalyptic texts are thoroughly theocentric in their interpretation of events that are seen as a whole, and viewed *sub specie aeternitatis*. What is provided thus amounts to a theodicy, since present suffering is

---

11. For portents accompanying the fall of Jerusalem, see Josephus, *War* 6.297-99. Plutarch's *Life of Julius Caesar* describes those associated with Caesar's death.

relativized by regarding it in the context of God's long-term salvific plan. In Luke–Acts, this is expressed by the repeatedly used verb δεῖ,[12] which emphasizes the divine control over human life. It is also used, and for the same reason, in Revelation and in John's Gospel.[13]

De la Potterie[14] suggests that John's key-word ἀλήθεια, which echoes throughout the Gospel and the Johannine Epistles, implies the divine plan as revealed to humanity, as is the case when it is used in both the Jewish Wisdom tradition and at Qumran:[15] the difference here is that as John sees it this 'plan' is Jesus. Though his terminology is not the same, Luke, too, talks of the βουλή of God at Lk. 7.30; Acts 2.23; 4.28; 5.38, and this plan is human salvation, the saviour being Jesus. Salvation history is itself a major Lukan theme: although σωτήριον/σωτηρία are not common words in the New Testament, we notice that Luke uses them for especial emphasis at both the beginning of his Gospel (Lk. 1.69, 77) and the end of Acts (Acts 28.28). And since in Luke's presentation salvation is offered first to the Jews and afterwards to the Gentiles, the time of the Gentiles is therefore after the resurrection.[16] The Parable of the Fig Tree in this context is programmatic; like the unfruitful tree, the Jews are to be given one last chance, which is the function of the preaching of the gospel to the Jews in Acts and the call to repentance it contains. The Jews acted 'in ignorance', says Peter (Acts 3.17): but if they reject the message a second time, the implication is that they, like the fig-tree, will be cut down.

We must perceive, however,[17] that Luke's view of historical events seems very different from that found in texts such as Revelation, where despite the portrayal of a future joy and glory in Heaven which could be seen to relativize to some extent the present earthly sufferings of Christians, there is nevertheless no effort to mute an agonized plea for retribution and justice, nor to hide the burning hostility felt by the author towards

12. Richardson, *Panorama*, p. 78, calculates that Luke–Acts accounts for almost half the New Testament uses of this word.

13. See Rev. 1.1; 4.1; 10.11; 17.10; 20.3; 22.6; Jn 3.7, 14, 30; 4.24; 9.4; 10.16; 12.34; 20.9.

14. I. de la Potterie, 'The Truth in St John', in J. Ashton (ed.), *The Interpretation of John* (London: SPCK; Philadelphia: Fortress Press, 1986), pp. 53-66. See especially pp. 54-56.

15. See Dan. 10.21, Wis. 3.9 and 1QH 7.26-27.

16. There is no Gentile mission as such in John's Gospel, either, although it may be similarly prefigured—in this case, by the arrival of some Greeks to see Jesus at Jn 12.20-21.

17. Cf. Wengst, *Pax Romana*, p. 127.

the 'harlot Babylon' because of what has been experienced. As we have seen above, Luke's treatment of Rome is relatively favourable; Pilate three times declares Jesus to be innocent, and Paul's experiences with later Roman governors are similar. It is significant that Acts closes not with Paul's martyrdom in Rome, but with the statement: 'And he lived there two whole years at his own expense…teaching about the Lord Jesus Christ quite openly and unhindered.'

It is therefore entirely typical that Acts 3.21 should speak of the restoration (ἀποκατάστασις) of all things at the End. Revelation, on the other hand, portrays the awful sufferings of a Rome subjected to God's final judgment with savage glee in ch. 18. It is a vindictive picture of destruction and chaos, not restoration, which in itself forms a powerful contrast to the equally graphic description of the new Jerusalem in ch. 21, the abode of the faithful, where there is a new Heaven and a new earth, 'for the old had passed away'.

6.2.2. *Personal Revelation*

As Rowland[18] emphasizes, eschatological ideas are not the only significant element in apocalyptic thought, because the concern is with the whole of history, not just its end. The word 'apocalypse' itself points to an important feature. Properly speaking, what the term implies is a vision or audition, framed by a narrative explaining the circumstances, and stressing the revealed message, although in the New Testament only John in the title ἀποκάλυψις and Luke in the related ἀποκαλύπτεται at Lk. 17.30 use it in the sense of 'revealed heavenly secrets'.[19] The modification made by Luke at 10.21-22 to Mt. 11.25-27 relates to this theme: no one knows who the Son *is*, except those to whom the knowledge has been revealed, such as Simeon in the birth narrative, or the disciples on the road to Emmaus, to whom Christ unfolds the Scriptures relating to himself.

In this context we should notice how important visions are in Luke–Acts;[20] not only are there those of the first two chapters, and perhaps the uniquely Lukan descent of the Holy Spirit σωματικῷ εἴδει ὡς περιστεράν at the baptism, but there is also the unparalleled Lk. 10.18 and maybe also 22.43 (though many authorities omit this verse). In Acts, too, not only Paul but also Stephen and Peter have visions, and the apostles are

18. Rowland, *Open Heaven*, pp. 136ff.
19. Thus Rowland, *Open Heaven*, p. 377.
20. Eleven of the twelve New Testament uses of ὅραμα are in Acts, and three of the four uses of ὀπτασία in Luke–Acts.

directed to action by angels. In John, of course, the main focus of Christ's preaching is himself as at once the revealer and the revelation. In Revelation, too, the open Heaven is a key image, occurring five times (see Rev. 3.8; 4.1; 11.19; 15.5; 19.11). This stress on direct personal revelation confers authority on the seer and on his interpretation of events; in Acts, for example, Stephen's vision confirms his preceding indictment of the Cult.[21] Thus, as Meeks[22] notes, the 'stick' of the Last Judgment is used in Revelation to sanction behaviour the seer finds acceptable and to condemn deviance (even if the criteria used to mark the distinction between acceptable and deviant are not always very clear). Since many apocalyptic texts are supposedly deathbed speeches,[23] this gives—as was surely intended—particular authority to what is said; and in this context, we note that in both Luke and John Jesus addresses his disciples in just such a 'farewell discourse' after the Last Supper.

6.2.3. *Witnessing*
Closely related to the theme of personal revelation, which is literally what 'apocalyptic' involves, is the importance of witnessing. This motif, which he did not derive from Matthew or Mark, links Luke to the entire Johannine tradition, since it is emphasized in John's Gospel, 1 John, and Revelation. Moreover, Luke and John both stress the importance of witnessing 'from the beginning' with $\dot{\alpha}\pi$' $\dot{\alpha}\rho\chi\hat{\eta}\varsigma$ being a repeated phrase,[24] and both regard witnessing as a counter to heresy, John setting Jesus' unique witness to God against mystical ideas[25] and Luke using the men and women from Galilee to validate the apostolic tradition. Talbert[26] sees this as a defence against incipient Gnosticism, and in support of this interpretation we notice that Luke stresses at Acts 1.3, 22 that the post-Resurrection teaching, contrary to Gnostic practice, was public instruction. He emphasizes its completeness,

21. Cf. Maddox, *Purpose*, p. 104.
22. W.A. Meeks, 'The Social Functions of Apocalyptic Language in Pauline Christianity', in D. Hellholm (ed.), *Apocalypticism in the Mediterranean World and the Near East* (Tübingen: J.C.B. Mohr [Paul Siebeck], 1983), pp. 687-705 (694, 700).
23. E.g. *T. Abr.*, *T. Levi*, *T. Naph.*, *Ass. Mos.*
24. See Lk. 1.2 (cf. Acts 11.15); Jn 15.27. See also 1 Jn 1.1 (cf. 2.7, 24; 3.11).
25. In Jn 3.31-36. See below.
26. Talbert, *Luke and the Gnostics*, pp. 17ff. It was pointed out to me by D.A.S. Ravens that whereas in John the main content of the witnessing is the relationship of Jesus to God, with the Father and the Son bearing witness to one another, Luke prefers to use witnesses to attest the corporeality of every event in Jesus' earthly history.

too, thus validating the later teaching of the Church.[27] The Scriptures them-selves testify to Jesus (Jn 5.39; Acts 10.43; compare also Lk. 24.27, 44), and the disciples witness from the beginning (Jn 15.27; Acts 1.22) what has been seen and heard (Jn 3.32; Acts 22.15). In both Gospels Jesus' disciples are witnesses after the resurrection (see Lk. 24.48; Jn 21.24); indeed, in both the two key witnesses are the apostles and the Holy Spirit (Jn 15.26-27; Acts 5.32), as Trites observes.[28] The 'signs and wonders' worked by the apostles in Acts bear testimony to Jesus and confirm the Johannine promise that, 'He who believes in me will also do the works that I do' (Jn 14.12).[29]

The theme of bearing witness (which links with the word αὐτόπται Lk. 1.2) thus pervades much of Acts. It is also of great importance to John; John the Baptist's function in this Gospel is not to baptize Jesus, but to witness to him as God's chosen, his Son. Jn 3.31-36 is a key passage, since it stresses that Jesus, because he has descended from Heaven, is uniquely able to testify of God. It is therefore quite plausible that the word οὐδεὶς earlier in this chapter (Jn 3.13) is to be seen as corrective, refuting the visions reminiscent of *Merkābāh* mysticism which occur quite frequently in Jewish Apocalypses.[30] Indeed, this verse also refutes the Old Testament.[31]

In Revelation μάρτυς is itself a key word, and it is used in an ambiva-lent way, involving both witness/testimony to the Christian message and the later understanding of 'martyr': one whose witness to Christ involved dying for him. Typically, this is linked back to Christ, who is the 'faithful witness' at Rev. 1.5,[32] and, to reinforce the connection, we notice that the two prophetic[33] witnesses of ch. 11 are raised by God and ascend to heaven, vindicated in the sight of all and enabled to loose torments such as earth-quakes on their persecutors; death in this life is thus only a prelude to

27. See Acts 20.20, 24, 27-30.

28. A.A. Trites, *The New Testament Concept of Witness* (Cambridge: Cambridge University Press, 1977), p. 121.

29. See Trites, *Witness*, p. 149.

30. Cf. H. Odeberg, *The Fourth Gospel* (Uppsala: Lundeqvist, 1929), pp. 72, 94ff.

31. See Gen. 5.24 and 2 Kgs 2.11. That Jesus surpasses the Old Testament prophets is a key Johannine theme.

32. Cf. Lk. 12.8-12, where Jesus, as Son of Man, acts as advocate and heavenly witness for Christians in the divine court.

33. There is a close connection drawn in Revelation between witnessing and proph-ecy: indeed, the days of the two witnesses' prophesying at 11.6 are interchangeable with the days of their witnessing at 11.7. In Jewish literature, the connection between proph-ecy and martyrdom was a recognized one; see, e.g., *Asc. Isa.* 1-5.

glory—and revenge. The function of this theme may well be paraenetic, since victory is through a suffering witness and it is the μαρτυρία as well as the blood of the Lamb that defeats Evil at Rev. 12.11.[34]

6.2.4. *Eschatological Speculations*
Even though, as argued above, the meaning of 'apocalyptic' is wider than just eschatology, eschatological speculations are nevertheless very common in apocalyptic texts. Such speculations usually concern an imminent catastrophe which separates this age from that to come. Cosmic calamities, severe distress, domestic strife, civic dissolution, wars, and the presence of false prophets and false teachers, which constitute the 'time of trial', ὁ πειρασμός, are a feature of many Jewish texts; they also occur throughout the New Testament in eschatological contexts, such as Mark 13 and parallels.

Typical vocabulary, which we also find in Luke–Acts and Revelation, includes μετανοέω, πειρασμός, θλῖψις, and γρηγορέω.

Table 1: *Verbal links between Luke 21 and Revelation found elsewhere in the New Testament not shared by the other Gospels*

Word	Luke	Acts	Revelation
πειρασμός (time of trial)	8.13; 11.4; 22.40, 46	–	3.10
γρηγορέω (be alert, watch)	12.37 (39: disputed in many mss.)	? maybe 20.31	3.2, 3; 16.15
Θλῖψις (tribulation)	–	14.22	1.9; 2.9, 10, 22; 7.14
μετανοέω (repent)	10.13; 11.32; 13.3, 5; 15.7, 10; 16.30; 17.34	2.38; 3.19; 8.22; 17.30; 26.20	2.5, 16, 21, 22; 3.3, 19; 9.20, 21; 16.9, 11
ὀργή (wrath)	3.7; 21.23	–	6.16, 17; 11.18; 16.19; 19.15

In this context it is perhaps worth noting that at 10.25, Luke uses the very Johannine ζωή, with its Johannine connotation of eternal salvation,

---

34. Similarly, R. Bauckham, *The Theology of the Book of Revelation* (Cambridge: Cambridge University Press, 1993), pp. 70ff., where the motif of the 'holy war', in which believers participate, is stressed.

although Luke characteristically links it to love; we may compare, too, Lk. 18.18, 30; Acts 13.46, 48.[35]

Table 2: *Verbal links between Luke 21 and Revelation found elsewhere in the New Testament not shared by the other Gospels*

Word	Luke 21	Revelation
Κοσμέω (put in order)	21.5 (Κεκόσμηται)	21.19 (κεκοσμένοι)
σημεῖα (sign)	21.11	13.13, 14; 16.14; 19.20
ὑπομονῇ (endurance)	21.19	1.9; 2.2, 19; 3.10; 13.10; 14.12
στρατόπεδον (army)	21.20	(19.19 στρατεύματα)
ἐρήμωσις (desolation)	21.20	(17.16, ηρημωμένην)
πατουμένη (trample, tread)	21.24	11.2; 14.20; 19.15
νεφέλη (cloud) [singular], in connection with the Son of Man)	21.27	14.14, 15, 16

Note 1. Both Luke (21.11) and Revelation (6.8) refer to pestilence as among the eschatological plagues.
Note 2. Both Luke (23.30) and Revelation (6.16) quote Hos. 10.8, in connection with God's Wrath.
Note 3. Lk. 21.25-26 and Rev. 6.12-13 are quite close, but could be conflating Joel and Isaiah in a similar way.
Note 4. The reference to Jerusalem being trampled by Gentiles at Lk. 21.24, Rev. 11.2 could be a shared allusion to Zech. 12.3.

In broad terms, in his rewriting of Mk 13/Mt. 24, Luke tones down the eschatological details; indeed, he splits them, putting some of the unquestionably eschatological ones in 17.22-37. Details apparently relating to the forthcoming destruction of Jerusalem, which Mark may have assumed would herald the Eschaton, are historicized; cf. Mk 13.14 and Lk. 21.20, where the 'abomination of desolation'[36] is replaced by the fall of Jerusalem. Luke also omits Mark's reference to 'false Christs' at Mk

---

35. J. Ashton, *Understanding*, p. 216, differentiates between the meaning of 'eternal life' found throughout the Johannine tradition and that occurring in texts like the *Psalms of Solomon*, where the stress is a temporal one; to John, the emphasis is on the different quality of the new life. This is also the implication of the Lukan σωτήριον.
36. Cf., too, Mt. 24.15 and Rev. 17.4, 5.

13.22.[37] This may well be, as Maddox[38] and Walaskay[39] conjecture, because he wished to cool apocalyptic fervour and perhaps a concomitant desire for martyrdom. Certainly there is little evidence in Luke–Acts of what seems in Revelation or Ignatius's *Epistle to the Romans* an encouragement to be martyred, although the account of Jesus' death shows how a Christian should behave under such circumstances. On the other hand, as Esler[40] points out, we do not have any direct evidence that such attitudes were a problem in Luke's community;[41] the omission could simply be because Luke's audience would not have understood the reference, which had in any case lost much of its impact after the destruction of the Temple.

It is evident that there were many ideas current concerning the 'Last Things', and contradictions abound, even within texts, as is particularly evident in the Gospels of John and Luke. Conzelmann[42] suggests that Luke's response to the 'delay' of the Parousia, and to the failure of the End to materialize after the catastrophe of the fall of Jerusalem, which was perhaps expected by Mark, was to show the Kingdom as already inbreaking in Jesus—the same point that is made in John by the 'signs' Jesus performs, which point to his significance as 'the Christ, the Son of God' (Jn 20.31). Nevertheless, Conzelmann[43] maintains that Luke did expect a climax and judgment, which was still inevitable, even if it was not necessarily imminent. The last Act had begun in Jesus' ministry, but it was not yet the last Scene, and therefore the distinction between history and eschatology is much more blurred in his Gospel than it is in Mark's. Hence, he removed from an eschatological context the obviously historical references to the events of the Romano-Jewish war which he found in Mark 13, since they had not presaged the End.

Luke was anxious to avoid any precise attempts to calculate the imminence of the Eschaton, as is evident from Lk. 19.11 and Acts 1.7. C.H. Talbert[44] argues convincingly that Lk. 17.20-36 is to be interpreted as implying that some were claiming that the eschatological Kingdom was

37. Cf. also Mt. 24.24; 1 Jn 2.18, 22; 4.3; 2 Jn 7.
38. Maddox, *Purpose*, pp. 96-96.
39. Walaskay, *Rome*, p. 67.
40. Esler, *Community and Gospel*, p. 209.
41. If there *is* a specifically Lukan community addressed by the work, which many critics doubt.
42. Conzelmann, *Theology, passim*.
43. Conzelmann, *Theology*, pp. 98-135, especially pp. 107, 132ff.
44. Talbert, *Reading Luke*, pp. 166-69.

already being experienced.[45] Luke stresses that the End will be quite unmistakable (Lk. 17.24, 30), but there are certain stages to be gone through first (Lk. 17.25; 21.24).[46] The implication of much of his Gospel is thus that the Parousia will arrive suddenly and unexpectedly, but it is not necessarily close at hand. This is the message of parables such as the Rich Fool, the Thief and the Householder, and the Ten Pounds (and see especially Lk. 12.40). A major difficulty for this interpretation, however, is Lk. 21.31-32, which seems to reflect an imminent expectation. Moreover, Acts 2.17-21 presents Pentecost as the fulfilment of Joel's prophecy relating to the Last Days.

We may conclude that no simple scheme can fully resolve all the inconsistencies in Luke's treatment of this particular theme.[47] Franklin argues that the Parousia in itself is not as significant or necessary to Luke as it was to Mark, since the Ascension, which was so important that he narrated it twice (at Lk. 24.50-51 and Acts 1.6-11) had already demonstrated the glorification of Christ.[48] But although it is true that Luke consistently excises references to the Parousia,[49] and modifies Mk 14.62 at Lk. 22.69 by the significant addition of $\dot{\alpha}\pi\grave{o}$ $\tauο\hat{υ}$ $ν\hat{υ}ν$, it would be equally possible to see these as attempts to cool an eschatological fervour which might have dangerous political implications.

Luke's real concern is less the timing of the Parousia than the question of who will enter the Kingdom.[50] Maddox argues that what we see in Luke 21 is less to be construed as a delayed Parousia than as evidence of a fundamental tension between statements that, though futurist, imply an

---

45. Cf. 1 Cor. 4.8 and 2 Tim. 2.18. Realized eschatology was characteristic of Gnosticism; see Irenaeus, *Against Heresies* 1.23.5 (and elsewhere).

46. Lk. 17.25, and the reference in 21.24 to the need to wait 'until the times of the Gentiles are fulfilled' are unparalleled in Matthew and Mark. Cf., however, Rev. 20–21 and *2 Baruch* 24–28.

47. Similarly Evans, *Luke*, p. 64.

48. E. Franklin, *Christ the Lord* (London: SPCK; Philadelphia: Westminster Press, 1975), pp. 28ff., 40-41. Franklin suggests that the Resurrection appearances in Luke are transitional; it is not until Jesus is taken to Heaven that he is glorified, as is demonstrated by Stephen's vision in Acts. But the implication of Peter's speech at Acts 2.33 is that it is the Resurrection that is significant; and in any case, Jesus is called $\acute{o}$ $κ\acute{υ}ριος$ by the disciples at Lk. 24.34. This confirms that it is the Resurrection which has transformed their respectful $κ\acute{υ}ριε$ to the absolute form of later Christian worship.

49. Cf. Mt. 24.27/Lk. 17.24; Mt. 24.37/Lk. 17.26; Mt. 24.39/Lk. 17.30.

50. Maddox, *Purpose*, pp. 49-50.

imminent End,[51] and those that imply already fulfilled expectations.[52] The lynchpin is the person of Jesus, who 'holds the present and the future aspects of eschatology together'.[53]

Since Jesus' followers receive the Spirit at Pentecost, they are participants in the Kingdom, the 'today' of salvation, which is inaugurated in Jesus' ministry[54] and is a present reality for believers (see Lk. 10.11; 19.9), even if the final consummation is 'not yet'. And the mission of the Church, which is directed by the Spirit, shows that this interim is to be creatively used 'until the times of the Gentiles are fulfilled' (Lk. 21.24). To talk of a 'delayed Parousia' is thus not only to oversimplify: it is to treat in negative terms something that Luke views very positively.

The inauguration of the Kingdom means, in the words of the Isaianic prophecy (Isa. 61.2) cited by Jesus at Lk. 4.18, 'good news to the poor …release to the captive…recovery of sight to the blind…liberty to those who are oppressed'.[55]

Christ's healings, and those performed by his emissaries, are hence seen as liberating those bound by Satan; this is obviously the case with exorcisms, which are important to Luke, but it is also explicitly stated with reference to the crippled woman. The Lukan stress on forgiveness, a recurrent theme which is expressed powerfully in the three parables of ch. 15, is relevant here since sin as well as disease oppresses humanity. Thus, the verb ἀφίημι, meaning 'forgive' as well as 'release, allow, leave', is consciously ambivalent, as is σώζω, meaning 'save' in an eschatological sense and also 'heal', and both are reiterated throughout Luke–Acts. Conzelmann[56] notes that Luke drops Mk 9.47 (and cf. also the omission of Mk 9.43, 45); to Luke, the Kingdom means healing and wholeness, so one cannot enter it 'maimed'. The evangelist associates the Kingdom with healing and behaviour, as is evident in Lk. 9.23-27, where only he adds

51. It is not quite accurate to say, as does S.G. Wilson, 'Lukan Eschatology', *NTS* 16 (1969), pp. 330-47 (343), that there are *no* examples of imminent expectation in Acts, but this aspect is only barely perceptible (see, e.g., Acts 13.41; 17.30-31) in Luke's second volume.

52. This is Maddox's interpretation of Lk. 21.19; Acts 11.14; 14.22 (*Purpose*, pp. 116-17, 136ff.).

53. Maddox, *Purpose*, p. 145.

54. σήμερον; see Lk. 4.21 ('Now is the acceptable year of the Lord'); Lk. 19.9; 23.43. Cf. the similar emphasis in John's use of νῦν Jn 4.23; 5.25; 12.31.

55. The verb εὐαγγελίζομαι includes them all. Acts 10.38 identifies the perpetrator of the oppression—the Devil.

56. Conzelmann, *Theology*, p. 116.

καθ᾽ ἡμέραν; at 12.32, too, he uses the Kingdom as an exhortation to right conduct. The effect of this is to ethicize and demythologize it; to Luke, it is not to be linked with the Passion/Resurrection or the Parousia.

The proper reaction to this message is 'repentance' and also 'joy'; both are key words in Luke's Gospel and both involve response. (Interestingly, the joy extends to heaven, too—see Lk. 15.7, 10; this is another example of the way Luke, like John, presents things on two levels at once.) And even though the full realization of the Kingdom remains in the future,[57] both responses are evidence that, in fulfilment of the prophecies, it is present proleptically in Jesus, with whom it is very closely identified. Those who have seen Jesus and responded to his message have indeed seen the Kingdom (Lk. 9.27); it is 'within [their] grasp' (Lk. 17.21). Thus at 21.31 Luke replaces Matthew/Mark's 'he' (i.e. the Son of Man) with 'the Kingdom'; similarly, at Acts 28.31, proclaiming the Kingdom is the same as teaching about Jesus. The unparalleled Lukan passage at 10.8-11 is especially interesting because it not only asserts the nearness of the Kingdom, but seems also to imply that to some extent it can be brought close by the disciples, too, presumably by their proclamation of Jesus.[58]

Luke's eschatological material thus shows evidence of differing traditions and expectations which he does not always succeed in reconciling, although in broad terms (and not just with relation to Luke 21, as Maddox suggests) it would be true to say that his presentation exhibits an attempt to hold together a predominantly future expectation such as that found in Mark and Matthew with one already realized, as is usually the case in John. It would be to oversimplifiy, however, not to recognize that there are also tensions within the Johannine literature on this topic. For example, nowhere in John's Gospel or the Johannine Epistles do we find any idea of renewed life at the Eschaton on a transformed earth in the messianic Kingdom that is inaugurated by the defeat of anti-Christ, as is the case in Revelation; to the evangelist at Jn 14.2-3 (although many would argue that this is uncharacteristic of John's usual interpretation elsewhere, which is that it is available for Christians here and now through belief in Jesus), eternal life is in Heaven, whither Jesus has gone to prepare abodes for believers. The same tension is evident if we compare 1 John and John's Gospel. Indeed, it is the case within the individual texts themselves, as we

57. The promises of Lk. 12.32 and Acts 14.22 clearly have a future reference.
58. Merk, 'Das Reich Gottes', p. 202, notes that preaching the Kingdom is a very important theme, which represents a Lukan addition at Lk. 4.43; 8.1; 9.2, 11 (see also Acts 1.3; 8.12; 19.8; 20.25; 28.23, 31).

have seen with regard to John's Gospel; even in Revelation there is tension between the emphatically future messianic Kingdom of the Millennium, and the implication of Rev. 1.9 or 2.11, where it seems to be in some senses realized in the seer's community, and linked to its suffering.

Unlike the Synoptic Gospels, where it is the main focus of Jesus' preaching, 'the Kingdom' is not a major Johannine theme, occurring explicitly only at Jn 3.3 and 3.5 in the dialogue with Nicodemus, although the kingship of Christ is another matter entirely. Like almost everything else in John's Gospel, the Kingdom is linked very closely with the person of Jesus (although the same is true in Luke, albeit in a different way, as was shown above). To enter the Kingdom is to have eternal life here and now in Christ; and it is characteristic of John's mode of presentation that Nicodemus fails completely to understand what Jesus means, just as later Pilate cannot understand in what sense he is a king. Like Luke, then, John also demythologizes the Kingdom, but by making it accessible in this world consequent only upon one's response to Jesus. Conduct is irrelevant.

Broadly speaking, there is in the Johannine Epistles more stress on future eschatology[59] than on one already realized,[60] whereas in the Gospel there are numerous indications that the new life is already here and that believers have been favourably judged (see, e.g., Jn 3.18; 5.24) and have eternal life in the present. The concept of judgment, like that of the Kingdom to which it is closely linked, is therefore usually removed from that of the End, so that although there are references to 'the last day'[61] and also to 'the hour',[62] which explicitly extend judgment to the already dead on the basis of whether they have done good or evil, John's thought centres more on the consequences of a response here and now to Christ and his message (see Jn 5.21, 24). The occasional reference to the prospect of inevitable future judgment (see Jn 5.25-29) perhaps represents a more 'orthodox' view, which John failed to integrate satisfactorily with his own.[63]

59. See, e.g., 1 Jn 2.28; 3.2, 3, and also 4.17.

60. It is thus possible that 1 John was written to reclaim John's Gospel for orthodoxy against heretical misappropriation, rather as it is suggested that the Pastoral Epistles attempt for Paul: cf. J.L. Houlden, *The Johannine Epistles* (HNTC; New York: Harper & Row, 1973), pp. 10ff.

61. See Jn 6.39, 40, 44, 54; 11.24; 12.48.

62. At Jn 5.28-29; 'life' and 'judgment' are used as antithetical terms here.

63. It is also possible that the inconsistencies are the result of differing interpretations in the source material and differing layers of redaction; both R.E. Brown, *Beloved Disciple*, and Martyn, *History and Theology*, regard traditional future eschato-

The concept of election, which is fundamental to Judaism, and which necessarily involves predestination, is closely related to this theme of judgment and is apparent throughout the New Testament, being drawn on by both Paul and all four evangelists to account for Jewish unbelief. The grim prophecy of Isa. 6.9-10 is used by all the Gospels in this connection: Luke uses it twice to emphasize its importance, once at Lk. 8.10 and again in a much fuller form in the climactic speech by Paul to the Jews in Rome at Acts 28.26-27. But although Jesus is ὁ ἐκλελεγμενος at Lk. 9.35 and ὁ ἐκλεκτός at Lk. 23.35 (cf. Jn 1.34: this title is not found in the other Gospels), the word ἐκλέγομαι itself is nevertheless rare in Luke, even though he repeatedly stresses the 'plan' (that is, predetermined purpose) of God, as we saw: there is little indication of the idea that we find especially in Revelation of a fixed number of the elect.[64] John, on the other hand, draws a clear distinction between those who are 'children of God' and the rest,[65] and it seems that no amount of effort can transfer a person from one category to another, as is strikingly demonstrated by Nicodemus.

In connection with the theme of judgment, we may note that there were many differing ideas in both the Jewish and the Gentile worlds concerning what happened after death, and naturally enough, tensions are evident in many texts. A common expectation (see, for example, *1 En.* 102.4–104.8; or *Jub.* 5.10-12), which may be related to Jewish reflections on texts like Isa. 53.; Dan. 7.14-18; 12.2-3, included a belief in a survival of some kind beyond death and a final judgment at the Eschaton. This was interpreted by many to imply the resurrection of the dead, as in Isa. 26.19.[66] Although a general resurrection of the dead and judgment at the Eschaton is not

logical ideas as a characteristic of the early period of the Johannine community, when links with Judaism were strong.

64. Acts 13.48 perhaps carries this implication, however, and the 'names written in Heaven' of Lk. 10.20 may be compared to the 'book of life' of Rev. 3.5. (Similar ideas occur in *1 En.* 103.1-3; 104.1, 7 and elsewhere.)

65. Cf. Rev. 11.17-18, or Rev. 22.11.

66. See, e.g., 2 Macc. 7.9, 23; 24.46. The resurrection of the dead was a belief shared by the Pharisees; see Acts 23.7-8, and cf. also Josephus, *War*, 2.162-63, although Josephus translates this belief into terms a Roman audience could relate to by referring to the 'immortality of the soul'. In other texts, too, such as *4 Maccabees* and *Jubilees*, although there is a survival of the spirit, there is not explicitly a resurrection of the dead. C. Rowland, *Christian Origins* (London: SPCK, 1985), p. 92, concludes that it is very difficult to draw a distinction between Palestinian texts uninfluenced by the Hellenistic belief in the immortality of the soul and Hellenistic Jewish texts which reflect it.

stressed by Luke, this idea is certainly to be detected on some occasions;[67] but there are also instances when judgment seems to take place at the moment of death. The most obvious examples are parables such as the Rich Man and Lazarus and the Rich Fool, but it may also be the implication of Stephen's vision in Acts, and likewise the words to the thief on the cross.[68]

Inextricably connected with the whole idea of judgment in the New Testament is that of Christ the judge, frequently as eschatological Son of Man;[69] a concept which seems to have been derived from Jewish apocalyptic, namely Dan. 7.9, 13-14.[70] John, like Mark, relates other christological titles to this one; but it is the exalted Son of Man,[71] the eschatological judge,[72] to whom 12 of the 13 references are made in John, and the 'suffering Son of Man' of the Synoptists finds little place. The Son of Man provides the only means of access to God: hence, perhaps, the 'ladder' symbolism of Jn 1.51.[73] In Revelation, the matter is rather more equivocal —it is not always possible to tell which prophecies relate to the Son and which to the Father, to whom the Son is subordinated at Rev. 2.27 and perhaps 3.14.[74] Nevertheless, the implication of Rev. 1.18 may be compared with *1 En.* 61.8-13; 69.29 where, as Rowland[75] points out, God's function of judgment is delegated to the Elect One/Son of Man. The

67. See, e.g., Lk. 14.14; 20.35; Acts 24.15.

68. Cf. *4 Macc.* 13.17; 15.3; 17.5, 18; 18.23, which present a life of eternal blessedness in Heaven, occurring immediately upon physical death for the virtuous.

69. See, e.g., Mt. 25.31-33; Acts 10.42; 17.31; Jn 5.30; 8.16, 26; 2 Tim. 4.1; Rev. 19.11.

70. *1 Enoch*, too, may perhaps have had some influence. The Son of Man in *1 En.* 37-71, as the Chosen One, is distinct from and above the archangels (40.5), and sits on the throne of glory (45.3); he judges (49.4), and is identified with the Messiah at 48.10. The difficulty here is that the dating of this section, which is not attested in the Qumran, is uncertain, and it may possibly reflect Christian influence, although many scholars disagree.

71. Jn 1.51; 3.13, 14; 5.27; 6.27, 53, 62; 8.28; 9.35; 12.23, 34 (twice); 13.31. We note, however, the profound Johannine irony of the reference in 3.14; 8.28; 12.23, 34; 13.31, where it is the crucifixion which exalts him.

72. See Jn 5.27 and compare, e.g., 5.22, 30; 8.16; 9.39.

73. Cf. Ashton, *Understanding*, pp. 345ff.

74. It is possible, however, that 'the beginning of God's creation' may mean that Jesus, as the Word, is seen as the originator of God's creative activity. This is argued by Bauckham, *Revelation*, pp. 55ff. Like God, Jesus is 'beginning and end', 'alpha and omega' (cf. Rev. 1.8; 21.6 and 22.13).

75. Rowland, *Open Heaven*, p. 106.

difference here is that in *1 Enoch*, this is Enoch; in Revelation, it is Christ (cf. Acts 17.31).[76]

The 'eschatological' Son of Man is found in all the Gospels, of course; and although there are five references in Luke's Gospel to the 'suffering Son of Man',[77] in general we may say that in his 25 references to the Son of Man (24 in his Gospel and one in Acts, ten of which are unparalleled in the other Gospels) the 'eschatological Son of Man' seems more important to Luke,[78] too, although he usually reserves the presentation of Jesus as judge for Acts (see Acts 10.42 and also Acts 17.31, where Jesus is the agent by whom God judges the world); this is a good example of the way he structures his narrative so as to keep for his second volume themes consistent with the post-Resurrection Lord.[79]

The 'Son of Man' reference at Lk. 21.27 is particularly interesting because it does not contain the usual idea of the Son of Man coming 'in clouds' and taking his people to Heaven. Luke here changes the plural ἐν νεφέλαις of Mk 13.26 (cf. 14.62 and also 1 Thess. 4.17), which is derived from Dan. 7.13, to a singular ἐν νεφέλη The reference is thus no longer a direct citation of Daniel; it reinterprets this verse in terms which link it both to the cloud of divine glory at the Transfiguration (see Lk. 9.34) and to that which receives Christ at the Ascension and will accompany him on his return (Acts 1.9-11);[80] similarly, it is *a* single cloud which receives the two witnesses into Heaven in Revelation 11. The only other reference in

76. There may be some typical Johannine anti-Peter polemic in Revelation here, since it is possible to read this verse as a refutation of Mt. 16.19: but this depends on the date we assign to the Apocalypse. An alternative explanation is that of D.E. Aune, 'The Apocalypse of John and Graeco-Roman Revelatory Magic', *NTS* 33 (1987), pp. 481-501. Aune sees John's target as Hecate, who was 'the primary mythological figure associated with the possession of the keys to the gates of Hades...the patron goddess of magic and sorcery' (p. 485).

77. At Lk. 9.22, 44 (cf. also 9.58); 18.31; and 22.22. All but the last can be paralleled in Matthew or Mark or both.

78. See Lk. 6.22; 9.26; 12.8, 10, 40; 17.22, 24, 26, 30; 18.8; 21.27, 36; Acts 7.56. At Lk. 5.24 and 6.5, too, Jesus has divine authority.

79. The only exception is in Luke's eschatological discourse at 21.36, where the reference is clearly to the future and Jesus' authoritative position then is presupposed.

80. F.L. Cribbs, 'The Agreements that Exist between John and Acts', in C.H. Talbert (ed.), *Perspectives on Luke–Acts* (Danville, VA: Association of Baptist Professors of Religion, 1978), pp. 40-61, notes that John at Jn 14.3 and 21.22-23 stresses that it is Jesus, not the Son of Man, who returns for believers, and the same is true of Luke at Acts 1.11; 3.20.

the New Testament to a cloud (singular) rather than clouds (plural) in connection with the Son of Man is at Rev. 14.14, 16, though it is also found in the *Apocalypse of Peter*, ch. 6.

6.2.5. *The Spirit*

As has often been pointed out, Luke and John place a much greater emphasis on the Holy Spirit than the other evangelists. In the gift of the Spirit, which both see in Septuagintal terms as bringing the consolation[81] to be expected in the messianic age, one aspect of the End-time has already been realized in the present. Thus, we notice that the Kingdom and the Spirit are very closely associated by Luke. At Lk. 11.13 the Father gives the Holy Spirit to those who ask, and in 12.32 he gives the disciples the Kingdom; similarly in Acts 1.6, when the apostles ask about the Kingdom, Jesus replies in vv. 7-8 in terms of the Spirit.[82] But the coming of the Spirit is nevertheless not to be equated with the Eschaton, even though its coming at Pentecost is unquestionably eschatological, as the Joel prophecy makes clear; it is, rather, the beginning of the End, which gives a proleptic assurance to believers.[83]

Luke conceives of the Spirit as anointing Jesus for ministry at the baptism, and until after the Ascension the two are very closely identified, so that to Luke, Jesus is not driven by the Spirit into the wilderness for the temptation, as in Mark and Matthew; he acts *in*[84] the Spirit, who is later seen at Acts 16.6-7 to mediate Christ's presence to Christians when he is in Heaven. The Spirit impels the Gentile mission, and directs the actions of Christians, confirming every stage in the spread of the Church—a leading concern of Acts; and by placing the motif of the Ascension at the beginning of Acts as well as the end of his Gospel, Luke firmly links the present of the Church to its founder, although in Acts the connection

---

81. John explicitly calls the Spirit ὁ παράκλητος in chs. 14–16: at Lk. 2.25 Simeon, with the Holy Spirit upon him, is waiting for the παράκλησις of Israel (and cf. also Acts 9.31, where we are told that the Church as it grows and thrives in Samaria is filled with the παρακλήσει of the Holy Spirit). This is a usage of παρακαλέω which seems to be restricted to Jewish Greek.

82. See Talbert, *Reading Luke*, p. 131.

83. The reception of the Spirit is not necessarily a concomitant of baptism, as Acts 8.15-16 and 19.2-6 make clear. It is possible that such incidents were narrated to reassure Christians in post-apostolic days, when charismatic phenomena were not in evidence. They were perhaps only to be expected at the beginning, being linked to the apostles.

84. Or perhaps 'by'; the Greek ἐν is frequently ambiguous.

between Jesus and the Spirit is usually assumed rather than stated. The two are not, however, indistinguishable, since Jesus, as Risen Lord, at Lk. 24.49 promises to send the Spirit.

Since he is responsible for the conception of Jesus, however, the Spirit is nevertheless also—as in the Old Testament—necessarily linked very directly to God. (Indeed, there is an interesting variation between the text of Acts [Acts 1.8], where the passive verb indicates that the Spirit is conferred by God and Lk. 24.49, where the giver is Jesus; this seemingly deliberate ambiguity about the precise identity of the donor suggests that it may be a serious mistake to view Luke's Christology as 'low'.) Luke therefore separates the activity of the Spirit who inspires prophets in the Old Testament (and characters like Anna, Elizabeth, Zechariah, Simeon, and John the Baptist are in a sense Old Testament-type figures) and the later 'age of the Spirit' in the Church after Pentecost: in the interim, only Jesus is identified with the Spirit, and it is Jesus, not the Spirit, who empowers the disciples at Lk. 9.1-6 and 10.1-12, 19. The connection which has been established in Luke between the Spirit and prophecy (see, for example, at Lk. 4.21) forms an important conceptual link with Revelation, where the author in the Spirit (Rev. 1.10) and, like Jesus in Luke, uttering the words of the Spirit (Rev. 3.22) is commanded to prophesy, referring to his work in these terms (Rev. 1.3; 10.11, and so on).

John also leaves it open whether the Spirit is primarily to be linked with—and sent by—God, as at Jn 14.16, 26, or with Jesus, as at Jn 16.7 and 20.22, where he is breathed (and the wordplay is clearly deliberate) into the disciples by the Lord, thus recalling and reinforcing the significant statement at 19.30 that at the moment of death Jesus παρέδωκεν τὸ πνεῦμα: for John, Passion and the coming of the Spirit at Pentecost are seemingly so tightly linked as almost to be fused. From their respective presentations, it would seem that both evangelists intended the distinction between God and Jesus to be somewhat blurred: and just as Jesus is sent by God and is his agent, so Jesus sends the Spirit to continue his work.[85]

There are nevertheless inconsistencies in John's attempt to define the nature of the relationship between believers, Jesus, and the Spirit, which are far more evident than those in Luke–Acts. Thus John sometimes sees Jesus' presence with Christians continuing after the Ascension via the indwelling Spirit[86] (see, for example, Jn 14.23). At Jn 14.16, 26, however,

---

85. Similarly Ashton, *Understanding*, p. 423.

86. This characteristic and distinctively Johannine conception is expressed in the repeated verb μένω.

the Father, at Jesus' request, is to give to the disciples another παράκ-λητος, the original one presumably being Jesus; at 16.7, too, the two (though akin) are distinguished, since it is Jesus who sends the Paraclete.[87] Although the Paraclete appears at these points in all respects to be an *alter ego* of Jesus, one with him in will and function, it seems that it is this other Paraclete who remains in the disciples mediating Jesus' presence at Jn 14.18-19, and continues his work of revelation and exposition, clarifying what is obscure (see Jn 16.13-14:[88] in this connection, we have already seen that in both John and Luke the Spirit teaches Christians what to say when they are put to the test).

These tensions are not necessarily to be seen as evidencing textual dislocations or a multiplicity of sources; the farewell discourse has patently undergone later revision. As suggested above, it is possible[89] that some statements primarily in the Johannine Epistles may be an attempt to pull the Johannine tradition back into line with a more orthodox main-stream Christianity, being a 'rearguard action' which was perhaps necessi-tated by the appropriation of the earlier Johannine material by heretics. Thus there is the statement in 2 Jn 9 about 'going beyond the teaching of Christ'; Diotrephes and the opposition party in 3 John may have wished to push the Johannine community further along a path leading directly to heresy,[90] since it was possible, using John's Gospel with only a few alterations and omissions, to present Jesus as a spiritual messenger from Heaven to a hopelessly and irremediably sinful world, which is an impres-sion that could very easily be drawn from Jn 5.37-47. 1 John staunchly

87. At 1 Jn 2.1-2 it is explicitly stated that ὁ παράκλητος, who intercedes in Heaven for Christians, is Jesus. D.L. Bock, *Proclamation from Prophecy and Pattern* (JSNTSup, 12; Sheffield: Sheffield Academic Press, 1987), pp. 224-25, argues that this is also the implication of Stephen's vision of Jesus as Son of Man standing in Heaven at Acts 7.55; cf. the role of the Son of Man in Lk. 12.8-12.

88. See Ashton, *Understanding*, p. 423. Ashton compares the function of angelic guides in apocalyptic literature.

89. See Houlden, *Johannine Epistles*, pp. 10ff., contra the very different interpreta-tion of J.M. Lieu, *The Second and Third Epistles of John: History and Background* (Edinburgh: T. & T. Clark, 1986).

90. Cf. Acts 20.29-31. It is possible that Luke may have encountered some tradition of problems concerning heresy—one that was becoming acute at the end of the first century, as we know from the Pastoral Epistles—at Ephesus, a city which Irenaeus later linked to the Johannine tradition. We note that Acts 20.29-30 reads like an *ex eventu* prophecy, and it clearly reflects a situation very similar to that recorded in the Johannine Epistles.

resists such a misinterpretation; and it is interesting to notice that Luke's conception of the Spirit remaining behind with the disciples as a substitute since Christ is now in Heaven (see Acts 7.55-56) is quite close to that of 1 John (see, e.g., 1 Jn 2.1-2, 28; 3.24; 4.13) and also to Jn 14.15-19, 26; 16.7, 16.13-14. Luke nevertheless plays down the near-mystical indwelling found in both John's Gospel (see especially Jn 14.16-17) and 1 John, which could perhaps have dangerous connections with the experiences of some 'fringe' groups; thus, in Acts, the Spirit is instead pictured in prophetic terms as 'coming upon' Christians at Pentecost. Despite the recognized charismatic phenomena that are generated, this is to be related far more directly to the wider mission of the Church and is ecclesiological rather than individual (although it is arguable that the giving of the Spirit at Jn 19.30 and 20.22 is to be interpreted in a similar way, and certainly Jn 17.18 refers explicitly to mission).

To sum up, in both the Johannine literature and Luke the Spirit imparts knowledge by revelation (Lk. 10.21; Jn 16.13-15) and prophecy (Lk. 4.21; Rev. 1.3, 10 for instance), instructs (Lk. 12.12; Acts 4, 6.10; Jn 14.25), witnesses (Acts 5.32; Jn 15.26) and enables Christians to bear witness (Acts 1.8; Jn 15.27) and to perceive the truth (Jn 14.17-26: Luke present this dramatically, *vide* Simeon, Stephen, Paul), empowers Christians (Acts 1.8; 8.14-20; Jn 16.13-14) and judges (Jn 16.8-11: once again, Luke presents this dramatically—lying to the Holy Spirit brings about Ananias' and Sapphira's deaths in Acts). It is a strikingly similar presentation.

In terms of purpose there are similarities, too. The need to reassure and encourage contemporary Christians seems to have been a major factor influencing the way both evangelists depict the activity of the Spirit; it is another example of 'double context'. Related to this paraenetic aspect— and there are often significant links between paraenetic literature and apocalyptic[91]—is the theme of endurance. Since Satan's time is short, and deliverance certain, either in this world or in the next, the message is 'Remain faithful; do not apostasize!' even in the face of the apocalyptic πειρασμός. Accordingly, Luke wishes to underline the need for patience, fortitude, perseverance in faith;[92] thus at Lk. 8.15 the words ἐν ὑπομονῇ (word and concept both being important in Revelation, too) are added to the Markan and Matthaean parallels. We may compare Jn 20.31, which states that his Gospel is intended to evoke faith, although we cannot be

---

91. The obvious example is a paraenetic epistle like 1 Thessalonians, where Paul uses apocalyptic to reinforce both its message and his authority.

92. On this theme, see especially S. Brown, *Apology.*

sure if the verb here, πιστεύω, was originally an aorist subjunctive, πιστεύσητε, in which case the object is to an extent missionary, 'so that they might come to belief', or a present, πιστεύητε, in which case the implication is that, like the Epistles, it was intended for insiders and was intended to help them continue in their faith. In any case, having and continuing in faith are what leads to eternal life in John.

6.2.6. *Messianic Expectations*
Another feature relating to eschatological hopes which links some Jewish apocalyptic texts with the New Testament is the belief in a Messiah who would be commissioned by God to effect the deliverance of his people. Expectations were by no means standardized or clear-cut, however; thus, the 'argument from testimony' of the early Christians, provided by combing the Old Testament for 'proof texts' which Christ could be seen to have fulfilled, failed to convince most Jews because many of the texts he did fulfil (such as the 'suffering servant' prophecies of Deutero-Isaiah) were not regarded as of messianic significance anyway. Broadly speaking, nevertheless, we can say that expectations clustered around three main figures of Israel's past: the hope of a new, victorious Davidic figure;[93] of a 'prophet like Moses', as promised in Deuteronomy 18.15; and of a 'second Elijah', 'Elijah *redivivus*'.[94] There are many connections between the presentations of Luke and John here, as will appear from the analysis below.

6.2.6.1. *Messiah*. First, there is the title 'Messiah' itself. At the beginning of his Gospel John emphasizes this title, which he gives in both Aramaic and Greek, and he ponders its significance and implications.[95] The same is true at the beginning of Luke's Gospel, as is most evident in the Canticles at Lk. 1.68-75, 77-79; 2.10-11; 2.30-32, 34-35, though Luke only explicitly calls Jesus Χριστός at 2.11. However, even though the kingship of Jesus is an important Johannine theme,[96] John also wishes to stress that his

---

93. Cf. Rev. 5.5.

94. Martyn, *History and Theology*, p. 11 observes that *Elijah redivivus* is actually a misnomer, since Elijah did not die, according to 2 Kgs 2.11; he was translated to Heaven in a whirlwind.

95. The 'unknown messiah' attested in Justin Martyr's *Dialogue with Trypho* (e.g. *Dial.* 8), is perhaps reflected in the narrative in John the Baptist's speech at Jn 1.31. It may also underlie the debate about Jesus' origins in Jn 7.27.

96. There are sixteen references to Jesus as king in John, as compared with five in Luke.

kingdom 'is not of this world'; it is not to be construed as an earthly one, as is made clear in Jn 18.36. (We may contrast the many images of kingship in Revelation, which clearly could have dangerous political implications; the evangelist wishes to correct expectations concerning a Davidic warrior Messiah, and this may be why he omits any reference to the Bethlehem birth, even though, as Jn 7.42 implies, this seems to be a tradition known to him.) Luke, like Matthew, shows Jesus' Davidic descent in his genealogy;[97] and he likewise places the birth in the city of David. On the other hand, he, too, does not wish to present Jesus in terms that might imply he is a threat to Rome, so he tends to play down this motif in comparison with Matthew.[98] Indeed, it is only the malice of the Jews in Luke which leads to the crucifixion, as it is to lead to Stephen's death in Acts, and to the repeated attacks on Paul.

In this context we may note that while all four Gospels lay the blame for the crucifixion squarely on the Jews, the references of Luke and John to οἱ Ἰουδαῖοι frequently seem particularly vitriolic. Thus, although both emphasize that 'salvation is from the Jews',[99] both also show that the Jews throughout their history have always rejected God's salvific plans—and murdered their prophets, adds Luke,[100] just as they are to reject and murder Jesus. Both, too, are fiercely hostile to those who allow niceties of Torah-observance to override love for others[101] (this was clearly a central plank of early Christian polemic); and by implication both are critical even of the Cult itself. Thus John consistently shows Judaism, represented by Jewish festivals, as being transcended by Jesus, who as the Paschal Lamb is the supreme and all-atoning Yom Kippur sacrifice taking away the sins of the world; Luke, via Stephen in Acts, effectively condemns the Temple

97. Since Joseph is not really his father, there is an anomaly here, as Luke himself acknowledges at 3.23.

98. Thus there are five occasions when Jesus is called 'Son of David' in Matthew by those who seek his help or greet him as Messiah (Mt. 9.27; 12.23; 15.22; 20.30, 31; 21.9, 15): Luke has only one (Lk. 18.38, 39).

99. This is only said explicitly at Jn 4.22, but it is one of the points made by the prophecy/fulfilment motif which shapes Luke–Acts and is especially evident in the birth narrative.

100. It is possible that there may be some connection between Rev. 16.6 and Lk. 11.50, although this could result from an independent allusion to Ps. 79.3 or 1 Kgs 19.10 (cf., too, Rom. 11.3).

101. See especially Jn 5; Jn 9; Lk. 7.36-50; Lk. 13.10-17; Lk. 14.1-6; the numerous occasions in Luke when Jesus dines with sinners; and the Parable of the Good Samaritan.

as idolatrous (the usual connotation of the term χειροποίητος when it is used in the Septuagint). Hence, when both stress the relative innocence of Rome in Jesus' death, evident in Pilate's three attempts to release him, this is probably more more to increase the guilt of the Jews than to offer an *apologia pro imperio*.

6.2.6.2. *The New Elijah*. There was also the expectation of the second, eschatological Elijah. The title 'Elijah' is the only one which is not specifically applied to Jesus in ch. 1 of John's Gospel, but Martyn argues[102] that v. 43 was originally on the same lines as vv. 41 and 45. He suggests that John's source presented Jesus in this way, too, but John did not wish to present Jesus as in any way secondary to anyone, and so he excised it. Another possibility is that he rejected it because Elijah in Jewish thought was translated into Heaven, and John wishes to stress that no one but Jesus has ascended; the two explanations are not mutually exclusive and both could be true. The usual practice in early Christianity was to apply this title to the Baptist, via Mal. 4.5-6, but we notice that neither John nor Luke presents John the Baptist in this role of precursor at the baptism,[103] although this is certainly implied in Luke's birth narrative, and both omit the description which links the Baptist with Elijah. In this context, we note the significant omission by Luke of Mk 9.11-13/Mt. 11.14, 17.9-13.

Martyn[104] suggests that the early Elijah typology in John has been muted by later stages of editing. He proposes that the wine at Cana recalls Elijah's actions to the widow of Zarephath in 1 Kgs 17.8-16, and the raising of the nobleman's son in Jn 4.50b echoes 1 Kgs 17.23. He also finds connections between the healing of the man was was born blind and 2 Kgs 5.10, 14; and between Jn 6.9 and 2 Kgs 4.42. But the resemblances he perceives are very faint, so his proposal must remain in doubt. If he is right, then in both John and Luke these three titles, explicitly denied to the Baptist in John, are embodied in Jesus, since the connections between the Elijah story

---

102. Martyn, *History and Theology*, pp. 33ff.

103. Conzelmann, *Theology*, pp. 22ff., sees John the Baptist in Luke as the last of the prophets: a bridge between the time of the prophets and that of Christ. But this is to oversimplify; it ignores the many occasions when the line between the two is much more blurred. Luke's rearrangement of the Markan material concerning John the Baptist's arrest, too, which Conzelmann regarded as confirming his 'periodization' scheme, could simply represent a deliberate simplification in order to focus more sharply on Jesus.

104. Martyn, *History and Theology*, pp. 33ff.

(1 Kgs 17.17-24) and the Lukan account of the raising of the Widow of Nain's son have often been noted.[105]

6.2.6.3. *The Prophet Like Moses.* Perhaps more widespread was the hope of the 'prophet like Moses':[106] indeed, the Jewish-Christian *Pseudo-Clementines* suggest that the main subject of dispute in the early days between Christians and Jews was whether Jesus fulfilled this criterion. In both John and Luke there are references to 'the Prophet',[107] which perhaps furnished a link with Samaritan theology, too—the Samaritan mission being an interest both share,[108] since the Samaritans may also have expected the Deuteronomic Prophet, if not the Davidic Messiah;[109] in this respect Galilee, which bordered the two, provided the perfect mixing ground for the blending of Jewish and Samaritan hopes.[110] In John's Gospel Jesus is himself active in Samaria, and this may well be implied by

105. Cf. also Lk. 9.51-56 and 2 Kgs 1.9-16, especially Lk. 9.54 and 2 Kgs 1.10; and also Lk. 9.61-62 and 1 Kgs 19.20. It should be observed, however, that in the other Gospels, too, Elijah traditions seem to be applied to Jesus. This is convincingly argued by C. Joynes, *Elijah, John the Baptist and Jesus in the Gospel Tradition* (M.St. dissertation, Oxford University, 1995). She suggests (p. 31) that Luke's Jesus nevertheless goes beyond the Elijah tradition at 9.61-62 (where Elijah allowed Elisha to return and bid farewell to his parents), in the same way that in Mark the Feeding of the Five Thousand surpasses the Elisha story in 2 Kgs 4.42-44. The tradition would thus have been used by all the evangelists to make a christological point.

106. See, e.g., 4QTestim. On the Moses-typology in John's Gospel, see especially W.A. Meeks, *The Prophet King* (NovTSup, 14; Leiden: E.J. Brill, 1967). On Moses and Luke, see D.P. Moessner, *Lord of the Banquet*; *idem*, 'Luke 9:1-50: Luke's Preview of the Journey of the Prophet like Moses of Deuteronomy', *JBL* 102 (1983), pp. 575-605.

107. See, e.g., Jn 6.14; 7.40; 9.17 (although the text is uncertain here); and compare Acts 3.22; 7.37 (and perhaps Lk. 7.16).

108. The Samaritans were descendents of the old Northern Kingdom, and they had their own cultic centre at Gerizim, to which John draws attention at 4.20; but there were centuries of hostility and prejudice between the two groups, which John explicitly remarks at 4.9. Luke comments on this, too, but obliquely, in the Parable of the Good Samaritan. Samaria is clearly regarded as a legitimate missionary outpost by Luke before the mission goes to the Gentiles. It is peripheral Judaism.

109. Unfortunately, the Samaritan sources which identify Moses and the Taheb are all late: few can be dated any earlier than the fourth century. It is therefore impossible to be sure that this was so.

110. Thus, Meeks, *Prophet King*, pp. 256-57.

Luke's account,[111] too, although opinions differ as to the significance of the odd description at Lk. 17.11 of Jesus 'passing along between Samaria and Galilee'.

In John's Gospel Jesus performs some Moses-type signs; for example, the miraculous feeding contains numerous references to manna, and likewise the 'living water' discourse recalls Moses striking the rock in the desert. John's intimation that Jesus surpasses Moses in both cases is entirely typical, since he stresses throughout that Jesus is incomparably greater than any of the figures in the Old Testament. Thus while he seems to accept that Jesus is to be identified in some respects as a prophet,[112] by implication he denies that this has any significance anyway in the dialogues between Jesus and the Jews in chs. 6 and 8. The authority that Jesus has for his teaching is that of God; and just as God gave the manna, so he gives the true 'bread from Heaven', Jesus.

Luke's method is slightly different. To emphasize the link between Moses and Jesus he uses not typology, but allusion.[113] At Lk. 11.20 (and contra Mt. 12.28) he therefore refers to 'the finger of God';[114] likewise, at 9.31, there is a reference to the ἔξοδος which Jesus is to accomplish at Jerusalem. To anyone well-versed in the Old Testament, this word encapsulates not only freedom/deliverance, as does Jesus' ministry in Luke's understanding, but also years of testing/trial in the wilderness. This may well be related to the situation facing the later Church: Jesus will, by implication, protect Christians as Moses protected the Israelites. There may also be some connection with the acceptance/rejection motif which extends throughout Luke–Acts, from the ominous words of Simeon at 2.35 onwards; Stephen's speech in Acts makes the connection between Moses and Jesus in this respect very plain. D.P. Moessner[115] points out that this

111. Although some Samaritans (Lk. 9.52-56) reject Christ, others, like the healed Samaritan leper at Lk. 17.16, accept him. Their divided response parallels that of the Jews.

112. See Jn 4.19.

113. There are allusions in Revelation, too, which compare Moses to Christ, such as Rev. 2.17; cf., too, Rev. 15.5 and Exod. 40.34. (The Plagues are of course meant to recall those of Egypt.) Because allusion is a literary device used by both Luke and Revelation we cannot necessarily infer that Revelation is copying Luke, if we propose that there is a literary connection between them (contra Vanni, 'Apocalypse').

114. Cf. Deut. 9.10; Exod. 8.19.

115. Moessner, *Lord of the Banquet*; see, too, *idem*, 'Jesus and the Wilderness Generation: The Death of the Prophet like Moses', in K.H. Richards (ed.), *SBLSP*, 21 (Chico, CA: Scholars Press, 1982), pp. 319-40.

same motif of the Deuteronomistic 'prophet like Moses', who travels, exhorts his stiff-necked people, is repeatedly rejected by them and suffers because of them—which means that he functions as both the prophet of their punishment by God and the cause of it—is evident in Luke's presentation of Paul, too. In this respect, Paul is following his Lord.

There seems to have been in later Judaism some conception of a suffering prophet, possibly[116] resulting from a conflation of Deuteronomy 9, where Moses interceded for a sinful Israel and suffered on her behalf, with the suffering *'ebed YHWH*, servant of Yahweh, of Deutero-Isaiah.[117] This is evident in *Jub.* 1.18-21 and also *Ass. Mos.* 3.11-14: Philo, too, presents Moses in the light of a redeemer and intercessor,[118] and evidence from the Qumran also suggests that Moses was seen as atoning for the sins of Israel.[119] 'The Messiah must suffer' is a constant theme of the preaching in Acts, and indeed it is only through suffering that he enters his glory, as Lk. 24.26 states;[120] the suffering Messiah seems to be a much more characteristically Lukan understanding than the suffering Son of Man of Mark and Matthew, and by this emphasis Luke removes any political implications from the title χριστός.

6.2.7. *The New Age*
Many New Testament writings see the coming Kingdom of God as heralding a new age; we may compare Jewish texts such as *1 En.* 1–5, which likewise offers a picture of a transformed world. Since the present age is regarded as wicked, there are obvious links with some of the ideas of later Gnosticism, although salvation in the New Testament is not construed as being available only apart from the world (cf. *1 En.* 5.9) because matter is inherently evil. It seems to have been taken for granted that the existing world order would be destroyed by God, maybe after a conflict in which God's ultimate victory was assured, and since God was going to intervene

116. This is suggested by Meeks, *Prophet King*, pp. 201-204.
117. That an identification of Jesus with the suffering servant of Deutero–Isaiah, interpreted messianically, underlies much of Luke's Christology (e.g. at Lk. 3.21-22; 4.17-19; Acts 3.13; 4.25-26, as well as in the more explicit citations at Lk. 22.37; Acts 8.32-33) is argued persuasively by Bock, *Proclamation, passim.*
118. See *Sacr* 3.69; or *Vit. Mos.* 2.166. The Rabbis, too, seem to have associated Moses' designation as Israel's shepherd with his intercessory activity; see *Mek. R. Ishmael*, Exod. 12.1.
119. See 4QDibHam[a].
120. Compare John's verb ὑψόω, where the two also coalesce.

to avenge the suffering righteous and punish the ungodly, Satan's time was short.

Thus in many apocalyptic texts it is assumed that at the Eschaton there will be a total alteration of the situation existing on earth at the time; the rich will become poor and the poor rich,[121] the weak will become strong, the suffering will rejoice, the captives will be freed, and so forth. This theme is strongly stressed by Luke, as we can see from the Magnificat[122] and the Parable of the Rich Man and Lazarus (both of which are unparalleled), and also Luke's version of the Beatitudes. Polar reversal is a major emphasis in Revelation, too; but here, although the two are closely related, the contrast is a vertical and not a temporal one. Things above are the opposite of what they seem on earth; just as the Smyrneans, though poor, are rich (in Heaven, presumably), so, too, the apparent powerlessness of the Philadelphians is deceptive—providing they remain firm in the faith.

6.2.8. *Dualism*

An essentially dualistic perception is expressed in the repeated antitheses occuring throughout many Jewish and Christian texts—so we find God and his angels/Satan and the demons; light/darkness; above/below; truth/falsehood; prophets/false prophets; apostles/false apostles; Christ/the world; Christ/Antichrist. The dualism inherent in the Johannine vision has often been regarded as Greek or Gnostic, but the Qumran has shown how similar was the thought-world of sectarian Judaism, even in Palestine.[123] It is, however, in both cases primarily ethical rather than cosmological and it is a qualified dualism, since God remains in control; it is never suggested that there are spheres outside God's dominion and, ultimately, his judgment. This is made clear in Jn 12.31 and we may compare 1QM 13.9-11 and also Lk. 4.6. There is no real ontological dualism in John's Gospel, although some passages such as the end of ch. 6 are very close to it.[124]

---

121. Thus, for example, *T. Jud.* 25.4. Such a belief would obviously encourage the poor and needy to accept their present lot, and await their eventual vindication by God.

122. Cf. *1 En.* 46.5-7 and Lk. 1.52.

123. It is, of course, characteristic of those facing what P. Berger, *A Rumour of Angels* (Harmondsworth: Penguin, 1970) terms 'cognitive minorities' (p. 18) when they feel themselves isolated from mainstream opinion and wish to defend their own ideas.

124. 1 John perhaps crosses the boundary at 3.7-10; 4.1-3. On the dualism of 1 John, see M.-E. Boismard, 'The First Epistle of John and the Writings of Qumran', in J.H.

We find, nevertheless, a separation of the 'sons of light' (Jn 12.36; cf., e.g., Jn 1.4, 5, 7; 3.19-21; see also Lk. 16.8) from the 'sons of darkness' (e.g. Jn 1.5; 8.12; 12.35; cf. Lk. 22.53), and from 'the world' (e.g. Jn 8.23; 15.18, 19; cf. Lk. 16.8).[125] J.H. Charlesworth[126] observes that although the symbolism of light/darkness is very common, the phrase 'sons of light', which occurs in both Luke and John, is in itself unusual, since there are no examples of such terminology in the Old Testament, the Apocrypha or the Pseudepigrapha; it occurs elsewhere only in the Qumran,[127] except for one instance at 1 Thess. 5.5 (where it links with Paul's reference to the dawning eschatological day).[128] Of Lk. 16.8, Charlesworth comments, 'It is peculiarly non-Lukan and appears to belong to his source.'[129] If this is so, then that source has presumably also influenced Lk. 22.53.

6.2.9. *Wealth*

Luke's gospel is regarded by many as a 'theology of the poor',[130] although it has often been noted that there seems to be some inconsistency[131] in his treatment of the theme of possessions. Thus at times he seems to condemn them unreservedly as incompatible with true Christianity,[132] whereas at others he seems, rather, to counsel sharing them (as in Acts 2 and 4), or to recommend using them to aid those in need (see Lk. 6.38, where he uses the present imperative of δίδωμι; or Lk. 19.9, where Zacchaeus is pronounced 'saved' by Jesus when he has resolved to give away half of what he owns).

Charlesworth (ed.), *John and the Dead Sea Scrolls* (New York: Crossroad, 1991), pp. 156-65, especially p. 164; and J.L. Price, 'Light from Qumran upon Some Aspects of Johannine Theology', in J.H. Charlesworth (ed.), *John and the Dead Sea Scrolls* (New York: Crossroad, 1991), pp. 9-37 (22).

125. Ashton (*Understanding*, p. 208) observes, however, that there is a slightly different nuance here: Luke's word αἰῶνος indicates a temporal distinction which is not present on John's κόσμος.

126. J.H. Charlesworth, 'A Critical Comparison of the Dualism in 1QS iii.13-iv.26 and the "Dualism" contained in the Fourth Gospel', in *idem* (ed.), *John and the Dead Sea Scrolls*, pp. 76-106.

127. E.g. at 1QS 1.9; 2.16; 3.13, 24.

128. There is also Eph. 5.8, which Charlesworth omits from consideration.

129. Charlesworth, 'Dualism', p. 101 n. 117.

130. Thus Pilgrim, *Good News*.

131. See, e.g., L.T. Johnson, *The Literary Function of Possessions in Luke–Acts* (SBLDS, 39; Missoula, MT: Scholars Press, 1977), *passim*.

132. See Lk. 14.33; or 5.11 and 18.22, where Luke adds 'all' to Mark.

The vehemence of Luke's attack on wealth, which informs parables like the Rich Man and Lazarus and the discourse with the Pharisees which precedes it, is unparalleled in the other Synoptic Gospels, although it is shared by Old Testament prophets such as Amos. It is also shared by the author of Revelation,[133] and in this context we notice that the apocalyptic term βδέλυγμα, which Luke applies to the Pharisees—who are lovers of money—at Lk. 16.15, is used in a similar way in Rev. 17.4, 5 and 21.27; Revelation regards wealth as evil, since it involves an acquiescence in idolatrous contemporary power structures (symbolized by the monstrous Beast) and thus alienation from God. This is the implication of the letter to Laodicea (Rev. 3.17-18); reliance on wealth means compromise with Rome, and Rome is attacked precisely because of the wealth of many of its inhabitants at Rev. 18.3, 11, 14-17, 19, in a chapter which links possessions to moral iniquity.[134] (We may compare John's Gospel, where Judas is explicitly said to be a thief, who steals money from the funds at Jn 12.6.) In Acts, the cautionary tale of Ananias and Sapphira, which is juxtaposed with the idealized picture of the κοινωνία of the early Church, illustrates a similar point. The message for the rich is very threatening in Luke; although hellfire is not particularly congenial to him as a theme and he seems to take little pleasure in vindictive speculations as to the sufferings of the damned, the grim parable in Luke 16 contains the most detailed picture of those torments[135] found in any Gospel, and they are experienced by the rich man upon his death.

The connection between the practice of magic and wealth was widely recognized in the ancient world,[136] where it was assumed that magicians were avaricious and exploited their powers for gain, as is evident in Acts

133. M. Hengel, *Earliest Christianity* (London: SCM Press, 1986), pp. 149-236, especially pp. 171ff., notes that a radical rejection of worldly wealth is common to many apocalyptic texts, both Christian and Jewish.

134. This linkage was not uncommon in Judaism; it is evident not only in apocalyptic texts like *1 Enoch* (where it occurs in both the Ethiopic section at 63.10-12, and in the final chapters) but also in Amos and First Isaiah, and in Wisdom literature such as Wis. 2.10-20; Sir. 13.3-7; 31.5. In the Qumran, too, the poor (= righteous) Sons of Light are praised and the mighty (and therefore rich) Sons of Darkness are castigated. See 1QpHab 12.3,10; 1QM 11.9, 13.

135. We may compare the horrific nightmarish visions of Revelation 9. Similar ideas are also reflected in *4 Ezra*, although this may post-date Revelation.

136. See Plato, *Laws* 10.909; Philo, *Spec. Leg.* 3.100; Lucian, *Lover of Lies* 15. (Cf. Garrett, *Demise*, p. 145 n. 39.)

16.19. It is significant that Judas, called the 'son of perdition' (ἀπώλεια) in Jn 17.12 and linked to Satan by Luke as well as John,[137] betrays Jesus for money, and in Acts 8.20 Simon Magus, along with his ill-gotten wealth, is similarly consigned to 'perdition' when he attempts to purchase the Holy Spirit. The love of money is closely associated with the root of all evil in both Luke and the Johannine literature.

There was, however, a strong current in Jewish thought prominent, for example, in the Deuteronomic tradition, which regarded riches as a blessing from God, and this continued, even though Wisdom writers (especially the later ones) modified it and stressed that wealth is only to be seen as a blessing if it does not result from the oppression of others;[138] see, for example, Prov. 1.12-13; 10.2; 11.16-18; Sir. 4.6; 5.8; 7.3, 18, 20; Wis. 2.1-12. This idea, too, is to be found in Luke, though he stresses even more emphatically than the Wisdom texts the need actively to aid the needy poor, as is evidenced by Lk. 1.52-53; 6.20-21; 12.33; 18.22; 19.8; 21.1-4.[139] There is therefore no condemnation in Acts of the clearly well-to-do Barnabas, nor of Lydia: the same is true in the Gospel of the women who maintain Jesus' ministry out of their own means at 8.3. Lk. 12.33, too, which can be compared with Mt. 6.19-20, does not appear to make absolute poverty a criterion for discipleship, even though Luke, like Matthew, clearly sets earthly against heavenly desires.

It seems to be the combination of this more positive attitude to possessions with material where they are regarded with loathing and disgust—material unparalleled among the other Synoptics but having clear connections with the Johannine tradition[140]—which is primarily responsible for the tensions in Luke, even if we argue that in his presentation the evangelist attempted to resolve it by relating the theme to a person's inner disposition.[141] We may compare Luke's eschatology, where his attempt to combine two conflicting streams of thought has arguably produced similar inconsistencies.

---

137. Cf. Lk. 22.3, Jn 13.2, 27.

138. See Johnson, *Sharing Possessions*, pp. 65-66.

139. Cf. also Tobit; Josephus, *Apion* 2.211 (where, as in Luke, caring for others and sharing with them is linked to salvation) and indeed Mt. 6.2.

140. And also Apocalyptic texts, such as *1 Enoch*. See the Excursus comparing Luke–Acts, Revelation and *1 Enoch* at the end of this chapter.

141. Thus Johnson, *Literary Function of Possessions*; and *idem, Sharing Possessions.*

6.2.10. *Christ versus Satan*

6.2.10.1. *The Conflict*. Although there are not many references to Satan in Luke–Acts, those that occur are very heavily emphasized by context.[142] In first-century Judaism, and throughout the New Testament, Σατανᾶς, a transliteration of the Hebrew *śāṭān*, is used interchangeably with ὁ διάβολος, as is often the case in the Septuagint.[143] In Job, however, where the framework may be pre-exilic, we find evidence of an earlier identification; here Satan is 'the Adversary', whose function is that of a prosecuting attorney, and this is clearly reflected in Lk. 22.31, where Satan demands to 'sift [Peter] like wheat'. We may compare, too, Rev. 12.10.

Satan, however, as well as 'testing' and 'accusing' people, is also seen in Jewish literature to lead them astray, most often by promoting idolatry.[144] The demonic world is assumed to be in perpetual conflict with Heaven, the battleground being humanity on earth. This idea, which is evident in *1 Enoch* and *Jubilees*, is presupposed by both Luke and John. Thus we notice that at Lk. 8.12 unbelief is the work of the Devil—and this, by implication, links the Jews who reject their Messiah to Satan (compare Rev. 3.9 and Jn 8.44). In this connection it is certainly significant that two of the magicians in Acts are Jewish, though in Gentile territory, and the other is a Samaritan.

Garrett[145] points out that there is quite a close verbal affinity between Lk. 4.5-7 and Rev. 13.7b-8: thus, unlike the Matthaean parallel at 4.8-10, both refer to ἐξουσία, to the fact that it is *all given* (Luke)/*given* over *all* (Revelation). We may compare, too, οἰκουμένης at Lk. 4.5 and οἱ κατα-οικοῦντες ἐπὶ τῆς γῆς at Rev. 13.8. (It should be noted, however, that both texts could be drawing on Dan. 7.14 [Septuagint] here.) That Satan's ultimate goal is worship[146] is made very plain in Rev. 13.4-8, where the blasphemy involved is clearly regarded with horror, and in this context we notice that Luke depicts the awful consequences of such a sin for humans at Acts 12.22-23:[147] it also underlies his treatment of Simon Magus, since

142. The importance of the theme of the conflict of Christ and Satan is emphasized by Garrett, *Demise, passim*.

143. In the Qumran, too, Satan is the Devil; see 1QM 13.2.

144. See *Jub.* 11.4-5; 22.16-17; *Asc. Isa.* 1.9; 2.4.

145. Garrett, *Demise*, p. 38.

146. Matthew uses προσκυνεῖσθαι at 4.9, too, so this parallel should not be over-emphasized.

147. Garrett, *Demise*, p. 43 suggests that there may be a link between Isaiah 14 and the account of Herod's death, since the King of Babylon was covered by worms

not even Jesus claims to be 'the power of God', as Lk. 22.69 shows. While it must be conceded that the connection between Luke and Matthew is very close throughout the whole Temptation sequence, so that a common source or direct dependence is accepted by all, that between Luke and Revelation at this point is nevertheless perceptible and should not be overlooked.

Using the 'Divine passive' which stresses the authority of God, Lk. 4.6 and Jn 12.31 both indicate that Satan is nevertheless permitted control over the kingdoms of the world; and, as Rev. 13.7-8 makes clear, this includes having permission to attack Christians. It must be emphasized that this conception is not truly dualistic, as Rowland[148] observes, because God is still in overall charge:[149] there is never any suggestion in Luke or the Johannine literature that there are two equal powers in heaven.[150] The theme of authority is underlined by Luke in his expansion of the Strong Man Bound parable at Lk. 11.21-22, and again—humorously—by the reaction of the demons to the Seven Sons of Sceva in Acts. Like most of his contemporaries Luke regards Satan as the authority behind all acts of magic, and hence victories over magicians, and likewise the healing of the possessed, represent Satan's kingdom being plundered.

The theme of magic and sorcery is in consequence considerably emphasized throughout Luke–Acts.[151] Thus the first healing Jesus performs (contra Matthew but not Mark) is an exorcism; the first action by the disciples outside Jewish territory involves them in a conflict with the magician Simon Magus; the first incident of Paul's career as a Christian missionary that is narrated in any detail is the clash with Elymas, a Jewish false prophet and magician. In the tradition on which Luke seems to have

---

(σκώληκες) and Herod is eaten by them (σκωληκόβρωτος); Josephus merely refers to severe stomach pains.

148. Rowland, *Open Heaven*, p. 92.

149. Cf. *Jubilees* 10.

150. Cadbury, *Making of Luke–Acts*, p. 216, notes that the linking of authority and power is characteristically Lukan (see Lk. 4.36; 9.1; 10.19; 19.15-17; Acts 1.7-8) and it is not common elsewhere, although it does also occur in Revelation (see Rev. 17.13).

151. Esler, *Community and Gospel*, pp. 49ff. suggests that this emphasis reflects a rejection of one of the ways sectarian groups attempted to legitimate themselves, the 'thaumaturgical' response which, 'is characterized by the individual's concern with relief from present and specific ills by magic' (p. 49). This ignores, however, the importance of the Christ/Satan conflict in Luke and the unquestionably apocalyptic nature of much of this material.

drawn,[152] magic is seen not only as Satanic (as in *1 En.* 65, for example; in *1 En.* 8, too, magic and sorcery come from the fallen angels) but also as characteristic of false prophets. Luke is very careful to distance Jesus and the Christians from charges of practising it; that this was a real danger[153] is evident from the accusations levelled at Jesus in all four Gospels.[154] Garrett[155] notes that Luke at 9.7-9 modifies Mk 6.14 to remove any intimation of necromancy; similarly, he avoids using the verb μεταμο-ρφόομαι, which had undesirable connotations, in the Transfiguration (compare Lk. 9.29 with Mk 9.2, Mt. 17.2). His account of Simon Magus, too, is very different from the picture of the proto-Gnostic found in Justin and Irenaeus; Luke stresses Simon's inferiority to the Christians, and his recognition of their superior power. Simon himself is subtly ridiculous as he pleads with Peter to revoke his curse.

In some important respects Luke's technique is similar to that of the author of Revelation. Thus Bar-Jesus, a false prophet who 'makes crooked the straight paths of the Lord' (Acts 13.10) is clearly meant to recall the true prophet, John the Baptist, who at Lk. 3.5 makes the crooked ways straight, just as the Seven Sons of Sceva mimic—with consequences disastrous to themselves—the actions of Paul when he exorcises demons.[156] In Revelation, too, parody informs the whole narrative. Indeed, almost every image of the world above has some obscene counterpart in that below: the Dragon and the Beast, for example, are devilish equivalents of God and Christ,[157] as is Babylon of the pure Bride of the Lamb. In all

152. See *Asc. Isa.* 1.8-9; 2.5; 3.1; *CD*-A. 5.17b-19; and Rev. 2.13-15; 13.11-18; 16.12-14, among others, for analogues/sources.

153. Aune, 'Apocalypse', pp. 481ff., has shown that throughout Revelation there is a continued polemic against pagan magical practices. See, e.g., Rev. 13.13-15; 16.13-14; 21.8. Babylon is explicitly linked to sorcery and to demons at 18.2, 23.

154. Accusations of sorcery against Jesus and leading people astray occur in Jewish sources; see *b. Sanh.* 43a. Jesus is called a λαοπλάνης in Justin Martyr, *Dial.* 69. This charge continued to be made and was taken very seriously; see Origen, *Against Celsus* 1.6.

155. Garrett, *Demise*, p. 3.

156. Garrett, *Demise*, p. 92, observes that the Jewish exorcists at Acts 19.13 are clearly copying what they have seen Paul doing, but the use of the verb ὁρκίζω links them with magic and hence with the Devil; cf. *PGM* 4.345; 1708. (Jesus commands demons using παραγγέλλω as does Paul at Acts 16.18, or ἐπιτιμάω.)

157. Thus it is stressed in Rev. 13.2 that the Dragon gives the Beast its power, throne and authority; and Christ is explicitly given these same attributes by God: power at 2.26 (and elsewhere); the throne at 3.21; and authority at 12.10.

cases the comparisons are shocking: but they also serve to emphasize the inferiority of the counterfeit, and Luke makes the same point.

6.2.10.2. The Defeat of Satan. Christ's victory over Satan is sure, as John's Prologue makes clear: 'The light shines in the darkness, and the darkness has not overcome it' (Jn 1.5). The same is true in Luke, as Lk. 10.18 (which is considered in more detail below) shows. It should nevertheless be stressed that Conzelmann[158] places far too much emphasis on the words ἄχρι καιροῦ at Lk. 4.13, since what is implied here is not a Satan-free ministry; it is rather to be compared with the victory of the righteous over Satan in works like *The Testament of Job* where Satan slinks away, temporarily worsted, meditating his next assault.[159] The temptation, however, demonstrates that the power of Christ is greater than that of Satan: Christ is the ἰσχυρότερός (Lk. 3.16; 11.22). Therefore, when he or his emissaries confront demons, the evil spirits obey; the verb νικάω which Luke substitutes for Mark's δέω at 11.22 is emphatic, and it echoes throughout Revelation, too, in a similar context.[160]

Closely related is the question of the authority conferred by Christ on believers. Throughout the New Testament (for example, in 1 John) there are numerous exhortations to Christians to remain faithful in persecution and not to be afraid: this is vividly expressed at Lk. 10.19, 'Behold, I have given you authority to tread upon serpents and scorpions, and over all the power of the enemy, and nothing shall hurt you'. Luke, however, in addition presents this dramatically, not only via the death of Christ, but through the narrative of Acts, where Peter is miraculously rescued in chs. 5 and 12, and Paul has numerous hairs breadth escapes, including an encounter with a serpent in Malta. It should be noted that Lk. 10.19, which in other respects is clearly an allusion to Psalm 91 (regarded as particularly efficacious in warding off evil powers and in consequence much used by exorcists) in its reference to scorpions, is independent of the psalm; there may be some connection here with Rev. 9.4, where scorpions are vividly presented as one of the torments visited on 'those who have not the seal of God on their foreheads'.[161]

158. Conzelmann, *Theology*, p. 28.
159. Thus Garrett, *Demise*, pp. 41-43.
160. At, e.g., Rev. 2.11; 2.26. See Bauckham, *Revelation*, pp. 88ff.
161. The two are, however, combined in Deut. 8.15, and both writers could be alluding to this verse. Other texts, such as *T. Sim.* 6.6; *T. Levi* 18.12; *T. Zeb.* 9.8 (cf. *T. Job* 43.8) and Ps. 91.13, refer merely to evil creatures/spirits/serpents being trampled underfoot.

Luke is aware, nevertheless, that there are no actual guarantees of safety or miraculous deliverance. Stephen and James are martyred, and Paul is obviously going to be; there are tensions between the assurances given and some of the actions depicted or predicted, and the same is true in John. In Revelation, too, the Seer presents the rewards in Heaven in very concrete terms in chs. 21 and 22, but does not attempt to conceal that many will suffer on earth first.

The success of Jesus' ministry, and that of his disciples, as seen in Acts, prefigures Satan's ultimate defeat, which Jesus himself envisions in the unequivocally apocalyptic and uniquely Lukan: 'I saw Satan fall like lightning from Heaven' (Lk. 10.18). This verse forms the climax to the Mission of the Seventy (Two),[162] when we are told that Jesus 'rejoiced', a word often used in Luke–Acts in connection with healings and other victories over malefic powers, and in its context it clearly implies Satan's defeat.[163] It seems to echo a myth like that recorded in Revelation 12, where Satan is defeated and cast out of Heaven by Michael and his hosts, which itself may reflect Isa. 14.12, a verse interpreted in later Jewish tradition as referring to the fall from Heaven of Lucifer, who was identified with the Devil.[164]

As to precisely when this fall occurred, there are two main possibilities. In *The Life of Adam and Eve* 13–16 Satan is cast down from Heaven when he opposes the creation of Adam, and in *1 En.* 10.4-6 the rebel angels/Watchers are cast out for seducing the daughters of men; if we follow either of these interpretations, Jesus could be referring to some pre-existent vision in Lk. 10.18. But Luke avoids any reference to the pre-existence of Jesus, and this would support the alternative, and more common, opinion concerning Satan's fall, which is that found in *The Testament of the Twelve Patriarchs*, Qumran and Revelation.[165] Here, Satan is still to be expelled in the last battle between the heavenly and the demonic

162. Whichever manuscript variant one reads, 70 or 72 emissaries, the incident represents a triumph for Christ against Satan.

163. Contra Vanni, 'Apocalypse', p. 18. Vanni's interpretation, that (as in Revelation 9) in this verse lightning/Satan falling to the earth is to be seen as destructive rather than defeated, takes insufficient account of the implication of Lk. 10.17

164. Cf. Rev. 2.28, and perhaps 6.13 and 9.1. There seems to have been a conflation of the judgment on the rebellious stars of *1 En.* 21.6 and the rebel angels/Watchers of Genesis 6 (who are servants of Satan in *1 En.* 54.6) and Isa. 14.12.

165. See *T. Jud.* 25.3; *T. Levi* 18.12; 1QS 3.20-24; Rev. 20.2. In *1 En.* 54, too, and *1 En.* 100.7, the final judgment on Azazel, committing him to eternal fire, is still to come.

powers. In this view, which is that accepted by most commentators,[166] the verb ἐθεώρουν relates to a vision which links the fall to his defeat in the exorcisms performed by the seventy (two) emmissaries and to Jesus' ministry (see Lk. 10.17-24).

But the vision is not necessarily fulfilled as yet; Garrett[167] points out that the context in which Luke has placed this verse is not solely retrospective. The demons *are* subject to the disciples (present tense, not past, at vv. 17, 20): 'nothing *shall* hurt you' (future tense, in v. 19). It is thus quite possible that the imperfect tense of the verb θεωρέω is proleptic, as is the case in Dan. 4.10; 7.2-15, and it refers to some future event when Satan's defeat and fall are to be accomplished. Clearly what is implied by the text is not another minor skirmish, such as are frequently recorded throughout Luke–Acts, but a definitive victory. Whereas Satan is active during the Passion sequence,[168] after the Ascension Christ is exalted to Heaven, as is confirmed by Stephen's vision, and by then we should presumably infer that in their conflict he has finally defeated Satan. Garrett[169] therefore argues that we should identify this victory as contemporaneous with the Resurrection, which has some affinities with the presentation in Revelation 12, where Satan is expelled after raising a rebellion in Heaven. The Accuser (Rev. 12.10) is thrown out from Heaven and conquered by the redeeming blood of Christ (Rev. 12.11); the Passion would therefore seem to be the deciding factor. There is, moreover, a clear connection in John's Gospel at 12.31-32 between Jesus' death/exaltation and Satan's ejection:[170] νῦν κρίσις ἐστὶν τοῦ κόσμου τούτου, νῦν ὁ ἄρχων τοῦ κόσμου τούτου ἐκβληθήσεται ἔξω· κἀγὼ ἐὰν ὑψωθῶ ἐκ τῆς γῆς, πάτας ἑλκύσω πρὸς ἐμαυτόν. It may be that this interpretation of events was simply presupposed in Luke, being so commonplace as to require no comment or explanation.

It should not be inferred that Luke or any of his contemporaries would have regarded his treatment of this theme as in any way metaphorical. As we have seen, like John's, Luke's narrative functions on more than one level: thus there is the metaphysical conflict of Christ and Satan (cf. Jn 12.31) as well as the actual conflict of Jesus in his ministry with opposing

166. E.g. Evans, *Luke*, pp. 454-55.
167. Garrett, *Demise*, pp. 49ff.
168. See, especially, Lk. 22.3, 31.
169. Garrett, *Demise*, pp. 51ff.
170. Symbolically, Christ's victory in his ministry over death, the raising of Lazarus, is the last of the signs in John.

forces. There may also be another layer of meaning. As was noted above, some modern interpreters[171] have convincingly argued that there is in John's Gospel an allegorical representation of the later difficulties facing the Johannine community. They suggest that John's implication is that the community, in its struggle with the world, lives out the moral conflict of good and evil evidenced in Jesus' battle with his opponents. Luke, too, presents the ministry of Jesus as a victorious battle with Satan, and this is echoed in Acts via a number of encounters between Christians and magicians (who represent the Devil) in which Christians, too, are equally victorious, as was promised at Lk. 10.19. What is implicit in John's allegorization Luke arguably draws out and develops in historical terms in the narrative of Acts.[172] Although details of their presentation differ, both Luke and John thus treat the archetypal conflict of good and evil inherent in the Christ/ Satan theme in a similar way.

6.2.11. *The Sea*

Associated with the demonic world was the sea, an association long-established in Judaism and probably linking with Canaanite myth,[173] since the sea represented primeval chaos, and the destruction of the Flood, which had the power to engulf creation.[174] It is noticeable that there are very few references to the sea in Luke; for example, the shore of Mk 3.7 is replaced by the plain, and at 5.27, too, Luke leaves out Mark's πάλιν παρὰ τὴν θάλασσαν (Mk 2.13), thus moving the call of Levi into the country. Moreover, we are never told that Capernaum is by the Sea of Galilee (or 'lake', as Luke prefers to call it[175]). As Conzelmann points out,

171. E.g. Martyn, *History and Theology*, and Ashton, *Understanding*.

172. Cf. the similar analysis of the techniques of Luke and John by O. Cullmann, *The Johannine Circle* (London: SCM Press, 1976), p. 14.

173. See Job 26.12; Isa. 27.1; 51.9. For the Canaanite background of this idea, see J. Day, *God's Conflict with the Dragon and the Sea* (Cambridge: Cambridge University Press, 1985). Day argues persuasively (pp. 162ff.) that the Danielic Son of Man who comes 'with the clouds of Heaven' in Dan. 7.13-14 seems to have affinities with a legend about Baal, the 'rider of the clouds' (*CTA* 2.4.8, 29), who defeated the sea-monster Yamm.

174. On the importance of this motif in Revelation, see Baukham, *Revelation*, p. 153.

175. It is perhaps significant that Revelation has several references to Hell as τὴν λίμνην τοῦ πυρὸς (Rev. 19.20; cf. 20.10, 14 [twice], 15; 21.8). Aune, 'Apocalypse', p. 495 n. 12, notes that this motif has no close parallel in Jewish or Graeco-Roman literature.

if we did not unconsciously harmonize with Matthew and Mark at this point we would have the impression from Luke's text that Capernaum, Jesus' 'centre of operations', was in the middle of Galilee. Conzelmann sees its significance, ultimately, as theological; in the Gospel it is a boundary: 'a place of manifestation which demonstrates the power of Jesus… which has mysterious features'.[176]

The pericope of the Stilling of the Storm in consequence has great impact in Luke's presentation;[177] the lake delimits the hostile demonic powers which Jesus subdues, using the significant verb ἐπιτιμάω. And this story is followed immediately by that of the Gerasene/Gadarene Demoniac, which is the only time in Luke's Gospel that Jesus definitely goes outside Jewish territory. The lake in this pericope is clearly identified as the home of demons; Luke at 8.31 uses the evocative and significant word ἄβυσσον, which is rare in the New Testament and only occurs in apocalyptic contexts referring to Hell. Seven of the nine recorded usages are in Revelation, and there may well be some relationship between the two texts here. It should perhaps be noted that the Beast (Rome), too, which is linked to Satan, in Danielic fashion rises from the sea at Rev. 13.1, being thereby associated with both Evil and chaos. It is no coincidence that in the vision of the new Heaven and new Earth in Revelation 21 we are explicitly told that 'the sea was no more'.

6.3. *Conclusion*

We may conclude that the conceptual correspondences between Luke and the Johannine tradition in their treatment of themes such as wealth, dualism, the Christ/Satan conflict, the Spirit, personal revelation and witnessing are manifold and striking, and there also seem to be significant affinities in their presentation of Jesus in relation to Jewish messianic expectations and in their eschatological speculations and conclusions. Many—indeed, most—of these reflect ideas current in other intertestamental Jewish writings, especially Apocalypses,[178] and their presence in Luke,

176. Conzelmann, *Theology*, p. 42.

177. We may also compare the shipwreck in Acts. Luke assumes the link between a supposed natural disaster and the demonic forces at liberty in the sea: he does not bother to spell it out again. But what is stressed here and in the stilling of the storm is that these evil forces do not have the last word. Jesus calms the storm; Paul survives the shipwreck; and so the gospel reaches Rome.

178. In this context the connections between the last chapters of *1 Enoch* and Luke have often been noticed, and I shall consider these in detail in the Excursus below.

popularly regarded as the most 'Gentile' of the Gospels, is somewhat surprising. Luke's inclusion of them means that it is a serious misinterpretation to regard him as 'unapocalyptic' simply because he modifies and historicizes Mark 13/Matthew 24. Luke's apocalypticism is not like that of Matthew and Mark; in many ways, it has closer links with the Johannine tradition, as has been shown above, and few critics seem to have appreciated that it therefore needs to be treated differently. From wherever he drew it, it is essential to a proper understanding of Luke's treatment of his sources and of his purpose that we take full account of this material, which he has consciously chosen to add to the other Synoptics.

Excursus

AN EXAMINATION OF THE CONNECTIONS BETWEEN LUKE–ACTS, *1 ENOCH* 92–105 AND REVELATION

Introduction

Professor S. Aalen[1] maintained that there are several significant parallels of expression and theme between the final chapters (92–105) of the Greek text of *1 Enoch* and Luke's Gospel; he regarded *1 Enoch* as a probable Lukan source. There are certainly many connections between Luke and Jewish apocalyptic generally, as has been shown, but Aalen a little over-stated his case. For example, many of the verbal affinities he noted between Luke and *1 Enoch* are unremarkable, such as the use of ἀπόλλυμι in the context of the punishment of the wicked which is also found in *Pss. Sol.* 12.6; 15.12-13 and Jn 3.16; 10.28; or of ὑποδείκνυμι ὑμῖν, which Nickelsburg[2] in his review of Aalen's article termed a cliché, common in apocalyptic contexts.[3] It is in any case used by Matthew as well at Mt. 3.7, so it need not have been derived from *1 Enoch*. Some of the parallels Aalen notes, too, such as δικαιόω plus reflexive pronoun at Lk. 10.29; 16.15 and *1 En.* 102.10, depend on conjecture,[4] since the text of *1 Enoch* is disputed at this point. (Aalen's reconstruction of it is not accepted by scholars such as Jeremias).[5] And the word ἐκλίπῃ at Lk. 16.9, which Aalen compared with ἐκλείπῃ in *1 En.* 100.5, may be used in a slightly different sense.[6]

---

1. S. Aalen, 'St Luke's Gospel and 1 Enoch', *NTS* 13 (1966), pp. 1-13.
2. Nickelsburg, 'Riches', p. 325.
3. Cf. *T. Naph.* 8.1; *T. Ash.* 1.2; Tob. 4.20; 12.11; Dan. 9.23; 10.21; 11.2.
4. So, too, that between *1 En.* 103.4 and Lk. 10.20, where there seems to have been an omission in the Greek text, and Aalen uses the Ethiopic one.
5. J. Jeremias, 'Beobachtungen zu ntl. Stelen an Hand des neuefund. griech. Henoch-Textes', *ZNW* 38 (1937), pp. 115-24 (117).
6. Luke's usage here may however imply 'fails', as in Heb. 11.32; Lk. 22.32; 12.33, rather than 'comes to an end' (cf. Heb. 1.12). There is in any case a different nuance to be given to the present and aorist subjunctives. (This form, which Aalen saw as a significant parallel feature, is regulated by context.)

There are, however, one or two more striking parallels, such as the word ὀδύνη in *1 En.* 102.11[7] and Luke's use of the verb ὀδυνάομαι in a similar context—namely, the pains of Hell—at 16.24, 25 (although Luke is not consistent in this respect, since he also uses βάσανος in the same context at 16.23, 28: cf. Wis. 1-5). Both *1 Enoch* and Luke use φλόξ for the flame, too, and hellfire is not a common theme until the late second century and beyond.[8] There is also what Aalen terms 'a further striking linguistic affinity'[9] between the two texts, in that *1 Enoch* at 99.9 has ἐπί μιᾶς, meaning 'together, as one', and Luke at 14.18 has ἀπὸ μιᾶς with the same meaning in a section which is a Lukan addition to the Parable of the Great Supper he shares with Matthew (compare Lk. 14.16-24; Mt. 22.1-10). Both forms, as Aalen notes, are rare and have few parallels. The contexts are, however, different: overall, we cannot, upon the verbal evidence offered by Aalen, regard the dependence of Luke upon the Greek text of *1 En.* 92-105 as proven.

Common Themes

Wealth

Nevertheless, there are some significant points of contact between the later chapters of *1 Enoch*[10] and Luke, and it is important that these should not be dismissed too readily on the grounds that the verbal 'parallels' between them are not quite as significant as Aalen seems to have believed. The obvious example is the treatment of wealth, a major Lukan emphasis which Luke frequently adds to his Markan/Matthaean sources. It has often

---

7.   And also in *1 En.* 22.10-11. Here, as elsewhere, there are many points of contact between the early sections of *1 Enoch* and the end.

8.   *1 Enoch* may perhaps be regarded as the ancestor of the 'tours of Hell' which were to be popular in Jewish, Christian and Muslim literature, being especially common in the Middle Ages. The first fully-developed example of this type is the second-century *Apocalypse of Peter*.

9.   Aalen, 'Luke', p. 3.

10.   R. Bauckham, *Jude and the Relatives of Jesus in the Early Church* (Edinburgh: T. & T. Clark, 1990), pp. 315-78, argues that Luke's genealogy of Jesus has affinities with the structure of *1 En.* 93.3-10, where world history is likewise periodized into units of seven. Enoch is the seventh member of the first heptad; Luke's Jesus is the seventh of the eleventh (the seventy-seventh from Adam; hence the climax of history). Bauckham may well be right that *1 Enoch* and Luke are to be linked here, although the significance of the number seven was widely recognized in the ancient world, as is attested by many writings, including Revelation.

been pointed out that both Luke (or his source) and *1 Enoch* have a strongly negative view of possessions and their relation to salvation. Thus what Aalen calls a 'common conception of rich and poor, mighty and lowly'[11] informs the only extensive series of verbal correspondences between the two, at *1 En.* 97.8-20 and Lk. 12.15-34, and the connection here relates to both idea and expression, whereas the links Aalen notes between Lk. 16.19-31 and *1 Enoch* are scattered throughout the latter text from ch. 94 onwards. Nickelsburg observes[12] that at this point there are also structural similarities to Sir. 11.18-19. The structure of all three comprises:

- introductory description (Lk. 12.16b/*1 En.* 97.8a/Sir. 11.18)
- quotation (Lk. 12.17-19/*1 En.* 97.8b-9/Sir. 11.19a, b)
- refutation/reversal (Lk. 12.20/*1 En.* 97.10/Sir. 11.19c, d).

Aalen notes the use of τὰ ὑπάρχοντα at *1 En.* 97.8; 98.3 and 101.5, which is something of a Lukan favourite (see Lk. 11.21; 12.33, 44; 16.1; 19.8; and also the cognate ὕπαρξις at Acts 2.45). Both texts, too, use ἀγαθά of goods, *1 Enoch* at 97.9 and Luke at 12.18; and there is also ποιήσωμεν at *1 En.* 97.9, which may be compared with ποιήσω at Lk. 12.17. Likewise, the verb θησαυρίζω occurs in both *1 En.* 97.9 and Lk. 12.21; and *1 En.* 98.1, 9 and Lk. 12.20 both stigmatize people who rely on possessions as ἄφρων, which Aalen thinks is significant, although there are many parallels in other Jewish sources, such as Wis. 2.1-9.

It should be stressed that the Parable of the Rich Fool, which concerns the folly of those who put their trust in wealth, and hence disregard the imminence of death and judgment, has other affinities with the Jewish Wisdom tradition found in texts such as Wis. 5.8 and also Sir. 11.18-19, the latter not only using a closely related term—ἀνάπαυσις—for 'rest' (cf. Lk. 12.19, ἀναπαύου), but also having a definite structural similarity to Luke's parable.[13] The folly of hoarding goods is in any case a Jewish commonplace.[14] It finds expression in Matthew as well as Luke; cf. Mt.

11. Aalen, 'Luke', p. 8.

12. Nickelsburg, 'Riches', p. 335.

13. Aalen, 'Luke', sees a further correspondence between Luke and *1 Enoch* in the use, with a strongly negative connotation, of the verb πείθω at *1 En.* 94.8 and Lk. 11.22, but the same verb is used in the same way in Ps. 49.6 and Prov. 11.28.

14. See, e.g., Sir. 29.11; *4 Ezra* 7.7; Tob. 4.9, where the stress is on storing up treasures in Heaven, rather than on earth.

6.19-21, 25-34. (It is worth noting that Luke at 12.18 uses the same term—
ἀποθήκη—for barn as does Matthew at 6.26, rather than *1 Enoch*'s
θησαυρός.)

A warning of the suddenness of the coming judgment has many
parallels, too. It is central to many of the eschatological parables in the
New Testament, such as Matthew's Foolish Virgins (Mt. 25.1-13) and
Luke's Watchful Servants (Lk. 12.35-40).[15] With regard to the Rich Fool,
Aalen seems to misinterpret Luke's parable: the emphasis here is not that
God's judgment leads to sudden death, although the Ananias and Sapphira
incident in Acts is another matter. In Luke 12 it is not so much that God
judges, and therefore the man dies suddenly, as that the man dies suddenly, and therefore the joke—albeit a sick one—is on him. It is less a
'parable of crisis' than a pointed contrast between human hopes and
expectations and the reality of the experience that frustrates them.

The complacent words of the Fool at Lk. 12.19, which are similar in
content and idea to *1 En.* 97.8-9; 102.9, have many analogues in both
Jewish and classical literature.[16] They may therefore be termed conventional. The same is true of the stress on the inability of riches to effect
salvation, pungently expressed in the words of God to the Fool at 12.20
(cf. *1 En.* 100.6-13), which occurs widely in Jewish texts.[17]

Nickelsburg concludes: 'It is clear that *Ben Sirach* and *1 Enoch* derive
from a common Wisdom tradition…if the author of the Lukan parable
knew the Enochic version of the passage, he was also aware of its broader
Wisdom context.'[18] Nickelsburg does, however, find it significant that
both Luke and *1 Enoch* stress the importance of sharing one's possessions
with those in need, this being his interpretation of Lk. 12.21, which
therefore has connections with *1 En.* 97.9 and also 96.6. It is a theme
congenial to Luke; sharing one's goods, or even giving most of them
away, is seen to bring salvation to Zacchaeus at 19.9. In this context, there
is a pointed but implicit contrast between the tax-collector who gives away
his wealth and so is saved, and the rich ruler at 18.18-22 who cannot quite
bring himself to make the sacrifice, and so cannot enter the Kingdom of
God. Aalen connects the second-person Woe over the rich at Lk. 6.24 with

15. In this context, we note that the 'thief in the night' motif is a common one in
the New Testament, occurring in Mt. 24.43-44; 1 Thess. 5.2; 2 Pet. 3.10; Rev. 3.3;
16.15.
16. See, e.g., Isa. 22.13 or Horace's *Odes*.
17. See, e.g., Sir. 11.24-28.
18. Nickelsburg, 'Riches', p. 335.

1 En. 94.8. Luke certainly shares *1 Enoch*'s hostility to the rich, but his attitude is much more positive, since, as the Zacchaeus pericope shows, he relates the theme to repentance.[19] In any case, this same hostility to the rich is to be found in prophets such as Amos and Isaiah: it is also a feature of James and Revelation in the New Testament.

The theme of wealth/possessions also informs the uniquely Lukan Parable of the Rich Man and Lazarus, and here Aalen finds many points of contact between Luke's Gospel and *1 Enoch*.[20] Thus *1 En.* 98 sets blessings (ἀγαθά) and evils (κακά) in the context of post-mortem judgment, and Luke does something similar at 16.19-31, although he stresses that the ἀγαθά and κακά relate to what has been experienced in this life, which affect the judgment afterwards. Both Luke and *1 Enoch*, too, emphasize the way the rich flaunt their wealth in fine clothes, and feast sumptuously,[21] while the poor starve in rags.[22]

The tale which forms the basis of the parable has analogues in both Egyptian and Jewish literature. The Egyptian tale[23] concerns Setme, who is sent from the sphere of the dead, Amnte, by Osiris, and who later provides his father with a tour of Hell to convince him that those who are poor in this life are blessed in the next one, while the rich suffer torment. The Jewish tale, which was widely known, occurs in the Palestinian Talmud[24] and concerns a pious man of Ashkelon, who is so outraged by the contrast he sees between the funeral of a rich tax-collector and that of his friend—who although devout and virtuous was very poor—that he demands an explanation. This is not simply that of the future punishment of the wicked and the reward of the virtuous, but also the statement that the virtuous are frequently punished in this world in order to spare them in the hereafter. (The story clearly reflects the struggle to find an adequate rationale for suffering when the so-called 'Deuteronomic fallacy' had been refuted for many by the events of the Seleucid period.) Both tales have points of contact with that told by Luke: the 'reversal' theme common in apocalyptic and a repeated Lukan emphasis[25] connects it with the Demotic

19.   Repentance is a theme of negligible significance in this section of *1 Enoch*; it is perhaps implied at 104.9.

20.   Similarly, Evans, *Luke*, pp. 614-17.

21.   See *1 En.* 98.1-3; Lk. 16.19, although we should remember that this charge is common in the Prophets, too, such as Isa. 3.18-26.

22.   *1 En.* 96.4-8; Lk. 16.20-21.

23.   It survives in a late first-century text, to which Evans, *Luke*, pp. 612ff., refers.

24.   *Ḥag* 2.77d. See Creed, *Luke*, p. 210.

25.   E.g. in the Lukan Beatitudes and the Magnificat.

text, whereas the 'burial' motif at Lk. 16.22 is closer to the story in the Talmud (although here we may note that Evans[26] finds the absence of any explanation consistent with normal Jewish morality for the reversal of fortune experienced in the next world by Lazarus and the Rich Man as telling against a Jewish origin).

To sum up, then, there do seem to be many points of contact between Luke and *1 Enoch* in their treatment of riches/the rich, but although the correspondences of idea, and occasionally of expression, should be recognized, we also need to bear in mind the many parallels to the material they share.[27]

In this context it is interesting to observe how very similar is the attitude to wealth and possessions in Revelation, where the implication for the rich at Rev. 18.14, 16-17 and elsewhere is similarly threatening, and where there is a similar motif of polar reversal (the Smyrneans, for example, though poor, are rich). Indeed, as noted above, both Lk. 16.15 and Rev. 17.4, 5 and 21.27 use the apocalyptic βδέλυγμα in this context, and both stigmatize the wearers of βυσσίνου καὶ πορφύρας (Rev. 18.12)/πορφύραν καὶ βύσσον (Lk. 16.19)—though this was clearly a 'stock phrase'.[28] Revelation regards wealth as evil, as we saw, and the theme underlying the letter to Laodicea at Rev. 3.17-18, and the words of the whore of Babylon at 18.7, are very similar in tone to those of *1 En.* 97.8-10 and the Rich Fool in Luke. Reliance on wealth, in Revelation, means compromise with Rome, which is attacked as immoral and idolatrous in a stinging and thoroughly prophetic indictment in ch. 18.

Thus when Nickelsburg[29] summarizes what he terms the 'consistent' factors connecting *1 Enoch* and Luke it should be noted that these could equally apply to Revelation:

- 'The rich and their possessions are always viewed in a bad light'—we have already noted in this context Rev. 18, the letter to Laodicea, and the word βδέλυγμα.
- 'In the judgment, the wealth and possessions in which they trusted will be swept away and will afford no help. The supposed

26. Evans, *Luke*, p. 612.
27. Nickelsburg, 'Riches', p. 343, points out that some of these ideas appear in the other Gospels, too; for example, the parallels to Lk. 9.5 at Mk 8.36-37/Mt. 16.26, where there is a common structure and vocabulary. He suggests that perhaps *1 En.* 92–105 not only finds echoes in the synoptic tradition, but may also reflect the teaching of Jesus.
28. See Prov. 31.22; Add. Est. 8.15.
29. Nickelsburg, 'Riches', p. 331.

blessings and happiness of this life will be of no account in the face of punishment'—see above; and also Rev. 2.9 and 19.1-3.
- 'which will be swift, sudden, and unexpected'—see, especially, Rev. 18.8, 14, 17.

There are, indeed, many points of contact between the grimly apocalyptic threats of this whole section of *1 Enoch* and Revelation; we may compare *1 En.* 94.9/Rev. 6.12; *1 En.* 96.6/Rev. 8.10-11; 16.12; *1 En.* 96.8/Rev. 2.9-10.

b. *Eschatology*
Aalen also detects a connection between the eschatology of *1 Enoch* and that of Luke. He claims that there is 'a far-reaching agreement between *1 Enoch* 91ff. and the peculiar matter of St Luke',[30] although detecting this involves simplifying some very complex and varied material and imposing a pattern which may not be consistently present in either text. As was noted above, the notion of 'sudden' death and judgment was fairly common. Aalen asserts that we see in Luke the separation of the righteous and sinners upon death (see 16.19-26; 23.43). The sinners are for the time being committed to ᾅδης, the Jewish Sheol, which in this case[31] amounts to an interim place of punishment, before the resurrection of all (see Lk. 14.14; Acts 24.15) and the final judgment at the Eschaton (Lk. 16.9; 20.35) when the righteous go to Paradise and the wicked to Hell, the γέεννα of Lk. 12.5. There is a 'two-stage' judgment in *1 Enoch*,[32] too, as Aalen points out, contra R.H. Charles,[33] who regarded Hades in *1 Enoch* as the final place of punishment. Aalen identifies a significant difference between the Greek text of *1 En.* 103.7-8 and the Ethiopic version, since the latter suggests that the great judgment takes place in Sheol.[34] The Greek text is rendered thus by Aalen:

---

30. Aalen, 'Luke', p. 10.
31. As in *1 En.* 22, there appear to be at least two apartments in the abode of the dead; the same separation of the virtuous and sinners is apparent in other texts, too, such as *2 Enoch*, but the 'great chasm' (cf. *1 En.* 18.11; 21.2) dividing them has no parallel in the latter text.
32. E.g. at 98.10; 99.15; 100.4, 5.
33. R.H. Charles, *The Apocrypha and Pseudepigrapha of the Old Testament* (2 vols.; Oxford: Oxford University Press, 1913), II, p. 271.
34. Sheol and Gehenna were consistently confused in later Christian tradition, it seems; indeed, this may be implicit even in Isa. 14.15.

> You yourselves know that they will take your souls down to Hades, and
> there they shall be in great anguish and in darkness and in boils and in
> burning flame. And your souls shall come into a great judgment in all the
> generations of the age.[35]

This 'great judgment' is clearly the Eschaton; so punishment in Hades
must precede it in 103.7.

The conclusion Aalen draws from his analysis of this theme in the two
texts is open to some objections, however. First, the notion of a 'two-stage'
judgment, to Sheol on death and to Gehenna at the Day of Judgment, is not
in any way unusual: it is cited as a Pharisaic idea by Josephus,[36] and it also
occurs in Revelation, where there is a millennial messianic Kingdom for the
virtuous before the End,[37] and in *2 Enoch*, too, as Nickelsburg points out
elsewhere.[38] It is debatable, however, whether this pattern is consistently
present in Luke. Aalen's assertion[39] that the reference to 'Abraham's
bosom' at Lk. 16.23 and to Paradise at 23.43 refers to an intermediate state
is refuted by Evans, who says that Lk. 16.31 implies, rather, that the return
to the earth 'would not be from an intermediate state, but after resurrection..."comforted" [v. 25] suggests a *permanent* rather than a temporary
consolation'.[40]

The picture Luke draws seems closer here to *4 Ezra* 7.36 and to *4 Macc.*
7.19 than to *1 Enoch*. Although the general thrust of the texts is that the
dead survive, it is by no means clear whether this is in Hades or not. And
there are a great many related references in other Jewish texts, such as the
Wisdom of Solomon; and also, indeed, in Christian ones, such as Revelation. In any case, as we have seen, Luke expresses many differing ideas
relating to the 'Last Days' throughout the course of Luke–Acts; it is to
oversimplify to the point of misinterpretation to acknowledge only those
which accord with the pattern one desires to perceive.

c. *Good versus Evil*
If, however, the dependence of Luke upon *1 Enoch*, though quite likely,
must remain somewhat in doubt from Aalen's evidence, we are left with a

35. Aalen, 'Luke', p. 9.
36. See Josephus, *War* 2.162-63; *Ant.* 18.14.
37. This could have some points of contact with the 'sweet sleep' of the just in
1 En. 100.5. See, too, *4 Ezra* 7.26-44.
38. Nickelsburg, 'Riches', p. 157.
39. Aalen, 'Luke', p. 10.
40. Evans, *Luke*, p. 614; emphasis mine.

need to find some other explanation for the presence in Luke of material which has clear connections with Jewish apocalyptic—most obviously, material relating to the fall of Satan and the angels (which is alluded to at Lk. 10.18);[41] to the activity of demons who oppress humanity and are clearly to be regarded as minions of Satan (see Lk. 11.18-23; 13.16); and to the torments of Hell (see Lk. 16.22-31). As shown above, the conflict of good and evil is personalized in Luke as a struggle between Satan and Christ; we may compare 2 Thess. 2, which represents a similar Christianization of the conflict of God and the Devil that we see in Jewish apocalyptic texts such as *Jubilees*, the *Ascension of Isaiah* and the *Testament of Job*.[42] We must assume, then, that either Luke himself was responsible for reinterpreting traditional Jewish material in this way, or that the material he drew from was already Christianized. There were numerous Christian apocalypses in the second century and beyond, the earliest probably being the mid-second-century *Apocalypse of Peter*;[43] but the first example of the genre in Christian literature is almost certainly the canonical Revelation, which may date from as early as 68–69 CE, although most critics place it later than this.

Revelation and Luke share many themes which are characteristic of apocalyptic literature as well as the good/evil conflict, such as the belief in God's direction of historical events (hence the importance of the verb $\delta\epsilon\hat{\imath}$ in both); the 'double context' in which incidents are relevant; the themes of endurance in the face of persecution and of repentance; and the emphasis on the importance of personal revelation/witness. The problem is that most—if not all—of these themes also occur in non-apocalyptic contexts, such as the Prophets. The correspondences noted merely serve to indicate ideas that were current at the time in Jewish religious literature. Most of the verbal connections between the two texts (which are often striking) are open to similar objections. Thus the verb $\delta\epsilon\hat{\imath}$ is used too frequently to be

41. The fall of Lucifer (Isa. 14.12) seems to incorporate a myth about rivalry between heavenly figures which has been assimilated into Judaism. It was combined with Gen. 6.1-4 in many Jewish texts. Garrett, *Demise*, p. 135 n. 54 and p. 130 n. 20, observes that by the first century CE the interpretation of laments such as Isa. 14.4-22 as references to the Devil/Satan/Lucifer was probably conventional in apocalyptic circles.

42. See *Jub.* 1.20; 48.15; *Asc. Isa.* 1.9; 2.4; *T. Job* 23.11; 26.6. (Most scholars believe that the *Ascension of Isaiah* and the *Testament of Job* probably reflect some Christian influence, even if in origin they were Jewish.)

43. Thus M. Himmelfarb, *Tours of Hell* (Pennsylvania: Pennsylvania University Press, 1983), pp. 8-9.

regarded as particularly significant in this respect, and the same applies to μετανοέω and μάρτυς. Phrases such as βυσσίνου καὶ πορφύρας, too, are evidenced elsewhere; and the same is true to a lesser degree of the word ἄβυσσον, which, although rare in the New Testament, is also used by Paul at Rom. 10.7 (although Paul does not link it to the sea, as do both Luke and the author of Revelation). Similarly, the addition by Luke at 10.19 of σκορπίοι to the list of harmful creatures over which Christians are to be given authority *may* have some connection with the scorpions so vividly described in Revelation 9 as one of the hellish punishments inflicted on the non-elect, but, on the other hand, scorpions are also mentioned in conjunction with serpents in Deut. 8.15.

Two other verbal connections between Revelation and Luke–Acts are perhaps more suggestive, although neither is in any way conclusive. First, there is the reference to the Son of Man coming on a (singular) cloud, which is unique to Luke and Revelation in the New Testament, although in the *Apocalypse of Peter* 6 Jesus again comes 'on a cloud' to judge sinners, as was noted above. Secondly, there is an interesting correspondence between Rev. 3.5 and Lk. 12.8:

Rev. 3.5	καὶ ὁμολογήσω τὸ ὄνομα αὐτοῦ ἐνώπιον τοῦ πατρός μου καὶ ἐνώπιον τῶν ἀγγέλων αὐτοῦ
Lk. 12.8	πᾶς ὃς ἂν ὁμολογήσῃ ἐν ἐμοὶ ἔμπροσθεν τῶν ἀνθρώπων, καὶ ὁ υἱὸς τοῦ ἀνθρώπου ὁμολογήσει ἐν αὐτῷ ἔμπροσθεν τῶν ἀγγέλων τοῦ θεοῦ

cf. Mt. 10.32:

| Mt. 10.32 | πᾶς οὖν ὅστις ὁμολογήσει ἐν ἐμοὶ ἔμπροσθεν τῶν ἀνθρώπων, ὁμολογήσω κἀγὼ ἐν αὐτῷ ἔμπροσθεν τοῦ πατρός μου τοῦ ἐν οὐρανοῖς |

In both Luke and Revelation we see a scene before God and his angels, and the reference to angels is not found in the Matthaean parallel. The connection between the two is actually closer than it appears, since Luke has added the reference to the Son of Man, and in Revelation it is the Son of Man, explicitly identified at 1.13, who is speaking at this point. In both Luke and Revelation we therefore have the Son of Man acting as an advocate for believers in Heaven, just as in both texts we see Satan as a prosecuting attorney (cf. Rev. 12.10 and Lk. 22.31) who is defeated by Christ (cf. Rev. 12.9 and Lk. 10.18). The affinity of ideas and vocabulary seems very close here, although we have no way of telling which came first.[44] If we propose the priority of Revelation, then Luke at this point would have been conflating Matthew and Revelation.

None of the correspondences noted can be considered as having proved literary dependence in either direction, since most reflect motifs and ideas current at the time, or which are evident in the Old Testament anyway. Even the very close parallel in meaning and expression between Lk. 4.5-7 and Rev. 13.7b-8 pointed out by Boismard[45] could be explained by a shared familiarity with Dan. 7.6 (cf. vv. 14, 27) and/or with related oral traditions concerning Satan and his activities, as Garrett[46] suggests, although it could perhaps indicate a literary relationship. The same is true of the correspondences between Rev. 3.5 and Lk. 12.8, and Rev. 12 (especially vv. 7-12) and Luke. We can only say that there is as much—if not more—to connect Luke with Revelation, in terms of theme and expression, as there is to postulate a link between Luke and *1 Enoch*.

44. Vanni, 'Apocalypse', p. 13, sees Revelation as using both Matthew and Luke, although the main evidence he offers, that ὁμολογήσω plus accusative in Rev. 3.5 is a later form than the 'Semitic' ὁμολογήσει ἐν used by Matthew and Luke, is not persuasive. Even if Luke elsewhere used Revelation, he might still have preferred the Matthaean form at this point.

45. M.-E. Boismard, 'Rapprochements littéraires entre l'évangile de Luc et l'Apocalypse', in J. Schmid and A. Vögtle (eds.), *Synoptische Studien* (Munich: Beck, 1953), pp. 53-63.

46. Garrett, *Demise*, p. 128 n. 8.

Chapter 7

THE GOSPELS OF LUKE AND JOHN

7.1. *Introduction*

As has been shown in the preceding chapters, there are many correspondences of idea and interpretation between Luke and the Johannine writings. In addition, those which connect Luke with apocalyptic texts,
particularly Revelation, are especially striking and perhaps suggestive.
However, to posit a literary relationship—in whatever direction it operated
—it is necessary to establish verbal links or correspondences of order
which are more definite than these. Detailed study of the Gospels of Luke
and John does indeed reveal many such links of subject-matter, chronology, and even wording, which are closer in certain passages than those
between Luke and the other Synoptics, as will be made clear in the
examination of parallel pericopes below. I shall briefly review critical
opinion on the relationship of John to the Synoptics, and then I shall focus
more specifically on the particular case of Luke, before I analyse in detail
all the pericopes shared by Luke and John.

7.2. *John and the Synoptics: A Review*

Although there were differing views as to whether John's Gospel was
supplementing[1] the Synoptics, complementing[2] them, or correcting them,[3]

---

1.   Thus Maddox, *Purpose*, p. 159: 'For the seventy years from H.J. Holtzmann in
1869 to P. Gardner-Smith in 1938, almost everyone agreed (with only various minor
qualifications) that Clement of Alexandria had been right in regarding John as a
supplementary gospel'. Maddox cites a survey of the evidence confirming this
statement is provided by J. Blinzler, *Johannes und die Synoptiker* (SBS, 5; Stuttgart:
KBW, 1965).
2.   Thus H. Scott Holland, *The Fourth Gospel* (ed. W.J. Richmond; London,
1923), p. 126.
3.   Thus H. Windisch, *Johannes und die Synoptiker: Wollte der vierte Evangelist*

the standard view of most nineteenth and earlier twentieth-century biblical scholars can be summed up in the words of E.K. Lee: 'The proposition that the author of the Fourth Gospel was acquainted with at least those of Mark and Luke is so generally accepted that there is no need to argue it out here…'[4]

This broad consensus was challenged by P. Gardner-Smith, R. Bultmann and later C.H. Dodd,[5] all of whom, as well as noting the many fundamental differences between the two traditions (as others such as Windisch had done), observed that there were other explanations for the partial verbal agreements between the Gospels besides the assumption of the literary dependence of one text upon another. They stressed the need to consider other factors which may have influenced the texts, such as oral traditions,[6] and also the use of non-canonical sources (oral and written); and they suggested that John's use of the Synoptic Gospels—if it occurred at all— was very marginal, and of far less significance in any study of his sources than that of other influences/sources.

This view, which has produced important insights into the Johannine tradition, still characterizes the work of the most influential North American scholars.[7] It has failed, however, to command similarly widespread support elsewhere. Many critics, especially in Europe, have questioned[8]

---

die älteren Evangelien ergänzen oder ersetzen? (UNT, 12; Leipzig: J.C. Hinrichs, 1926); F.W. Worsley, 'The Relation of the Fourth Gospel to the Synoptists', *ExpTim* 20 (1908), pp. 62-65.

4.   E.K. Lee, *The Religious Thought of St John* (London: SPCK, 1950), p. 22.

5.   P. Gardner-Smith, *Saint John and the Synoptic Gospels* (Cambridge: Cambridge University Press, 1938); R. Bultmann, *The Gospel of John* (Oxford: Basil Blackwell, 1971); C.H. Dodd, *Historical Tradition in the Fourth Gospel* (Cambridge: Cambridge University Press, 1963).

6.   This was emphasized by J. Schniewind, *Die Parallelperikopen bei Lukas und Johannes* (Leipzig: J.C. Hinrichs, 1914; repr. Hildesheim: G. Olms, 1958) although Schniewind also believed that John's account presupposed (p. 99) that of the Synoptic Gospels.

7.   E.g. R.E. Brown, *The Gospel According to John* (AB; 2 vols.; Garden City, NY: Doubleday, 1966, 1970); Martyn, *History and Theology*; D.M. Smith, *Johannine Christianity: Essays in its Setting, Sources and Theology* (Columbia, SC: University of South Carolina Press, 1984), although in his more recent book, *John Among the Gospels* (Minneapolis: Augsburg–Fortress, 1992), Smith leaves the question open.

8.   See, e.g., A. Dauer, *Johannes und Lukas* (FzB, 50; Würzburg: Echter Verlag, 1984), p. 35. Dauer believes that the Synoptics have influenced the (possibly written) tradition which forms John's source.

whether common oral traditions would so often agree so minutely. They instead propose that there may be some more direct relationship between the texts, which must remain the most economical of the explanations offered. Thus even though some scholars would regard the connections between John and the Synoptics as probably to be explained by the use of common traditions,[9] others have maintained that there is a direct literary connection,[10] and some[11] have argued for the existence of a (lost) common source. A combination of any or all of these positions is possible; they are not mutually exclusive, and each could be true in some instances. It must be emphasized that the three Synoptic Gospels are not necessarily to be grouped together, in any case. The connection between any one Synoptic and John could be of a literary nature, whereas that between the others could be at the level of common traditions. We can only hypothesize, and select the model which in statistician's terminology would be called the 'best fit' for the evidence we have.

9.   E.g. J.A. Bailey, *Traditions Common to the Gospels of St Luke and St John* (NovTSup, 7; Leiden: E.J. Brill, 1963); D.W.C. Robinson, *Selected Material Common to the Third and Fourth Gospels* (MLitt dissertation, Oxford University, 1979). It should be noted that both Bailey and Robinson also consider that in some cases the relationship may be a literary one.

10.   E.g. C.K. Barrett, 'John and the Synoptic Gospels', *ExpTim* 85 (1974), pp. 228-33; *The Gospel According to John* (London: SCM Press, 2nd edn, 1978); *idem*, 'The Place of John and the Synoptists within the Early History of Christian Thought', in A. Denaux (ed.), *John and the Synoptics* (Proceedings of the 1990 Leuven Colloquium; BETL, 101; Leuven: Leuven University Press, 1992), pp. 63-79; W.G. Kümmel, *Introduction to the New Testament* (Nashville: Abingdon Press; London: SCM Press, 1975); F. Neirynck, *Jean et les Synoptiques* (BETL, 49; Leuven: Leuven University Press, 1979); *Evangelica*, I (BETL, 60; Leuven: Leuven University Press, 1982), pp. 297-455; 'John and the Synoptics, 1975–1990', in A. Denaux (ed.), *John and the Synoptics* (Proceedings of the 1990 Leuven Colloquium; BETL, 101; Leuven: Leuven University Press), pp. 3-62; M. Sabbe, *Studia neotestamentica* (BETL, 98; Leuven: Leuven University Press, 1991), pp. 355-88, 409-513; H. Thyen, 'Johannes und die Synoptiker', in A. Denaux (ed.), *John and the Synoptics* (Proceedings of the 1990 Leuven Colloquium; BETL, 101; Leuven: Leuven University Press), pp. 81-107.

11.   E.g. V. Taylor, *Behind the Third Gospel* (Oxford: Clarendon Press,1926); *idem*, *Passion Narrative*; H. Klein, 'Die lukanische-johanneische Passionstradition', *ZNW* 67 (1976), pp. 155-86; I. Buse, 'St John and the Passion Narratives of St Matthew and St Luke', *NTS* 7 (1960), pp. 65-76; A.R.C. Leaney, 'The Resurrection Narratives in St Luke', *NTS* 2 (1955), pp. 110-14.

7.3. *Luke and John*

7.3.1. *Introduction*

Many critics (including most of the above) have observed how numerous are the points of contact between the Gospels of Luke and John. It was calculated by Pierson Parker[12] that whereas John agrees with Mark 19 times, Matthew 24 times and both against Luke 23 times, he agrees with Luke alone 124 times. On the basis of these figures, he seems to mean not merely common ideas and/or the odd detail and isolated word, but also close verbal agreements extending to a phrase or more, since he estimates that phrases in common between Luke and John exceed by a ratio of 5:1 those connecting John with Matthew or Mark. The evidence offered by Parker shows that the agreements between Luke and John alone extend throughout both Gospels.[13] And although some of the contacts between John and Luke cited by Parker are not made sufficiently precise,[14] and hence fail to carry conviction, the sheer quantity of them would seem to require some explanation. Taylor regarded the Markan material in Luke as a later insertion into an original and related Johannine/Lukan core; Klein, too, saw a fixed common pre-Markan Passion tradition underlying John and Luke. Parker,[15] who examined the many correspondences between the two in detail, and showed that it is very difficult to argue convincingly that John used Luke,[16] still maintained the literary independence of the two Gospels, despite the evidence to the contrary that his own article had highlighted. But since, to him, some tangible link between their Gospels was self-evident, he concluded that the two men must have met frequently

12. Parker, 'Luke', pp. 317-36.

13. Contra L. Morris, *Studies in the Fourth Gospel* (Grand Rapids: Eerdmans, 1969), p. 41, we should not dismiss them as limited to 'the resurrection appearances… and a number of smaller points'.

14. E.g. Parker, 'Luke', p. 330: 'The circumstances in Matthew (Mt. 28.16-20) and John are totally different… John 21 is, in fact, much more like Lk. 5.1-11'. There is no detailed analysis of the text to support this assertion and to explain the many points of contact between Luke and John in this pericope.

15. Parker, 'Luke', pp. 331ff. His arguments are very similar to those which led Gardner-Smith, Bultmann and Dodd to maintain the complete independence of the Johannine tradition.

16. H. Klein, 'Die lukanische-johanneische Passionstradition', p. 167, calls this proposal 'ausgeschlossen'.

on missions.[17] I shall look at those sections where the two Gospels are acknowledged to be very close, namely their accounts of Jesus' Passion and Resurrection, before considering the question of chronology and the change in Luke's usual practices in Quadruple Tradition passages with regard to usage of Mark and citations from Scripture, and then finally reviewing critical opinion on the order Luke and John were written. This forms a necessary prelude to my detailed analysis of the parallel pericopes which follows.

7.3.2. *Passion/Resurrection*

The correspondences between Luke and John are most evident in their presentations of the Passion and Resurrection, where there are some striking shared omissions of material included by Mark and Matthew, as the following summary will show:[18]

Items in Mark's Passion which are shared by Matthew but not Luke or John

1. The quotation of Zech. 13.7 by Jesus, and the accompanying predictions (Mk 14.27-28; Mt. 26.31-32).
2. Jesus' statements to Peter, James and John after he has left them and returned in Gethsemane (Mk 14.38-42; Mt. 26.41-46).
3. The fact that Judas had arranged to give the crowd from the Jewish authorities a sign (Mk 14.44; Mt. 26.48).
4. The action of the crowd, seizing Jesus before the disciples struck out in his defence (Mk 14.46; Mt. 26.51b).
5. The flight of the disciples (Mk 14.49-52; Mt. 26.55b-56).
6. The night 'hearing' conducted by the Sanhedrin, and the presence there of false witnesses who tell of Jesus' threats against the Temple (Mk 14.55-59; Mt. 26.59-61).
7. The High Priest's command to Jesus to answer the charge, and Jesus' silence (Mk 14.60-61; Mt. 26.62); the reference to the Son of Man coming with/on the clouds of heaven (Mk 14.62; Mt. 26.64).

17. Parker, 'Luke', p. 336. Cf. the view of E. Osty, 'Les points de contact entre le récit de la Passion dans S. Luc et dans S. Jean', *RSR* 39 (1951), pp. 146-54, who suggested that Luke must have heard John preach (p. 154).

18. This summary is adapted from M. Soards, *The Passion According to Luke: The Special Material of Luke 22* (JSNTSup, 14; Sheffield: Sheffield Academic Press, 1987), pp. 14-15.

8. The explicit statement that Jesus has committed blasphemy (though this is implied by Lk. 22.71), and the unanimous verdict —death—by the Council (Mk 14.64; Mt. 26.65-66).
9. Peter's invocation of a curse on himself and swearing (Mk 14.71; Mt. 26.74).
10. An accusation by the Chief Priests before Pilate; Pilate's command to answer, and Jesus' silence (Mk 15.3-5; Mt. 27.12-14).
11. Pilate's offer to release Jesus, since he perceives the Chief Priests' envy; the Chief Priests' incitement to the crowd to call for Barabbas (Mk 15.10-11; Mt. 27.17-20).
12. The mocking of Jesus by the onlookers, with a repetition of the charge against the Temple, and the injunction to come down from the cross (Mk 15.29-32; Mt. 27.39-42).
13. The unqualified statement (Mk 15.32; Mt. 27.44) that those crucified with him also reviled him (John makes no mention of this at all; Luke takes the opportunity to draw a contrast between the two malefactors and illustrate his favourite theme of repentance/forgiveness).
14. The 'cry of dereliction' and the crowd's misinterpretation of it (Mk 15.34-36; Mt. 27.46-49).
15. The naming of the women who saw where Jesus was buried (Mk 15.40; Mt. 27.56).

It must, however, be acknowledged that arguments which are based on shared omissions like these are of doubtful value when one is attempting to demonstrate a relationship between two texts, even when they are as striking as nos. 4-6, or 10-12, for which some explanation is clearly required. More significant, and suggestive of a more direct connection between Luke and John than that of a common tradition, are the many occasions when both share material that Mark and Matthew lack, especially since in many cases this shared material is expressed in the same or similar words. The following is a summary of the main points of correspondence:

Items in Luke's Passion which are shared
by John but not Mark or Matthew

1. A 'farewell discourse' (Lk. 22.14-38; Jn 13.31–17.26).
2. The reference to Satan/the Devil in connection with Judas (Lk. 22.3; Jn 13.2, 27).

3.   Jesus' behaviour at the arrest: in both he is in control (Lk. 22.49; Jn 18.8).

4.   The reference to the *right* ear being cut off. (In addition, although Luke's οὖς at Lk. 22.50 is a stylistic improvement on the vulgar Markan/Johannine ὠτάριον [Mk 14.47; Jn 18.10], both Luke and John in their second reference to the ear use ὠτίον [Lk. 22.51; Jn 18.26]).

5.   The reference at Lk. 22.53 to the ὥρα[19] (which John consistently applies to the Passion; e.g. Jn 12.27) and to the 'power of darkness' (a frequent Johannine symbol; see, e.g., Jn 1.5; 3.19; 8.12, and cf. 13.30).

6.   Both Luke and John portray Judas as more active in Jesus' arrest. In John, he has procured a cohort of soldiers (Jn 18.3) and also Jewish officers: in Luke, he leads the arresting party, as the verb προέρχομαι at 22.47 shows (contra Mark's παραγίνομαι at Mk 14.43; or Matthew's ἔρχομαι at Mt. 26.47).

7.   The threefold declaration of Jesus' innocence by Pilate (Lk. 23.4, 15, 22; Jn 18.38; 19.4, 6).

8.   The presence of two angels at the tomb (Lk. 24.4; Jn 20.12).

9.   More than one disciple go to investigate the woman's/women's report (Lk. 24.24; Jn 20.3-8).

10. The circumstances of Peter's visit to the tomb (Lk. 24.12; Jn 20.3-8).

11. The Jerusalem Resurrection appearances, and the display of Jesus' wounds to the disciples (Lk. 24.36-43; Jn 20.19-29).

12. The bestowal of the Holy Spirit (Jn 20.22; Acts 2.3).

13. The Ascension (referred to, Jn 20.17; narrated, Lk. 24.50-51; Acts 1.9-10).

---

19.   While it is true that Mk 14.41 (cf. Mk 14.35) and Mt. 26.45 both use ὥρα with reference to the Passion, it is nevertheless characteristically Johannine to qualify it and make it specific. Thus only John has 'my hour'/'his hour' in this context (see Jn 2.4; 7.30; 8.20; 13.1; cf. 12.27). Similarly, Luke here says '*your* hour', and he combines it with a very Johannine symbol in a sentence which has no parallel in Mark or Matthew. We may note that if John at this point were using Luke (or a source shared by Luke) his omission of such a sentence, which one would have expected to be congenial to him, seems almost inexplicable, as R.E. Brown, *Gospel According to John*, II, p. 817, observes.

7.3.3. *Chronology*

It will be noted that many of these points of contact relate to chronology, since Luke and John often agree as to placement and timing, even when the words they use differ, and this is the more remarkable in view of Luke's fidelity to Mark's order (often against Matthew) elsewhere. Luke is very careful about chronology; his prologue states that putting existing narratives about Jesus 'in order' (καθεξῆς, Lk. 1.3) is his purpose in writing.[20] F. Lamar Cribbs, who reached conclusions similar to my own concerning the relationship of the Gospels of Luke and John,[21] pointed out[22] that in the blocks of Triple Tradition material, of the 71 shared pericopes, Luke follows Mark's order in 64, of which only 42 are in the same position in Matthew. But in the 24 narrative pericopes shared also by John the situation is very different. In 11 cases (John the Baptist; his Messianic Preaching; the Baptism; the Entry into Jerusalem; Jesus is Taken to Pilate; the Death Sentence; the Journey to the Cross; the Crucifixion; the Death of Jesus; the Burial; the Resurrection),[23] there is no problem, since the sequence is the same in all four Gospels. In three cases, however—the Call of the Disciples, the Anointing of Jesus, and the Mocking of Jesus—where the Johannine and the Markan/Matthaean material conflict, Luke rewrites the incident and places his own version of it at a different point in the narrative:[24]

20. A.M. Perry, *The Sources of Luke's Passion Narrative* (Chicago: University of Chicago Press, 1920), p. 5, notes that Luke is careful to avoid suggesting temporal connections which are not explicitly made by Mark but could have been inferred from his text: cf. Mk 2.1/Lk. 5.17; Mk 3.1/Lk. 6.6; Mk 3.13/Lk. 6.12.

21. See F.L. Cribbs, 'St Luke and the Johannine Tradition', *JBL* 90 (1971), pp. 422-50; *idem*, *'A Study of the Contacts Between St Luke and St John'*, in G.W. MacRae (ed.), *SBLSP*, 12 (Cambridge, MA: Scholars Press, 1973), I, pp. 1-93; *idem*, 'Agreements between John and Acts', pp. 40-61. The same points are made by Cribbs, and supported by more statistical data, in *idem*, 'The Agreements that Exist Between Luke and John', in P.J. Achtemeier (ed.), *SBLSP*, 18 (Missoula, MT: Scholars Press, 1979), I, pp. 215-61.

22. Cribbs, 'Study of the Contacts', p. 9.

23. I have omitted from consideration the 'Words of Institution', since Luke's text is disputed here, Lk. 22.19b-20 being a notorious crux. If we accept the authenticity of the longer version, then Luke on this occasion, too, follows Matthew and Mark, although it could be argued that the footwashing, which is of comparable significance, occupies a similar place in John.

24. In these examples Luke not only rewrites the material, but also places it differently from all the other evangelists. Cribbs ('Study of the Contacts', pp. 37, 61) also instances the Prediction of Peter's Denial at Lk. 22.31-34, and the Hearing by

	Luke	Matthew	Mark	John
Call of the Disciples	5.1-11	4.18-22	1.16-20	1.35-50
Anointing	7.36-50	26.6-13	14.3-9	12.1-8
Mocking	23.6-12	27.27-31	15.16-20	19.2-5

Luke shares features of John's order in 7: the Feeding of the Five Thousand; Peter's Confession (which in both Luke and John is placed very close to the Feeding, without much other Galilaean and non-Galilaean material intervening); the Last Supper[25] (where the prediction of the betrayal occurs during the meal in Mark/Matthew, but after the cup/foot-washing in Luke and John, who both share a farewell discourse after the meal and before the arrest); the Prediction of Peter's Denial (which both Luke and John place at the supper rather than in the garden later); the Arrest (which both Luke and John place at the end of the scene); the Sanhedrin Trial (which does not take place at night in either Gospel: their placement of Peter's denial is similar, too); and the Hearing by Pilate (where there are numerous correspondences of presentation, including the thrice-repeated declaration of innocence). In only three cases—the Betrayal, the Cleansing of the Temple, and the Conspiracy to Capture Jesus—does Luke follow Mark/Matthew against John for the entire pericope, and even here Luke is vague at 19.47 about when precisely the conspiracy sequence took place, unlike Mark/Matthew, and he thus avoids directly contradicting John. Such a departure from Luke's normal practice in pericopes shared by John would therefore strongly suggest that Luke is indeed following another tradition here, which he considered more reliable in some respects.[26]

If John were using Luke, it is rather remarkable that in so many cases he used precisely those pericopes where Luke's chronology and/or placement differed from those of Mark/Matthew, and that he failed to use so many of

Pilate at 22.66-71; the denial sequence itself is similar, since the order of John's narrative at Jn 18.25-27 is different from that in Mark and Matthew, and Luke recasts it altogether. The last three examples show Luke more or less in agreement with John and therefore I have considered them below.

25. Although the timing of the Supper in relation to Passover is probably that of Mark/Matthew rather than that of John, Luke's verb ἐγγίζω at Lk. 22.1 is much less precise than Mark's and Matthew's μετὰ δύο ἡμέρας (we recall that John simply says πρὸ). It is thus quite possible, as is suggested by Taylor, *Passion Narrative*, p. 37, that Lk. 22.16 implies an unfulfilled wish to eat the Passover, which may have some connection with John's chronology.

26. Similarly Perry, *Sources*, p. 5.

the others. If, however, Luke was secondary, his purpose is clearer; he was trying to mediate between two conflicting traditions and thus to give ἀσφάλειαν (Lk. 1.4) to his audience.[27]

7.3.4. *Verbal Relationship with Mark*

There is evidence, too, that Luke is departing from his usual practice in other respects in pericopes shared by John as well as by Matthew and Mark, namely the pronounced reduction in the verbal agreements between Mark and Luke, which occasioned comment from V. Taylor.[28] Cribbs observes[29] that whereas verbally Luke is quite close to Mark in Triple Tradition pericopes which have no Johannine parallel (such as Lk. 4.38-44; 5.12–6.11; 8.4-56; 9.23-36)—where the percentage for agreement normally exceeds 51 per cent,[30] and sometimes 75 per cent[31]—in passages where all four Gospels[32] contain parallel material the verbal agreement with Mark seldom exceeds 25 per cent, and is occasionally under 12 per cent,[33] as Taylor showed. He concludes that Luke had preferred a non-Markan source here.[34] Moreover, the agreement with John in these

27. B. Weiss, *Die Quellen des Lukasevangeliums* (Stuttgart: J.G. Cotta, 1907), pp. 276ff. also saw Luke as attempting to harmonize three different sources: Q, Mark, and his special source, L (which had many connections with the Johannine tradition, especially in the Passion).

28. Taylor makes this observation in both *Behind the Third Gospel*, *passim*, and *Passion Narrative*, pp. 41ff.

29. Cribbs, 'Study of the Contacts', p. 8.

30. There are a very few exceptions: in the Transfiguration, for example, the figure is 37.2 per cent (cf. Lk. 9.28-36; Mk 9.2-10), and in healing summaries, such as those at Lk. 4.40-41; 6.17-19, it is around 34 per cent. But these are atypical.

31. Taylor, *Behind the Third Gospel*, p. 84, estimates that the agreement between Lk. 9.23-27 and Mk 8.34–9.1, on discipleship, is 83.9 per cent.

32. See especially Lk. 19.37-40; 22.14-23, 31-34, 39-71; 23.1-5, 13-38, 50-56; 24.1-12.

33. See Taylor, *Behind the Third Gospel*, pp. 35ff. Thus in the (Markan) Preparations for the Passover (Lk. 22.7-13), he calculates that the agreement is 65.2 per cent; but in the Approach to Jerusalem (Lk. 19.37-40) it is 11.4 per cent, and in the Journey to the Cross at Lk. 22.26-33 it is less than 13 per cent, with 11 of the 14 common words occurring in v. 36, a verse where Luke follows Mark in the reference to Simon of Cyrene since this suits the theme of discipleship the two evangelists share. Elsewhere, Luke rewrites Mark.

34. Taylor, *Behind the Third Gospel*, e.g. pp. 37, 40, 42. B. Weiss, *Die Quellen*, regarded Mark as a secondary source for Luke. P. Winter, *On the Trial Of Jesus* (ed.

pericopes is frequently appreciably higher than 12 per cent; thus in the approach to Jerusalem at Lk. 19.37-40, where words shared with Mark amount to only 11.4 per cent, the agreement with John is 23 per cent—granted that there is some variation in the grammatical cases of the references to the Pharisees and the disciples (both of which groups, significantly, are mentioned at this point only by Luke and John). Similarly, the agreement between Lk. 24.1-11 and Mk 16.1-8 is 21.4 per cent; but if we uphold the authenticity of Lk. 24.12, as I shall argue below on manuscript evidence that we should, then Lk. 24.1-12 has 41 out of 181 words in common with Jn 20.1-18, which is nearly 24 per cent.

7.3.5. *Scriptural Citations*

There is a similar discrepancy between Luke's treatment of citations from Scripture in Triple Tradition pericopes and in those shared also with John. In Triple Tradition passages, Luke follows Mark/Matthew quite closely. Thus he reproduces ten:[35]

	Matthew	Mark	Luke
Isa. 42.1; Gen. 22.2	3.17b	1.11	3.22b
Lev. 13.49; 14.2-9	8.4	1.44	5.14
Isa. 6.9-10	13.13-15	4.12	8.10b
Deut. 6.5; Lev.19.18	22.37-39	12.30-31	10.27-28
Exod. 20.12-16	19.18-19	10.19	18.20
Deut. 5.16-20;			
Ps. 118.22	21.42	12.10-11	20.17
Deut. 25.5	22.24	12.19	20.28
Exod. 3.6	22.32a	12.26	20.37b
Ps. 110.1	22.44	12.36	20.42-43
Dan. 7.13-14	24.30b	13.26	21.27

Two others are alluded to by Luke, and quoted in Mark/Matthew:

Isaiah	Matthew	Mark	Luke
5.2	21.33	12.1	20.9
13.10	24.29	13.24-25	21.25-26

T.A. Burkill and G. Vermes; SJ, 1; Berlin: W. de Gruyter, 2nd edn, 1974); and Perry, *Sources*, also believed that Luke seems to have followed a non-Markan source for much of his Passion.

35. Adapted from the list given by Cribbs, 'Study of the Contacts', p. 23. It should be noted that Isa. 42.1; Gen. 2.22, a composite citation, is replaced in many Lukan texts by a quotation from Ps. 2.7.

while another two are allusions in all three evangelists:

	Matthew	Mark	Luke
Dan. 4.21	13.32	4.32	13.19
Gen. 19.17	24.18	13.16	17.31

The only omissions[36] in Luke are in the apocalyptic discourse, which he modifies and extensively rewrites, splitting the material into two speeches at Lk. 17.20-37; 21.8-36.[37]

In the 24 narrative pericopes shared by all four evangelists, however, Luke almost always uses only those which John either alludes to:

Psalms	Matthew	Mark	Luke	John
69.21	27.48	15.36	23.36	19.29
38.11	27.55	15.40	23.49	19.25

(where Luke shares μακρόθεν at 23.49 with Mark/Matthew and εἱστ-ήκεισαν with John)

Isaiah	Matthew	Mark	Luke	John
50.6	20.19	10.34	18.32, 33	18.22

or cites explicitly; thus:[38]

	Matthew	Mark	Luke	John
Isa. 40.3	3.3	1.3	3.4	1.23
Ps. 118.26	21.9	11.9	19.38	12.13
Ps. 41.9	26.23	14.20	22.21	13.18
Ps. 22.18	27.35	15.24	23.34	19.24

The only exceptions are an allusion to Ps. 110.1 at Lk. 22.69 (cf. Mt. 26.64; Mk 14.62)[39] and the citation of Isa. 56.7; Jer. 7.11 at Lk. 19.46 (cf. Mt. 21.13; Mk 11.17) in the Cleansing of the Temple pericope which Luke, like Mark and Matthew, places at the end of Jesus' ministry rather than at the beginning like John. (Prayer is in any case a favourite Lukan theme, as is censure of the rich: this conflation would have been

36. Dan. 9.27; 12.11 in Mt. 24.15, Mk 13.14; Dan. 12.1 in Mt. 24.21, Mk 13.19; Deut. 13.2 in Mt. 24.24, Mk 13.22.

37. The 'sheep without a shepherd' citation of Num. 27.17 is used by Mark and Matthew in different contexts (which may be why Luke has omitted it), and I have therefore ignored it.

38. Adapted from Cribbs, 'Study of the Contacts', pp. 24-25.

39. Christ's exaltation, which is how the synoptic evangelists interpreted this reference, is in any case assumed by John's repeated wordplay on the verb ὑψόω, even if he does not quote this verse.

particularly congenial to him.) Luke uncharacteristically omits the other five shared by Mark and Matthew,[40] as well as all the citations which appear in only one of the other Gospels. Here, too, we see evidence that Luke is acting differently in pericopes common to all four evangelists than in those when he is simply following Mark and Matthew, which suggests that some other influence is at work. And since this other influence is only apparent in material shared also by John, the obvious inference is that it is John. Luke is seemingly attempting to reconcile conflicting Synoptic and Johannine traditions, and in some respects the connections between Luke and John here are at least as close as those linking Luke with the other Synoptics.

7.3.6. A Critique of Scholars' Views on the Relationship of Luke and John
It would, nevertheless, be true to say that detailed studies of the connections between the Gospels of Luke and John, such as those by A. Dauer, E. Osty, M.-E. Boismard, J.A. Bailey and F. Neirynck, all assume rather than prove that Luke was written before that of John.[41] Dauer's view, which is shared by many (including Schniewind), is that John's Gospel

---

40. Zech. 13.7 at Mt. 26.31, Mk 14.27; Ps. 42.6, 11 at Mt. 26.38, Mk 14.34; Dan. 7.13a at Mt. 26.64, Mk 14.62 (no 'coming on/with the clouds of Heaven' in Lk. 22.69; the reference is only to the enthronement); Ps. 22.7 at Mt. 27.39, Mk 15.29; Ps. 22.1 at Mt. 27.46, Mk 15.34.

41. Dauer, *Johannes und Lukas*; Osty, 'Points de contact'; J.A. Bailey, *Traditions*; M.-E. Boismard, 'S. Luc et la rédaction du quatrième évangile', *RB* 69 (1962), pp. 185-211; Neirynck, *Jean et les Synoptiques*. An exception is W. Gericke, 'Zur Enstehung des Johannes-Evangeliums', *TLZ* 90 (1965), Nr.11, pp. 807-20. Gericke believes that John's Gospel was written before Nero's death in 68 CE, and that it served as an inspiration—though not a direct source (see p. 816)—for Luke's. But his argument is concerned with establishing an early date for John; with regard to Luke, he confines himself almost entirely to a consideration of Luke's prologue and barely mentions the rest of his Gospel. Gericke reverses the usual pattern; he asserts rather than demonstrates Johannine priority. A. Loisy, *L'Evangile selon Luc*, regards some portions of Luke's Gospel—the post-Resurrection accounts, and the Miraculous Catch—as reflecting Johannine influence on a later redactor, who considerably expanded and modified Luke's original narrative to Theophilus. The 'Johannine redactor' is also assumed by others such as F.C. Grant, 'Was the Author of John Dependent upon the Gospel of Luke?', *JBL* 56 (1937), pp. 285-307; K. Curtis, 'Luke 24:12 and John 20:3-10', *JTS* NS 22 (1971), pp. 512-15; and R. Mahoney, *Two Disciples at the Tomb* (TW, 6; Bern-Frankfurt: H. Lang, 1972), to explain why on occasions Luke's account seems secondary to John's.

presupposes[42] the Lukan account, which Dauer believed had already influenced the material John used and reworked: Similarities between the Johannine story and the Lukan account(s) have in consequence come about in this way; the latter, in the course of the oral tradition, have influenced the pre-Johannine story, which will itself have been developed from the Markan.[43]

It is thus typical that, in his very full consideration of the changes in critical opinion since the publication of Schniewind's book in 1914, Dauer[44] does not even consider the possibility that Luke may have used John, rather than the reverse. In his review of the various explanations which can be offered for the connections between Luke and John—Johannine dependence on Luke; Johannine reminiscences of Luke (though not written dependence); John's knowledge and use of Luke's source; a written source common to both evangelists; a common or related oral tradition used by both— the suggestion that perhaps John could have been a source for Luke is never made. That some (he cites, especially, Cribbs) have proposed that Luke may have been acquainted with the developing Johannine tradition[45] he acknowledges briefly, but does not discuss further. The same is true in his consideration of individual pericopes: he does not consider the suggestion that Luke's Gospel could have been secondary to John's, except when he is defending the authenticity of certain disputed passages of the text of Lk. 24.34-39 against a charge of possible (Johannine) interpolation. Luke's possible secondariness to John elsewhere he ignores.

Critics such as Dauer do not realize, apparently, that the evidence they offer, far from demonstrating Lukan priority to John, in many cases seems to suggest the opposite. A typical example is J.A. Bailey's consideration of Lk. 22.31-34, where he finds Luke's presentation somewhat awkward, in that Jesus' intercessory prayer at v. 31 is followed in v. 34 by a prediction of Peter's denial.[46] Bailey believes that Luke has combined here two differing written fragments, which explains the variation between Σίμων in v. 31 and Πέτρε in v. 34. He suggests that John has recast Luke's narrative, placing Jesus' prayer for Peter later in his text (at Jn

42. Dauer, *Johannes und Lukas*, p. 35.
43. Dauer, *Johannes und Lukas*, p. 206; my translation.
44. Dauer, *Johannes und Lukas*, pp. 15-38.
45. This phrase, although it is certainly used by Cribbs ('Study of the Contacts', p. 3), is actually a quotation from R.E. Brown, *Gospel According to John*, II, p. 791.
46. See Bailey, *Traditions*, pp. 37-42, especially p. 38 n. 4, where he refers to the 'odd composition' of vv. 31-34.

17.15), and has reworked the whole account to accord with his own emphasis—that where Jesus is going the disciples cannot follow (see 13.33). John therefore reserves the 'rehabilitation' of Peter until after the Resurrection. But although Bailey's explanation could be correct, it is equally possible that Luke has modified John's account to mitigate Peter's guilt by the insertion of vv. 31-32, which Bailey himself sees as in some tension with vv. 33-34. Indeed, this explanation would be in line with Luke's practice elsewhere, since he repeatedly softens Markan criticism of the disciples, especially Peter.

The Anointing of Jesus is another case in point. Although many would regard Luke's text as the more coherent here, the tensions which some critics have found in John's version do not necessarily show that his is secondary[47] (at least in respect of Luke's), and that he or his hypothetical source has made a very clumsy attempt to combine differing traditions. The argument, as is so often the case, is reversible; Luke could equally have woven the two accounts together—the Johannine and the Markan— and integrated them skilfully into his own text by using the pericope to illustrate his favourite theme of repentance/forgiveness. A narrative which is secondary is not *ipso facto* inferior.

It is possible that the question may hitherto have been considered from the wrong angle. If we examine the evidence offered by the two Gospels without any preconvictions as to priority, then we must conclude that the case for the secondariness of John to Luke is still unproven, as has been consistently argued by Cribbs in all his articles. J.F. Coakley, too[48] has made this point regarding the Anointing. Indeed, V. Taylor,[49] in his consideration of the Lukan Passion narrative, and J.M. Creed, in his commentary on the miraculous catch, both thought that on occasions John's use of the material appeared 'more original',[50] even though they regarded the connection between the two texts as being the result of a related or common source.[51] R.E. Brown, too, who felt that the many connections

47. Cf. R. Schnackenburg, *The Gospel According to St John*, II (New York: Crossroad, 1980), p. 367; Fortna, *Gospel of Signs*, pp. 150 n. 3, p. 152.

48. J.F. Coakley, 'The Anointing at Bethany and the Priority of John', *JBL* 107 (1988), pp. 241-56.

49. Taylor, *Passion Narrative*.

50. Creed, *Luke*, p. 73.

51. Thus, too, Leaney, 'Resurrection Narratives', p. 111, '*Unless* we are to believe that Luke was based on John, we must recognize the existence of similar sources used by the two independently...' (emphasis mine). Leaney does not appear to consider the first possibility.

between the Lukan and the Johannine Passion accounts were 'too precise to be accidental', suggested that Luke may have been acquainted with 'an early form of the developing Johannine tradition'.[52]

It will become clear from the following analysis that any assumption of Lukan priority on literary grounds rests on very shaky foundations, since it is quite impossible on most occasions to tell which came first, Luke's account or John's. There are, however, some suggestive indications, and the nature and number of these are such as to make it appear worthwhile to challenge the hypothesis that Luke is prior to John, and to consider what are the implications for our appreciation of Luke's technique and purpose if the reverse is true. Although it is not possible to prove the case either way, just as it is not possible to prove the existence (or otherwise) of linked traditions, my proposal that Luke is secondary to John is consistently supported by the evidence of the material they share in their Gospels. I shall begin by reviewing those pericopes where, despite many similarities, it is not possible to say which Gospel came first, and then I shall consider those where the connections between them are less apparent. Next, I shall study one pericope that might suggest Johannine dependence on Luke, and finally, I shall examine in detail those pericopes where the evidence seems to point very clearly in the other direction.

7.4. *Comparison of Parallel Passages in Luke and John*

7.4.1. *John the Baptist (Luke 3.2-22; John 1.19-36)*

It is evident that the baptism of Jesus proved an embarrassment to the early Church, especially as christological thinking developed, since the implication of the act is the washing away of sins. Thus Matthew at 3.14-15 modifies Mark's account both to stress Jesus' superiority and to remove any imputation that Jesus was a sinner (compare, too, Jn 1.19-30); his baptism, on the contrary, fulfils all righteousness. John omits any reference to the Baptist actually baptizing Jesus; his account presents the recognition by the Baptist of Jesus as 'The Lamb of God who takes away the sins of the world', which emphasizes that it is not baptism which removes our sins, but the sacrificial death of Jesus. Luke treats the baptism in a participial phrase which one can almost overlook, Καὶ Ἰησοῦ βαπτισθέντος might so that, as in John, one is merely left to assume that it was performed by the Baptist. Luke prefers to stress the descent of the Spirit at the

---

52. R.E. Brown, *Gospel According to John*, II, p. 791.

baptism, because this connects with the later spread of the Church; it is a link forward to Acts.

It seems clear that both Luke and John have modified the narrative in accordance with their own particular concerns, and at first sight Luke seems much closer to Mark and Matthew than he is to John.[53] Nevertheless, there are some important thematic links between Luke and John, and these are often overlooked. Thus both present the Baptist as God's witness to Jesus; John's text emphasizes the Baptist's witness and subordination to Jesus at 1.30-34, and Luke presents this dramatically as beginning *in utero* in his birth narrative.[54] 'Witnessing' is a theme which Luke does not derive from Mark/Matthew. It is repeated throughout Luke–Acts from the αὐτόπται in 1.2 onwards, being especially important in Acts, and it is heavily emphasized throughout the entire Johannine tradition, too.[55] In John's Gospel, this is the function of the Beloved Disciple, who witnesses everything from the beginning, if we assume that the unnamed 'other disciple' of the Baptist who follows Jesus at Jn 1.35-42 is to be identified with him, as many critics suppose.[56]

It is noticeable that in their accounts of the baptism neither Luke nor John associates the Baptist with Elijah, even though this is certainly implied in Luke's birth narrative at 1.17, 76, and later at 7.27: there are tensions in Luke here. Cribbs suggests that in his Gospel Luke seems to be 'taking a middle position between the Matthacan/Markan and the Johannine positions'.[57] Thus while John firmly refutes the identification of the Baptist and Elijah at Jn 1.21 Luke is less explicit, although he, like John, omits the description of the Baptist given in Mk 1.6; Mt. 3.4 which alludes to that of Elijah in 2 Kgs 1.8, just as he later omits the Coming of Elijah pericope after the transfiguration, contra Mark and Matthew, and he provides no parallel to Mt. 11.14, where John the Baptist is quite positively identified with Elijah. Moreover, Luke does not include the ὀπίσω μου

53. Cf. Lk. 3.3, Mt. 3.5b, Mk 1.4b; Lk. 3.16b, Mk 1.7b; Lk. 3.7b-9, Mt. 3.7b-10; Lk. 3.17, Mt. 3.12.

54. This emphasis was perhaps especially necessary to counter claims made by followers of John the Baptist, which may be reflected in Acts 18–19.

55. As noted in the preceding chapter, there are marked similarities in the treatment of this theme by Luke and John.

56. See, e.g., H. Thyen, 'Entwicklungen der johanneische Theologie', in M. de Jonge (ed.), *L'Evangile de Jean* (BETL, 44; Leuven: Leuven University Press, 1977), pp. 259-99, esp. pp. 274ff.

57. Cribbs, 'St Luke', p. 429. Joynes, pp. 25, 27, 32 also finds evidence of a conflict of traditions in Luke on this topic.

reference (Mk 1.7; Mt. 3.11, cf. Jn 1.27)[58] which presented the Baptist as Jesus' precursor, perhaps because many expected Elijah to return in the Last Days (see Mal. 3.1; 4.5; Sir. 48.10) and he wished to avoid the identification of the two here.[59]

There are other features peculiar to Luke and John. Both include speculations by the Jews as to John's identity and significance (cf. Jn 1.19-22; Lk. 3.15); both include a denial by the Baptist that he is the Messiah (Jn 1.20; Acts 13.25); both imply some kind of an itinerant ministry by the Baptist (Lk. 3.3; Jn 1.28; 3.22-23, 26; 10.40). And although Luke is very close verbally to Mk 1.7; Mt. 3.11 at Lk. 3.16, Cribbs[60] has demonstrated that the Lukan version is in some respects as close to John as it is to Mark or Matthew:

Lk. 3.16a	ἀπεκρίνατο λέγων πᾶσιν ὁ Ἰωάννης
Jn 1.26a	ἀπεκρίθη αὐτοῖς ὁ Ἰωάννης λέγων
Lk. 3.16b	Ἐγὼ μὲν ὕδατι βαπτίζω ὑμᾶς
Mt. 3.11a	ἐγὼ μὲν ὑμᾶς βαπτίζω ἐν ὕδατι
Lk. 3.16c	ἔρχεται δὲ ὁ ἰσχυρότερός μου
Mt. 3.11b	ἐρχόμενος ἰσχυρότερός μού ἐστιν
Mk 1.7b	ἔρχεται ὁ ἰσχυρότερός μου
Lk. 3.16d[a]	οὗ οὐκ εἰμὶ ἱκανὸς λῦσαι τὸν ἱμάντα τῶν ὑποδημάτων αὐτοῦ
Mk 1.7c	οὗ οὐκ εἰμὶ ἱκανὸς κύψας λῦσαι τὸν ἱμάντα τῶν ὑποδημάτων αὐτοῦ
Lk. 3.16e	αὐτὸς ὑμᾶς βαπτίσει ἐν πνεύματι ἁγίῳ καὶ πυρί
Mk 1.8b	αὐτὸς δὲ βαπτίσει ὑμᾶς ἐνπνεύματι ἁγίῳ
Mt. 3.11d	αὐτὸς ὑμᾶς βαπτίσει ἐν πνεύματι ἁγίῳ καὶ πυρί

Note:
a. Jn 1.27b is similar here, though Luke is closer to Mark

Moreover, the connection between Jn 1.27 and Acts 13.25 is much closer than it is between this Johannine verse and Lk. 3.16. We may compare:

58. Although Luke uses Mal. 3.1 and applies it to John the Baptist at 7.27, he omits the specific description of John's clothes and diet which reinforce the identification: the contrast drawn between John's garments and those of people living in kings' courts at 7.25 could be read as a simple statement of fact, with perhaps a veiled thrust at Herod in terms which reflect Luke's preoccupation with the theme of riches, even if we assume that he recognized the implication of Matthew's allusion.

59. In Acts 13.25, where Luke says that Jesus came after the Baptist, the reference is removed from any Elijah associations and is purely temporal (as in John).

60. Cribbs, 'St Luke', p. 432.

Acts 13.25   οὗ οὐκ εἰμὶ ἄξιος τὸ ὑπόδημα τῶν ποδῶν λῦσαι
Jn 1.27   οὗ οὐκ εἰμὶ ἄξιος ἵνα λύσω αὐτοῦ τὸν ἱμάντα τοῦ ὑποδήματος

Here Luke has ἄξιος, like John, not ἱκανός; he uses the singular of
ὑπόδημα (as against the earlier plural form he shares with Mark and
Matthew), and he drops the reference to the ἰσχυρότερός and the baptism
with fire. It seems that Luke, faced with conflicting details in his sources
for this pericope, adopts two strategies. Sometimes he avoids a clash, such
as that concerning the identification of the Baptist and Elijah, or the description of the descent of the Spirit, which is witnessed by Jesus in
Mark/Matthew, and by the Baptist in John; in Luke it is left unstated who
saw it, although the phrase 'in actual bodily form' could well be a Lukan
compromise which makes it possible for both to have done so. On other
occasions, he splits the details between two accounts much as he is later to
do with the mass of tradition concerning Mary, sister of Martha, and the
Anointing. (The same is true in the hearing before the Jewish authorities.
In Mark/Matthew, false witnesses tell of Jesus' threats against the Temple,
but in John no such threat is recorded, and Luke postpones both the false
witnesses and the threat until the trial of Stephen in Acts.)

The conclusion Cribbs draws from this is that Luke seems to conflate
the two traditions. He observes that there are in Luke at least nine passages
where a phrase or detail paralleled in Mark/Matthew but not found in
John, and a Johannine phrase which similarly does not appear in Mark/
Matthew, are combined in a single Lukan statement.[61]

> We are suggesting that at least some of Luke's alterations of his Matthaean
> and Markan source were due to his knowledge of another tradition that was
> different…and that here (Lk. 3.16-22) and elsewhere, in attempting to write
> an orderly[62] *Vita Jesu*, Luke may have sought to mediate between these two
> traditions at the points at which they were in conflict.[63]

We may conclude that from the evidence in this pericope there is no real
reason for assuming that Luke is prior to John; indeed, since we see in
Luke–Acts what appears to be an attempt to reconcile two conflicting
accounts, the reverse would seem more likely.

---

61. Cribbs, 'Study of the Contacts', p. 87. The examples he gives are Lk. 3.16;
7.37-38; 22.3; 22.59-60; 22.67-70; 23.3-4; 23.22; 23.53; 24.1-3. All are considered in
the pages below.

62. καθεξῆς, Lk. 1.3.

63. Cribbs, 'St Luke', pp. 429-30. A similar point is made by Weiss, *Die Quellen*,
p. 294.

7.4.2. *The Entry into Jerusalem (Luke 19.29-40; John 12.12-19)*

Another example is provided by the entry into Jerusalem, where, although Luke's details concerning the collection of the colt are those of Mark/Matthew,[64] as is the timing of the incident in relation to the priests' plot, there are also some less obvious but nevertheless perceptible links between Luke and John, such as the acclamation of Jesus as a miracle worker. (In Luke, his 'mighty works' are referred to; in John, the raising of Lazarus. This link is a significant one, and cannot be explained as merely reflecting common traditions used by both evangelists, since Jn 12.9 is clearly redactional.) The words of acclamation, too, with βασιλεὺς following εὐλογημένος ὁ ἐρχόμενος, are similar, though Luke inserts βασιλεὺς between this and ἐν ὀνόματι κυρίου, and John puts it afterwards. We can also observe that in both the Pharisees react very negatively, even though in John they merely murmur amongst themselves.

The presence of the Pharisees, which both Luke and John recount, unlike Mark and Matthew, is more intelligible in John, because of the raising of Lazarus and the reaction which this provoked. In John, the Pharisees are consistently active in Jerusalem, and they are linked with the Chief Priests at 7.32, 45; 11.46, 47; 18.3. They are the group that John most frequently singles out as Jesus' main opponents among the Jews. In Mark's Gospel they fade out almost completely once Jesus has left Galilee: they are mentioned only at 12.13, and Jesus' leading enemies are the Chief Priests and Scribes.[65] Matthew's Pharisees are much more in evidence, being the subject of the Woes in ch. 23, and being mentioned as opponents at Mt. 21.45 (cf. Mk 12.12: Matthew splits Mark's more general statement here and uses the reference to the Pharisees in Mk 12.13 again at Mt. 22.15-16); they are also named in Mt. 22.34, 41. But they are not Jesus' main enemies in Matthew's Passion narrative, either: these are the Chief Priests and the Elders.[66]

Luke's attitude to the Pharisees is less consistently hostile—especially in Acts, as we have seen, where many are sympathetic, and there are even some who are Christians (Acts 15.5). It is therefore notable that they appear at Lk. 19.39, especially since elsewhere he follows Mark and does

---

64. Verbally, Lk. 19.28-31 is very close to Mk 11.1-3, although there are occasional correspondences with Mt. 21.1 3, such as ἀπέστειλεν in Lk. 19.29, Mt. 21.1 (contra Mk 11.1 ἀποστέλλει); λύσαντες in Lk. 19.30, Mt. 21.2 (contra Mk 11.2 λύσατε); ἀγάγετε in Lk. 19.30, Mt. 21.2 (contra Mk 11.2 φέρετε).

65. See Mk 11.27; 12.12; 14.1, 10, 43.

66. See Mt. 21.23; 26.3; 27.1.

not present them as participating in the Passion: indeed, he even omits them from the Lukan parallel to Mk 12.13 at Lk. 20.19. In Luke's Passion Jesus' main opponents are the Chief Priests and Scribes (Lk. 19.47; 20.19; 22.2) and also the Elders (Lk. 20.1; 22.52). In this respect he seems to be combining Matthew and Mark. Neither Mark nor Matthew was Luke's source for their presence at the entry into Jerusalem, and this particular detail is inconsistent with Luke's presentation elsewhere in his Passion. It is therefore significant that he is here in agreement with John, whose treatment is, on the contrary, perfectly consistent since the Pharisees are active in Jerusalem in John.

Similarly, the 'whole multitude of the disciples' (cf. Mark's πολλοὶ) which is at the scene in Luke does not seem to accord with the intimation that Jesus has had no contact with Jerusalem during his ministry. In John's narrative there is a significantly longer ministry, and several trips to Jerusalem at major Jewish festivals: it is therefore more credible that Jesus would have amassed some considerable following in the city.

John has added the reference to the 'King of Israel' to the citation of Ps. 118.26. He presents the story as the exact opposite of a planned demonstration, which is what the pre-arranged details about the colt seem to be in the Synoptics. In John, it is emphasized that the colt is an *ad hoc* proof of Jesus' humility; only thus is he to be seen as King of Israel, even though this is not understood until afterwards (Jn 12.16). From John's narrative it appears as if Jesus himself is acted upon here; the verb ἐποίησαν in v. 16 implies that the crowd initiates the action, and we may compare Lk. 19.35, where the multitude of disciples sets Jesus upon the colt. The incident in John is a rebuke to Jewish nationalism; we recall that at Jn 6.15 some of the people have already tried to make Jesus their king. (In this context, Luke, too, is anxious to show that Jesus is no threat to Rome.)

There is some difficulty with the mention of the 'crowd' in John, since the many who flock to Bethany because of the raising of Lazarus in v. 9 do not seem to be the same as those in v. 12 who come because they hear that Jesus is approaching Jerusalem. In vv. 12, 18 John seemingly attempts to knit together two separate strands of tradition. Since Luke does not mention the people coming out from Jerusalem to meet Jesus (and indeed Jesus has not had any significant previous contact with Jerusalem in Luke), he cannot have been John's source at this point.[67] Moreover the features Luke shares with him, such as the reference to miracles, to the Pharisees, and to the crowds, seem secondary insertions in Luke.

67. Similarly, Bailey, *Traditions*, p. 26.

D.W.C. Robinson points out[68] that it would be very unusual for Luke to alter a reference to the βασιλεία (Mk 11.10)—a major Lukan theme (46 instances)—into an acclamation of Jesus as βασιλεύς, which is used of Jesus only five times in the whole of Luke's Gospel, on occasions where there is a parallel in at least two of the other Gospels. We may compare:

Luke	Matthew	Mark	John
23.3	27.11	15.2	18.33
23.37	27.42	15.32	–
23.38	27.37	15.26	19.19
19.38	21.5	–	12.13

One wonders if perhaps Luke agreed with John and Mark here because they provided a 'double witness'. Moreover, while it is true that in this sequence Matthew has the term a little earlier, at 21.5,[69] Luke's structure at 19.38 is nevertheless closer to Jn 12.13 than to Mt. 21.9, and we notice that neither Luke nor John has any reference to David at this point, unlike Matthew and Mark. Both Luke and John seem to wish to refute the wrong sort of expectations, and thus they connect Jesus' kingship with his coming in the name of the Lord. Luke, indeed, focuses only on this aspect, as Lk. 19.38b—which is peculiar to his Gospel and seems to link with the birth narrative[70]—makes clear.

We may conclude that in this pericope Luke is in many ways as close to John as he is to Matthew or Mark.

7.4.3. *The Conspiracy to Capture Jesus (Luke 19.47-48; 20.19-20; John 7.30-36)*

All four Gospels emphasize that Jesus spends much time teaching in the Temple, and the response of the people clearly poses a threat, as is implicit at Mk 11.18, 32; Mt. 21.26 and Lk. 19.48. What the Jewish leaders fear is made quite explicit at Lk. 20.6—they are afraid they will be stoned to death! (The speech of Caiaphas in Jn 11.49-52 represents their anxieties, in terms much more flattering to themselves, as being civic disorder. This is a motif which is also present in Luke, who is careful to play down the political aspect of Jesus' clashes with the Jews, and to stress the Jews' culpability, for apologetic reasons.)

In John, Jesus' ministry extends over more than two years, so that there

---

68. D.W.C. Robinson, *Selected Material*, pp. 60-61.
69. This is a citation of Zech. 9.9, which is used by John, too, at 12.15.
70. See Lk. 2.14.

are frequent trips to Jerusalem for major Jewish festivals. The motif of the
Jews' fury and their intention to kill Jesus[71] can therefore be expressed in
several vivid clashes.[72] All of these precede the Passion week, where in
John's Gospel there is little interaction between Jesus and the Jewish
authorities; the dice here are already cast.

This event is therefore differently placed by John and Luke, although
we notice that whereas Mk 11.18-19 and Mt. 21.46 both imply that the
initial conspiracy takes place the day after Jesus' arrival in Jerusalem, Luke
is less precise. Jesus teaches 'daily' in the Temple, and the Chief Priests
and Scribes and the leaders of the people wish to destroy him (Lk. 19.47).
It could well be the case here, as was evident in the account of the baptism,[73] that Luke is taking a middle position which avoids explicitly
contradicting either Mark/Matthew or John.

There are, however, verbal correspondences between Luke and John
which should not be ignored. Thus Mk 12.12 and Mt. 21.46 talk of the
Jews' resolve to seize (κρατῆσαι) Jesus. Luke and John render this more
dramatic, using the same expression, ἐπιβαλεῖν ἐπ' αὐτὸν τὰς χεῖρας, at
Jn 7.30, Lk. 20.19, though it must be acknowledged that this phrase is
something of a cliché, and it occurs on numerous occasions in all four
Gospels. More significant is the fact that both Luke and John follow this
by a reference to the ὥρα, and in both this is qualified and made specific:
in John, it is *his* hour, in Luke, *that* hour. 'The hour'/'my hour' is a key
term in John.[74] It is neither so common nor so profoundly meaningful in
Luke, but it is used with this particular connotation at Lk. 22.14, 53. The
difference in the present instance is that John says that Jesus' hour has not
yet come (οὔπω), since the conspiracy, as we saw, takes place long before
the final trip to Jerusalem. In Luke, there is only one such gathering—in
the Passion week: and the time is therefore now. In consequence, Luke
refers in 20.19 to 'that very hour' (RSV).[75] It is quite possible that the use
of the term by one evangelist sparked it off in the other at this point, so

71. This occurs in the climax to the Markan 'conflict' stories, at Mk 3.6.

72. See, e.g., Jn 5.16; 7.19, 25-30; 7.45–8.20; 8.39-40, 58-59.

73. We may compare the technique of Jewish historians such as the author of
1 Maccabees and Josephus when their sources are at odds,

74. See Jn 2.4, 7.30; 8.20; 12.23, 27; 13.1; and cf., too, Jn 5.25, 28; 7.6, 8; 16.25, 32.

75. Luke's ἐν αὐτῇ τῇ ὥρᾳ is probably to be regarded as emphatic here. αὐτός
used in Greek before the article, or outside the noun/article unit, as here, usually carries
the meaning 'itself'. 'The hour itself' is not normal English, but it can perhaps best be
rendered as the RSV suggests.

that it is one more example of the 'verbal reminiscences' that often con-nect the two Gospels;[76] we cannot say with certainty which one came first, but the term in this context is nevertheless Johannine rather than Lukan.

7.4.4. *The Last Supper (Luke 22.14-38; John 13-17)*

In the Passion, there are numerous alterations by both Luke and John to the sequence of events recorded by Mark, as noted above; there is, for example, the timing of the prediction of Peter's denial, which Luke and John place during the Last Supper but Mark and Matthew depict as taking place on the way to Gethsemane, or the prediction of Judas's betrayal which Luke presents as occurring after the blessing and sharing of the bread and cup, as does John after the footwashing, which is similarly symbolic in his Gospel. Luke's placement, which reinforces the ideal of fellowship and communion in the powerful image of the shared food and blessing, points up Judas's subsequent act of treachery even more than the accounts in Mark or Matthew. Cribbs[77] points out that in both Luke and John either the disciples question one another as to who will betray Christ (Luke), or they look at one another in inquiry (John);[78] in Mark and Matthew they ask Jesus to whom he is referring.

Both Luke and John have a 'farewell discourse', too, which comes after the meal but before the arrest, though John's is much longer, extending from 13.31–17.26, with a hiatus at the end of ch. 14; presumably this was the ending of the original discourse which was later expanded. But we cannot assume that because John's account has undergone revision and development it is necessarily later than Luke's; Luke may equally have abbreviated it as he did the Sermon on the Mount. He disliked long, uninterrupted blocks of teaching, and at this point he did not wish to retard the action or to lessen the impact of the last meal.

Another point of contact is the dispute about greatness, which Luke,

76. Cf. Schürmann, 'Sprachliche Reminiszenzen'.

77. Cribbs, 'Study of the Contacts', pp. 52-53.

78. M.D. Goulder, 'An Old Friend Incognito', *SJT* 45 (1992), pp. 487-513 (502), points out that both Jn 13.24 and Lk. 22.23 use the optative form of εἰμί; this is the only optative in John, although Luke has several examples. Goulder believes this suggests that John used Luke here, but we must remember that supposedly 'obsolete' forms survive much longer in irregular verbs such as 'to be' (we may compare the otherwise archaic modern English subjunctive in phrases like 'if I were a rich man'). The optative of εἰμί here in John may therefore be of less significance than it might at first appear.

who has softened it in its Markan context in the journey to Jerusalem,[79] uses again here at the Supper in a somewhat muted form.[80] There seems to be some connection between Lk. 22.27, τίς γὰρ μείζων, ὁ ἀνακείμενος ἢ ὁ διακονῶν; οὐχὶ ὁ ἀνακείμενος; ἐγὼ δὲ ἐν μέσῳ ὑμῶν εἰμι ὡς ὁ διακονῶν, and the footwashing in John 13, which portrays the same point in a powerful and dramatic way; but we cannot conclude, since Mark makes a similar point in Mk 10.43, that Luke's account is necessarily earlier than John's and inspired it. We may note that Luke does not show Jesus waiting at table, as the verb διακονέω in v. 27 perhaps implies; thanking God, breaking the bread, and sharing the cup do not count as serving.[81] Washing the feet of the guests most certainly does, but Luke had already presented a footwashing which is peculiar to his Gospel at Lk. 7.38, in the tears of the sinner woman,[82] and he probably did not wish to repeat it in this context. The action recounted in Jn 13.4-12 is nevertheless presupposed in Luke's words. I. Buse comments, 'The most striking feature is the curious way in which the narrative of one seems to refer to that of the other'.[83]

In addition, the verb ἀνάκειμαι only occurs in Luke here in v. 27 (twice). Luke normally uses ἀναπίπτω (see Lk. 22.14; and also 11.37; 14.10; 17.7), or συνανάκειμαι (see Lk. 7.49; or 14.10, 15), or κατακλίνω (twice in Lk. 9.14-15). John, however, uses ἀνάκειμαι on two separate occasions in this sequence (at Jn 13.23, 28) and twice elsewhere, too (see Jn 6.11; 12.2), so it could reasonably be considered more characteristically Johannine. John also uses ἀναπίπτω four times, twice at Jn 6.10, and elsewhere at 13.25 and 21.20; but he does not use συνανάκειμαι or κατακλίνω at all.[84]

79. Cf. Mk 9.33-37, Lk. 9.46-48.

80. The presentation of Jesus' death as a vicarious sacrifice in Mk. 10.45 was clearly uncongenial to Luke and he does not use it in either context.

81. See Bailey, *Traditions*, p. 36.

82. The connection between these two events was also noted by Klein, 'Die lukanische-johanneische Passionstradition', p. 171 and M. Sabbe, 'The Footwashing in John 13 and its Relation to the Synoptic Gospels', in *Studia neotestamentica* (BETL, 98; Leuven: Leuven University Press, 1991), pp. 409-11.

83. Buse, 'St John and the Passion Narratives', p. 75. We may compare the observations of Schürmann, 'Sprachliche Reminiszenzen'.

84. This was pointed out to me by Mark Goodacre, whose recently published book *Goulder and the Gospels: An Examination of 'A New Paradigm'* (JSNTSup, 133; Sheffield: Sheffield Academic Press, 1996) considers evidence for Luke's secondariness to Mark and Matthew.

The prediction of Peter's denial looks like Luke's free rewriting of material when John and Mark/Matthew diverge. There are verbal correspondences between Luke and John here, such as the οὐ…ἕως[85] construction (which neither Mark nor Matthew uses at this point, and which also occurs in Jn 9.18), and also the use of the nominative of ἀλέκτωρ. There is also a structural similarity in that Peter's protestations of continuing loyalty precede the concluding prophecy.[86] But the verbal differences between the two are perhaps more striking than the similarities, since Luke is closer to Mark than to John in some respects:

Lk. 22.34   οὐ φωνήσει σήμερον ἀλέκτωρ ἕως τρίς με ἀπαρνήσῃ εἰδέναι
Jn 13.38   οὐ μὴ ἀλέκτωρ φωνήσῃ ἕως οὗ ἀρνήσῃ με τρίς
Mk 14.30   σήμερον ταύτῃ τῇ νυκτὶ πρὶν ἢ δὶς ἀλέκτορα φωνῆσαι τρίς με
            ἀπαρνήσῃ
Mt. 26.34   ἐν ταύτῃ τῇ νυκτὶ πρὶν ἀλέκτορα φωνῆσαι τρίς ἀπαρνήσῃ με

Thus, when Cribbs says, 'Luke's version…is verbally considerably closer to John than it is to either Mark or Matthew',[87] this would seem to be an overstatement, although the verse nevertheless does offer evidence of a conflation of differing traditions. Equally suggestive of a combination of traditions is the address by Jesus to Peter in v. 31 as Σίμων (which is very unusual after Lk. 6.14: the only other example is at 24.34) and as Πέτρε (cf. Mk 14.29; Mt. 26.33) in v. 34. The Johannine parallel uses John's favourite 'Simon Peter' (Jn 13.36), and this may be significant.

This whole section has been considerably revised by Luke. Thus only Luke has the reference to Satan sifting Peter like wheat, though John at 17.15 has a prayer to God to protect Jesus' followers ἐκ τοῦ πονηροῦ (here, probably 'The Evil One', rather than 'from evil'). Bailey suggests[88] that Lk. 22.36-37 may have inspired Jn 13.33, but the two statements are so far apart that it is difficult to claim dependency. The same is true of the correspondence between Jesus' injunction to Peter to 'strengthen his brethren' after he has 'turned again' (Lk. 22.32), and the three times reiterated command in Jn 21.15-17 to 'feed my sheep'. We seemingly have here a commissioning of Peter before his denials in Luke, and a *re*-commissioning afterwards in John, with the threefold declaration of love to atone for

85. Thus Bailey, *Traditions*, p. 37.
86. Thus D.W.C. Robinson, *Selected Material*, p. 91.
87. Cribbs, 'Study of the Contacts', pp. 53-54.
88. Bailey, *Traditions*, p. 39.

the threefold denial.[89] The settings, however, are so different that it is possible only tentatively to suggest some possible connection.

7.4.5. *The Arrest (Luke 22.39-53; John 18.1-12)*

Features concerning Jesus' arrest which are common to these two Gospels include first an explicit statement that the disciples are with Jesus, and secondly the fact that the τόπος to which he goes, which neither Gospel names as Gethsemane, is his usual preferred location. It is interesting that Luke, like John, does not name the place (just as neither locates Peter's confession in Caesarea Philippi), since Luke elsewhere in Triple Tradition passages uses almost all the place names given by Mark and Matthew.[90] Once again, we have an example of Luke acting against his usual practice in passages shared by John, and this would suggest that the variation is more likely to be the result of Johannine influence on Luke than the reverse.

Both Luke and John abbreviate the confrontation with Judas, with John omitting the kiss altogether and Luke's narrative leaving it unclear what it is supposed to signify; we may compare their earlier treatment of the baptism. Cribbs sums up: 'Luke 22.47-49 would thus seem to represent a middle position between Mt. 26.48f/Mk 14.44f, which explicitly describe Judas's kiss of betrayal, and Jn 18.3-7, which makes no mention of the incident'.[91]

The portrayal of Jesus is similar in Luke and John, too; he is not the almost passive Markan figure. Indeed, in John's narrative he seems to take charge of his own arrest, and in both accounts this does not happen until the end of the scene. Bailey finds a definite verbal link in the use of the verb συλλαμβάνω in this pericope; he observes[92] that the verb is relatively common in Luke, with the meaning 'arrest, seize', but this is the only instance in John (who prefers πιάζω).[93] It must, however, be noted that συλλαμβάνω is used at both Mt. 26.55 and Mk 14.48; it could therefore have been derived from one of these.

There is also the detail that is the right ear which is severed from the High Priest's servant, whom only John names as Malchus, just as only

---

89. Thus Bailey, *Traditions*, p. 41.
90. Cf. Cribbs, 'Study of the Contacts', p. 19.
91. Cribbs, 'St Luke', p. 443.
92. Bailey, *Traditions*, p. 50 n. 4.
93. See Jn 7.30, 32, 44; 8.20; 10.39; 11.57.

John states that the deed was done by Peter.[94] Bailey sees some correspondence between the detail that it was the right ear[95] and the earlier reference to the withered right arm of the man in Lk. 6.6, which Luke adds to Mark. He seems to think that the specification 'right' is characteristically Lukan. But the two cases are in no way comparable. Luke stresses that it is the right arm that is affected since this would limit the man's capacity for work; it increases the pathos. To lose either ear is certainly a misfortune, but it really makes no difference whether it is the right or the left one.[96]

Bailey[97] also sees a verbal link between ἰδόντες δὲ οἱ περὶ αὐτὸν τὸ ἐσόμενον (Lk. 22.49) and Ἰησοῦς οὖν εἰδὼς πάντα τὰ ἐρχόμενα ἐπ' αὐτὸν (Jn 18.4), but it is almost imperceptible. The omission of the flight of the disciples by Luke, to which Bailey also refers, is a piece of typical 'rehabilitation', which conflicts not only with Matthew and Mark but also with Lk. 22.32. John's account, too, is confused at this point; Jn 16.32 presupposes the disciples' flight, even though it is not narrated.

There are, however, some striking differences between the two accounts, notably the words of Jesus to his assailants, where Luke characteristically heightens the pathos: in Mark, Jesus is silent; in Matthew, he says, Ἑταῖρε, ἐφ' ὃ πάρει; in John, τίνα ζητεῖτε; and in Luke, Ἰούδα, φιλήματι τὸν υἱὸν τοῦ ἀνθρώπου παραδίδως. It is only in Luke, too, that the disciples ask if they may use force, and that Jesus heals the wounded ear. The stress on the injustice of the proceedings at 22.53 is also Lukan; we may compare Lk. 23.47; Mk 15.39.

Features peculiar to John include the reaction of the company to Jesus' statement ἐγώ εἰμι; his intercession for his disciples; and the fact that Judas is accompanied by officials of the judicial Sanhedrin, whom John quite correctly calls ὑπηρέται. (These perhaps correspond to the officials Luke describes as being present, who are somewhat abruptly introduced into the narrative in Lk. 22.52.) It is characteristic of John's presentation of Jesus that the charge of being a λῃστής, which is levelled at him in Matthew, Mark, and Luke, is in John reserved for Barabbas; Jesus is not to be seen as a brigand even by those opposed to him in this Gospel.

---

94. This is perhaps another example of John's repeated downvaluing of Peter. It also serves to substantiate his implicit claim that the 'disciple Jesus loved' had the *entrée* at the High Priest's palace.

95. Bailey, *Traditions*, p. 49.

96. Similarly, Buse, 'St John and the Passion Narratives', pp. 70ff.

97. Bailey, *Traditions*, p. 51.

Although it is quite possible that John's account of the arrest and Luke's are linked, there is no strong evidence; neither are there grounds for Bailey's contention that John used Luke to frame his account of its timing.[98] It is also hard to understand how he arrives at the conclusion[99] that John's statement at 18.2 that Jesus and his disciples often met at a garden in the Kidron valley is necessarily based on Lk. 22.39, καὶ ἐξελθὼν ἐπορεύθη κατὰ τὸ ἔθος εἰς τὸ Ὄρος τῶν Ἐλαιῶν. Indeed, D.W.C. Robinson comes to the opposite conclusion and says that clearly Luke has used John or a source like John;[100] certainly, given John's emphasis on the continuing contact between Jesus and Jerusalem, we might well maintain that the words ἔθος suggest that the dependence, if such there be, is the other way round. M. Sabbe,[101] who also assumes Lukan priority, notes that the combination in John of πέραν τοῦ (Jn 18.1), τὸν τόπον and ἐκεῖ (Jn 18.2) is found earlier at Jn 10.40 (and at Jn 19.41, too, τόπος occurs in conjuction with κῆπος, as is the case in Jn 18.2). This would support Robinson's contention; there is no reason why John's use of τὸ τόπος should not have influenced Luke, rather than the reverse. And since there is a conflict here between Matthew/Mark, who name the place as Gethsemane, and John, who writes of a garden across the Kidron, Luke[102] follows John's suggestion that the place was frequented by Jesus and locates the arrest at the Mount of Olives, to which Jesus was accustomed to go in Luke's own Gospel (see Lk. 19.29, 37; 21.37).

We should also take note of the very Johannine vocabulary of Lk. 22.53: ἀλλ' αὕτη ἐστὶν ὑμῶν ἡ ὥρα καὶ ἡ ἐξουσία τοῦ σκότους. If John were using Luke or a source which Luke shared, then he must have excised this statement, which one would have thought would have appealed to him. It seems more likely that Luke is secondary to John here.

---

98. Bailey, *Traditions*, p. 51.

99. Bailey, *Traditions*, p. 53.

100. D.W.C. Robinson, *Selected Material*, p. 117.

101. M. Sabbe, 'The Arrest of Jesus in Jn 18:1-11 and its Relation to the Synoptic Gospels: A Critical Evaluation of A. Dauer's Hypothesis', in M. de Jonge (ed.), *L'Evangile de Jean* (BETL, 44; Leuven: Leuven University Press, 1977), pp. 203-34 (209-10). Sabbe shows that, contra Dauer, it is unnecessary to postulate a pre-Johannine source.

102. We have noted above that when there is a conflict in his services Luke often rewrites freely.

7.4.6. *The Trial Before Pilate (Luke 23.1-5, 13-25; John 18.29–19.16)*
An obvious link between Luke and John in this section is the threefold
declaration by Pilate of Jesus' innocence. Sherwin-White[103] notes that,
under Roman law, those accused who did not defend themselves were
given three opportunities to change their minds and offer a defence before
they were sentenced; and that may be reflected here. In Luke, only the first
declaration is unqualified, as against all three of John's; the other two in
Luke state that Jesus is innocent of any capital crime. It is, however, very
unlikely that Luke meant to suggest that Jesus could have been considered
guilty of lesser charges; we see, rather, Luke's liking for variety—even at
the expense of historicity.[104]

For apologetic reasons both Luke and John are anxious to stress the
culpability of the Jews and the relative innocence of Rome. This is
presumably the explanation for the impression given by Luke at 23.25 that
the crucifixion itself was carried out by the Jews. Luke omits Mk 15.20,
which states that the Roman soldiers led Christ out, and he never explicitly
says that the responsibility was Rome's; he seems to be deliberately vague,
even though he is forced to concede that Pilate is in possession of Jesus'
body after death, and that the Romans are present at the crucifixion (see
Lk. 23.36, 47). In John, too, at 19.16, Pilate hands Jesus over to the Jews
to be crucified, though this is not to be taken literally since at Jn 19.23 it is
acknowledged that the soldiers, not the Jews, executed him.

There is a close verbal parallel which many have noted between Lk.
23.4 and Jn 18.38, although there seem to be tensions in Luke's account at
this point. Thus it is difficult to see how Jesus' equivocal reply Σὺ λέγεις
at Lk. 23.3 leads Pilate immediately to proclaim his innocence; the
dialogue which takes place between the two in John provides a much more
convincing setting for these words. I. Buse, indeed, concludes: 'The only
way in which we can make sense of this is to assume that Luke knew a
story such as that in the Fourth Gospel, in which Jesus showed Pilate that
his kingship was of a non-revolutionary type.'[105]

D.W.C. Robinson suggests[106] that the juxtaposition of Lk. 23.4 and 23.3
is explicable if we assume that Luke at this point has omitted some
conversation of the type that John records at 18.37, which was preserved

---

103. Sherwin-White, *Roman Society*, p. 25.
104. Cf. the differing accounts of Paul's conversion in Acts. *Variatio* was a common
rhetorical device; it was part of *imitatio*.
105. Buse, 'St John and the Passion Narratives', p. 72.
106. D.W.C. Robinson, *Selected Material*, p. 145.

in a common tradition used by both, in order for Luke to conform his account more closely to that of Mark. But we have seen that Luke feels free to depart from Mark elsewhere in his Passion; the hearing before Herod, for example, occurs only in Luke. A more likely explanation is that the speech of the Johannine Jesus, with its very characteristic reference to Christ bearing witness to the truth, does not accord with Lukan presentation, where the 'witnesses' are the disciples who can testify to Jesus. The verb μαρτυρέω is never used by Jesus of himself in Luke's Gospel.

Having examined this pericope with the usual presupposition that if there is any direct dependence it must be of John upon Luke, F.C. Grant[107] is driven to conclude that the evidence points the other way. Since the language of Lk. 23.4 is too close to John for this to be coincidental, he suggests that the verse must be one of many later insertions into Luke, made under the influence of the Johannine narrative.[108] He seems to see this as one more piece of evidence that there must have been a later revision of Luke's text by a Johannine glossator, but a simpler explanation is that Luke's text was composed in the knowledge of John's Gospel.

Other links between Luke and John include Pilate's three efforts to release Jesus (see Lk. 23.16, 20, 22 and compare Jn 18.39, 19.6, 12), which was perhaps a logical development from Pilate's question at Mk 15.12. In addition, Jesus is explicitly charged with claiming to be a king in Luke and John, though this is certainly implicit in both Mark and Matthew, too, being on the inscription nailed to the cross. Moreover, both Luke and John present the scourging as a warning, rather than as the prelude to crucifixion, as is the case in Mark and Matthew—a Roman practice attested elsewhere by Josephus and Livy. Structurally, too, both Lk. 23.22 and Jn 19.12 show Pilate attempting to release Jesus one last time after his final proclamation of Jesus' innocence. Moreover, Cribbs[109] points out that Lk. 23.22,

τί γὰρ κακὸν ἐποίησεν οὗτος; οὐδὲν αἴτιον θανάτου εὗρον ἐν αὐτῷ

seems to be a conflation of

τί γὰρ κακὸν ἐποίησεν (Mt. 27.23; Mk 15.14) and
Ἐγὼ οὐδεμίαν εὑρίσκω ἐν αὐτῷ αἰτίαν (Jn 18.38).

In addition, we notice that neither John nor Luke explains who Barabbas is (nor, indeed, in many of the best Lukan manuscripts, does Luke explain

107. F.C. Grant, 'Author of John', p. 298.
108. Cf. the view of Loisy, *L'Evangile selon Luc*.
109. Cribbs, 'St Luke', p. 445.

his significance in relation to Pilate's Passover custom, which is unmentioned) until after the Jews demand his release.[110] John at this point is actually closer to Mark than to Luke, and he agrees with Mark in the placement of Pilate's explanation. The powerful Johannine irony of Barabbas being a λῃστής depends for its impact on Jesus' words to those who arrest him, which Mark, Matthew and Luke all record, though John himself does not.

Bailey[111] observes that the verb αἴρω is used by the crowd calling for Jesus' destruction in both Lk. 23.18 and Jn 19.15; he notes that this particular use is characteristically Lukan, occurring in the New Testament only here and in Acts 21.36; 22.22. But the two uses in Acts are attacks on Paul which Luke has clearly modelled on the experience of Jesus. There is no way of proving that his use of it was not suggested by John, rather than *vice versa*.[112] Bailey also sees the repetition by the crowd of the call to crucify Jesus (see Lk. 23.21; Jn 19.6) as evidencing John's use of Luke. But although double vocatives[113] may be a Lukan characteristic, the examples here are imperative verbs, not vocative nouns. In any case, repetition can be typically Johannine, too: Ἀμὴν, ἀμὴν λέγω ὑμῖν...(see, e.g., Jn 1.51), so that if this is to be regarded as an echo it could operate in the reverse direction. It hardly suggests Johannine dependence.

7.4.7. The Crucifixion and Burial (Luke 23.25-56; John 19.17-42)
Some common features of Luke's and John's accounts of the crucifixion can be termed positive—such as the verb εἱστήκεισαν for the action of the people who watch Jesus, some of whom were men, which was necessary in Jewish law to provide valid evidence.[114] The verb used here is actually a significant parallel, since it is an allusion to Ps. 38.11, and the Septuagint

---

110. Lk. 23.17 is not attested in some manuscripts, and its placement varies in others, presumably because it seemed intrusive and clumsy.

111. Bailey, *Traditions*, p. 77.

112. Evans, *Luke*, p. 855, calls Αἶρε the usual shout of angry crowds.

113. E.g. Μάρθα, Μάρθα at Lk. 10.41; or Σίμων, Σίμων at Lk. 22.31.

114. Contra Thyen, 'Johannes und die Synoptiker', pp. 102-104, it is necessary for John's presentation of the Beloved Disciple, who succeeds when Peter fails, that the witness of the death is that disciple: the reference in v. 27 is not to be taken to imply that he leaves the scene at this point. The emphasis on the water and blood may be John's reaction to his source, as Thyen supposes (cf. the repetition of 'his feet' in the Anointing), but it is to substantiate the reality of the death, with perhaps an anti-docetic thrust (see v. 17).

at this point has ἔστησαν (Mark and Matthew have ἦσαν).[115] In addition, both inform us that the tomb of Jesus was previously unused.[116] Both Luke and John, too, follow this description of Jesus' burial with a reference to the 'day of preparation' for the Sabbath, beginning their accounts of the Resurrection morning itself in the same words, τῇ δὲ μιᾷ τῶν σαββάτων. Indeed, there are tensions in Luke's story here because Luke, like John, but unlike Mark, refers at 23.55 to the embalming of the body in spices before the mention of the Sabbath at 23.56. But he also refers to the Sabbath at 23.54, before he describes the embalming, and this would have meant that the women were breaking the Sabbath restrictions. Luke has here deliberately changed the 'very satisfactory'[117] order of the Markan narrative which explains that it is not until after the Sabbath that the women buy the herbs, and it is difficult to see why he would have done so, thus creating a problem, unless he was following another tradition at this point.[118]

There are also what could be called 'negative agreements'; no reference in either account to the Markan wine mixed with myrrh, nor to the bystanders who make mocking reference to Jesus' threats against the Temple. The most significant omission, however, is the cry of dereliction, which both presumably found unacceptable, since Luke sees Jesus as an example of the perfect martyr and in John he is totally in control throughout. We notice, too, that neither Luke nor John mentions that the tomb is sealed with a stone, though this is presupposed later by both (Lk. 24.2; Jn 20.1).[119]

---

115. See Buse, 'St John and the Passion Narratives', p. 73.

116. In this case, there is an interesting line of development. In Mark, the tomb is λελατομημένον ἐκ πέτρας. A detail added by Matthew is that it is καινόν. Both Luke and John expand this rather bald statement: ἐν μνήματι λαξευτῷ οὗ οὐκ ἦν οὐδεὶς οὔπω κείμενος (Lk. 23.53); μνημεῖον καινὸν ἐν ᾧ οὐδέπω οὐδεὶς ἦν τεθειμένος (Jn 19.41). Despite an overall similarity of meaning at this point, the wording is not very close, which could suggest memory rather than direct dependence, although we cannot say in which direction it operated.

117. Thus Taylor, *Behind the Third Gospel*, p. 61. Inconsistencies of this type often occur when Luke is combining sources.

118. This is also the conclusion of Taylor, *Behind the Third Gospel*, p. 61.

119. P. Borgen, 'John and the Synoptics in the Passion Narrative', *NTS* 5 (1958), pp. 246-59, notes that although only John in his crucifixion account has 'the Jews' asking Pilate that Jesus be taken down from the cross, and the burial as such performed by Joseph of Arimathea and Nicodemus (in the Synoptic Gospels the action is performed by Joseph alone), in Acts 13.29 Luke says, '*they* took him down from the tree and laid him in a tomb' (emphasis in original). Here we have another example of

There are, however, many equally striking differences in the two Passion narratives, which reflect the themes important to each evangelist; thus, for example, it is characteristic that only in John, where the suffering of the Passion receives little emphasis, does Jesus carry his own cross.[120] Luke, who similarly avoids Mark's depiction of the lonely agony of Jesus, nevertheless includes Simon of Cyrene, perhaps because, as Evans[121] suggests, discipleship is a Lukan theme,[122] and Simon here represents to Luke later disciples who need to take up their cross and follow their Lord.

Likewise, the pathos of the words to the 'daughters of Jerusalem' is Lukan, as is the stress on repentance evident in the appeal of the thief on the cross. Forgiveness, too, has been a leading theme throughout Luke's Gospel, and it is expressed here in both Jesus' words to the thief and his first words on the cross. Although Lk. 23.34 is not attested in all manuscripts, its authenticity is supported by the parallel at Acts 7.60.

As both Bailey and Robinson[123] conclude, there are so many differences between Luke's and John's narratives at this point that we cannot assume any common oral or written source; in both cases, there seems to be an independent creative rewriting of Mark. Nevertheless, there are several occasions where Luke's and John's accounts are closer to one another than either is to Mark's; a very powerful example is the actual death of Jesus, which both present in terms of perfect resignation to God's will. John, indeed, goes even further: the last word of Jesus in his Gospel is a cry of triumph. Jesus' death itself is expressed as παρέδωκεν τὸ πνεῦμα: Luke dramatizes this by presenting, as Jesus' final words, a citation of Ps. 31.5: Πάτερ, εἰς χεῖράς σου παρατίθεμαι τὸ πνεῦμά μου (Lk. 23.46). The resemblance is certainly striking: what we cannot say with any certainty is which evangelist thought of it first, and in any case Matthew says ἀφῆκεν τὸ πνεῦμα (Mt. 27.50), which could have contacts with either or both. Nevertheless, it is Luke who has replaced Mark/Matthew's scriptural

---

the phenomenon that was evident in the baptism at Lk. 3.16, where Luke is closer to John in Acts than he is in his Gospel. This is pointed out by Cribbs, 'Agreements between John and Acts', pp. 40-61 (45): cf. also F.F. Bruce, *The Acts of the Apostles* (Grand Rapids: Eerdmans, 2nd edn, 1951), pp. 50; 266 n. 1; 354; P. Parker, 'Mark, Acts and Galilean Christianity', *NTS* 16 (1970), pp. 295-304.

120. There may be an anti-docetic thrust here; some had suggested that Simon of Cyrene was crucified, and not Jesus, and John wished to refute such a claim.

121. Evans, *Luke*, p. 860.

122. Luke emphasizes this aspect; cf. Mk 15.21 or Mt. 27.32.

123. Bailey, *Traditions*, p. 79; D.W.C. Robinson, *Selected Material*, p. 171.

citation of Ps. 22.1 with another, and one that includes the sense of both
Mt. 27.50 and Jn 19.30, and this is suggestive.

But as well as all these examples of linked material where it is almost
impossible for us to decide in which direction any dependence operated—
although there are some indicative details, as has been shown—in the next
three cases what we have is similar material where the wording is so
different that we can understand why many have seen the connection as
arising from a related oral tradition, rather than literary dependence.

7.4.8. *The Centurion's Servant/Nobleman's Son (Luke 7.1-10; John 4.46-54)*

As we have already shown, when Luke's sources conflict he often rewrites
very freely; thus, Lk. 7.3-6, which is not paralleled in Matthew, is entirely
Lukan in sentiment, the centurion being endowed with a generosity to 'our
people' that has earned him the approval of the local community. The
vocabulary, too, is Lukan.[124] In this case, there is a discrepancy between
the Matthaean account of the incident at Capernaum, which he attributed
to a centurion,[125] and that of John, where the chief character is a βασι-
λικός. Luke, who has a fondness for sympathetic Gentiles,[126] especially
Roman ones, and prefers ordinary people to aristocrats,[127] naturally
chooses to follow Matthew here. Similarly, there is a discrepancy over the
precise identification of the sick person. In Matthew he is consistently
described[128] as παῖς; but unfortunately this term is ambiguous in Greek,
and can mean either 'servant' or 'lad' (i.e. 'son'). In John the boy is
explicitly called υἱὸς at Jn 4.46, 47, 50, 53; παιδίον/παῖς is used in this

---

124. Thus σώζω is also used in the sense 'heal' at Lk. 8.36 (unparalleled in
Matthew) and at Acts 4.9. The use of a verbal compound (here, διασώζω) is a Lukan
characteristic. Σπουδαίως, haste, is very Lukan; cf. Lk. 1.39; 2.16; 19.5, 6; Acts
20.16; 22.18; ἀγαπάω is much more common in Luke than in the other Synoptics (13
uses, as compared with 8 in Matthew, and 5 in Mark). Σὺν αὐτοῖς is Lukan. He likes
σύν + dative (23 examples in Luke, 41 in Acts, as against 4 in Matthew and 6 in Mark).
Λαός is a Lukan favourite (36 uses in Luke, 14 in Matthew, 3 in Mark and John).

125. Thus raising historical questions about the precise nature of any Roman
garrison in Capernaum, which have exercised the ingenuity of many commentators.

126. The connection between the centurion of Luke 7 and Cornelius in Acts has
often been noted.

127. Thus he 'downscales' the king in Matthew's Great Banquet parable so that he is
merely ἄνθρωπός (cf. Mt. 22.2 and Lk. 14.16).

128. See Mt. 8.6, 8, 13.

7. The Gospels of Luke and John   235

sense at Jn 4.49, 51. Luke again prefers the identification that most trans-lators have inferred was intended by Matthew,[129] and to make the matter quite clear he changes Matthew's παῖς to δοῦλος, which he uses through-out,[130] although he takes over Matthew's ὁ παῖς μου at Lk. 7.7, in what is surely to be construed as a very typical example of the phenomenon Goulder terms 'Lukan fatigue'.[131]

In many ways, Matthew's treatment of the story was more congenial to Luke than was John's. Hence as well as the identification of the chief characters, the ringing declaration of faith in Jesus by a Gentile, which forms a powerful and explicit contrast with the unbelief of the Jews in Mt. 8.9-10, was so much to Luke's taste that he copied it almost word for word; John's rebuke at 4.48 would have been quite out of place in Luke's presentation.

There are, nevertheless, features which Luke shares with John rather than with Matthew. Thus in Matthew the servant is suffering grievously (δεινῶς βασανιζόμενος, Mt. 8.6), but although his condition is serious it is not explicitly critical. In John and Luke, however, where a similar idiom is used for his illness,[132] we are told that the man is at the point of death: ἤμελλεν τελευτᾶν (Lk. 7.2); ἤμελλεν ἀποθνήσκειν (Jn 4.47).

In both, too, we are told that the man hears about Jesus: ἀκούσας δὲ περὶ τοῦ Ἰησοῦ (Lk. 7.3); ἀκούσας ὅτι Ἰησοῦς ἥκει (Jn 4.47). There is no mention of this in Matthew. Moreover, in Luke and John, others besides the two men and Jesus are involved, and find that the sick man is cured (cf. Lk. 7.10 and Jn 4.51; Mt. 8.13 is very different). There are a few other faint verbal echoes connecting the two texts, such as ἐρωτῶν at Lk. 7.3, ἠρώτα at Jn 4.47; οἶκον at Lk. 7.10, οἰκία at Jn 4.53; and perhaps ὁ δὲ Ἰησοῦς ἐπορεύετο at Lk. 7.6, ὁ Ἰησοῦς καὶ ἐπορεύετο at Jn 4.50[133]—although these are much less significant than the very close verbal corre-spondence between Matthew and Luke.

129. Perhaps by unconsciously harmonizing with Luke?
130. See Lk. 7.2, 8 and 10.
131. Goulder, *Luke*, p. 110.
132. κακῶς ἔχων at Lk. 7.2 is the reverse of John's κομψότερον ἔσχεν (Jn 4.52) once the man is recovering, as is pointed out by B. Lindars, 'Capernaum Revisited: Jn. 4:46-53 and the Synoptics', in F. van Segbroeck (ed.), *The Four Gospels: Festschrift Frans Neirynck* (BETL; Leuven: Leuven University Press, 1992), III, pp. 1985-2000 (1995), although Lindars assumes that this phrase must have been in the source used by all three evangelists, which he tentatively identifies as Q.
133. The difference here is that in John, it is the man who is going; in Luke, it is Jesus.

Once more, we cannot tell which came first, Luke's version or John's,[134] but it is the introduction of features that are shared with John, such as hearing about Jesus and the presence of others, which produce the Lukan 'muddle' at Lk. 7.6, where at the instigation of the centurion, Jesus is requested by the Elders to come and help the sick man, but on his way there the centurion sends out others to tell him not to trouble himself. Even though vv. 4-6 serve to make a very Lukan point about the centurion, and they also keep Jesus out of any direct contact with a Gentile since to Luke the time of the Gentiles is after the Resurrection, these verses are undeniably awkward. John's version is perfectly coherent and affords us no evidence of the intrusion of disparate material; this is consistent with its priority to the Lukan account, where the evangelist seems to be attempting to reconcile two differing sources.

7.4.9. The Feeding of the Five Thousand (Luke 9.10-17; John 6.1-14)
Another example is provided by the feeding of the multitude, which Luke has rewritten very freely; verbally, vv. 10b, 11b, 12a, 13b, 14b and 15 are almost without parallel among the other evangelists. This is characteristic in Quadruple Tradition sections when his sources conflict—in this case, over the location of the miracle and when it occurred in relation to the other events of Jesus' ministry. Although, unlike Mark (and John), he does not mention the actual distribution of the fish among the crowds,[135] in which respect he resembles Matthew, in the main Luke's wording is nevertheless closest to Mark's in this pericope. Thus both use κύκλῳ and ἀγρούς (Lk. 9.12; Mk 6.36), contra Matthew; similarly, the words κατέκλασεν...καὶ ἐδίδου and the verb παρατίθημι are common to Lk. 9.16 and Mk 6.41 but do not occur in Matthew. Verbal connections with Matthew are for the most part relatively minor and mainly stylistic, with the possible exception of τὸ περισσεῦον (Mt. 14.20), τὸ περισσεῦσαν (Lk.

---

134. Both Dauer, *Johannes und Lukas*, and Boismard, 'S. Luc', assume the former. Although he later abandoned the idea, Boismard proposed that Luke was the final redactor of John's Gospel, who was responsible for the introduction at Jn 4.48 of the 'faith should not need signs' theme, which Boismard regarded as un-Johannine. (Boismard concluded that Luke must also have composed the pericope of Doubting Thomas and vv. 14-18 of the prologue, where the same theme recurs.) But Luke himself is not consistent on this matter; in Acts 8.6, the signs performed by Philip promote faith. Should we therefore assume that this verse was written by John?

135. The words used for fish by Mark and John differ, so there is not a noteworthy parallel between them here.

9.17). There is also a reference to 'healing' at the beginning of both Matthew and Luke, as opposed to Mark's 'teaching'. This may be significant since John, too, talks of the signs that Jesus has performed on the sick as his introduction to the incident, and we would therefore have an example of 'double witness', which could explain why Luke has followed Matthew against Mark here.

Points of contact between Luke and John concern structure and placement. Thus both place the reference to 'about five thousand men' before the distribution of the food. In Matthew and Mark, the number of the fed is not given until the very end of the pericope, after the left-overs have been collected. Parker[136] points out that in both Lk. 9.10-22 and Jn 6.1-71 Peter's confession is placed in close proximity to the miraculous feeding (and the linked discourse, in John), whereas in Mark and Matthew much other material separates them.[137] In addition, Luke, like John, has only one feeding. This is usually explained away as an example of Luke's supposed dislike of doublets, despite the acknowledged fondness for deliberate parallelism which is evident throughout the whole of Luke–Acts, but actually Luke includes more narrative doublets[138] than any other evangelist. He may dislike verbal doublets—although there are 12 examples of these in his text[139]—but he is quite prepared to repeat material. To argue for Luke's aversion to doublets on the basis of his inclusion of only one feeding is an example of circular reasoning and it does not accord with the evidence of the text.

Cribbs[140] notes that in both Luke and John the crowd follow Jesus rather than preceding him, as they do in Mark. And while it is true that Matthew, too, talks of the crowds following—the verb ἀκολουθέω occurring in Mt. 14.13 as well as Lk. 9.11 and Jn 6.2—they nevertheless appear to be awaiting him in Mt. 14.14, so that Luke's presentation is closer to John's in this respect. There is also an interesting agreement between Luke and

---

136. Parker, 'Luke', p. 319.

137. It is perhaps worthwhile to recall that καθεξῆς (Lk. 1.3) normally refers to chronological order.

138. Thus Cribbs, 'Study of the Contacts', p. 37. He instances: Lk. 9.46/22.24 (dispute about greatness); 7.11-17/8.49-56 (raising of the dead); 5.12-14/17.11-19 (healing of a leper); 5.29-32/19.1-10 (eating with a tax-collector); 6.6-11/13.10-17/14.1-6 (Sabbath healings); 4.31-36/8.26-39/9.37-43/11.14 (exorcism of demons); 9.1-6/10.1-11 (mission charge).

139. See Chapter 3.2.3 above.

140. Cribbs, 'Study of the Contacts', p. 41.

John concerning the actual location of the feeding miracle, which both
seem to set on the eastern side of the Sea of Galilee. Thus John, at 6.1,
specifically says that they went 'to the other side' of the sea, and at 6.16-
17 says they returned across the sea to Capernaum; and Luke at 9.10
mentions Bethsaida, which was on the eastern shore, although he very
typically does not mention a sea-crossing—the sea, to Luke, seems to have
been associated with evil, as was argued above. Both Luke and John (Jn
1.44; 12.21) mistakenly regard Bethsaida (in reality in Gaulanitis) as being
in Galilee, which was perhaps conceived as including this eastern shore. It
is possible that the reference to Bethsaida in Luke may have arisen
because in John's Gospel, Philip (who is from Bethsaida) is asked by Jesus
to procure the bread for the multitude. Parker[141] suggests that such a
reference in his source was interpreted by Luke to imply that they must
therefore be near Philip's home town—Bethsaida—since they were on that
side of the lake. The 'town of Bethsaida' in Luke is in clear tension with
the reference to the 'lonely place' in which the feeding is said to take
place.[142] Indeed, it contradicts Mk 6.45, which talks of Jesus and the
disciples withdrawing by boat and going to Bethsaida, on the other side of
the sea, a verse which in Mark immediately follows the account of the
feeding, and which Luke is surely unlikely to have overlooked or misread.

It must be conceded, however, that the verbal agreements between John
and Luke are negligible in this pericope; indeed, John is closest to Mark in
details like the sum of two hundred *denarii* to be spent on the bread, which
Matthew and Luke both omit.[143] It is impossible to tell which came first,
Luke or John, or even to show convincingly that the two accounts are to be
linked. Nevertheless, it is Luke's pericope which evidences a very obvious
conflict between a source which locates the feeding near the city of
Bethsaida and one which refers to a 'lonely place', and seems to be trying
to reconcile the two; this is perhaps significant.

7.4.10. *The Miraculous Catch (Luke 5.1-11; John 21.1-14)*
A similar case is that of the Miraculous Catch, although the connections
here between Luke and John are rather more perceptible. Once again, there
is an obvious link in subject-matter between their two accounts, even
though the only common vocabulary is the unavoidable use of the word

141. Parker, 'Luke', p. 321.
142. Cf. Mk 6.35; Mt. 14.15; Lk. 9.12, contra John.
143. Cf. the omission of Mk 14.4-5; Luke seems to have disliked precise financial
calculations of this kind.

for fish, and that for net. Luke in this pericope seems to combine material from John[144] with that from Mark and Matthew,[145] but since there is a wide divergence in his sources he feels free to pursue his own course, and his version differs significantly from all three.

Luke uses the story to motivate the response of the disciples to Jesus' call, and he places this after the sermon in Nazareth. But there are tensions in the narrative here;[146] Jesus has already healed Simon's mother-in-law at 4.38 before we are introduced to Simon. John places the material differently; he treats it as a post-Resurrection account. But this whole chapter in John appears to be an afterthought, since 20.31 seems to be an ending; and it is perhaps somewhat strange that the disciples, after their enormous catch, come ashore and eat some other fish (the word used at Jn 21.10 is ὀψάριον, whereas at 21.6 it is ἰχθύς).

Some have suggested that Luke's account is clearly prior because there is a symbolic relationship in Luke between the events of the fishing miracle and the call to discipleship; but this also applies to a post-Resurrection commissioning, as in John. On the other hand, it has equally been claimed that Peter's 'Depart from me, for I am a sinful man, O Lord' is more suited to a post-Resurrection narrative, (especially in view of Peter's denials), but it is just as possible that Luke intends the speech as an example of awe at the numinous; Peter's κύριε seems definitely christological rather than merely respectful. Once more, it is difficult to tell which account came first, assuming they are linked,[147] but it is nevertheless suggestive that Luke only here calls Peter by the Johannine appellation Simon Peter.

We can, moreover, understand why Luke would not have wished to take over the reference to the Beloved Disciple, who appears only in John and to whom Peter is firmly and consistently subordinated. Luke chooses to

144. See Jn 21.3c-6, 8 and Lk. 5.3c-9.

145. Cf. Mk 1.17/Mt. 4.19 and Lk. 5.10b; Mk 1.19/Mt. 4.21b and Lk. 5.10a; Mk 1.20/Mt. 4.22 and Lk. 5.11.

146. Contra F. Neirynck, 'John 21', *NTS* 36 (1990), pp. 321-36, especially p. 326, these tensions cannot necessarily be taken to demonstrate Lukan priority to John, who attempts here to tidy up Luke's somewhat awkward temporal sequence. They may instead show Luke's attempt to reconcile conflicting sources.

147. T.L. Brodie, *The Quest for the Origin of John's Gospel* (Oxford: Oxford University Press, 1993), p. 170, believes that at this point Luke's original text (a proto-Luke–Acts, which was used by John and lacked Lk. 4.31–6.49; 8.4–9.50; 10.21–15.32; 16.10-18; 17.1-10; 19.11–21.38; 22.31-65; and Acts 15.36–28.31) has been revised to incorporate Markan, Matthaean and Johannine material. There is unfortunately no evidence that such a truncated form of Luke–Acts ever existed.

stress Peter's obedient faith (v. 5) and reverence (v. 8). He repeatedly rehabilitates Peter, as we can see if we compare his Gospel with Mark's, or even Matthew's. We notice that in this scene attention is concentrated on him and there is no mention of his brother Andrew (who is not mentioned in John's account either, contra Mark and Matthew[148]). This provides a further tension in Luke, since the plural verbs in vv. 5, 6 and 7 show that Peter is not fishing alone. James and John are in the other boat (5.10); so who *is* Peter's fishing companion? Matthew (Mt. 4.18) and Mark (Mk 1.16) say Andrew, but John (Jn 21.6-7) implies that it was the Beloved Disciple. Although Luke's text indicates that Peter had a partner, here as elsewhere he avoids openly contradicting any of his sources if possible, and does not identify the man.[149]

It may also be significant that there is no evident motive for Luke's modification of Mark's reference to Galilee at Mk 1.39, which becomes 'all the synagogues of *Judaea*' at Lk. 4.44 and is therefore in some tension with Lk. 5.1, which is located back in Galilee. The transition in John's Gospel is similarly abrupt, but the resurrection appearance in Jerusalem was important to John (and Luke) and that in Galilee a part of the early tradition (cf. Mk 16.7; Mt. 28.16). It is less clear why Jesus is in both Judaea and Galilee at this point in Luke, and this could suggest his account is secondary here.

7.4.11. *Satan and Judas (Luke 22.3; John 13.2, 27)*
The one instance which could seem on linguistic grounds to support Bailey's assumption that John is dependent on Luke concerns the possession of Judas by Satan, which only Luke and John record. Some[150] have regarded Jn 13.27 as a late gloss, since nowhere else in John is the Devil called Satan, although Luke has five uses of it.[151] It would, however, be a

---

148. It is worth noting that this is the only time that John (Jn 21.2) and Luke (Lk. 5.10) mention Zebedee, contra Matthew (Mt. 4.21; 10.2; 20.20; 26.37; 27.56) and Mark (Mk 1.19, 20; 3.17; 10.35). Cf. Parker, 'Luke', p. 322.

149. Cf. his treatment of the High Priest in the trial sequence in 7.4.13, below, and also his vagueness over the timing of the conspiracy in 7.3.3, above, and over who saw the dove at the baptism in 7.4.1.

150. E.g. O. Zürhellen, *Die Heimat des vierten Evangeliums* (Tübingen: J.C.B. Mohr, 1909), p. 52.

151. At Lk. 10.18; 11.18; 13.16; 22.3, 31. There is no parallel in Mark or Matthew for any of these except the second, although they have other uses of the term Satan which Luke omits.

somewhat desperate expedient to claim it is a later interpolation assimilating John's text to Luke's, especially where there is no supporting manuscript evidence; the reading is very well attested.

The placement is a little different, since in Luke the incident occurs in the account of Judas's plot with the Chief Priests and Scribes, before the preparation for the Passover—which agrees with Mark's and Matthew's location of the betrayal—whereas in John it occurs during the meal itself. The wording is nevertheless quite close:

Lk. 22.3   εἰσῆλθεν δὲ Σατανᾶς εἰς Ἰούδαν τὸν καλούμενον Ἰσκαριώτην.
Jn 13.27   καὶ μετὰ τὸ ψωμίον τότε εἰσῆλθεν εἰς ἐκεῖνον ὁ Σατανᾶς.

There is also a statement concerning the devil and Judas at Jn 13.2: τοῦ διαβόλου ἤδη βεβληκότος εἰς τὴν καρδίαν ἵνα παραδοῖ αὐτὸν Ἰούδας Σίμωνος Ἰσκαρίωτου. Barrett points out that if this is translated, as Bauer suggests, 'the devil, having already put it into the heart of Judas Iscariot to betray him',[152] this means that in John there is another very close link, Jn 13.2 being closer both to what occurs in Luke and to where he places it. But this interpretation is syntactically difficult, and Barrett prefers the reading, 'the devil, having already resolved in his heart that Judas should betray him',[153] though this interpretation is in some tension with Jn 13.27.

On the face of it, then, this verse could seem to suggest that John used Luke. Bailey[154] proposes that Jn 13.2 was a Johannine composition inspired by a meditation on Lk. 22.3; Jn 13.27 is a repetition of the same incident in the even more shocking context of the Last Supper. Thus the only person who is explicitly said to share food with Jesus at the Supper in John's Gospel is—Judas. The evangelist could not have provided a more terrible parody of the Eucharist.[155] Indeed, it seems from John's presentation that Jesus arranged for Satan to enter Judas. Morton Smith says, 'The notion that a demon can be sent into food so as to enter anyone who eats the food is common'.[156] As we saw, Luke consistently strove to dissociate

152. Barrett, *Gospel According to John*, p. 439, refers to W. Bauer, *Das Johannesevangelium* (Tübingen: J.C.B. Mohr, 3rd edn, 1933).

153. Barrett, *Gospel According to John*, p. 439. He cites in support of this translation Lk. 21.14; Job 22.22 (LXX); and 1 Sam. 29.10 (LXX).

154. Bailey, *Traditions*, pp. 30-31.

155. Similarly, J.C. Fenton, *Finding the Way Through John* (Oxford: A.R. Mowbray, 1988), p. 61.

156. M. Smith, *Jesus the Magician* (London: Victor Gollancz, 1978), p. 110. He cites *PGM* 7.385ff.; 620ff.; 643ff.; and 970f.

Jesus from any connection with the practice of magic,[157] which was a charge that the early Church sought emphatically to refute, and he therefore chose to omit the detail about the piece of bread. That John deliberately modified the Lukan account in the opposite direction, in a way which would lend support to this accusation, is much less likely.

We should note that there are some inconsistencies in Luke's account. Thus Satan is associated with Peter at Lk. 22.31, and in a context where Satan's function seems closer to that of a prosecuting attorney, as in Job, than to that of the Devil. John is perfectly consistent throughout his Gospel, and it is appropriate that his only mention of Satan should be in association with the archetypal traitor, Judas, whom he has already identified as 'a devil' at Jn 6.70.[158] The conflict between Good and Evil is thus personalized; we note that there are no other cases of demon-possession in John.

It is quite conceivable that the early Judaea-based Church, wrestling with the almost incomprehensible act of betrayal by one of the Twelve, had concluded that it must have been the work of Satan; and this interpretation was reflected in oral tradition which was later used by John and/or Luke. D.W.C. Robinson[159] observes that if John were following Luke at this point, it is very strange that he used only a fraction of a Lukan verse (Lk. 22.3a) and ignored the rest of Luke's basically Markan material. It accords with what we have observed of Luke's practice elsewhere that he has at this point combined the synoptic placement of the betrayal with the Johannine explanation for it, which was one that he would have found entirely congenial. (It is also worth noting that the word ὥρα at Lk. 22.14—contra Mk 14.17 and Mt. 26.20—seems Johannine rather than Lukan, and this verse corresponds in its placement to the Johannine reference to the Devil/Judas in Jn 13.2.)

We may conclude that the evidence offered here, namely the unprecedented use of the term 'Satan' by John, does not seem sufficient to justify an assumption of Lukan priority, especially when there are other factors which would allow the reverse to be argued with equal plausibility.

---

157. It is perhaps significant that he omits Jesus' Walking on the Water and the Cursing of the Fig-tree, both of which have parallels in the recorded activities of contemporary magicians.

158. Contra Goulder, 'Incognito', p. 501, (see n. 91), who maintains that since Satan does not enter Judas until 13.27, διάβολος at Jn 6.70 should be translated 'slanderer'. But this ignores Jn 13.2: the Devil/Judas/the act of betrayal form a tightly linked complex in John.

159. D.W.C. Robinson, *Selected Material*, p. 71.

There are, on the other hand, pericopes where there are features which strongly suggest Lukan dependence on John. This is the case in the Anointing of Jesus, the Hearing Before the Jewish Authorities/Peter's Denial, and the post-Resurrection narratives, and I shall examine each of these in detail. (There is also the inscription on the cross, though there are manuscript discrepancies here.)

7.4.12. *The Anointing of Jesus (Luke 7.36-50; John 12.1-8)*

The basic story of the Anointing of Jesus by a woman is found in all four Gospels, although Luke places the incident much earlier in Jesus' ministry than do the other evangelists. John and Mark disagree over the timing of the incident in relation to the Passion, the identity of the host, and the portion of Jesus' body anointed; and it is characteristic of Luke that if there is a discrepancy between pericopes in Mark/Matthew and John, he often rewrites freely and inserts the material elsewhere in his narrative.

John's account of the Anointing is nevertheless closest to Mark's in many ways. He shares with Mark/Matthew the location in Bethany, the reproach to Jesus about extravagance, Jesus' statement about the poor, and the intimation that Jesus' body is being prepared for burial; there is also a reference to the sum of three hundred *denarii*, and the rare phrase νάρδου πιστικῆς, which are found only in Mark and John. Luke's 'theology of the poor' presumably rendered Mk 14.4-5; Jn 12.5/Mk 14.6-7; Jn 12.7-8 unacceptable to him (and perhaps, too, the financial calculation in Mk 14.5; Jn 12.5);[160] the reference to 'pistic nard' may have been incomprehensible to an audience unfamiliar with the customs and products of Palestine, and perhaps to the evangelist himself. And since Luke placed this episode earlier in his narrative, to illustrate the theme of repentance, he therefore could not locate it in Bethany, nor refer to Jesus' imminent burial.

Luke does, however, share with John an account of two sisters who were followers of Jesus, and the characterization of Mary and Martha is similar. But Luke does not include any reference to the raising of their brother Lazarus[161] (which is of crucial importance to John since it sparks

---

160. Cf. Lk. 9.13; Mk 6.37.

161. There is nevertheless a Lukan parable concerning a poor man, Lazarus, who is unique among parabolic characters in being given a name. Some connection between the two texts here, at least of the order of a verbal reminiscence, seems probable. We may note that even the raising of one from the dead (Lazarus, in John's pericope) does not persuade the Jews; Lk. 16.31 thus serves as a comment on both his own parable and the Johannine story.

off the Passion), and he drops the identification of the woman who anoints Jesus.[162]

Obvious similarities between John and Luke include first, the anointing of Jesus' feet rather than his head; second, the wiping of Jesus' feet by the woman's hair; and last, the reluctance of either John or Luke to present the action as a royal anointing, although this might perhaps have been inferred from Mark's account.[163]

We should first consider why there is the divergence between anointing Jesus' head and his feet. J.F. Coakley suggests[164] that the original incident probably involved feet rather than head, but it was changed by Mark, either out of respectful reserve or to serve as the anointing of the 'King of the Jews'. (Thus although in both Mark and Matthew we are told that the woman pours ointment over Jesus' *head*, Jesus refers to the anointing of his *body* for burial; the two are in some tension.) Bailey[165] finds the repetition of τοὺς πόδας in Jn 12.3 clumsy, and therefore suggestive of a conflation of differing traditions—and, hence, secondary; but it is possible that because John is altering the story as told in Mark and Matthew, he has repeated the noun for emphasis. We should note that although it is very unusual, it is by no means completely unprecedented[166] in ancient literature for the feet to be anointed.

Some critics have suggested that the action of the woman anointing

---

162. Jn 11.2 appears to be a later addition, which attempts to structure a superfluity of material concerning Mary and is difficult to reconcile with John's knowledge of Luke. One assumes that neither evangelist would have wished there to be an identification of Mary of Bethany and the sinner of Luke 7. (Cf. Cribbs, 'St Luke', p. 440). It is nevertheless possible that Luke was influenced here by the Johannine story of the Samaritan woman of questionable morality at the well, which he omitted because it conflicted with his careful geographical structuring. (Goulder, 'John 1:1–2:12 and the Synoptics', pp. 210-37 [232-34], who assumes Lukan priority, suggests the reverse.)

163. D.A.S. Ravens, 'The Setting of Luke's Account of the Anointing: Luke 7:2–8:3', *NTS* 34 (1988), pp. 282-92 (293), and Coakley, 'Anointing', pp. 248ff., both point out that the verb used in the Septuagint for royal anointing is never ἀλείφω, as in Lk. 7.38, 46 and Jn 11.2; 12.3 (contra Mk 14.8, μυρίζω). Indeed, this verb is only rarely used to translate the Hebrew *māšaḥ* (see Gen. 31.13; Exod. 40.15; Num. 3.3), which is normally rendered by χρίω, as at Isa. 61.1 (see, too, Lk. 4.8). Luke himself uses χρίω at Acts 10.38: ἀλείφω is not his normal vocabulary.

164. Coakley, 'Anointing', pp. 248ff.

165. Bailey, *Traditions*, p. 3.

166. As Coakley, 'Anointing', pp. 246-49 shows, contra R.E. Brown, *Gospel According to John*, p. 451, and A. Legault, 'An Application of the Form-Critique Method to the Anointings in Galilee and Bethany', *CBQ* 16 (1954), pp. 131-45.

Jesus' feet is more appropriate in Luke's presentation, being a mark of penitence rather than what Coakley terms an 'extravagant gesture of love',[167] as
in John. But the 'excess' element of Mary's action is completely Johannine;
we recall the enormous quantity of wine at Cana. It has also been regarded
as improbable that Mary, having applied costly ointment to Jesus' feet,
immediately removes it with her hair (Jn 12.3). But since the substance
seems to be conceived as a liquid, as it is in Mk 14.3 where the same words
occur, we can appreciate that such a vast quantity, a λίτρα,[168] would inevitably require some action to cope with the surplus.[169] It is entirely fitting,
given John's portrayal of Jesus, that whereas in ch. 13 the disciples have
their feet bathed in water by Jesus and wiped (the same verb ἐκμάσσω is
used at 12.3 and 13.5) with a towel, Jesus' are anointed in costly ointment
and wiped with Mary's hair;[170] the parallelism is deliberate and the point is
christological. It is worth remembering that, from the evidence of 1 Cor. 11,
in Jewish thought a woman's hair was her 'pride', her 'crowning glory'.
This action of Mary's, letting down her hair to mop up the spilled unguent,
in itself indicates the extent of her love for Jesus and is by no means
illogical.

There are, however, inconsistencies in Luke. It is difficult to imagine
tears of repentance sufficiently copious to wet Jesus' feet enough to require
drying, and Jesus would hardly have needed to be a prophet (see Lk. 7.39)
to deduce the likely profession of a woman who appeared in public with
unbound hair. In addition, Coakley points out[171] that in Lk. 7.44 the
reference to wiping Jesus' feet with the woman's hair unbalances the
structure of the verse, where elsewhere there is a repeated contrast—no
kiss/kissed feet; no water/tears; no oil/anointed feet. Hair seems an addition not properly integrated into the text, which Luke has derived from his
source.

It has also been proposed[172] that because Luke's story takes place at an
unspecified time and place in Galilee, this shows that it is more primitive.
But we must remember that Luke's temporal and geographical references

167. Coakley, 'Anointing', p. 254.
168. A litre is about 325 ml, and there are approximately 568 ml to the pint.
Expensive perfume is still today sold by the ounce (approximately 28.5 ml).
169. Similarly, Maddox, *Purpose*, pp. 166-67, and Coakley, 'Anointing', p. 251.
170. The connection between the two incidents is also noted by Sabbe, 'Footwashing', pp. 409-41.
171. Coakley, 'Anointing', pp. 250-51.
172. See Coakley, 'Anointing', p. 244.

are often vague, especially when his sources are at odds;[173] and precise details are quite likely to drop out as a story is retold. In other respects Luke's account does not seem primitive. It seems, rather, to represent an attempt to simplify a hotch-potch of tradition concerning Mary[174] by splitting the material into two separate incidents concerning different people. It is conceivable that the picture of Mary sitting at the feet of Jesus, a devoted disciple, in Lk. 10.39 was inspired by John's story; but Luke preferred to use the Anointing of Jesus pericope to illustrate his own favourite theme of repentance.

It should perhaps be observed that because Luke's pericope is more coherent than some critics[175] will grant regarding that of John, this does not in any way prove Luke's priority: he could quite easily have taken over John's story and adapted it to accord with his own particular emphases. Some critics argue[176] convincingly that Luke has adapted Matthew's birth narrative in a far more radical way in the composition of his own, and they propose the same type of action for the derivation of Luke's Parable of the Fig-tree from the Markan/Matthaean account of its cursing.

There is nothing in this story that enables us to affirm that John used Luke; indeed, since the word 'hair' seems an insertion in Lk. 7.44, at this point at least Luke appears secondary. Moreover, there is evidence that Luke is splicing together differing strands of material. As at Lk. 3.16, almost every phrase in Lk. 7.37-38 has a parallel somewhere in Mark/ Matthew or John. Luke seems to be attempting to reconcile two differing views, using Mark but also reflecting Johannine material, and this accords with his practice elsewhere when they conflict. Reconciliation of differing accounts is not, however, characteristic of John, who usually prefers to go his own way. This would support the contention that here John is prior to Luke, if not to Mark.

---

173. See, e.g., Lk. 20.1-8 and cf. Mt. 21.23-27; Mk 11.27-33; Jn 7.14-24 (the question of authority). Matthew places the discussion the day after Jesus' entry into Jerusalem; in Mark's account, it is *two* days after; in John, it takes place much earlier in the narrative; and Luke carefully avoids saying precisely when it occurred: ἐν μιᾷ τῶν ἡμερῶν. The conspiracy sequence is similar: cf. Lk. 19.47; Mt. 21.45-46; Mk 12.12-17 and Jn 11.45-53.

174. Similarly, Cribbs, 'Study of the Contacts', p. 38.

175. E.g. R.T. Fortna, *The Fourth Gospel and its Predecessor: From Narrative Source to Present Gospel* (Philadelphia: Fortress Press, 1988).

176. E.g. Drury, *Tradition*, pp. 62ff.

7.4.13. *The Hearing Before the Jewish Authorities and Peter's Denial (Luke 22.54-71; 23.6-12; John 18.12-28)*

Since there is a conflict in his sources, Luke recasts the denial sequence which in Mark and Matthew follows the trial and mocking and in John is split, with the first denial preceding the questioning and the second and third succeeding it; in Luke, all three occur before the trial and mocking. Some features of this sequence are characteristically Lukan, such as the presumably reproachful glance Jesus directs at Peter in 22.61, which provokes his immediate remorse. The whole scene is thus at once more pathetic and it provides a more direct illustration of the favourite Lukan theme of repentance. But there are nevertheless features Luke shares with John; both mute the denials to some extent and also omit the curse Peter invokes on himself in Mark and Matthew, and they further agree that the second accuser is male. There are also the words of Peter's second denial, ἄνθρωπε, οὐκ εἰμί, at Lk. 22.58 (cf. Jn 18.17, 25) which Bailey concedes is a point of contact between the two Gospels, although we would be rash to conclude, as he does, 'It is possible that this influenced John in the phrasing of the first and second denials.'[177] It is true that both use οὐκ εἰμί, but any connection is perhaps more likely to be the other way round when we remember how important to John's Jesus is the assertion ἐγώ εἰμι Indeed, we have already noted the effect of this, 'I am' being the name of God, on the crowd. There is thus in John's narrative a powerful ironic contrast between two of Peter's denials and the two balancing positive declarations of Jesus to the soldiers who arrest him. Irony is a characteristically Johannine trait; there is no reason why John should be secondary to Luke here.

Cribbs observes[178] that Lk. 22.59, ἐπ' ἀληθείας καὶ οὗτος μετ' αὐτοῦ ἦν, καὶ γὰρ Γαλιλαῖος ἐστιν, seems to contain echoes of both γὰρ Γαλιλαῖός εἶ (Mk 14.70), and οὐκ ἐγώ σε εἶδον ἐν τῷ κήπῳ μετ' αὐτοῦ (Jn 18.26). There seems to be a combination of differing traditions in Lk. 22.55, too, as Cribbs also notes,[179] since Luke agrees with Jn 18.18 in describing the actual kindling of a fire in the High Priest's courtyard even if the words used are different; Luke has περιαψάντων δὲ πῦρ whereas John has ἀνθρακιὰν πεποιηκότες. (In Mk 14.54 we simply assume that one is alight, since Peter warms himself at it.) On the other hand, the detail of Peter sitting down with the others by the fire, which is not in Matthew

177. Bailey, *Traditions*, p. 55 n. 1.
178. Cribbs, 'Study of the Contacts', p. 60.
179. Cribbs, 'Study of the Contacts', p. 59.

at all, clearly shows Luke following Mark, since in John they stand. (Mark at 14.54 and Luke at 22.55 both use the verb συγκαθίζω, while John at 18.18 has ἵστημι.)

Luke and John both agree (against Matthew and Mark) that there was not a formal trial of Jesus in the night by the Jewish authorities. In Luke, Jesus is taken to the High Priest's palace, where Peter's three denials take place; in John, he is taken at night to the house of the ex-High Priest Annas (Ananias), father-in-law of the present High Priest, for interrogation, and in the morning to Caiaphas himself. Since Jesus had already been sentenced *in absentia* in Jn 11.47-53, what happened at night amounted to a questioning by Annas of Jesus, followed by some 'coercive action' performed by those in charge of him. Although Luke knows of Annas (see Lk. 3.2; Acts 4.6) and of his continuing influence, which is confirmed by Josephus in *Ant.* 20.198, there is nevertheless a conflict in his sources here, since neither Mark nor Matthew mentions Annas, although Matthew does refer to Caiaphas. Luke typically attempts to avoid the contradiction; he condenses the two hearings into one, and does not identify the High Priest in question at all, just as he does not name Peter's partner in the fishing expedition at Lk. 5.7.

It is noticeable that in both Lk. 22.63 and Jn 18.22 (probably) Jesus is struck by those who arrest him, not by members of the Council, contra Mk 14.65 and Mt. 26.67; and in neither text are the required witnesses, who appear in Mark and Matthew, present. (It is interesting that it is these two features which Luke, in accord with John, omits from his Passion, that appear in the trial of Stephen in Acts. Here, too, Luke seems to have split his material, just as he did with the Anointing of Jesus/Mary and Martha. We should note in this context that although the words of the High Priest's official at Jn 18.22 do not form part of Luke's Passion, there is a close connection with the words spoken to Paul in a similar situation at Acts 23.4.)[180]

A night trial would in any case have been quite unprecedented, in historical terms. It could therefore be argued that both Luke and John are perhaps following a better, more accurate tradition than that used by Mark/Matthew.[181] The sequence of events, as recorded in Lk. 22.66–23.1,

180. This parallel was noted by H. Klein, 'Die lukanische-johanneische Passionstradition', pp. 181-82. It should be noted that the High Priest in question at Acts 23.4 is Ananias (Annas), as in Jn 18.22.

181. This was the view of Taylor, *Passion Narrative.*

certainly seems to flow more smoothly; but there are, nevertheless, inconsistencies in it.[182] Hence it is unclear why in Luke, Jesus is taken to the High Priest's house at all; that the whole Council at v. 66, speaking as one (v. 70), question him in the same words is highly improbable (and it conflicts with 23.51); and the reference to further testimony in v. 71, which has not been sought in the first place in Luke, is obscure.

Evans[183] suggests that Luke has condensed the Markan narrative, freely revising Mk 14.55-64; but this ignores the far closer parallel between Lk. 22.67-71 and Jn 10.24-25, 36, where, in both, there are two separate questions concerning Jesus' Messiahship (Lk. 22.67, Jn 10.24) and his Sonship (Lk. 22.70, Jn 10.36), with other material intervening. This differs from Mk 14.61 or Mt. 26.63, where there is only one question which combines both elements. The connection between Luke and John is very evident in the close parallel between Lk. 22.67 and Jn 10.24-25:

Lk. 22.67   Εἰ σὺ εἶ ὁ Χριστός, εἰπὸν ἡμῖν. εἶπεν δὲ αὐτοῖς, Ἐὰν ὑμῖν εἴπω, οὐ μὴ πιστεύσητε

Jn 10.24-25   Εἰ σὺ εἶ ὁ Χριστός, εἰπὲ ἡμῖν παρρησία. ἀπεκρίθη αὐτοῖς ὁ Ἰησοῦς, Εἶπον ὑμῖν καὶ οὐ πιστεύετε

These two verses in John are much closer to Luke's account than any in the later Johannine passage (Jn 18.19-23), and they do not have any parallel in Mk 14.61 or Mt. 26.63. Bailey[184] does not see this very close verbal connection as displaying John's use of Luke; on the contrary, he thinks that what we see here is evidence of a source that was common to both the evangelists. John, according to Bailey, uses only the material which Luke does not derive from Mark[185]—that is, he omits the reference to the Son of Man coming in power, to witnesses, and to the death sentence. But it is equally possible that what we see here is a Lukan combination of John and Mark, especially since this hypothetical source has a somewhat Johannine vocabulary.[186] (D.W.C. Robinson, indeed, concludes that either Luke and John were at this point drawing from a common written source, or that Luke at 22.67 used John.)[187]

---

182. This is pointed out by Evans, *Luke*, pp. 823ff.

183. Evans, *Luke*, p. 833.

184. Bailey, *Traditions*, p. 56.

185. Bailey, *Traditions*, p. 60 n. 3.

186. E.g. πιστεύω, which is very common in John (98 uses) although it is quite rare in Luke, and also, perhaps, ἐρωτάω (15 uses in Luke; 27 in John).

187. D.W.C. Robinson, *Selected Material*, pp. 131-32.

Moreover, there is no evidence that at this point Luke is striving to use a better, more complete tradition than that used by Mark. Evans notes, 'Luke does not furnish additional or alternative information for clarifying the issues whether the Sanhedrin did pass a formal sentence of death for blasphemy, or had the power of capital punishment in such a case.'[188] These are precisely the points that John's account does cover; but whatever may have been Luke's normal practice elsewhere, in this instance his desire to exonerate Rome as much as possible from responsibility for Jesus' death took precedence over any urge to answer historical questions of the kind addressed by John's narrative. Luke therefore concentrates on the political nature of the charges laid by the Jews (see Lk. 23.2,5), which would carry the most weight with Pilate, who even so declares Jesus innocent. Since the reader knows from Luke's presentation that these charges are malicious lies, the effect is to emphasize further the culpability of the Jews and the (relative) innocence of Rome.

The 'mocking' as such[189] is done by Herod and his soldiers at Lk. 23.11, in an incident which is only in Luke. His account seems to reinterpret events in terms reflecting his own interests,[190] which is supported by the parallel to the hearing by Herod in Acts 25. Even though it would be possible to argue on the basis of the unparalleled Lk. 13.1, 31, 23.12, that both men were tarred with the same brush, Luke's presentation underlines that it is the Jews, not the Romans, who are culpable; Luke consistently goes out of his way to exonerate Rome. We may note that according to Taylor's analysis,[191] this pericope contains at least 15 characteristically Lukan words and phrases; there is little to suggest the use of a source here.

The Herod sequence seems, therefore, to be a free creation by Luke;[192] it is characteristic of what has been shown of Luke's practice elsewhere that since there is a conflict between Mark/John (where Jesus is attired in an imperial purple cloak) and Matthew (whose soldiers use the regulation red), Luke avoids the difficulty by merely saying that he is dressed in 'splendid' ($\lambda\alpha\mu\pi\rho\grave{\alpha}\nu$) garments. Cribbs points out[193] that there are nevertheless certain features which relate the mockery by Herod's soldiers in

188. Evans, *Luke*, p. 839.

189. Cf. Mt. 27.27-31; Mk 15.16-20; Jn 19.2-5.

190. It is possible that this incident may have been constructed by Luke to fulfil Ps. 2.2, which is quoted in Acts 4.25-26, as Evans, *Luke*, p. 849 suggests.

191. Taylor, *Passion Narrative*, p. 87.

192. There may perhaps be a connection with the question Pilate poses at Jn 19.9, Πόθεν εἶ σύ.

193. Cribbs, 'Study of the Contacts', p. 69.

Luke rather more closely to the account of the mockery by the soldiers in John 19 than to the Markan and Matthaean versions. In both Luke and John, the incident occurs during the somewhat protracted hearing before Pilate which takes place before the sentence whereas in Mark and Matthew, it is a prelude to crucifixion; similarly, in both Luke and John, Pilate's second declaration that Jesus is innocent immediately succeeds the account of the mocking (compare Jn 19.1-4 and Lk. 23.10-11, 14). It is noticeable, too, that unlike Mark and Matthew, who mention it earlier in their accounts, it is at this point that Luke and John stress the silence of Jesus; and their terminology is quite similar (cf. Lk. 23.9 and Jn 19.9). Both refer to the Chief Priests in this connection, too (Lk. 23.10; Jn 19.6), which is not the case with Mark or Matthew. And both Lk. 23.11 and Jn 19.2 use the verb περιβάλλω, contra ἐνδιδύσκω (Mk 15.17) and περι-τίθημι (Mt. 27.28).

Taylor concludes that 'some knowledge of Johannine tradition'[194] is implied here; I would agree with Cribbs and put it more strongly than a mere linked tradition. There are too many verbal connections between Luke and John which support the likelihood of there being some literary relationship between the two at this point, and Luke's version seems to me to offer more convincing evidence of the attempted reconciliation of differing strands of material.

7.4.14. *The Cross Inscription (Luke 23.38; John 19.20)*
It is noteworthy that some manuscripts at Lk. 23.38 relate that upon the cross the inscription is written Ἑλληνικοῖς καὶ Ῥωμαϊκοῖς καὶ Ἑβρ-αϊκοῖς which is very close to Jn 19.20: Ἑβραϊστί, Ῥωμαϊστί, Ἑλλη-νιστί. It is difficult to see why if this reading were genuine it was omitted later, though we should note Luke's order here is the one which was usual, and if it is authentic it represents a definite correction of the Johannine text, as Bailey notes.[195]

7.4.15. *The Post-Resurrection Narratives (Luke 24; John 20 and 21)*
It is generally acknowledged that the connections between Luke and John are strongest in their Resurrection narratives. Indeed, from the very first we seem to see evidence of a combination of Markan/Matthaean and Johannine material in Luke.[196] Thus Mt. 28.1 says that dawn was drawing

---

194. Taylor, *Passion Narrative*, p. 87.
195. Bailey, *Traditions*, pp. 78-79 n. 2.
196. Cf. Weiss, *Die Quellen*, p. 233.

near (ἐπιφωσκούσῃ); Mk 16.2 that the sun had risen (ἀνατείλαντος τοῦ ἡλίου); Jn 20.1 that it was still dark (πρωῒ σκοτίας ἔτι οὔσης); and Lk. 24.1 that it was *very early dawn* (ὄρθρου βαθέως), which sounds suspiciously like a Lukan compromise. The same may be true of his account of the visit of the woman/women to the tomb. At the tomb Mary Magdalene and the other women find the stone rolled away (cf. Mk 16.4), and see two angels (cf. Jn 20.12) dressed in garments (plural, cf. Jn 20.12) which are dazzlingly bright (ἀστραπή, Mt. 28.3; ἀστραπτούσῃ Lk. 24.4). In John, Mary Magdalene is alone, but we are given the substance of her conversation with Simon Peter; in Mark and Matthew, she is accompanied by another Mary but no conversation is recorded (indeed, in Mark, the women flee in terror); in Luke, she is one of a group including the two Marys, as in Mark and Matthew,[197] who tell the apostles of the empty tomb, as in John, although they are not believed. Unlike John and Matthew, Luke does not report a conversation between Mary and Jesus; but both Luke and John use Mary's report to motivate the subsequent visit of Peter to the tomb. There are clearly numerous variations between all the accounts, and since his sources conflict Luke has rewritten freely. His version reflects the other three, and he synthesizes their differing elements.

An obvious link between the post-Resurrection stories recorded in Luke 24 and John 21[198] is that in both Jesus cooks fish, but whereas in John's account we are told that he cooks the fish for the disciples but not that he eats it—which could leave the pericope open to the possible assumption that the Resurrection was not truly corporeal—Luke instead stresses that Jesus, rather than the disciples, ate the fish.[199] This particular emphasis is in some tension with Acts 10.41, where the definition given would thus disqualify the disciples as witnesses, since no other shared meals are recorded. The pericope was no doubt intended in both Gospels to demonstrate that the Risen Lord was not a spirit, despite no longer being subject

---

197. The presence of Joanna is a deliberate link back to 8.3.

198. Even though John 21 is clearly an appendix, which was presumably added by members of the Johannine circle (as is intimated by Jn 21.23-24), the parallel to Jn 21.1-8 at Lk. 5.2-10, as well as to Jn 21.9-14 at Lk. 24.36-43, strongly suggests that it was known to Luke.

199. Contra R.J. Dillon, *From Eye-Witnesses to Ministers of the Word: Tradition and Composition in Luke 24* (AnBib, 82; Rome: Pontifical Biblical Institute, 1978), Dauer, *Johannes und Lukas*, p. 270, observes, 'Die Tendenz der vv 41-43 liegt klar auf der Hand: urchristlichen Apologetik'. Dauer argues that it is not quite correct to classify this incident as antidocetic.

to the normal laws of time and space (see Jn 20.19; Lk. 24.31, 36). If, however, we propose that there is a literary relationship between the two texts, then the incident is explicable only if we assume Johannine priority and Lukan modification. John would hardly have altered the story in the opposite direction unless he wanted to imply that Jesus was indeed a spirit, rather than flesh. And in that case, he would surely have dropped it altogether.

There are also some very close verbal links between Luke and John, although these do not appear in all the main Lukan manuscripts. Examples are: καὶ λέγει αὐτοῖς 'Εἰρήνη ὑμῖν' at Lk. 24.36 (cf. Jn 20.26); and in the same verse in the same manuscripts, ἔστη ἐν μέσῳ αὐτῶν (cf. ἔστη εἰς τὸ μέσον [Jn 20.19]).

There is also at Lk. 24.40, καὶ τοῦτο εἰπὼν ἔδειξεν αὐτοῖς τὰς χεῖρας καὶ τοὺς πόδας,[200] which we may compare with Jn 20.20—the only difference here is that τοὺς πόδας seems to conform to Luke's crucifixion account[201] and πλευρὰν to John's.[202] The first of these passages is the Greek translation of the usual Jewish greeting *šālôm*, so that it proves nothing, even if it is authentic, and the second is the obvious way to describe the situation. Lk. 24.40 is different; many have rejected it as a later gloss, but Lk. 24.39, which contains the very Johannine ἐγώ εἰμι αὐτός,[203] is not disputed, and here Jesus clearly shows his wounds to the disciples. In John's Gospel, the same point is made dramatically in the story of Doubting Thomas,[204] so there would seem to be another example

200. These phrases, which are omitted from many Lukan manuscripts, are considered very fully by Dauer, *Johannes und Lukas,* and also by D.W.C. Robinson, *Selected Material*, pp. 188ff.

201. Luke does not explicitly mention Jesus being nailed to the cross in his Gospel, unlike Jn 20.25, but this seems to be implied by Lk. 24.39, although in Acts 5.30; 10.39, the stress is on Jesus being hanged on a tree. There is also a reference to his blood at Acts 20.28 (and also at Lk. 22.20, if the longer text is authentic), which would perhaps support the interpretation that his flesh was pierced—especially since in Luke, Jesus is neither scourged nor crowned with thorns, both of which would also have drawn blood. Where did the blood Luke refers to come from, if not wounds made by nails?

202. Although Lk. 2.35 is clearly figurative, one wonders whether the stress there on Mary, too, being pierced may also reflect a familiarity with John's crucifixion account (see Jn 19.34; 20.27).

203. This seems an obvious 'verbal reminiscence' of John in Luke.

204. It is interesting that the verb used in Lk. 24.39, ψηλαφάω, is also used in the same sense and in a similar context at 1 Jn 1.1.

of the way the narrative of one Gospel appears to reflect that of the other.[205]

None of these phrases, then, proves Lukan or Johannine priority; they only suggest that there is a connection between the two Gospels. It is worth noting that a very rare example in Luke of the historic present, λέγει (Lk. 24.36),[206] also occurs in Jn 20.19 (historic presents are even more common in John than they are in Mark).[207]

But the most notable example of all, the one which supports most strongly the contention that Luke is using John here, rather than vice versa, is Lk. 24.12: ὁ δὲ Πέτρος ἀναστὰς ἔδραμεν ἐπὶ τὸ μνημεῖον καὶ παρακύψας βλέπει τὰ ὀθόνια μόνα, καὶ ἀπῆλθεν πρὸς ἑαυτὸν θαυμάζων τὸ γεγονός. This verse clearly summarizes the incidents described in Jn 20.3-8. Its vocabulary was termed Johannine by Curtis,[208] who regarded it as a Johannine interpolation. He cites as evidence the word ὀθόνια[209] (when Luke earlier, in common with Matthew and Mark, has σινδών) and also μνημεῖον, παρακύπτω and ἀπέρξεσθαι πρὸς ἑατὸν. Muddiman, however, points out that John's use of ὀθόνια is not consistent either, since at 11.44 he uses κειρίαις.[210] He also disputes that ἀπέρξεσθαι πρὸς ἑαυτὸν is any more Johannine than Lukan, and observes that the supposedly Johannine μνημεῖον is characteristic of Luke, too, except where he is following Mark. As far as παρακύπτω is concerned, there are only two examples of this verb in John, both in ch. 20 (vv. 5 and 11), so one can hardly term it Johannine, although here Mahoney[211] argues that

205. Thus, Buse, 'St John and the Passion Narratives', p. 75.

206. There are four examples in narrative sections: at 7.40 (the Anointing); at 8.49 (when Luke follows Mark); and at 24.12, 36 (the post-Resurrection stories, both of which have Johannine parallels). There are also seven examples in 'sayings' material, at 11.37, 45; 13.8; 16.7, 23, 29; 19.22.

207. Hawkins, *Horae synopticae*, pp. 143ff., estimates that there are 151 in Mark, 78 in Matthew and 162 in John, compared with Luke's 11.

208. Curtis, 'Luke 24:12', pp. 512-15.

209. Cf. Jn 19.40; 20.5. Although there are two uses of the related ὀθόνη in Acts 10.11; 11.5, the meaning there is 'sheet', not shroud.

210. J. Muddiman, A Note on Reading Lk. 24:12', *ETL* 48 (1972), pp. 542-48.

211. Mahoney, *Two Disciples*, p. 246. Mahoney regards Lk. 24.12 as inauthentic, but his arguments, which are similar to those of Curtis, are not convincing. His article is criticized by W.L. Craig, 'The Inspection of the Empty Tomb', in A. Denaux (ed.), *John and the Synoptics* (Proceedings of the 1990 Leuven Colloquium; BETL, 101; Leuven: Leuven University Press, 1992), pp. 614-19, although Craig nevertheless draws the strange conclusion, 'The failure of Mahoney's extensive argument against

παρακύψας is more necessary to John's account than it is to Luke's, since it delays matters until Peter arrives and enters the tomb. It is not really relevant to Luke, and this could suggest that it is secondary.

Curtis also draws attention to the historic present βλέπει in Lk. 24.12, and points out that this tense is very rare in Luke, who consistently corrects Mark's almost habitual use of it. It is not, however, unusual in John, as I have noted above (see n. 206); indeed, there are six examples of it in the first three verses of ch. 20, including βλέπει at 20.1. Curtis regards this verb as a final and conclusive proof that Lk. 24.12 is inauthentic and a Johannine addition. But there are a few examples of the historic present in Luke (see n. 206); Muddiman[212] concludes that we cannot, contra Curtis, dismiss the verse as a Johannine interpolation on the strength of this verb and some not fully substantiated claims about vocabulary, especially since there are inexplicable tensions between this verse and Jn 20.3-10 if we assume it was written by a 'Johannine' interpolator—why, for example, would such an author omit the Beloved Disciple? If we assume the author is Luke, however, his motive is clear; as in the Miraculous Catch, he wishes to avoid any implicit downvaluing of Peter. In no way does Luke's omission prove his independence of John.[213]

Nevertheless, because of its similarity to the Johannine account, many have rejected this particular verse as a later gloss. But here we should note that there are some characteristically Lukan touches as well, such as θαυμάζων, τὸ γεγονός, and the participial use of ἀνίστημι followed by another verb. It is suggested by Curtis that even though the pleonastic ἀναστὰς is unquestionably Lukan, the position of the participle after the proper noun is unique; Luke habitually places the proper noun after the participle. But Muddiman points out that Luke's usage of the participle ἀποκριθείς frequently follows this pattern.[214] The verse seems therefore to represent a fusion of John and Luke, in linguistic terms, and it is well-integrated into Luke's account. There is, on the contrary, no evidence of Lukan vocabulary in Jn 20.3-8.[215]

---

the authenticity of Lk. 24.12 makes it plausible that John is not the source of Luke's story' (p. 615). Why a weak argument should have such an effect is unclear.

212. Muddiman, 'Lk. 24:12', p. 548.

213. Contra Fortna, *Fourth Gospel*, p. 196.

214. E.g. at Lk 9.20, against his usual order, which on this occasion is found in the Markan parallel. This syntatical change may be to emphasize the noun Peter.

215. This is pointed out by Muddiman, F. Neirynck, D.W.C. Robinson and others. Indeed, attempts to detect Lukan vocabulary elsewhere in John have been equally

In his detailed consideration of Lk. 24.12 Neirynck sees the entire verse, which is a creative elaboration of Mk 16.4, as a Lukan editorial composition used and amplified by John.[216] Thus the repetition of πρὸς in Jn 20.2 and the singular verb ἐξῆλθεν in v. 3, even though the subject is actually plural—Peter and the 'other disciple'—is evidence that the presence of the Beloved Disciple here is clearly a secondary insertion, and John's account is therefore later than Luke's. It seems indeed an insertion, but perhaps into the Markan account rather than the Lukan.[217] Similarly, the plural verb οἴδαμεν at Jn 20.2 could reflect Mark's version of the visit of the women to the tomb, not Luke's.

There are elements in the text which do not necessarily support Neirynck's assumption of Lukan priority. The arguments are reversible, and the evidence may, if viewed from a different perspective, instead suggest Lukan dependence on John. Thus John's verb προέδραμεν at 20.4 is necessitated by his account, where the other disciple outruns Peter and, seeing the empty tomb, is the first to believe. Luke, who uses the related verb ἔδραμεν at 24.12, does not need Peter to perform this action since he omits all mention of the other disciple; thus the action could be typical Petrine impetuosity, or it could be secondary. There is no reason why Luke's account should be prior here.

There is also the mention by John of the σουδάριον in v. 7, which links with the earlier reference in the raising of Lazarus at 11.44. John's point is that Jesus did not need anyone to unbind him or remove the headcloth; it is christological. Thus while it is possible that the mention of the headcloth was suggested to John by Luke's τὰ ὀθόνια μόνα, by which Luke meant 'only the gravecloths' (i.e. not the body), whereas John understood this as meaning 'the gravecloths, not the headcloth', it is equally possible that the situation was the other way round: John's account of the gravecloths lying on the ground apart from the headcloth, expressed in the words τὰ ὀθόνια κείμενα, καὶ τὸ σουδάριον...οὐ μετὰ τῶν ὀθονιῶν κείμενον, was reinterpreted by Luke as meaning that the body was not there; and this

unsuccessful; see A. Harnack, *New Testament Studies*. III. *The Acts of the Apostles* (London: Williams & Norgate, 1909), p. 231.

216. Neirynck, *Evangelica*, I, pp. 313-34; 401-55. Neirynck, too, regards Lk. 24.12 as authentic (see, especially, pp. 313-28). A similar conclusion is reached by Thyen, 'Johannes und die Synoptiker', pp. 288ff.

217. To Mark's Empty Tomb story, John has added the traditional first appearance to Peter (cf. 1 Cor. 15.5); but in his version, as usual, Peter is cast into the shade by the Beloved Disciple.

linked with his treatment of the empty tomb and the reference to it in 24.3. The headcloth was essential to the comparison John wished to make between Jesus and Lazarus; it was irrelevant to Luke, and so he dropped it.

The problem about this verse is that it, too, is not attested in all manuscripts. Though almost all the major ones, including the very early third-century papyrus 75, contain it, Marcion—perhaps not surprisingly—and some Old Latin and Syriac texts and the *Codex Bezae* do not. Mahoney[218] and Bailey[219] also reject it, as a later scribal assimilation to John's text; but the weight of the manuscript evidence is against them.[220]

In addition, if we reject v. 12 we are left with the statement of the disciples' disbelief in v. 11, which contradicts v. 34. There is also v. 24, which is in some tension with 24.12, as D.W.C. Robinson points out,[221] and which seems to reflect John's account, since it mentions *disciples* (plural) going to the tomb, as is the case in John but not Luke. Even if Lk. 24.12 were not original, this verse, which is not disputed, corresponds only with John's version. Lk. 24.24 presupposes the visit described by John which is omitted altogether from Luke's narrative if we delete v. 12.

In either case, it seems that this is a very clear example of 'Lukan fatigue'. As with the changed location of the feeding miracle (where the addition of Bethsaida in Lk. 9.10 is inconsistent with the reference at 9.12 to the 'lonely place' which is derived from Mark and Matthew), in his account of the Resurrection, too, Luke makes changes at the beginning of a pericope which he fails to sustain. The content of the original source is discernible in the later verse, just as the language of that source may be apparent in the historic present tense of the verb βλέπει at 24.12.[222]

218. Mahoney, *Two Disciples*, pp. 67ff.

219. Bailey, *Traditions*, p. 85 n. 3.

220. See Metzger, *Text of the New Testament*. Metzger calls the Alexandrian text, of which papyrus 75 is a very early witness, 'on the whole the best ancient recension and the one most nearly approximating to the original' (p. 216). K. Aland, 'The Significance of the Papyri for Progress in New Testament Research', in J. Philip Hyatt (ed.), *The Bible in Modern Scholarship* (Nashville: Abingdon Press, 1965), p. 334 (cited by K. Snodgrass), says that the 'Western non-interpolations' should not be regarded as authoritative; see the detailed study by K. Snodgrass, which reaches the same conclusion after a consideration of examples including Lk. 24.12 (K. Snodgrass, '"Western Non-interpolations"', *JBL* 91 [1972], pp. 366-79).

221. D.W.C. Robinson, *Selected Material*, pp. 182ff.

222. Grant, 'Author of John', p. 301, who assumes that 24.12 is an interpolation, is driven to suggest that Lk. 24.22-24 is a further (and presumably very careless) one; but there is no manuscript evidence at all to support this contention.

Verse 34, which records the traditional Peter protophany, is itself in some tension with v. 37; Luke is clearly trying to unite differing sources and traditions, and to tie up all the loose ends in the final chapter of his Gospel, even though he modifies some of these details later at the beginning of Acts.[223] He seems to wish to present all the Resurrection appearances—beginning with that to the travellers to Emmaus, the similarity of which to the account of Philip and the Ethiopian eunuch would suggest it is a Lukan creation—and to end with the Ascension in the very congested evening of that first Easter Sunday.

7.5. *Conclusion: A Combination of Traditions*

I have attempted to show some of the more definite verbal links which exist between John's Gospel and Luke's; and although many of these are echoes which perhaps suggest memory, or maybe related traditions, some suggest either a hypothetical shared written source, of which we have no evidence, or a direct dependence. We must concede that it is hardly ever possible to be sure which came first, John's account or Luke's. Although in some ways Lk. 22.3 would seem compatible with Lukan priority, we have seen that there is nevertheless much evidence which points in the other direction in this pericope. Moreover, all the other very close correspondences—especially the Hearings by the Jewish Authorities and Pilate, the Empty Tomb story, and the Resurrection appearances—suggest that Luke is later than John, and this seems to offer a better explanation for common features in the Baptism, the Anointing, the Miraculous Catch, the Entry into Jerusalem, the Arrest and the Crucifixion. If we accept the weight of manuscript evidence, and uphold the authenticity of Lk. 24.12, we may regard the matter as more or less settled. Luke knew and used John, and not vice versa, and what he is repeatedly doing, in Quadruple Tradition passages, is effecting a confluence of the two separate streams of Jesus material; in simple terms, he is combining the two.

In this context D. Moody Smith, who concedes that Cribbs has presented a 'surprisingly strong'[224] case for Luke's secondariness to John, observes that if we propose that Luke is attempting to combine the Johannine and the Markan traditions, then it is very strange that he has omitted

---

223. Cribbs, 'St Luke', p. 446, observes that the account of the time preceding the Ascension given in Acts 13.31 agrees more closely with John 20 than with Luke 24. Here, as elsewhere, Luke is sometimes closer to John in Acts than he is in his Gospel.
224. D.M. Smith, *John Among the Gospels*, p. 99.

almost all the very close verbal parallels between Mark and John, which would seem to provide a ready-made conflation of the two streams. But in reply it should be noted that all the omissions are consistent with Luke's editorial practices and emphases. Thus two relate to the theme of kingship: see Mk 15.9; Jn 18.39/Mk 15.17-18; Jn 19.2-3, which Luke plays down for political reasons. (The purple cloak reference in particular would have been deeply offensive to Roman sensibilities.) The parallel at Mk 6.50; Jn 6.20 comes in the Walking on the Water pericope which Luke omits altogether, since he keeps Jesus away from the sea, which he seemingly associated with evil, whenever possible. The parallel between Mk 2.9; Jn 5.8/Mk 2.12; Jn 5.9, where the narrative context is actually significantly different, consists of the command to the paralytic, ἆρον σου τὸν κράβ-αττον Luke follows Mark/Matthew's context here, and like Matthew he avoids the vulgar Markan/Johannine κράβαττον, just as he avoids their later ὠτάριον. The other parallels that Luke omits are in the Anointing sequence and have been considered above. In no case is Luke's omission of the material shared by Mark and John inconsistent with the contention that he is nevertheless throughout his Gospel trying to reconcile the two traditions.

What, then, are we to conclude? The nature of the relationship between John and the Synoptics has long been debated, since there has been no really satisfactory explanation that has commanded wide critical support to account for both the similarities between the two traditions—which are manifold—and also the numerous differences—which are striking. Perhaps what is needed is a new hypothesis.[225] I suggest that Luke, as well as using Mark and Matthew, in addition used John. He did so mainly for narrative purposes, without feeling in any way obliged to include all of John's material[226] when it conflicted with his own interpretation. (We may compare his omission of the Markan and Matthaean material which he finds uncongenial, such as Mark's criticisms of Jesus' family and the disciples; or the Matthaean stress on hellfire and judgment; or, indeed, any evidence of a Gentile mission which either one records, since this does not square with Luke's view that the time of the Gentiles is after the Resurrection.)

Luke is throughout prepared to alter and rearrange his material, and to add to it or cut it if necessary, in order to achieve his aim of an 'ordered' (καθεξῆς) narrative, which will give 'certainty', or 'accurate information,

225. Similarly D.M. Smith, *Johannine Christianity*, pp. 124ff.
226. See Gericke, 'Johannes-Evangeliums', p. 816. I offer my own explanation for Luke's omission of much Johannine material in the following chapter.

the truth' (ἀσφάλειαν)[227] to his readers. Thus when Soards says: 'The greatest differences between Luke and Mark may be the result of Luke's strongest motives for writing his Gospel',[228] I would suggest that this also applies to his use of Matthew and John. The 'many' sources that Luke refers to in his prologue (Lk. 1.1) are therefore to be taken seriously, and not dismissed as a mere rhetorical commonplace. The ὑπηρέται[229]...τοῦ λογοῦ of Lk. 1.2 would thus refer at least to Mark, and maybe also to Matthew, and the αὐτόπται would include John,[230] who certainly claims eyewitness testimony at 21.24,[231] in a verse which concludes with the verb, like the αὐτόπται, in the plural, καὶ οἴδαμεν ὅτι ἀληθὴς αὐτοῦ ἡ μαρτυρία ἐστιν. Luke 'ha[s] gathered the story of Jesus from the αὐτόπται[232] and in Acts he adds to this the history of the early Church, which he himself (Lk. 1.3) as a conscientious historian has investigated.

227. The καθεξῆς is thus demonstrated by the concern for chronology which we have seen in Luke, and by his attempt to reconcile conflicting chronologies, if possible. The ἀσφάλεια is evidenced by Luke's attempt to include both Johannine and Markan/ Matthaean material when he can, and perhaps, also, to guard against heretical misinterpretation. The facts which Luke gives provide the security.

228. M. Soards, *The Passion According to Luke: The Special Material of Luke 22* (JSNTSup, 14; Sheffield: Sheffield Academic Press, 1987), p. 123.

229. Gericke, 'Johannes-Evangeliums', p. 816 observes that the only parallel in the New Testament for ὑπηρέται as applied to the disciples is at Jn 18.36.

230. Cf. Gericke, 'Johannes-Evangeliums', p. 816.

231. See also Jn 19.35. Alexander, *Preface*, p. 121, notes that in ancient prologues αὐτόπται is normally used to mean personal contact with a living tradition (i.e. the original witness) and μάρτυς to bearing testimony.

232. Thus C.K. Barrett, 'The Third Gospel as a Preface to Acts? Some Reflections', in F. van Segbroeck (ed.), *The Four Gospels: Festschrift Frans Neirynck*, II (3 vols.; BETL; Leuven: Leuven University Press, 1992), pp. 1451-66 (1462).

Chapter 8

LUKE'S AIM: A CORRECTIVE GOSPEL

8.1. *Introduction*

It has been shown in the preceding pages that Luke is to some extent writing a 'corrective' Gospel. Indeed, this might be said of the other evangelists, too.[1] Mark, through the motif of the disciples' failure to understand, is in part perhaps seeking to correct mistaken ideas which did not emphasize sufficiently the radical break with Jewish traditions and Judaism which was involved in Christianity. Matthew rewrites Mark to stress that Jesus is the fulfilment of Jewish prophecy, the teacher and authentic interpreter of the Torah to his followers. John has significantly reinterpreted the Jesus material to accord with his own very different views. All four Evangelists have their own agenda to pursue.[2] It is for this reason that the ἀσφάλεια of Lk. 1.4 may be deliberately ambiguous.[3] Luke is aiming both to correct erroneous ideas so that his readers will know 'the truth' (thus, RSV) and also to reassure doubters that the teaching is 'well-founded' (so, JB). Confidence comes from a knowledge of the facts; the two are closely related. For Luke, to be an adequate witness one must first be properly taught: Apollos in Acts 18.28 cannot show from the

---

1.   Similarly, J.C. Fenton, 'Why Are There Four Gospels?' (unpublished paper read to the Oxford Society of Historical Theology).

2.   Whether or not John knew Mark's Gospel is disputed by Johannine scholars. Even though with C.K. Barrett and others I believe that he probably did, the point is irrelevant, strictly speaking, to my contention that Luke knew and used both. Nevertheless, I would suggest that John's proposed use of Mark, which scholars such as Barrett believe was significantly different from the way Luke and Matthew used the second Gospel, provides an analogy for the way Luke could have used John.

3.   Cadbury, 'Preface', pp. 509-11, makes a similar suggestion for ἀκριβῶς and καθεξῆς (Lk. 1.3). Ambiguity was a recognized rhetorical device: see Pseudo-Cicero, *Rhetorica ad Herrenium* 4.53.67; cf. Quintilian, *Institutio Oratoria* 8.3.83, on 'emphasis', or meaning more than one says.

Scriptures that 'the Christ was Jesus' until he has been 'more accurately'[4] instructed by Priscilla and Aquila.

In her consideration of Luke's prologue, in which the author states his purpose in writing, L. Alexander notes that the verb ἐπιχειρέω (cf. Lk. 1.1) almost always serves to 'damn with faint praise' when it is used in the third person, although in the first person it can convey modest self-deprecation;[5] it is significant that Luke's uses of it elsewhere are in hostile contexts.[6] Others had attempted to write a narrative of the events concerning Jesus and this encouraged Luke to offer his own version, which by its mere existence suggests that he felt some dissatisfaction with the earlier accounts.[7] Since I am assuming, on the basis of the evidence presented in the preceding pages, that Luke's, not John's, is the fourth Gospel,[8] I shall review the other three canonical Gospels, and attempt in the light of Luke's treatment of them to deduce what particular features he wished to interpret differently. This is inevitably a highly speculative exercise, but it is nevertheless a very important one, since usually why an author includes or omits material will explain what is included or omitted. As V. Taylor remarks: 'Unless we can give our theories regarding the use of sources some rational explanation of the writer's purpose and intention, our hypothesis remains precarious indeed. No writer worthy of the name will utilize sources at random; he will have a reason for what he does...'[9]

8.2. *Luke's Use of Mark*

8.2.1. *Order*
Almost all critics believe that Mark was Luke's main source for much of his narrative. With a very few exceptions, most of which occur in the

---

4. ἀκριβέστερον, Acts 18.26; cf. ἀκριβῶς Lk. 1.3.

5. See Alexander, *Preface*, pp. 110, 115, although she is cautious about assuming that Luke necessarily intends any criticism of his predecessors.

6. At Acts 9.29; 19.13. This is pointed out by Cadbury, 'Preface', p. 493.

7. Contra du Plessis, 'The Purpose of Luke's Prologue', pp. 259-71, and R.J. Dillon, 'Previewing Luke's Project from his Prologue (Lk. 1:1-4)', *CBQ* 43 (1981), pp. 205-27. Although Luke's κἀμοὶ links him to his predecessors in terms of genre, there would have been no point in his writing another account if he had felt that existing versions were adequate. This is also the conclusion of G. Klein, 'Lukas 1:1-4 als theologisches Programm', in E. Dinkler (ed.), *Zeit und Geschichte: Dankesgabe an R. Bultmann zum 80 Geburtstag* (Tübingen: J.C.B. Mohr, 1964), pp. 193-216 (195ff.)

8. Similarly, Gericke, 'Johannes-Evangeliums', p. 818.

9. Taylor, *Behind the Third Gospel*, p. 31.

Passion, he follows Mark's order. This to Luke was an important consideration, as is evident from the word καθεξῆς in his prologue (Lk. 1.3). It normally implies chronological order,[10] as is the case elsewhere in Luke.[11] Chronological order is not, however, Mark's main concern,[12] which is to present the 'good news of Jesus Christ, Son of God'.[13] His narrative begins abruptly at the Baptism and ends without an explicit post-Resurrection appearance in Mark's text: the Resurrection is only foretold and implied.[14] Luke, like Matthew, provides both a birth and a post-Resurrection narrative, although (unlike Matthew) he fills the gap between infancy and maturity by including a story of the boy Jesus in the Temple.[15]

In this context we may observe that Luke has a historian's eye for causality; thus the connection between the actions of the Jews against Jesus and the coming doom of Jerusalem (which is only implied in Mark 13) is made clear not only at Lk. 13.31-35[16] but very powerfully in the context of the Passion itself at Lk. 23.27-31. Moreover, he motivates actions which often seem arbitrary in Mark, such as the response of the disciples to Jesus' call. Similarly, he groups related events together, so that his narrative proceeds in a less disjointed fashion; for example, he links the reference to the later imprisonment of John the Baptist with the account of the Baptism at Lk. 3.19-20, rather than separating them, as at Mk 1.9-11; 6.17-29. He carefully connects his two volumes, too, so that things predicted in his Gospel form part of the narrative of Acts.[17]

Luke nevertheless feels free to alter the sequence of events to suit his

---

10. Thus, e.g., W. Bauer, *A Greek–English Lexicon of the New Testament and Other Early Christian Literature* (Chicago: University of Chicago Press, 2nd edn, 1958), *ad loc*. This is also the interpretation of L. Alexander and H.J. Cadbury, albeit in a very general, broad sense, which could therefore include the prophecy/fulfilment motif and the salvation history schema, both of which are central to Luke's presentation. Similarly, Baarlinck, 'Die zyklische Struktur', *passim*.

11. At Lk. 8.1; Acts 3.24; 11.4; 18.23.

12. Papias (c. 60–c. 130 CE) said that Mark's narrative was not 'in order'.

13. Jesus and 'the gospel' are very closely linked in Mark.

14. Like very many scholars, I believe that Mark's Gospel was meant to end at 16.8.

15. We may compare other ancient biographies, such as Plutarch, *Life of Alexander* 5; or Philostratus, *Life of Apollonius* 1.7, where the precocious wisdom of the hero even in childhood is stressed; cf. Josephus, *Life* 8-9.

16. Cf. Mt. 23.37-39.

17. Among other examples, Drury, *Tradition*, p. 108, notes that there is a close connection between Lk. 21.15 and Acts 6.10; and also Lk. 21.18 and Acts 27.34.

own purposes when necessary; the obvious example is the shifting of the rejection at Nazareth to the very beginning of Jesus' ministry, with Jesus' speech in the synagogue providing a programme for the mission as Luke sees it, in the same way that the Joel prophecy and Pentecost are programmatic in Acts. Jesus, anointed by God with the Spirit at his baptism, proclaims that the time is now: now is the 'acceptable year of the Lord', and this has profound implications for all, Gentiles as well as Jews.

8.2.2. *Narrative Technique*

Like Mark, Luke is a born storyteller, as is evident in parables such as the Prodigal Son, the Pharisee and the Tax-collector, and the Good Samaritan. Unlike Matthew, therefore, who obliterates most of the distinguishing features from the different healing narratives, perhaps because he wishes instead to stress their representative character,[18] Luke takes over many of the details which enliven Mark's narrative, such as the attempt to penetrate the roof by the bearers of the paralytic,[19] or the description of the fetters and chains used to secure the Gerasene/Gadarene demoniac. He even provides some touches of his own to add pathos—the withered arm is the man's right; Jairus's daughter and the Widow of Nain's son are only children.

Like Mark, too, Luke is fond of presenting the material dramatically, using dialogue and vividly contrasting scenes; in both Gospels we see the demoniac after the exorcism ἱματισμένον καὶ σωφρονοῦντα, and then the evangelist focuses on the fear this arouses in the crowd. Similarly, in their accounts of the woman with the haemorrhage, Jesus asks who among the thronging crowd has touched him, and this is followed by an interview between Jesus and the fearful and trembling sufferer. In the latter example, however, Luke's readiness to alter details which conflict with his own emphases is also apparent. (This is a consistent feature of his response to his sources; Luke is not afraid to make changes if necessary.)[20] Thus

18. This would also explain why he doubles the number of those healed at Mt. 8.28; 9.27; 20.30.

19. Luke modifies Mark's account in line with the building practices to which he was accustomed, however; roofs in Luke are tiled.

20. To call such a treatment 'conservative' does not accord with the facts: even in terms of content, there is the 'Greater Omission' of Mk 6.45–8.26 by Luke; the different placement of the Anointing and the Rejection of Jesus at Nazareth pericopes (and substantial differences of presentation in these, too); and the addition of Birth and post-Resurrection stories.

whereas in Mk 5.33 the woman tells only Jesus what has happened, in Lk. 8.47 she testifies to it publicly before all the people and hence serves as a witness, an important theme which Luke shares with the Johannine tradition.

8.2.3. *Style*

Stylistically Luke frequently polishes up Mark's accounts, improving the concord[21] and replacing Mark's Semitic parataxis with subordinate adverbial clauses which use participles in the Greek manner. He usually chooses to avoid the historic present tense and also Mark's favourite εὐθύς, both of which impart a breathless pace to much of Mark's narrative. Likewise, Luke omits vulgarisms such as κράβαττον (Mk 2.11; cf. Lk. 5.24), κοράσιον (Mk 5.42; cf. Lk. 8.54) and ὠτάριον (Mk 14.47; cf. Lk. 22.50). Mark's Aramaic expressions, too, such as *Talitha cumi* at Mk 5.41 and *Ephphatha* at Mk 7.34, and the name *Boanerges* at Mk 3.17, which would presumably have sounded strange to Luke's audience, find no place in his narrative. There is an interesting contrast here between Luke's Gospel and Acts, where on three occasions Luke uses Aramaic terms[22] and provides some sort of translation of them, albeit one which has baffled generations of scholars. The explanation for this change of Lukan policy may be that Luke wishes to distance his readers from Judaea and things Jewish in Acts, and he effects this by using unfamiliar terms, emphasized by editorial asides which draw attention to their strangeness.[23]

8.2.4. *Themes*

8.2.4.1. *Discipleship.* Some of Mark's emphases Luke accepts with only minor modifications. Although he prefers Matthew as his main source for teaching material,[24] his concerns, like Mark's, are pastoral ones, and he follows Mark's structure in this respect. He therefore places Matthaean teaching (plus much material peculiar to him) within Mark's context of the last journey to Jerusalem, which is also a course on discipleship. It should

---

21. E.g., cf. Mk 4.41; Lk. 8.25.

22. Namely, '*Akeldama*, that is, Field of Blood' (Acts 1.19); '*Barnabas*, which means Son of encouragement' (Acts 4.36); '*Elymas* [is] the meaning of his [i.e. Bar-Jesus'] name' (Acts 13.8).

23. Cf. S.M. Sheeley, *Narrative Asides in Luke–Acts* (JSNTSup, 72; Sheffield: Sheffield Academic Press, 1992), p. 126.

24. Most obviously, in the Sermon on the Plain, and throughout nearly all the central section.

be noted that although Luke reserves ἡ ὁδός as a title for Christianity in Acts (see Acts 9.2; 19.9, 23; 22.4; 24.14) and in consequence avoids Mark's use of the term,[25] he nevertheless follows Mark very closely in his understanding of the implications of discipleship. V. Taylor[26] estimated that the verbal agreement between Mk 8.34-9.1 and Lk. 9.23-27 on the conditions of discipleship is 83.9 per cent, which is a very high figure.

8.2.4.2. *Attitude to Judaism*. Luke's attitude to Jewish exclusivity, too, is in many ways as critical as Mark's. Hence although all three synoptic evangelists stress that Jesus eats with tax-collectors and sinners, Mark and Luke lay greater emphasis on his reluctance to let minutiae of Torah-observance override personal need when it comes to touching those classified as unclean or healing on the Sabbath, since the Torah's true intention is to do good, not harm; to save life, not to kill.[27]

Luke nevertheless omits the clashes between Mark's Jesus and the Pharisees over the tradition of the Elders and the abuse of Corban,[28] and he transfers the threats against the Temple which Jesus is said to have uttered at Mk 14.58 to Stephen in Acts. He carefully avoids any direct contradiction of the Torah by Jesus, who in his Gospel does not explicitly 'declare all foods clean',[29] any more than he does in Matthew's. Although from its context this is the implication of Lk. 10.8, the problem is not solved in Luke–Acts by explicitly abrogating the Torah.[30] Thus at Acts 10.28, Peter interprets the heavenly command at Acts 10.15, Ἃ ὁ Θεὸς ἐκαθάρισεν, σὺ μὴ κοίνου, to refer to the cleansing of the Gentiles—presumably, by baptism[31]—not to Jewish food laws and unclean animals. Moreover, the Apostolic Decree of Acts 15.19-20 relies on the Torah, although for Luke the crucial factor is the initiative of the Spirit, through whose direction Peter is brought to perceive the significance of his vision, so that the mission is extended to the Gentiles.

25. Cf. Mk 8.27/Lk. 9.18; Mk 9.33-34/Lk. 9.46; Mk 10.52/Lk. 18.43.
26. Taylor, *Behind the Third Gospel*, p. 84.
27. Mk 3.4; Lk. 6.9 (cf. Mt. 12.12).
28. These would have been irrelevant in a non-Jewish environment, so that Luke's omission of them could be seen to offer support to the common perception of Luke as a Gentile writing for Gentiles. This may be to oversimplify, however, as is argued by Esler, *Community and Gospel*, pp. 121ff. Esler notes that Luke deals with the question of ritual washing in Lk. 11.37-41 (cf. Mt. 23.25-28).
29. See Mk 7.19 (although there are textual variations here).
30. See D. Juel, *Luke–Acts* (Atlanta, GA: John Knox Press, 1983), pp. 105ff.
31. Cf. the cleansing function of the Spirit in the Dead Sea Scrolls (e.g. 1QH 16).

Luke sees Christianity as the fulfilment of Judaism; it is what Judaism is aiming at, and he is therefore obliged to present a positive picture of what it should be. The piety of Anna and Simeon is emphasized in the birth narrative, and moreover his Jesus, like Paul in Acts, is a very good and devout Jew. It is significant that Luke's Gospel begins and ends in the Temple, the heart of Judaism. The continuation of the story into a second volume, however, allowed Luke to impose a clear temporal structure on his material: God's promises to Israel were fulfilled in Jesus (Luke), and then extended to the Gentiles (Acts), as had always been intended (see Lk. 2.32). Without presenting Jesus as being in conflict with the faith of his people, which would have been offensive to Jewish-Christians, Luke was thus able to show Judaism and the salvation offered by the Covenant as belonging to the past; the future lay with Christianity.

8.2.5. *Treatment of Jesus' Family and the Disciples*

Luke treats the disciples and Jesus' family differently, too. Mark is implicitly critical of Jesus' family, who do not understand his mission any more than do the disciples, and indeed at 3.21 think he is insane.[32] Luke treats Mary in particular with sensitivity; hence although Jesus gently rebukes her when she fails to understand why he has tarried in Jerusalem,[33] Luke takes care to stress afterwards both Jesus' obedience to her and her own subsequent reflection on what has taken place, which removes much of the sting from the reproof. Luke drops Mk 6.4d,e too (cf. Lk. 4.24), and whereas in Mk 3.33-35 Jesus excludes his family from the circle of Christian disciples, Luke's modification of this at Lk. 8.21, omitting the harsh τίς ἐστιν ἡ μήτηρ μου καὶ οἱ ἀδελφοί μου (Mk 3.33), serves rather to include Jesus' disciples in his family.

If Mark's treatment of Jesus' family is at best equivocal,[34] his attitude to the disciples, whose incapacity to understand his teaching and the nature of his mission frequently exasperates Jesus,[35] sometimes seems to verge

32. οἱ παρ' αὐτοῦ is ambiguous, but it is usually interpreted, from its context, as meaning 'his family'; see Bultmann, *History of the Synoptic Tradition*, p. 29. (Bultmann links Mk 3.20-22 and vv. 31-35.). See also J.D. Crossan, 'Mark and the Relatives of Jesus', *NovT* 15 (1973), pp. 81-113.

33. See Lk. 2.49. Strictly speaking, in view of the revelations about his birth made to Mary, she should not have been concerned. Her maternal anxiety, though natural, is misplaced.

34. Crossan, 'Relatives', sees his treatment as straightforwardly hostile.

35. See especially Mk 8.17-21. The disciples never see more than 'through a glass, darkly' in Mark.

on open hostility.[36] Luke's presentation of the disciples, who were after all the leaders of the early Church, which he portrays in idealized terms in Acts, was necessarily more positive. Although he accepts, with considerable reservation,[37] the motif of the disciples' incomprehension, he emphasizes that it was not their fault—they were not meant to: οἱ δὲ ἠγνόουν τὸ ῥῆμα τοῦτο καὶ ἦν παρακεκαλυμμένον ἀπ' αὐτῶν ἵνα μὴ αἴσθωνται αὐτό, καὶ ἐφοβοῦντο ἐρωτῆσαι αὐτὸν περὶ τοῦ ῥήματος τούτου (Lk. 9.45).

Other Markan criticism of the disciples is modified or omitted; thus Luke drops the incident in Mark's journey narrative[38] where James and John ask to sit in a place of honour in the Kingdom, retaining only the general lesson in humility addressed to all the disciples which concludes the episode—although since the point is important to Luke[39] he places this for maximum effect in the context of the Last Supper.[40] He also omits that stinging rebuke to Peter: Ὕπαγε ὀπίσω μου, Σατανᾶ, ὅτι οὐ φρονεῖς τὰ τοῦ Θεοῦ ἀλλὰ τὰ τῶν ἀνθρώπων (Mk 8.33).

In Luke, Satan demands to sift Peter like wheat, but Jesus intercedes for him, and even though his denials are recounted (albeit in a softened form), his rehabilitation, too, is anticipated.[41] Most telling of all, whereas in Mark Jesus' disciples fail him on three separate occasions by sleeping when he has commanded them to watch, and then scatter in terror when he is arrested, leaving him to face the ordeal of crucifixion alone, in Luke they sleep (from grief!)[42] only once, they do not flee, and they even watch the crucifixion from afar (Lk. 23.49).

36. Thus T. Weeden, *Mark: Traditions in Conflict* (Philadelphia: Fortress Press, 1971). It should be noted, however, that Weeden, who believed that the disciples' misconceptions represent heretical attitudes which Mark's community opposed, greatly overstates his case.

37. In Lk. 8.10 (and Mt. 13.11) the disciples are not merely given the secret(s) of the Kingdom: they know them. Luke requires the disciples to have understood sufficiently to preach the Kingdom at Lk. 9.2 (cf. Mk 6.12). Luke also provides excuses for some of their lapses: Peter is too drowsy at the Transfiguration to know what he is saying, and later, they disbelieve the astonishing news of the Resurrection 'for joy' (Lk. 24.41).

38. See Mk 10.35-41.

39. See, most obviously, the Magnificat (Lk. 1.52).

40. Similarly, R.C. Tannehill, 'A Study in the Theology of Luke–Acts', *ATR* 43 (1961), pp. 195-203.

41. See Lk. 22.32. The same presentation, muted denials by Peter and subsequent rehabilitation, is also found in John.

42. Grief was, however, a negative quality to Greek philosophical schools such as

8.2.6. *Presentation of Jesus*

Luke's modifications to Mark's portrayal of Jesus are partly to be attributed to the same tendency to idealize that is apparent in his presentation of both the disciples and the Church. Luke's Jesus, like a Greek σοφός, is fully in command of his emotions; we see little evidence of anger, irritation, compassion, or indeed of love such as that felt by Mark's Jesus for the rich young would-be follower.[43] His death is that of the perfect martyr;[44] instead of Mark's anguished cry of dereliction, Luke's Jesus forgives his enemies, commits his Spirit to God in perfect trust, and then expires.

Mark focuses much more sharply on the suffering of Jesus than does Luke, who (like John) plays down this motif. Mark makes no attempt to mitigate the sheer horror of Jesus' agonized, lonely death on the cross, which takes place in an atmosphere of unrelieved metaphorical and cosmological gloom. The heart of Mark's message is encapsulated in the confession/transfiguration sequence at Mk 8.27–9.13: 'The Son of Man *must* (δεῖ) suffer';[45] the way to glorification lies only through suffering. It is only possible really to know who Jesus is—namely, the Son of God (and it is this identity that is concealed consistently in Mark's Gospel until the time is right to proclaim it, after the Passion/Resurrection)[46]—by accepting the necessity for his death. The title 'Messiah', which may represent an attempt by others to impose their hopes on Jesus (see, especially, Mk 8.29-31), is treated with great reserve by Mark;[47] it is not that the title is wrong, but it is inadequate, and it arouses the wrong expectations. Mark defines 'Messiah' in terms of a role, that of the Son of Man who must

the Stoics; see Diogenes Laertius, *Lives of the Eminent Philosophers* 7.111-112. The same was true elsewhere, too; see Horace, *Odes* 1.33; 2.9, and Longinus, *On The Sublime* 8. So, too, in Hellenistic Judaism (Philo, *Rer. Div. Her.* 270). Here, it implies a failure in faith. We note that in Luke Jesus is not 'deeply sorrowful', as he is in Mk 14.33-34; Mt. 26.37-38.

43. Cf. Mk 10.21; Lk. 18.22.

44. Cf. Plato's portrait of Socrates.

45. Mk 8.31.

46. Thus 1.1 is credal; 1.11 and 5.7 are said only to Jesus; the revelations of 1.24 and 3.11 are silenced; 12.6 is parabolic and hidden; 14.61 is ironic and so, in my opinion, is 15.39, where the οὗτος ὁ is contemptuous, and likewise functions at the expense of the speaker since what is said is true, although he does not perceive it.

47. Contra W. Wrede, *The Messianic Secret* (Cambridge: James Clark, 1971), however, it is not Jesus' Messiahship that is the main focus of Mark's interpretation: it is his Sonship.

suffer and will afterwards be exalted; the two are so tightly fused that they almost coalesce. And at 10.45; 14.24 Mark stresses that Jesus' suffering is *for us*. Although there are only two specific references to the atoning power of his death, both are heavily emphasized by context, as Hengel[48] observes.

Luke's understanding is rather different. The redemptive significance of Jesus' death is not a motif that he finds congenial, and he either plays it down or omits it altogether from his Gospel.[49] The 'suffering Son of Man' is less important to him than is the exalted Son of Man, as we have seen; Luke's distinctive emphasis is that, in fulfilment of the prophecies, the *Messiah* must suffer[50] (thus removing any dangerous implications from the title), and then must be raised from the dead and enter into his glory, which in Luke's narrative takes place at the Ascension. The most significant of Jesus' titles in Luke–Acts is that of Lord;[51] 'Jesus Christ and him risen', rather than Mark's more Pauline 'Jesus Christ and him crucified', is the core of Luke's Christology.

8.2.7. *Other Modifications and Alterations*

There are many of Mark's other points which Luke wishes to modify substantially or avoid altogether. Thus he greatly reduces the extent of the ministry in Galilee, which is important to Mark, and instead, as we have seen, places more emphasis on Judaea. Teaching in Luke is more public, too; he omits Mark's repeated inside/outside contrast, so that Jesus never takes the disciples inside the house for private instruction, as is frequently the case in Mark's Gospel.[52] Similarly, he does not take over Mark's 'secrecy' motif, except in a greatly abbreviated way at Lk. 4.41; 5.14. Although Luke is as anxious as Mark (Mk 8.31-32; 9.9) to underline the

---

48. M. Hengel, *The Gospel of Mark*, p. 37.

49. He omits Mk 10.45, and the 'words of institution' (Lk. 22.19-20) are a textual crux. (Acts 20.28 is Luke's attempt to sound Pauline.)

50. At Lk. 24.26; Acts 2.36; 3.18; 4.26; 17.3; 26.23.

51. As argued convincingly by Franklin, *Christ the Lord*.

52. See Mk 7.17; 9.28, 33; 10.10. At 8.27; 10.23, 32-45; and 13.3, too, it is stressed that what is given is private teaching. Although Luke deliberately varies the audience for Jesus' teaching in his narrative, so that there are inevitably occasions when the disciples alone are taught, the emphasis is quite different. We notice that Luke usually omits Mark's revelatory formula κατ' ἰδίαν, perhaps because it seemed too exclusive. It may also have had unwished associations with the private instruction given to initiates by some heretical groups. (It was to be a feature of many of the differing Gnostic systems.)

crucial importance of the Resurrection in changing the perception of the disciples and others, since it is the supreme testimony that Jesus is God's Chosen, Luke (like John) prefers to do so by showing that Jesus is only recognized as *the* Lord, ὁ κύριος, after the Resurrection.[53] He also wishes to remove any doubts about the actuality of the Resurrection, which Mark's open-ended narrative had done nothing to dispel. Thus whereas Mark's account is a delicate invitation to faith, so sketchy that it requires to be believed 'on the basis of sheer trust', as Houlden says,[54] Luke's version approaches crude early Christian apologetic.

8.3. *Luke's Use of Matthew*

An explanation for the modifications Luke made to Matthew has been offered in the preceding pages, so the main points can be briefly summarized here. We should note at the outset an important structural feature; Luke dislikes long, uninterrupted blocks of teaching, and therefore he breaks up Matthew's five great discourses, relocating material into appropriate contexts in his narrative.[55] The concept of order, καθεξῆς, is irrelevant here, since Matthew's discourses clearly do not represent actual sermons; Luke was therefore free to recast the material in them.

8.3.1. *Inclusiveness*
With regard to content we observe, firstly, that Luke does not wish any of his readers to suppose that Jesus intended his message to be confined specifically to Israel; Luke therefore omits Mt. 10.5-6; 15.24. And since he carefully keeps Jesus out of Gentile territory during his ministry,[56] it does not appear that Jesus is reluctant to heal Gentiles who are in need; he simply fails to encounter many. Luke's aim is to provide a truly inclusive Gospel which will not needlessly offend any group's sensibilities, and will

53. Although ὁ κύριος is a Lukan editorial favourite (see, e.g., 1.43; 7.13; 10.39, 41; 11.39, being especially common in pericopes peculiar to Luke, such as Zacchaeus or the Healing of the Crippled Woman, it is not used by disciples until after the Resurrection (at Lk. 24.34 and throughout Acts): cf. Jn 20.2, 18, 25, 28 where the same is true.

54. J.L. Houlden, *Backward into Light* (London: SCM Press, 1987), p. 56.

55. This is argued at length in my review of Luke's central section. Jesus as teacher and interpreter of the Torah is Matthew's conception, and he characteristically begins his ministry with the Sermon on the Mount; Luke instead commences with the 'Nazareth Manifesto' (Lk. 4.18-27).

56. Hence his 'greater omission' of Mk 6.45-8.26.

be acceptable to as many as possible,[57] and he therefore rejects material in Matthew with a particularly Jewish orientation.[58] Luke's emphasis from the beginning is that in Christ is salvation for *all people*, πᾶσα σάρξ (Lk. 3.6: cf. Mt. 3.3), as is asserted in the Birth narrative, the Baptism, and the Sermon at Nazareth. Indeed, it is the offer of salvation to all, including Gentiles, that alienates the Jews from the first, as the incident at Nazareth shows. Their murderous spite, arising from the same cause, is paralleled repeatedly in Acts. The problem, as Luke sees it, is Jewish exclusivity. He is *including* Gentiles, rather than excluding Jews: to the Jew first, and after, to the Greek.[59]

It is also evident that Luke does not share Matthew's relish for the theme of separation and judgment. Luke clearly finds hellfire and damnation uncongenial, and he wants to include as many as possible within the Christian fold; Matthaean parables such as the Wheat and the Tares, the Dragnet, and the Sheep and the Goats therefore find no place in his Gospel. He does not wish to deny that there will be a judgment, as is evidenced by the (shared) Parable of the Wicked Tenants, and also by the (Lukan) Parable of the Fig-tree:[60] but nevertheless, like 1 Peter,[61] Luke apparently hopes that most will be acquitted. Even at the Baptism there is a contrast between Matthew's ἐν πνεύματι ἁγίῳ καὶ πυρί (Mt. 3.11), which is understood in a judgmental way, and Luke's use of the image at Lk. 3.16, where it seems to be connected to the coming of the Holy Spirit at Pentecost and provides a link forwards to his second volume.[62]

Luke normally prefers carrots to sticks, and he stresses patience, fortitude, and endurance (primarily, in faith; see Lk. 8.15, which probably reflects the continuing danger of apostasy in the face of persecution). And like the author of Hebrews, he is careful to distinguish between sins committed knowingly[63]—for example, the rejection of their Messiah by the Jews, which merits a 'severe beating' at Lk. 12.47—and those which were

---

57. Though with some qualifications; Luke wishes to rule out any heretical misinterpretation.

58. See Mt. 5.47; 6.32; 7.6; 10.18; 18.17. Although Jesus at Mt. 28.19 commands his disciples to take the gospel to 'all nations', Gentiles are 'swine' and 'dogs' at 7.6 (cf. 15.26), and are grouped with the hated tax-collectors at 18.17.

59. Cf. Rom. 1.16.

60. Lk. 13.6-9.

61. See 1 Pet. 3.19.

62. Thus Tannehill, *Narrative Unity*, I, p. 57.

63. See Heb. 10.26-27.

done unwittingly, and therefore receive a less harsh punishment. Indeed, ignorance is a key theme not only in Luke's Gospel,[64] but also in Acts,[65] and much of the tragedy of Luke's Passion is because the Jews have failed to recognize the 'time of their visitation'. All together call for Jesus' death at Lk. 23.18 (παμπληθεὶ is a Lukan addition); all alike will suffer the consequences (Lk. 19.43-44), unless they repent of their mistake.[66]

8.3.2. *Ethics*
Many features characteristic of Lukan ethics, such as his recognition of the supreme importance of love, and the need to respond to God's love for us by actions which demonstrate our love for others,[67] and also Luke's sympathy for the downtrodden and underprivileged (especially women) and for the poor, whose actual physical needs he stresses, are apparent when we compare Matthew's version of the material which the two evangelists share. We also notice that the Matthaean exhortation in the Sermon on the Mount (Mt. 5.48) to 'Be perfect' (and the antitheses included by Matthew and omitted by Luke, presumably because they made the Torah so much stricter, are indeed a counsel of perfection), is at Lk. 6.36 typically modified to 'Be merciful'. Luke also omits the rather chilling commission to bind and loose, given to the disciples by Matthew's Jesus,[68] which we infer that he found unacceptable.

8.3.3. *Other Differences*
As many have recognized, the treatment of the Torah by Luke shows some inconsistencies. Hence although at Lk. 16.17 he retains Matthew's assertion[69] of its continuing validity, and he presents Jesus (and Paul) as Torah-observant Jews, nevertheless, since to do good to others is always to do God's will, in practice Luke's Jesus is prepared to interpret the law flexibly when it conflicts with compassion.[70] In the main, therefore, Luke

---

64. Most obviously, in Jesus' words from the cross at Lk. 23.34.

65. See, especially, Acts 3.17; 13.27.

66. See Lk. 13.9. The preaching of the gospel to the Jews in Acts is their last chance.

67. The two commands to love God and to love one's neighbour, which both Mark and Matthew treat as separate, are combined at Lk. 10.27.

68. Mt. 18.18-19; cf. Jn 20.23.

69. See Mt. 5.18. Since the Law was unitary, breach of one requirement nullified observance of the rest.

70. E.g. at Lk. 13.15-16.

places much less emphasis on legal matters than does Matthew, and he leaves out Matthew's rather Rabbinic consideration[71] of which aspects of the Torah are most weighty. Likewise, he omits items such as the prohibition on travelling on the Sabbath even if it coincided with a catastrophe like the end of the world (Mt. 24.20), which perhaps sounded as bizarre to a non-Jew in the first century as they do to us today. In addition, he cuts most of Matthew's discourse on church discipline,[72] which he presumably felt was anachronistic; and he characteristically reinterprets the Parable of the Lost Sheep in a universalistic way as an example of God's grace in saving the lost rather than as aimed at the correction of an erring (Christian) brother. He alters, too, the ecclesiological instruction at the end of Matthew's Gospel (Mt. 28.19) to baptize in the name of the Father, the Son, and the Holy Spirit, even though the baptism of converts is important in Acts; the command of Luke's Jesus instead reflects very Lukan preoccupations, the preaching of repentance and the forgiveness of sins to all nations (see Lk. 24.47).

Material concerning the disciples is treated differently, too. Even though Luke's presentation is, on the whole, a positive one, as we have seen, so that Matthew's censure of their ὀλιγόπιστία receives little emphasis,[73] there are nevertheless no keys to the gates of heaven and authority on earth for Peter in Luke, perhaps because this seemed to denigrate Paul, his hero; the two men are clearly paralleled in Acts.[74] In this context we notice that the courage and resolution which Paul displays in his farewell speech at Miletus form a powerful contrast with the threefold denial of Jesus by Peter, following the bold words he speaks at Lk. 22.33, which find an echo in Acts 20.23. This deliberate paralleling of characters in Luke–Acts provides resonances both forwards and backwards; we are perhaps meant to weigh Paul against Peter here, although if so Luke leaves his readers to draw that inference for themselves.

---

71. Cf. Mt. 23.23, Lk. 11.42.
72. Cf. Mt. 18.15-22, Lk. 17.3-4.
73. The only use of this Matthaean concept is at Lk. 12.28.
74. Thus both have visions (Acts 10.10-16; cf. Acts 9.3); both have miraculous escapes from prison (Acts 12.7-10; cf. Acts 16.26); both impart the Holy Spirit by their touch (Acts 8.17; cf. Acts 19.6); both heal the lame (Acts 3.7; cf. Acts 14.10); both raise the dead (Acts 9.40; cf. Acts 20.10-12). Another possibility is that Mt. 16.18 may have seemed to conflict with 1 Cor. 3.11; Christ, not Peter, is the Church's foundation.

8.4. *Luke's Use of John*

8.4.1. *Introduction*

It is clear from the above that Luke has used Mark and Matthew differently,[75] although in both cases his response is in some respects a critical one. I would suggest that his use of John is different again. John served as a major inspiration for his distinctive presentation of the Baptism, the Miraculous Catch, the Anointing, the Hearings Before the Jewish Authorities and Pilate, the Empty Tomb, and the Jerusalem Resurrection appearance, but direct verbal agreements are on a small scale. They do, however, extend throughout the whole of Luke's two volumes, which suggests that he has treated John as a source with even more emphatic reserve than he accorded Matthew. He nevertheless knew and remembered it, however, as has been argued on the basis of the many correspondences of conception, presentation, chronology[76] and vocabulary. Even though Mark was the source which he seems to have valued most highly elsewhere for incident and order, if not for expression and teaching, Luke often seems to have chosen to use the historical details provided by John rather than by Mark, especially in his Passion, so that Mark is Luke's main source for his Passion account in only a modified way;[77] he is frequently as close (or closer) to John here.

As was observed above, however, there is rarely any direct verbal correspondence between Luke and John for more than a verse or so; John is usually paraphrased and alluded to rather than copied almost verbatim as Luke often copies Mark or Matthew. This suggests that Luke is perhaps working from his own notes on John[78] rather than directly from a copy of the text. Under these circumstances, it is almost inevitable that Luke would have retained some memory of John while using another source, which would have been reflected in his own version. Indeed, it is very likely that the echoes of Matthew when he is using Mark as his main

75. Similarly Green, 'Luke's Transformation of Matthew'.

76. John's Gospel was regarded as the more accurate, chronologically, by some early Christians. It was placed first in some Gospel collections, and Tatian used it as his primary source (in terms of order) in much of the *Diatessaron*.

77. G.B. Caird, *Saint Luke* (Pelican Commentary; Harmondsworth: Penguin, 1963), calculates that in Lk. 22.14-24.53, out of a total of 163 verses, there are only 20 where there is a close verbal correspondence between Luke and Mark. See, too, Taylor, *Behind the Third Gospel*; and *idem, Passion Narrative*.

78. Pliny the Younger's mention of this practice was referred to earlier, in 5.3.2.

source (and *vice versa*) are to be explained in a similar way. It is less probable that Luke was consistently attempting consciously to harmonize his three sources (although this is not as impossible a task as some[79] have supposed, since Tatian achieved it in his *Diatessaron*);[80] there would surely be more direct evidence of John in Luke if this were the case. Because there is so much less textual evidence to support the hypothesis that Luke used John, it is both more difficult and more risky to attempt to deduce his response to it. But if Luke is the fourth evangelist, as I have argued above, then we have the evidence provided by the other two Synoptic Gospels with which we can compare Luke's in order to determine where he has followed them and where he is closer to John.

8.4.2. *Narrative Content*
As far as content is concerned, it is noticeable that surprisingly few of the main sections of John's narrative find no echo at all in Luke–Acts, and this would support the contention that Luke valued John as a source in this respect. Luke is aiming at completeness; Klein[81] argues that καθεξῆς (Lk. 1.3) is a reference to the comprehensive nature of his account, and although it would not be true to claim that there are no omissions,[82] Luke nevertheless includes as much as possible of the material found in the other Gospels, very often taking a mediating position between divergent presentations, as has been shown in the preceding chapter. The only episodes unique to John[83] that he drops completely are the Marriage at Cana,

79. E.g. Wenham, *Redating*, pp. 206ff.

80. There were apparently other Gospel harmonies, too, which have not survived; Jerome (*Epistles* 121.6.15) refers to a possible list by Theophilus of Antioch.

81. G. Klein, 'Lukas 1:1-4', p. 210; see too, A. Wright, *The Gospel According to St Luke [in Greek]* (London: Macmillan, 1900), p. xvii, Section 7, where Luke's attempts to dovetail his sources and omit as little as possible are compared with Livy's practice. Cadbury, *Making of Luke–Acts*, p. 346, says that ἀκριβῶς (Lk. 1.3), when combined with verbs of knowing and finding out such as παρακολουθέω, implies that the information given is full and explicit, rather than meagre.

82. Contra F. Mussner, ' "καθεξῆς" im Lukasprolog', in E. Ellis and E. Grässer (eds.), *Jesus und Paulus: Festschrift für W.G. Kümmel zum 70 Geburtstag* (Göttingen: Vandenhoeck & Ruprecht, 1975), pp. 253-55, this cannot be the implication here.

83. Jn 7.1-10 has some connection with Mk 3.21-35 (and in both, the reference to the disbelief of Jesus' family is followed by an accusation that Jesus is possessed by a demon, which would support the suggestion that the two texts may be linked here). It is omitted by Luke because of its hostility to Jesus' brothers, one of whom was the head of the Jerusalem church in Acts; the Walking on the Water pericope, which occurs in

where the treatment of Mary is far from sympathetic (in Luke's pre-ministry story, the rebuke is considerably softened; compare Jn 2.4 and Lk. 2.49-51), and the Samaritan Woman at the Well, which conflicted with Luke's careful geographical and temporal structuring of his material (Luke omits Mark's story of the Syrophoenician Woman, and much else, for the same reason. It is possible, nevertheless, that the Johannine story has influenced Luke's account of the Anointing of Jesus).

Luke does not, however, narrate the incidents described by John as he narrates those in Mark and Matthew, where the verbal correspondence is often very close, and this again suggests that he did not have John's Gospel open/unrolled in front of him as he worked. In some cases he briefly summarizes the Johannine account; examples are the race to the tomb (cf. Jn 20.3-10 and Lk. 24.12) and the footwashing (cf. Jn 13.4-15 and Lk. 12.35, 37; 22.26-27). In other cases incidents in John do not connect directly with Luke's Gospel but have echoes in Acts, such as the healing in the portico at Bethzatha in Jerusalem (Jn 5.2-13), which is followed by an injunction to repentance (Jn 5.14) and a dispute with the Jews (Jn 5.19-47). This may be compared with the healing of the lame man in Solomon's portico in Jerusalem in Acts 3.1-11 (described at Acts 4.22 in the Johannine term σημεῖον), which is likewise followed by a call to repentance (3.17-26) and a dispute with the Jews (Acts 4.1-20). The words of the High Priest's official in Jn 18.22, too, are picked up in Acts 23.4; and Luke's treatment of Gamaliel at Acts 5.34-39 recalls Nicodemus,[84] who although an important Pharisee (Jn 3.1) is relatively sympathetic to Jesus and opposes the imposition of harsh measures against him (Jn 7.50-51).

Sometimes Luke refers to Johannine incidents in related parables,[85] such as the further allusion to the footwashing in the Parable of the Unworthy Servants at Lk. 17.7-10; or the reference to the three-year ministry in the Parable of the Fig-tree at Lk. 13.9; or to the healing at Siloam and the associated discussion of sin at Lk. 13.2-5. (It is also possible that there may be an allusion to the Marriage at Cana pericope in the Lukan addition

all three other Gospels, is omitted because he associates the sea with evil and prefers to keep Jesus away from it.

84. Martyn, *History and Theology*, pp. 161-63, notes the connection here, and suggests a common tradition.

85. Compare Luke's treatment of sayings in the Sermon on the Mount, where, as has been suggested above, some are turned into parables; cf. Mt. 5.44 and the Good Samaritan; Mt. 6.5-6 and the Pharisee and the Tax-Collector in Luke 18.9-13.

to Mk 2.22; Mt. 9.17 at Lk. 5.39, οὐδεὶς πιὼν παλαιὸν θέλει νέον λέγει γάρ ὁ παλαιὸς χρηστός ἐστιν, which is in some tension with the attached parable.)

The Lazarus story needs fuller consideration. Luke's parable emphasizes that even a resurrection from the dead does not make the Jews repent, and its point is clearly polemical, like John's narrative, where it precipitates the Passion. But Luke perhaps felt that John's story came too close to presenting Jesus as a wonder-worker,[86] and he was anxious to dissociate Christianity from any connection with pagan magic. In its place, as his account of the raising of a man from the dead, he presents the entirely Lukan story of the widow of Nnain's son, where Jesus is linked not to magic but to the Old Testament. But Luke not only alludes to the Johannine story in his own text, at Lk. 16.19-31; there are also many lexical parallels between the Lazarus story in John and the Raising of Tabitha in Acts 9.36-42. Fortna[87] notes: τις ἦν, ἀσθενήσασαν, ἀποθανεῖν, ἐγγὺς, ἀκούσαντες, ἀπέστειλαν, πρὸς αὐτόν, κλαίουσαι, ἔξω, ἐπίστευσαν. This is a sizeable list.

8.4.3. *Differing Emphases*
Luke's critique of John, however, is most obvious not in his treatment of John's narrative material, but in his omission of the Johannine discourses. Here the differences between Luke's interpretation of the significance of the Jesus event and John's are immediately apparent. Although some of John's themes—such as the importance of witnessing, believing, and the presence of the Spirit with believers, and also his interest in Judaea and Samaria and his hostility to οἱ Ἰουδαῖοι—are also to be found in Luke–Acts, many of John's emphases are uncongenial to Luke, and he either omits them altogether or considerably modifies them, as he does with Matthaean teaching material that he finds unacceptable.

8.4.3.1. *The Kingdom.* There is a wide divergence between Luke's and John's respective treatments of the theme of the Kingdom; a connection between the coming Kingdom of God and the behaviour to be expected of Jesus' disciples is entirely absent from John's Gospel. As John sees it, the

86. C. Bonner, 'Traces of Thaumaturgic Technique in the Miracles', *HTR* 20 (1927), pp. 171 81, shows from classical literature that the verbs ἐμβριμάομαι (Jn 11.33, 38) and ταράσσω (Jn 11.33) were associated with the frenzy of magicians; he cites Menander, *Corpus scriptorum historiae byzantii XIV*, p. 381, and the Paris *PGM* (suppl.gr. 574; 620ff.).
87. Fortna, *Gospel of Signs*, p. 84 n. 2.

Kingdom, the implication of which is summed up in the repeated metaphor of ζωή αἰώνιος,[88] is already present in Jesus. He therefore replaces Jesus' proclamation of the Kingdom with his own distinctive conception of Jesus as the Revealer, who proclaims himself the revelation of God (see, especially, Jn 14.9, ὁ ἑωρακὼς ἐμὲ ἑώρακεν τὸν πατέρα).

Although Luke shares John's conviction that the Kingdom is already present in some sense in Jesus, so that proclaiming the Kingdom and proclaiming Jesus are the same at Acts 28.31, it is nevertheless essentially a future reality[89] for Jesus' followers, as far as Luke is concerned. He prefers the ethical teaching of Mark and Matthew;[90] at Lk. 9.23-27, 12.32-40 the Kingdom is firmly linked to the behaviour expected of a disciple. The Kingdom is the core of Jesus' message: there are 46 'Kingdom' references in Luke–Acts, 18 occurring in material peculiar to him and 6 more being additions to the Markan/Matthaean parallels. Indeed, this theme is so important to Luke that he places two references to it within the context of the Last Supper, as opposed to only one in Mark and Matthew. It is connected by Luke to the giving of both the bread (Lk. 22.16) and the wine (Lk. 22.18), and, whichever text of Luke is authentic, there is clearly at least an implicit reference here to the later liturgical practice of the Church, which is thereby linked to its Lord and the Kingdom he embodies.[91]

8.4.3.2. *The Spirit.* The 'today' of salvation is in some respects a present reality for both Luke and John, in which Jesus' followers participate through their reception of the Spirit. But Luke wishes to dispel any idea that the Eschaton has already arrived, which might possibly be inferred from John's presentation; Luke is perhaps not so much trying to accommodate a Parousia delay here, as Conzelmann suggested, as to correct an over-realized eschatology. And although he shares John's interest in the Spirit, he views it in ecclesiological rather than individual terms. Luke avoids any suggestion of mystical indwelling, which perhaps had dangerous associations with the experiences of heretical groups.[92] In a similar

88. See Ashton, *Understanding*, pp. 216ff.

89. See, especially, Lk. 19.11; Acts 1.7.

90. It is perhaps worth noting that Mark and Matthew confirm each other in this respect; this provides a double testimony. John's interpretation seems unique.

91. If the longer text is authentic, Luke also alters Mark/Matthew's ὑπὲρ/περὶ πολλῶν to ὑπὲρ ὑμῶν. The new covenant sacrifice to be commemorated is for the Church.

92. We notice that Luke does not describe Paul's conversion experience/vision as taking place in an ecstatic state.

way, at Acts 2.4-12 he reinterprets the unquestionably eschatological 'gift of tongues' as an ability to communicate in other languages, thus emphasizing its significance for the Church, although Acts 10.46 shows that he is aware of the real meaning of the phrase.

8.4.3.3. *Love.* The theme of love is also treated differently by Luke, where it is central to Lukan ethics and the main focus of the Sermon on the Plain. As noted above, ethics as such are almost totally ignored in John's Gospel; the evangelist concentrates on the saving knowledge of the new life available here and now in Jesus. And this knowledge is the privilege of a chosen few: thus although love is important, it is exclusive, the love of Jesus for 'his own' (Jn 13.1),[93] who keep his commandments (Jn 14.21), and theirs for him and for each other (i.e. members of the community; see Jn 13.35; 15.12-17).[94] In Luke, love is demonstrated by one's behaviour to all one's neighbours, and the radical definition of 'neighbours' in Luke 10 also includes enemies, not just one's Christian brothers. This, to Luke, is the proper response to God's love for us, which extends to all humanity. It is not to be limited to a chosen few who keep the Commandments (Jn 14.21; 15.10), as is made evident in the three parables of Luke 15. His is a very inclusive Gospel; it is instructive to compare the universal application of the love principle found in Luke's two best-known parables, the Prodigal Son and the Good Samaritan, with the emphasis in John's Good Shepherd, which is narrowly aimed at Jesus' flock who hear his voice; those 'outside this fold', i.e. outside the Johannine community,[95] will also be saved if they respond to his commands, but they receive only the barest of acknowledgements.

8.4.3.4. *Christology.* As far as their respective Christologies are concerned, the differences between Luke and John in both interpretation and emphasis are very apparent; although both evangelists choose to concentrate on the glory, their focus is quite different. In John, Jesus is the pre-existent Son of Man, in whom the divine and the human coalesce, so that he is uniquely

---

93. See also Jn 17.20-23.

94. The same exclusive love for one's brother (and, as a correlative, hatred for everyone else!) is found in the Qumran. See, for example, 1QS 1.9-10; 2.24; 5.24. Both Josephus and Philo stress the importance of the love commandment to the Essenes.

95. This is usually thought to refer to the Gentile mission, though this is not explicit in the text.

the means for the descent of the divine and the ascent of the human.[96] Jesus' crucifixion is reinterpreted as exaltation, via the repeated and deliberately ambiguous verb ὑψόω; it is also glorification (see, for example, 12.27-32). The cry from the cross in John is one of triumph; 'the hour' represents victory, not defeat. In John, the Resurrection is, strictly speaking, superfluous. He puts Jesus firmly on the God side of the divide; as Jn 14.9-13 makes clear, he belongs above, and has been sent to earth to reveal the truth, which is himself as the supreme revelation of God.

Luke retains some of the glory retrojected into the earthly ministry, as the significant and Johannine δόξαν in the unparalleled Lk. 9.32 makes clear; at 9.51, too, the word ἀνάλημψις fuses crucifixion and exaltation much as does John's ὑψόω. Usually, however, Luke prefers to separate them and reserve the glory for the post-Resurrection Lord; once more, Luke's two-volume structure enables him to historicize his material by imposing a temporal framework onto it. Thus whereas in John Jesus, like God, has the power to judge,[97] and he likewise has the power to give life (Jn 5.21), even to a rotting corpse, in Luke Jesus is judge primarily when he is exalted to God's right hand after the Resurrection (see Acts 10.42; 17.31). The Passion in Luke represents Jesus' obedient acceptance of God's will, since it is necessary for the Messiah to suffer, but the narrative of the Passion is not itself presented as a victory; victory comes with the Resurrection.

Moreover, while both Luke and John play down the humiliation and suffering of Christ, John, like Mark, makes the atoning nature of that sacrificial death[98] explicit (see Jn 1.29). Luke, on the other hand, makes no connection between the forgiveness of sins and the actual death of Christ, even though forgiveness is a major Lukan theme. He stresses the salvific significance of the entire Jesus event from birth onwards, but not specifically the death; it is the trust in Jesus of the dying thief that saves him at Lk. 23.43.[99]

In addition, John's conception of Jesus as Revealer of heavenly secrets, expressed in language which veers close to ditheism at Jn 5.19-29; 10.30; 15.9-10, is alien to Luke, who prefers the direct pastoral guidance offered

96. This is perhaps the point of the ladder symbol in Jn 1.51.
97. See, e.g., Jn 5.22, 27, 30.
98. This is also the obvious interpretation of the Good Shepherd, who lays down his life for his friends.
99. See Lk. 5.20; 7.9-10, 50; 8.48; 18.42.

by Matthew's teacher. Although visions are important throughout Luke–Acts as a means of divine communication, John's presentation perhaps seemed too close to the ideas of some burgeoning heretical groups; Ashton[100] says:

> What we have…is a series of vignettes that encapsulate the view of the gospel as revelation. They say almost nothing of the content of this revelation: it is to be delivered by a divine envoy, charged with the task of carrying it to the world, the object of God's salvific love. The effect of this revelation will be dramatically divisive. Those who reject it *ipso facto* pronounce judgment on themselves. Those who accept it are granted a new life—the life of the new age. Having fulfilled his mission, the purpose of his entry into the world, the Son will return to the Father who sent him. If this is not gnosis it is remarkably close.

Luke prefers to keep the focus on the humanity of his Jesus, who provides a model for believers of the right way for a Christian to live and to die. He studiously avoids any intimation of Jesus' pre-existence; he therefore does not use John's above/below paradigm at all, and he separates Jesus from either a Wisdom or a Logos[101] Christology, which depicts Jesus as the pre-existent self-expression of Yahweh's Word. Wisdom, to Luke, is reserved for God;[102] indeed, Jesus is explicitly said to *grow* in wisdom at Lk. 2.52. Luke prefers to historicize (with an emphasis on the flesh) statements like 'the Word became flesh' in his birth narrative, just as he historicizes the Resurrection and the Ascension. Jesus' birth is the result of God's creative activity through the Spirit, the last and greatest in a long series of similar miraculous interventions, and this links it not to a metaphysical speculation which was to prove a fertile seedbed for developing Gnosticism, but to the Old Testament.

8.5. *Gnostic Speculations*

It is usually agreed that fully developed Gnostic systems cannot be dated any earlier than the mid-second century. Christianity and Gnosticism evolved at approximately the same time, there being much cross-fertiliza-

---

100. Ashton, *Understanding*, p. 545.

101. The transformation of Wisdom, who assisted God in creation in Prov. 3.19; 8.22-31, into the Logos (a concept found also in Philo) was prepared for by Sir. 24.3, who identified the creative Spirit of God in Gen. 1.2 with the expression of God's word in the Torah (cf. also *Jub.* 12.4).

102. Cf. Lk. 7.35/Mt. 11.19; Lk. 11.49/Mt. 23.34.

tion, so that scholars are divided as to how far it is primarily a second-century Christian heresy,[103] and how far its origins are independent of Christianity, to be found in the Hellenistic-Jewish culture which also nurtured the Gospels.[104] Gnosticism's cradle may have been Jewish Wisdom speculation combined in a highly syncretistic way with a middle Platonic philosophy,[105] and clearly the ideas it reflects must have been in the air for some time past.

8.5.1. *Modification of Proto-Gnostic Trends in Luke*

A desire to refute developing proto-Gnostic speculation—if not fully fledged Gnosticism—must therefore remain a plausible explanation for some of the modifications Luke makes to the other Gospels, especially if his is to be dated late, but we cannot be more definite than that. F.C. Baur believed that Luke's Gospel was extended to oppose the version used by the heretic Marcion: although none today would accept dating Luke as late as this (i.e. probably after 140 CE), Luke could nevertheless have been refuting already-current ideas which were drawn on later by Marcion.

In that case it may be significant that Luke avoids any intimation of Jesus' pre-existence. Moreover, his Jesus does not reveal heavenly secrets to an elect few, thus enabling them to participate in a new life here and now, such as we find in John.[106] Conduct is what matters to Luke, and the

---

103. Thus, for the most part, B. Layton, *The Gnostic Scriptures* (London: SCM Press, 1987), although he concedes that we cannot be sure.

104. The Jewish background of Gnosticism is supported by many, including R.McL. Wilson, *The Gnostic Problem: A Study in the Relations Between Hellenistic Judaism and the Gnostic Heresy* (London: A.R. Mowbray, 1963); B.A. Pearson, 'Jewish Sources in Gnostic Literature', in M. Stone (ed.), *Jewish Writings of the Second Temple Period* (CRINT, 2.2; Assen: Van Gorcum; Philadelphia: Fortress Press, 1984), pp. 443-81; G.W. MacRae, 'The Jewish Background of the Gnostic Sophia Myth', *NovT* 12 (1970), pp. 86-101; and P. Perkins, *Gnosticism and the New Testament* (Minneapolis: Fortress Press, 1993).

105. Thus Layton, *Gnostic Scriptures*, p. 8, says, 'The Gnostic myth seems to pre-suppose this speculative tradition' (i.e. a creation myth derived from a combination of Genesis and middle Platonism).

106. We may compare what we can deduce of the teachings of Valentinus, especially if *The Gospel of Truth* is his work, as Layton and others believe. Some critics, such as M.J. Edwards, 'Gnostics and Valentinians in the Church Fathers', *JTS* NS 40 (1989), pp. 26-47, maintain that Valentinus, while certainly classified as a heretic by Irenaeus, is not explicitly called a Gnostic, but many of his ideas are comparable to those regarded as Gnostic, and the distinction is irrelevant to my argument.

Eschaton is in any case a future event. As we have seen, too, Luke stresses
the universality of the salvation in Christ at Lk. 2.30-31; 3.6. There is no
suggestion that matter/the world, created by God (to whom Jesus is firmly
subordinated in Luke's presentation), is inherently evil and hostile, which
was the belief of heretics such as Marcion, although one could misinterpret John's Gospel and arrive at this conclusion.[107] Luke emphasizes that
Christianity is the fulfilment of Old Testament prophecy, and the promised
saviour is the human Jesus, with every stage in his story from gestation to
Ascension avouched by witnesses. Luke connects this firm base to the
present day of the Church by the bridge of the apostolic tradition, which is
confirmed by the Spirit; it would be difficult to establish a Christianity
upon more secure (ἀσφάλειαν, Lk. 1.4) foundations.

Elsewhere, too, Luke may be regarded as correcting ideas which were
developed by later heretics. We know from Irenaeus[108] that Basilides, who
was maybe an influence on Valentinus during his education in Alexandria,[109] omitted all mention of Christ's suffering and death in his teaching;
Simon of Cyrene, not Jesus, was crucified, and therefore confessing Christ
was unnecessary, since he did not really die and his followers were already
saved.[110] Luke's crucifixion account, like John's, does not dwell on the
suffering, but although he reinstates Simon of Cyrene (who is missing
from John's version) he is careful to stress (cf. Lk. 23.26/Mk 15.21) that
Simon, who carries Jesus' cross, follows behind Jesus. It would not be
possible to claim that he and not Jesus was crucified and that Jesus some-
how escaped; the journey to the cross is witnessed by the following crowd
(Lk. 23.27), who are peculiar to his Gospel. Furthermore, he emphasizes
through the experiences of Stephen, James, Peter, and Paul that being a
Christian by no means exempts one from the need to suffer for Christ. One

---

107. See, e.g., Jn 1.10-13; 7.7; 15.18-24. It is the hostility to the God of the Old
Testament shown in works like *The Apocalypse of Adam* or *The Apocryphon of John*
which is so difficult to reconcile with a Jewish origin for Gnosticism, since the creator of
such an imperfect world was seen as evil and identified with Satan (Saklas). But Perkins,
Gnosticism, pp. 41-42, points out that since some Gnostics regarded themselves as the
true descendants of Eve/Seth, they were nevertheless still dependent on Jewish traditions. She concludes, 'Gnosticism may well have emerged among nonobservant [*sic*],
assimilating Jews' (p. 42).

108. Irenaeus, *Against Heresies* 1.24.3-6.

109. At c. 120 CE. This is suggested by Layton, *Gnostic Scriptures*, p. xvi.

110. Not all Gnostic works deny the suffering of Christ; see *The Gospel of Truth*
18.24; 20.19-20.

must be prepared to confess him, whatever the cost, and one is promised aid from the Holy Spirit for this purpose.[111]

The potential for misinterpretation of the event which is arguably the most central of all to the Christian faith—the Resurrection itself—had long been apparent.[112] John himself affirms its corporeality (which was a concept abhorrent to Gnostics, since they regarded the flesh as inherently evil) almost as emphatically as does Luke. Only Luke, however, also presents the Ascension in corporeal form; it is visible to those present at Acts 1.9-10. John does not attempt to narrate it as Luke does, even though the descent/ascent model is central to his whole presentation. The closest he comes—and one can only applaud his literary tact—is the allusion at Jn 20.17. Since few would bother to defend points that were not under attack,[113] and Luke is manifestly defending both of these, one must assume that some at the time were denying them. This is certainly true of Basilides, and also the Jewish-Christian Docetist Cerinthus,[114] whose views Luke opposes more directly than does John.[115] In addition, Luke asserts a general resurrection of the dead at Lk. 20.33-38, and also at Acts 23.6; 24.15, 21, where it forms part of Paul's preaching. Although John does not deny that there will be one (see Jn 11.24),[116] there is little emphasis on it. The stress is on the new life available now; Jesus himself qualifies Martha's words to this effect at Jn 11.25. We should note that although many Jews, including possibly Cerinthus,[117] did not deny a general bodily resurrection at the End, Gnostics such as Basilides and Valentinus did. The Valentinian *Epistle to Rheginus* depicts this resurrection exclusively in spiritual terms; it was 'an upward movement in a metaphorical sense, which was a transformation of the soul into another state of being'.[118]

---

111. Cf. Mk 13.11/Lk. 12.12, where in Mark the Spirit of God speaks through the Christian (cf. Mt. 10.20), whereas in Luke the Holy Spirit teaches him what to say.

112. See 1 Cor. 15.

113. Thus C.H. Talbert, 'An Anti-Gnostic Tendency in Lukan Christology', *NTS* 14 (1967), pp. 259-71 (265).

114. See Irenaeus, *Against Heresies* 1.26.1. Irenaeus believed that John wrote, in part, to oppose Cerinthus; Gaius on the other hand thought Cerinthus wrote Revelation (see Eusebius, *Ecclesiastical History* 3.28.2).

115. Thus R.M. Grant, 'On the Origin of the Fourth Gospel', *JBL* 69 (1950), pp. 305-22 (313).

116. Cf. Jn 5.28-29, and the references to the 'Last Day' in ch. 6.

117. See R.M. Grant, *Gnosticism and Early Christianity*, p. 98.

118. Thus Layton, *Gnostic Scriptures*, p. 317.

The difficulty for us is that most of the evidence we have about Gnosticism and its contacts with orthodox Christianity is inconclusive and late, and much is drawn from hostile sources such as Irenaeus. All we can say is that the development of some Gnostic systems (such as those of Valentinus) seems to be related, in part, to a creative reflection on John's Gospel, with Platonic and (maybe) Stoic philosophy thrown in; it is perhaps significant that the first commentators on John's Gospel, Heracleon and Ptolemaeus, were both Valentinian Gnostics. This is not to say that John is Gnostic (or even proto-Gnostic), even if his work was congenial to them; but it remains quite possible nevertheless that Luke, writing a little later than John, could see the writing on the wall and tried to wipe it clean.[119]

8.5.2. *Evidence of False Ideas in Acts*

Actual evidence of problems directly caused by 'heresy' in Acts is, however, extremely scanty. Luke idealizes the early Church; true doctrine exists prior to error.[120] This may explain why Simon Magus is treated as he is by Luke. Far from being a dangerous heretic, as Irenaeus and Justin Martyr believed (Irenaeus called him the first Gnostic), he is ridiculed by Luke as a money-grabbing, power-hungry magician, who instantly recognizes—and fears—the superior power of Peter and John. We should remember that there was an assumed connection between Satan (and hence, magicians) and false teachers/false prophets; Luke is not necessarily at odds with later interpretation, but his presentation accords with his own emphases.

The other example in Acts is rather different. Acts 20.29-30 is quite explicit about the activities of heretical teachers within (and without) the Church and their pernicious effect, expressed in terms that recall the Johannine Epistles. Ignatius of Antioch describes a similar situation in Asia Minor, and we may also compare Rev. 2.6, which is addressed to the church at Ephesus and concerns the Nicolaitans. Acts 20.29-30 is one more example of a prediction in the Lukan narrative which is confirmed by later

119. It is perhaps significant that whereas John's Gospel has connections with later heresy, the orthodox old Roman Creed is virtually a summary of Luke's.

120. Similarly, the later teaching of Tertullian. See Tertullian, *Prescription Against Heresies* 29, 30, 31. (Thus, Talbert, *Luke and the Gnostics*, p. 88.) The same idealizing tendency is evident in *1 Clem.* 1.2–2.8, in Clement's description of Corinth in the apostolic age, which is at variance with Paul's Epistles.

events; the only difference is that in this case the events probably relate to the time when Luke was writing.

It is interesting that Luke places these words in the context of Paul's discourse to the Ephesian Elders at Miletus, and in Ephesus there may have been a community connected with the disciples of John the Baptist (see Acts 19.2-6). Many scholars, following ancient tradition going back to Irenaeus and Papias, believe that the Johannine community was later located in Ephesus,[121] even if it originated in Judaea or Syria.[122]

With regard to Ephesus, which was a centre for magical practices as well as for the Artemis cult,[123] Sherwin-White has pointed out how accurate are the historical details which Luke includes in his account.[124] The importance of the Town Clerk, γραμματεύς (see Acts 19.35) in control over the Council is well-documented in a series of inscriptions dating from 103–104 CE concerning the actions of a Roman, Viblius Salutaris. The same source confirms the use of the theatre as a meeting-place. The technical term for the assemblies of the Council is given, too, and it agrees with Acts 19.39, ἔννομος ἐκκλησία. The existence of the proconsular assizes at Acts 19.38 is also confirmed, and the Asiarchs (Acts 19.31) would also seem to have been correctly styled, the plural here being significant since in other cases the '-arch' suffix referred to a single official: thus there was only one Pontarch of Bithynia or ethnarch of Damascus.[125] As a conscientious historian, Luke would have performed his research thoroughly, and this may well have involved visiting the places about which he wrote to verify such details. Ancient historians preferred to rely on direct contact with people and places whenever possible. Luke probably visited or lived in Ephesus for a while, and it may have been there that he encountered the Johannine material which he used as a source for his Gospel.[126] It may also have been at Ephesus that he became acquainted

121. See, for example, G. Quispel, 'Qumran, John, and Jewish Christianity', in J.H. Charlesworth (ed.), *John and the Dead Sea Scrolls*, pp. 137-55 (140); Hengel, *Johannine Question, passim*.

122. The connections which many scholars have noted between John and the Dead Sea Scrolls lead Ashton (Ashton, *Understanding*, p. 205) to suggest that the founder of the Johannine community may himself have been an ex-Essene, or a former disciple of the Essene John the Baptist (see Jn 1.35-37).

123. See C.E. Arnold, *Ephesians: Power and Magic* (SNTSMS, 63; Cambridge: Cambridge University Press, 1989), pp. 14-40.

124. Sherwin-White, *Roman Society*, pp. 84ff.

125. Strabo, *Geography* 14.1.2 refers to the *Asiarchs* (plural) of Tralles.

126. Cf. H. Gaussen, 'The Lukan and Johannine Writings', *JTS* 9 (1908), pp. 563-68,

with Paul's letters, some of which I have argued that he probably knew, if this was where they were first collected.[127]

8.6. *Conclusion*

It can be seen from the above analysis that Luke has responded with varying degrees of approval to each of his three predecessors. The κἀμοὶ of his prologue (Lk. 1.3) is generic: it does not imply that he thought his version was on a par with theirs. Although he was quite prepared to correct it when it conflicted with his own ideas, Mark's was the Gospel he knew best and valued most;[128] his reaction to Matthew and John was much more critical and his use of them accordingly more sparing and hence less immediately apparent.

although Gaussen suggests that the contact was more direct; in Ephesus Luke met the 'Beloved Disciple' (identified as the author of John's Gospel) and also Mary.

127. See Goodspeed, *New Solutions*, pp. 11-20. It is a view shared by J. Knox, *Marcion*, and C.L. Mitton; see C.L. Mitton, *The Formation of the Pauline Corpus of Letters* (London: Epworth Press, 1955), pp. 50, 263ff.

128. Cf. E. Franklin, *Luke: Interpreter of Paul, Critic of Matthew* (JSNTSup, 92; Sheffield: Sheffield Academic Press, 1994).

Chapter 9

CONCLUSION

It remains to consider whether it is possible to determine Luke's overall purpose in the composition of his two-volume work. Any such attempt inevitably involves over-simplification, since a writer's motives are usually many,[1] and there is obviously a danger that a literary examination like this may focus overmuch on literary questions at the expense of other issues. In view of the indications noted in the preceding pages, however, we can infer that a main concern of Luke's was a theological/historical one: to set out via his narrative what he thought it was appropriate for Christians to believe, in as inclusive a way as was compatible with his interpretation of 'the facts' (ἀσφάλειαν, Lk. 1.4).[2] To some extent, therefore, he wished to reconcile differing streams: the Gentile-oriented/ Pauline, represented among the Gospels by Mark; the Jewish-Christian (Matthew); and the very distinctive Johannine brand of early Jewish Christianity. As G. Lüdemann rightly says: 'Luke's activity as a writer consists of linking traditions together'.[3]

It has been suggested in the preceding pages that Luke may be combining traditions from all the other canonical Gospels. To this end he has placed Matthaean teaching into appropriate contexts in a basically Markan narrative, and inserted into his text Johannine details, such as the presence of the Pharisees at the entry into Jerusalem, or the entry of Satan into Judas, or the way the disciples look *at each other* when Jesus predicts his betrayal, or the information that the severed ear was the man's right. He has also sometimes taken a position midway between the other Gospels when they conflict, as in his presentation of John the Baptist, or Judas's

1. Gasque, *History*, p. 126, remarks how often this self-evident truth is overlooked.
2. This is H.J. Cadbury's interpretation of the meaning of ἀσφάλεια; see Cadbury, *Making of Luke–Acts*, p. 346.
3. Lüdemann, *Earliest Christianity*, p. 9. We may compare the views of Weiss, *Die Quellen.*

kiss, or the location of the feeding miracle, even though this can produce inconsistencies in his own narrative.

Luke seemingly aims to incorporate as much as possible of the material at his disposal, provided that it is not seriously discordant with his own interpretation,[4] thereby ensuring that Christians who are familiar with some of the information given, but not all of it, may be reassured and therefore prepared to accept the rest. He omits material which would have been offensive either to Gentiles or to Jewish Christians. In this respect, his deliberate and careful combination of the other Gospels into a harmonious whole is indeed putting them in order, in terms of both presentation and content, and it offers security to believers.

Christianity in this pre-canonical period was very diverse, however, as we know from the surviving literature,[5] and while Luke wanted to include as many as possible within the Christian fold, he nevertheless aimed to do so within the bounds set by 'the facts', as expounded after the Resurrection by Christ to his followers, who carried on the tradition, duly authenticated by the Spirit. Luke's is a truly catholic Gospel[6] and he idealizes both the early Church (which was by no means as unified as he portrays it; nor were its internal disputes so amicably settled) and its representatives, including Peter, Stephen, Philip, Barnabas, James and most obviously Paul.

Luke's central concern in his treatment of all his now canonical sources —the other three Gospels and Paul—is summed up in those two polyvalent terms καθεξῆς and ἀσφάλεια. 'Order' to the evangelist covers the breadth of his material, its overall inclusiveness, and its structuring, in that incidents are suitably placed and contain appropriate teaching. And since the material in Paul's letters is inappropriate in Luke's missionary context, he instead prefers to weave a little into the events he describes, and a little into Paul's longer speeches.[7]

---

4.   A similar suggestion is made about John by Brodie, *Quest*. Brodie argues that John has systematically used Mark, Matthew, a truncated (and hypothetical!) proto-Luke–Acts, and also Ephesians, and the Pentateuch, in order to produce a text 'which appeals to everyone' (p. 143). But the evidence offered for John's use of Matthew and Ephesians is not persuasive, and John's use of Luke–Acts is assumed rather than tested.

5.   See the analysis by Layton, *Gnostic Scriptures*, pp. xvii-xviii.

6.   Luke shares this 'early Catholic' tendency with much of the New Testament; cf. U. Luz, 'Erwägungen zur Enstehung des "Frükatholizismus": Eine Skizze', *ZNW* 65 (1964), pp. 88-111 (89).

7.   This fulfilled the requirement for speeches to contain what the speaker might, in

But it is even more important to Luke to justify the faith to interested outsiders; and to those inside, to define normative Christianity,[8] and to present via his narrative, in terms which would be acceptable to most, what should be believed about Christ.[9] The word ἀσφάλεια, which Luke places for especial emphasis at the end of his opening sentence, a stylistic *tour de force* unmatched elsewhere in Luke–Acts, thus qualifies the inclusive connotation of καθεξῆς. Luke provides teaching which will resist heretical misinterpretation and promote a secure, well-grounded faith. This is the 'truth' he offers.

the circumstances, be supposed to have said. In this context, it is perhaps significant that the Pauline echo at Acts 20.28, and the use here of the very Pauline ἐκκλησία τοῦ θεοῦ, are reserved, like Paul's epistles, for believers.

8. Cf. Aune, *Literary Environment*, p. 137.

9. Cf. Barrett, 'The Third Gospel as a Preface to Acts? Some Reflections', in F. van Segbroeck (ed.), *The Four Gospels*, II, pp. 1451-66 (1462).

BIBLIOGRAPHY

Aalen, S., 'St Luke's Gospel and 1 Enoch', *NTS* 13 (1966), pp. 1-13.

Achtemeier, P.J. (ed.), *SBLSP*, 18 (Missoula, MT: Scholars Press, 1979).

Aland, K. (ed.), *SE I* (TU, 73, Berlin: Akademie Verlag, 1959).

Alexander, L., *Luke–Acts in its Contemporary Setting* (DPhil thesis, Oxford University, 1977).

—*The Preface to Luke's Gospel* (SNTSMS, 78; Cambridge: Cambridge University Press, 1993).

Alter, R., *The Art of Biblical Narrative* (New York: Basic Books, 1981).

—*The World of Biblical Literature* (London: SPCK, 1992).

Arnold, C.E., *Ephesians: Power and Magic* (SNTSMS, 63; Cambridge: Cambridge University Press, 1989).

Ashton, J., *Understanding the Fourth Gospel* (Oxford: Oxford University Press, 1991).

Ashton, J. (ed.), *The Interpretation of John* (London: SPCK; Philadelphia: Fortress Press, 1986).

Attridge, H.W., 'Josephus and his Works', in Stone (ed.), *Jewish Writings of the Second Temple Period*, pp. 185-232.

Aune, D.E., 'The Apocalypse of John and Graeco-Roman Revelatory Magic', *NTS* 33 (1987), pp. 481-501.

—*The New Testament in its Literary Environment* (Cambridge: James Clarke & Co., 1988).

Baarlinck, H., 'Die zyklische Struktur von Lukas 9.43b–19.28', *NTS* 38 (1992), pp. 481-506.

Bailey, J.A., *Traditions Common to the Gospels of St Luke and St John* (NovTSup, 7; Leiden: E.J. Brill, 1963).

Bailey, K.E., *Poet and Peasant: A Literary Cultural Approach to the Parables in Luke* (Grand Rapids: Eerdmans, 1976).

Balch, D.L., 'Acts as Hellenistic Historiography', in Richards (ed.), *SBLSP*, 24 (1985), pp. 429-32.

Barr, D.L., and J.L. Wentling, 'The Conventions of Classical Biography and the Genre of Luke–Acts: A Preliminary Study', in Talbert (ed.), *Luke–Acts*, pp. 63-88.

Barrett, C.K., *Luke the Historian in Recent Study* (London: Epworth Press, 1961).

—'Things Sacrificed to Idols', *NTS* 11 (1964), pp. 138-53.

—*New Testament Essays* (London: SPCK, 1972).

—'John and the Synoptic Gospels', *ExpTim* 85 (1974), pp. 228-33.

—' "The Father is Greater than I" (Jn. 14:28); Subordinationist Christology in the New Testament', in Gnilka (ed.), *Neues Testament und Kirche*, pp. 144-59.

—*The Gospel According to John* (London: SCM Press, 2nd edn, 1978).

—'The Place of John and the Synoptists within the Early History of Christian Thought', in Denaux (ed.), *John and the Synoptics*, pp. 63-79.

—'The Third Gospel as a Preface to Acts? Some Reflections', in van Segbroeck (ed.), *The Four Gospels*, II, pp. 1451-66.

Barton, J., *People of the Book* (Bampton Lectures; London: SPCK, 1988).

Batey, R., 'The Destination of Ephesians', *JBL* 82 (1963), p. 101.

Bauckham, R., *Jude and the Relatives of Jesus in the Early Church* (Edinburgh: T. & T. Clark, 1990).

—'The *"Acts of Paul"* as a Sequel to Acts', in Winter and Clarke (eds.), *The Book of Acts in its First Century Setting*, I, pp. 105-52.

—*The Theology of the Book of Revelation* (Cambridge: Cambridge University Press, 1993).

Bauer, W., *Das Johannesevangelium* (Tübingen: J.C.B. Mohr, 3rd edn, 1933).

—*A Greek–English Lexicon of the New Testament and Other Early Christian Literature* (Chicago: University of Chicago Press, 2nd edn, 1958).

—*Orthodoxy and Heresy in Earliest Christianity* (Philadelphia: Fortress Press, 1971).

Beck, B., *Christian Character in the Gospel of Luke* (London: Epworth Press, 1989).

Becker, J. (ed.), *Christian Beginnings* (Louisville, KY: Westminster/John Knox Press, 1993).

Bell, H. Idris, *Cults and Creeds in Graeco-Roman Egypt* (Liverpool Monographs in Archaeology and Oriental Studies; Liverpool: University Press, 1953).

Berger, P., *A Rumour of Angels* (Harmondsworth: Penguin, 1970).

Best, E., *One Body in Christ* (London: SPCK, 1955).

Betori, G., 'Preaching to the Pagans in Acts', in O'Collins (ed.), *Luke and Acts*, pp. 103-20.

Betz, H.D. (ed.), *The Greek Magical Papyri in Translation* (Chicago: University of Chicago Press, 1986).

Bilde, P., *Flavius Josephus: Between Jerusalem and Rome* (JSPSup, 2; Sheffield: Sheffield Academic Press, 1988).

Blackman, E.C., *Marcion and his influence* (London: SPCK, 1948).

Blass, F., *The Philology of the Gospels* (London: Macmillan, 1898).

Blomberg, C.L., 'Midrash, Chiasmus, and the Outline of Luke's Central Section', in France and Wenham (eds.), *Gospel Perspectives*, pp. 217-61.

Bock, D.L., *Proclamation from Prophecy and Pattern* (JSNTSup, 12; Sheffield: Sheffield Academic Press, 1987).

Boismard, M.-E., 'Rapprochements littéraires entre l'évangile de Luc et l'Apocalypse', in Schmid and Vögtle (eds.), *Synoptische Studien*, pp. 53-63.

—'S. Luc et la rédaction du quatrième évangile', *RB* 69 (1962), pp. 185-211.

—'The First Epistle of John and the Writings of Qumran', in Charlesworth (ed.), *John and the Dead Sea Scrolls*, pp. 156-65.

Bonner, C., 'Traces of Thaumaturgic Technique in the Miracles', *HTR* 20 (1927), pp. 171-81.

Booth, W., *The Rhetoric of Fiction* (Chicago: University of Chicago Press, 2nd edn, 1983).

Borgen, P., 'John and the Synoptics in the Passion Narrative', *NTS* 5 (1958), pp. 246-59.

—'From Paul to Luke', *CBQ* 31 (1969), pp. 168-82.

—'God's Agent in the Fourth Gospel', in Ashton (ed.), *The Interpretation of John*, pp. 67-78.

—'John and the Synoptics', in Dungan (ed.), *The Inter-relations of the Gospels*, pp. 408-37.

Bornkamm, G., 'The Missionary Stance of Paul in 1 Corinthians 9 and Acts', in Keck and Martyn (eds.), *Studies in Luke–Acts*, pp. 194-207.

Bovon, F., *Luke the Theologian: Thirty-Three Years of Research* (Pennsylvania: Pickwick Publications, 1987).

Brawley, R.L., 'Paul in Acts: Lucan Apology and Conciliation', in Talbert (ed.), *Luke–Acts*, pp. 129-47.

Brodie, T.L., 'Greco-Roman Imitation of Texts as a Partial Guide to Luke's Use of Sources', in Talbert (ed.), *Luke–Acts*, pp. 17-46.

—*The Quest for the Origin of John's Gospel* (Oxford: Oxford University Press, 1993).

Broughton, T.R.S., 'The Roman Army', in Jackson and Lake, *The Beginnings of Christianity*, V, pp. 427-45.

Brown, R.E., *The Gospel According to John* (AB; 2 vols.; Garden City, NY: Doubleday, 1966, 1970).

—' "Other Sheep Not of This Fold": The Johannine Perspective on Christian Diversity in the Late First Century', *JBL* 97 (1978), pp. 5-22.

—*The Birth of the Messiah* (New York: Doubleday, 1979).

—*The Community of the Beloved Disciple* (New York: Paulist Press, 1979).

—*The Epistles of John* (AB; Garden City, NY: Doubleday, 1982).

Brown, R.E., and J.P. Meier, *Antioch and Rome* (Garden City, NY: Doubleday, 1983).

Brown, S., *Apology and Perseverance in the Theology of Luke* (AnBib, 36; Rome: Pontifical Biblical Institute, 1969).

—'The Role of the Prologues in Determining the Purpose of Luke–Acts', in Talbert (ed.), *Perspectives on Luke–Acts*, pp. 99-111.

Bruce, F.F., *The Acts of the Apostles* (Grand Rapids: Eerdmans, 2nd edn, 1951).

Bultmann, R., 'The History of Religions Background of the Prologue to the Gospel of John', in Ashton, *The Interpretation of John*, pp. 18-35.

—*The History of the Synoptic Tradition* (Oxford: Basil Blackwell, 1968).

—*The Gospel of John* (Oxford: Basil Blackwell, 1971).

Burkill, T.A., *Mysterious Revelation* (Ithaca, NY: Cornell University Press, 1962).

Burkitt, F.C., *The Gospel History and its Transmission* (Edinburgh: T. & T. Clark, 1906).

Burridge, R.A., *What Are the Gospels?* (SNTSMS, 70; Cambridge: Cambridge University Press, 1992).

Buse, I., 'St John and the Passion Narratives of St Matthew and St Luke', *NTS* 7 (1960), pp. 65-76.

Butler, B.C., *The Originality of St Matthew* (Cambridge: Cambridge University Press, 1951).

Cadbury, H.J., 'A Commentary on the Preface of Luke', in Jackson and Lake (eds.), *The Beginnings of Christianity*, II, pp. 489-510.

—'The Speeches of Acts', in Jackson and Lake (eds.), *The Beginnings of Christianity*, V, pp. 402-27.

—' "We" and "I" Passages in Luke–Acts', *NTS* 3 (1956), pp. 128-32.

—*The Making of Luke–Acts* (London: SPCK, rev. edn, 1958).

—'Four Features of Lukan Style', in Keck and Martyn (eds.), *Studies in Luke–Acts*, pp. 87-102.

Caird, G.B., *Saint Luke* (Pelican Commentary; Harmondsworth: Penguin, 1963).

—'The Study of the Gospels I: Source Criticism', *ExpTim* 87 (1976), pp. 99-104.

Callan, T., 'The Preface of Luke–Acts and Historiography', *NTS* 31 (1985), pp. 576-81.

Carroll, J.T., 'Luke's Portrayal of the Pharisees', *CBQ* 50 (1988), pp. 604-21.

Cassidy, R.J., *Jesus, Politics and Society* (Maryknoll, NY: Orbis Books, 1978).

Cassidy, R.J., and P.J. Scharper (eds.), *Political Issues in Luke–Acts* (Maryknoll, NY: Orbis Books, 1983).

Catchpole, D.R., *The Trial of Jesus* (SBS, 18; Leiden: E.J. Brill, 1971).

—*The Quest for Q* (Edinburgh: T. & T. Clark, 1993).

Charles, R.H., *The Apocrypha and Pseudepigrapha of the Old Testament* (2 vols.; Oxford: Oxford University Press, 1913).

—*Revelation* (Edinburgh: T. & T. Clark, 1920).

Charlesworth, J.H., 'A Critical Comparison of the Dualism in 1QS iii.13-iv.26 and the "Dualism" contained in the Fourth Gospel', in *idem* (ed.), *John and the Dead Sea Scrolls*, pp. 76-106.

—'Qumran, John and the Odes of Solomon', in *idem* (ed.), *John and the Dead Sea Scrolls*, pp. 107-36.

Charlesworth, J.H. (ed.), *John and the Dead Sea Scrolls* (New York: Crossroad, 1991).

Chilton, B., 'Announcement in Nazara: An Analysis of Lk. 4:16-21', in France and Wenham (eds.), *Gospel Perspectives*, pp. 147-72.

—*Profiles of a Rabbi* (Atlanta, GA: Scholars Press, 1989).

Coakley, J.F., 'The Anointing at Bethany and the Priority of John', *JBL* 107 (1988), pp. 241-56.

Coggins, R.J., 'The Samaritans and Acts', *NTS* 28 (1982), pp. 423-34.

Collins, A. Yarbro, 'The Political Perspective of the Revelation to John', *JBL* 96 (1977), pp. 241-56.

—'Persecution and Vengeance in the Book of Revelation', in Hellholm (ed.), *Apocalypticism in the Mediterranean World and the Near East*, pp. 729-49.

—*Crisis and Catharsis: The Power of the Apocalypse* (Philadelphia: Fortress Press, 1984).

Collins, J.J., *The Apocalyptic Imagination* (New York: Crossroad, 1984).

Conzelmann, H., *The Theology of St Luke* (London: SCM Press, 1960).

—'The Address of Paul in the Areopagus', in Keck and Martyn (eds.), *Studies in Luke–Acts*, pp. 217-30.

—'Luke's Place in the Development of Early Christianity', in Keck and Martyn (eds.), *Studies in Luke–Acts*, pp. 298-316.

Cook, M.J., 'The Mission to the Jews in Acts: Unraveling Luke's "Myth of the Myriads"', in Tyson (ed.), *Luke–Acts and the Jewish People*, pp. 102-23.

Cosgrove, C.H., 'The divine 'δεῖ' in Luke–Acts', *NovT* 26 (1984), pp. 168-90.

Craig, W.L., 'The Inspection of the Empty Tomb', in Denaux (ed.), *John and the Synoptics*, pp. 614-619.

Creed, J.M., *The Gospel According to Luke* (London: Macmillan, 1930).

Cribbs, F.L., 'St Luke and the Johannine Tradition', *JBL* 90 (1971), pp. 422-50.

—'A Study of the Contacts Between St Luke and St John', in G.W. MacRae (ed.), *SBLSP*, 12 (1973), II, pp. 1-93.

—'The Agreements that Exist between John and Acts', in Talbert (ed.), *Perspectives on Luke-Acts*, pp. 40-61.

—'The Agreements that Exist between Luke and John', in Achtemeier (ed.), *SBLSP*, 18 (1979), I, pp. 215-61.

Crockett, L.C., 'Lk. 4:25-27 and Jewish–Gentile Relations in Luke–Acts', *JBL* 88 (1969), pp. 177-83.

Cross, F.L. (ed.), *SE II* (TU, 87; Berlin: Akademie Verlag, 1964).

Crossan, J.D., *In Parables: The Challenge of the Historical Jesus* (New York: Harper & Row, 1973).

—'Mark and the Relatives of Jesus', *NovT* 15 (1973), pp. 81-113.

Cullmann, O., 'The Significance of the Qumran Texts for Research into the Beginnings of Christianity', *JBL* 74 (1955), pp. 213-26.

—'The Plurality of the Gospels as a Theological Problem in Antiquity', in Higgins (ed.), *The Early Church*, pp. 39-58.

—*The Johannine Circle* (London: SCM Press, 1976).

Curtis, K., 'Luke 24:12 and John 20:3-10', *JTS* NS 22 (1971), pp. 512-15.

Dahl, N., 'The Story of Abraham in Luke–Acts', in Keck and Martyn (eds.), *Studies in Luke–Acts*, pp. 139-58.

—'The Johannine Church and History', in Ashton (ed.), *The Interpretation of John,* pp. 122-40.

Danker, F.W., 'The Endangered Benefactor in Luke–Acts', in Richards (ed.), *SBLSP*, 20 (1981), pp. 39-48.

—'Graeco-Roman Cultural Accommodation in the Christology of Luke–Acts', in Richards (ed.), *SBLSP*, 22 (1983), pp. 391-414.

—'Reciprocity in the Ancient World and in Acts 15:23-29', in Cassidy and Scharper (eds.), *Political Issues in Luke–Acts*, pp. 49-58.

—*Jesus and the New Age* (Philadelphia: Fortress Press, 2nd edn, 1988).

Darr, J.A., *On Character Building: The Reader and the Rhetoric of Characterization in Luke–Acts* (Louisville, KY: Westminster/John Knox Press, 1992).

Dart, J., *The Jesus of Heresy and History* (San Francisco: Harper & Row, 1988).

Dauer, A., *Die Passionsgeschichte im Johannesevangelium* (SANT, 30; Munich: Kösel, 1972).

—*Johannes und Lukas* (FzB, 50; Würzburg: Echter Verlag, 1984).

Davies, J.G., 'The Prefigurement of the Ascension in the Third Gospel', *JTS* NS 6 (1955), pp. 229-33.

Davies, J.H., 'The Purpose of the Central Section of Luke's Gospel', in Cross (ed.), *SE II*, pp. 164-69.

Davies, W.D., and D.C. Allison, *A Critical and Exegetical Commentary on the Gospel According to St Matthew*, I (Edinburgh: T. & T. Clark, 1988).

Day, J., *God's Conflict with the Dragon and the Sea* (Cambridge: Cambridge University Press, 1985).

De la Potterie, I., 'The Truth in St John', in Ashton (ed.), *The Interpretation of John*, pp. 53-66.

Denaux, A. (ed.), *John and the Synoptics* (Proceedings of the 1990 Leuven Colloquium; BETL, 101; Leuven: Leuven University Press, 1992).

Derrett, J.D.M., 'Fresh Light on St Luke 16: The Parable of the Unjust Steward', *NTS* 7 (1961), pp. 198-219.

—*Law in the New Testament* (London: Darton, Longman & Todd, 1970).

—'The Rich Fool: A Parable of Jesus Concerning Inheritance', *HeyJ* 18 (1977), pp. 131-51.

Dibelius, M., *From Tradition to Gospel* (London: Ivor Nichols & Watson, 1934).

Dillon, R.J., *From Eye-Witnesses to Ministers of the Word: Tradition and Composition in Luke 24* (AnBib, 82, Rome: Pontifical Biblical Institute, 1978).

—'Previewing Luke's Project from his Prologue (Lk. 1:1-4)', *CBQ* 43 (1981), pp. 205-207.

Dinkler, E. (ed.), *Zeit und Geschichte: Dankesgabe an R. Bultmann zum 80 Geburtstag* (Tübingen: J.C.B. Mohr, 1964).

Dodd, C.H., *The Interpretation of the Fourth Gospel* (Cambridge: Cambridge University Press, 1953).

—*Historical Tradition in the Fourth Gospel* (Cambridge: Cambridge University Press, 1963).

—'The Fall of Jerusalem and the "Abomination of Desolation"', in C.H. Dodd, *More New Testament Studies* (Grand Rapids: Eerdmans, 1968), pp. 69-83.

Donahue, J.R., *The Gospel in Parable: Metaphor, Narrative and Theology in the Synoptic Gospels* (Philadelphia: Fortress Press, 1988).

Douglas, M., *Purity and Danger* (London: Routledge & Kegan Paul, 1966).

Dowell, T.M., 'Why Luke Rewrote the Synoptics', in Denaux (ed.), *John and the Synoptics*, pp. 453-57.

Downing, F.G., 'Redaction Criticism: Josephus's "Antiquities" and the Synoptic Gospels II', *JSNT* 9 (1980), pp. 29-48.

—'Common Ground with Paganism in Luke and Josephus', *NTS* 28 (1982), pp. 546-59.

—'Contemporary Analogies to the Gospels and Acts: Genres or Motifs?', in Tuckett (ed.), *Synoptic Studies*, pp. 51-65.

—'Compositional Conventions and the Synoptic Problem', *JBL* 107 (1988), pp. 69-85.

Drury, J., *Tradition and Design in Luke's Gospel* (London: Darton, Longman & Todd, 1976).

—*The Parables in the Gospels: History and Allegory* (New York: Crossroad, 1985).

Dungan, D.L., 'Mark: The Abridgement of Matthew and Luke', in Miller (ed.), *Jesus and Man's Hope*, I, pp. 51-97.

Dungan, D.L. (ed.), *The Inter-relations of the Gospels* (BETL, 95; Leuven: Leuven University Press, 1990).

Dunn, J.D.G., *Jesus, Paul and the Law* (London: SPCK, 1990).

—*The Partings of the Ways* (London: SCM Press, 1991).

Du Plessis, I.I., 'Once More: The Purpose of Luke's Prologue (Lk. 1:1-4)', *NovT* 16 (1974), pp. 259-71.

Dupont, J., *The Sources of Acts* (Paris: Cerf, 1960; London: Darton, Longman & Todd, 1964).

—'La portée christologique de l'évangélisation des nations d'après Luc 24:47', in Gnilka (ed.), *Neues Testament und Kirche*, pp. 290-99.

—*The Salvation of the Gentiles* (Paris: Cerf, 1967; New York: Paulist Press, 1979).

—'La mission de Paul d'après Actes 26:16-23 et la mission des apôtres d'après Luc 24:44-49 et Actes 1:8', in Hooker and Wilson (eds.), *Paul and Paulinism*, pp. 290-99.

Easton, B.S., *Earliest Christianity: The Purpose of Acts* (rev. by F.C. Grant; New York: Seabury, rev. edn, 1954).

Edwards, M.J., 'Gnostics and Valentinians in the Church Fathers', *JTS* NS 40 (1989), pp. 26-47.

Edwards, O.C., *Luke's Story of Jesus* (Philadelphia: Fortress Press, 1981).

Edwards, R.A., *A Theology of Q* (Philadelphia: Fortress Press, 1976).

Elliott, J.H., 'A Catholic Gospel: Reflections on "Early Catholicism" in the New Testament', *CBQ* 31 (1969), pp. 213-23.

Ellis, E.E., and E. Grässer (eds.), *Jesus und Paulus: Festschrift für W.G. Kümmel zum 70 Geburtstag* (Göttingen: Vandenhoeck & Ruprecht, 1975).

Enslin, M.S., 'Luke and Matthew: Compilers or Authors?', *ANRW* II.3 (1985), pp. 2357-88.

Epsztein, L., *Social Justice in the Ancient Near East and the People of the Bible* (London: SCM Press, 1986).

Esler, P.F., *Community and Gospel in Luke–Acts: The Social and Political Motivations of Lukan Theology* (SNTSMS, 57; Cambridge: Cambridge University Press, 1987).

Evans, C.F., 'The Central Section of St Luke's Gospel', in Nineham (ed.), *Studies in the Gospels*, pp. 37-53.

—*St Luke* (London: SCM Press; Philadelphia: Trinity Press International, 1990).

Farmer, W.R., *The Synoptic Problem: A Critical Analysis* (London: Macmillan, 1964).

—'A Fresh Approach to Q', in Neusner (ed.), *Christianity, Judaism and Graeco-Roman Cults*, I, pp. 39-50.

—'Certain results reached by Sir John Hawkins and C.F. Burney, which make more sense if Luke knew Matthew, and Mark knew Matthew and Luke', in Tuckett (ed.), *Synoptic Studies*, pp. 75-98; see also pp. 105-109.

Farrer, A.M., *A Re-birth of Images: The Making of St John's Apocalypse* (Westminster: Dave Press, 1949).

—'On Dispensing with Q', in Nineham (ed.), *Studies in the Gospels*, pp. 55-88.

Feldman, L.H., and G. Hata (eds.), *Josephus, Judaism and Christianity* (Leiden: E.J. Brill, 1987).

Fenton, J.C., *St Matthew* (Pelican Gospel Commentaries; Harmondsworth: Penguin, 1963).

—*Finding the Way Through John* (Oxford: A.R. Mowbray, 1988).

Fiorenza, E. Schüssler, 'The Phenomenon of Early Christian Apocalyptic', in Hellholm (ed.), *Apocalypticism in the Mediterranean World and the Near East*, pp. 295-316.

—*The Book of Revelation: Justice and Judgment* (Philadelphia: Fortress Press, 1985).

Filoramo, G., *A History of Gnosticism* (Oxford: Basil Blackwell, 1990).

Filson, F.V., 'The Journey Motif in Luke–Acts', in Gasque and Martin (eds.), *Apostolic History*, pp. 68-77.

Fitzmyer, J.A., 'The Priority of Mark and the "Q" Source in Luke', in Miller (ed.), *Jesus and Man's Hope*, I, pp. 131-70.

—*The Gospel According to St Luke* (2 vols.; AB; Garden City, NY: Doubleday, 1981, 1985).

—*Luke the Theologian: Aspects of his Teaching* (London: Geoffrey Chapman, 1989).

Fortna, R.T., *The Gospel of Signs* (SNTSMS, 11; Cambridge: Cambridge University Press, 1970).

—'Christology in the Fourth Gospel', *NTS* 21 (1974), pp. 489-504.

—*The Fourth Gospel and its Predecessor: From Narrative Source to Present Gospel* (Philadelphia: Fortress Press, 1988).

France, R.T., and D. Wenham (eds.), *Gospel Perspectives* (Sheffield: JSOT Press, 1983).

Franklin, E., *Christ the Lord* (London: SPCK; Philadelphia: Westminster Press, 1975).

—*Luke: Interpreter of Paul, Critic of Matthew* (JSNTSup, 92; Sheffield: Sheffield Academic Press, 1994).

Freed, E.D., 'The Entry into Jerusalem in the Gospel of John', *JBL* 80 (1961), pp. 329-38.

—'John 1:19-27', in van Segbroeck (ed.), *The Four Gospels*, III, pp. 1943-1961.

Fuks, A., 'The Jewish Revolt in Egypt, A.D. 115–117, in the Light of the Papyri', *Aeg* 33 (1953), pp 131-58.

—'Aspects of the Jewish Revolt in A.D. 115–117', *JRS* 51 (1961), pp. 93-104.

Fusco, V., 'Problems of Structure in Luke's Eschatological Discourse (Lk. 21:7-36)', in O'Collins (ed.), *Luke and Acts*, pp. 72-91.

Gallagher, E.V., *Divine Man or Magician?: Celsus and Origen on Jesus* (SBLDS, 64, Chico, CA: Scholars Press, 1982).

Gardner-Smith, P., *Saint John and the Synoptic Gospels* (Cambridge: Cambridge University Press, 1938).

Garrett, S.R., *The Demise of the Devil: Magic and the Demonic in Luke's Writings* (Minneapolis: Augsburg–Fortress, 1989).

Gasque, W. Ward, 'The Speeches of Acts', in Longenecker and Tenney (eds.), *New Dimensions in New Testament Studies*, pp. 232-50.

Gasque, W. Ward, and R.P. Martin (eds.), *Apostolic History and the Gospel* (Exeter: Paternoster Press, 1970).

—*A History of the Criticism of the Acts of the Apostles* (BGBE, 17, Tübingen: J.C.B. Mohr [Paul Siebeck], 1975).

Gasse, W., 'Zum Reisebericht des Lukas', *ZNW* 34 (1935), pp. 293-98.

Gaussen, H., 'The Lukan and Johannine Writings', *JTS* 9 (1908), pp. 563-68.

Gempf, C., 'Public Speaking and Published Accounts', in Winter and Clarke (eds.), *The Book of Acts in its First Century Setting*, I, pp. 259-304.

Gericke, W., 'Zur Enstehung des Johannes-Evangeliums', *TLZ* 90 (1965), pp. 807-20.

Gill, D., 'Observations on the Lucan Travel Narrative and Some Related Passages', *HTR* 63 (1970), pp. 199-221.

Gnilka, J. (ed.), *Neues Testament und Kirche: Für Rudolf Schnackenburg* (Freiburg: Herder, 1974).

Goehring, J.E. *et al.*, *Gnosticism and the Early Christian World* (Sonoma, CA: Polebridge Press, 1990).

Goldstein, J.A., *1 Maccabees* (AB; Garden City, NY: Doubleday, 1976).

—2 Maccabees (AB: Garden City, NY: Doubleday, 1983).

Goodacre, M., *Goulder and the Gospels: An Examination of 'A New Paradigm'* (JSNTSup, 133; Sheffield: Sheffield Academic Press, 1996).

—'Fatigue in the Synoptics', *NTS* 44 (1998), pp. 45-58.

Goodenough, E.R., 'John, a Primitive Gospel', *JBL* 64 (1945), pp. 145-82.

Goodspeed, E.J., *New Solutions to New Testament Problems* (Chicago: University of Chicago Press, 1927).

—*The Meaning of Ephesians* (Chicago: University of Chicago Press, 1933).

Goodwin, C., 'How Did John Treat his Sources?', *JBL* 73 (1954), pp. 61-75.

Goulder, M.D., 'The Chiastic Structure of the Lucan Journey', in Cross (ed.), *SE II*, pp. 195-202.

—'Mark XVI.1-8 and Parallels', *NTS* 24 (1978), pp. 235-40.

—'On Putting Q to the Test', *NTS* 24 (1978), pp. 218-34.

—'From Ministry to Passion in John and Luke', *NTS* 29 (1983), pp. 561-68.

—'The Beatitudes: A Source-Critical Study. An Answer to C.M. Tuckett', *NovT* 25 (1983), pp. 207-16.

—'Some Observations on Professor Farmer's "certain results"', in Tuckett (ed.), *Synoptic Studies*, pp. 99-104.

—'The Order of a Crank', in Tuckett (ed.), *Synoptic Studies*, pp. 111-30.

—*Luke: A New Paradigm* (Sheffield: JSOT Press, 1989).

—'Nicodemus', *SJT* 44 (1990), pp. 153-68.

—'An Old Friend Incognito', *SJT* 45 (1992), pp. 487-513.

—'John 1:1–2:12 and the Synoptics', in Denaux (ed.), *John and the Synoptics*, pp. 201-37.

—*A Tale of Two Missions* (London: SCM Press, 1994).

Grant, F.C., 'Was the Author of John Dependent upon the Gospel of Luke?', *JBL* 56 (1937), pp. 285-307.

Grant, R.M., 'On the Origin of the Fourth Gospel', *JBL* 69 (1950), pp. 305-22.

—*Gnosticism and Early Christianity* (New York: Harper & Row, 2nd edn, 1966).

—*Greek Apologists of the Second Century* (London: SCM Press, 1988).

—*Jesus after the Gospels* (London: SCM Press, 1990).

Grassi, J., 'Emmaus Revisited (Lk. 24:13-35 and Ac. 8:26-40)', *CBQ* 26 (1964), pp. 463-67.

Green, H.B., 'The Credibility of Luke's Transformation of Matthew', in Tuckett (ed.), *Synoptic Studies*, pp. 131-55.

—'Matthew, Clement and Luke: Their Sequence and Relationship', *JTS* NS 40 (1989), pp. 1-25.

Haenchen, E., 'The Book of Acts as Source Material for the History of Early Christianity', in Keck and Martyn (eds.), *Studies in Luke–Acts*, pp. 258-78.

—*The Acts of the Apostles* (trans. Bernard Noble; Philadelphia: Westminster Press, 1971).

Hahn, F., 'Die Jüngerberufung: Jn. 1:35-51', in Gnilka (ed.), *Neues Testament und Kirche*, pp. 172-90.

Hanson, P.D., *The Dawn of Apocalyptic* (Philadelphia: Fortress Press, 1975).

Harnack, A., *Luke the Physician* (London: Williams & Norgate, 1907).

—*The Sayings of Jesus: The Second Source of St Matthew and St Luke* (London: Williams & Norgate, 1908).

—*New Testament Studies*. III. *The Acts of the Apostles* (London: Williams & Norgate, 1909).

Harrison, P.N., *Polycarp's Two Epistles to the Philippians* (Cambridge: Cambridge University Press, 1936).

Hawkins, J.C., *Horae synopticae* (Oxford: Oxford University Press, 2nd edn, 1909).

Head, P., 'Acts and the Problem of its Texts', in Winter and Clarke (eds.), *The Book of Acts in its First Century Setting*, I, pp. 415-44.

Hellholm, D. (ed.), *Apocalypticism in the Mediterranean World and the Near East* (Tübingen: J.C.B. Mohr [Paul Siebeck], 1983).

Hemer, C.J., *The Book of Acts in the Setting of Hellenistic History* (Tübingen: J.C.B. Mohr [Paul Siebeck], 1989).

Hengel, M., *The Son of God* (London: SCM Press, 1976).

—*Between Jesus and Paul* (London: SCM Press, 1983).

—*Studies in the Gospel of Mark* (trans. J. Bowden; London: SCM Press, 1985).

—*Earliest Christianity* (London: SCM Press, 1986).

—*The Johannine Question* (trans. J. Bowden; London: SCM Press; Philadelphia: Trinity Press International, 1989).

Hennecke, E., and W. Schneemelcher (eds.), *New Testament Apocrypha* (trans. R.M. Wilson; 2 vols.; Philadelphia: Westminster Press, 1963, 1965).

Higgins, A.J.B. (ed.), *The Early Church* (Philadelphia: Fortress Press, 1956).

Hill, C., *Hellenists and Hebrews* (Minneapolis: Augsburg–Fortress, 1992).

Hillard, T., A. Nobbs and B. Winter, 'Acts and the Pauline Corpus, 1: Ancient Literary Parallels', in Winter and Clarke (eds.), *The Book of Acts in its First Century Setting*, I, pp. 183-213.

Himmelfarb, M., *Tours of Hell* (Pennsylvania: Pennsylvania University Press, 1983).

Holland, H. Scott, *The Fourth Gospel* (ed. W.J. Richmond; London: John Murray, 1923).

Hooker, M.D., *Continuity and Discontinuity* (London: Epworth Press, 1986).

Hooker, M.D., and S.G. Wilson (eds.), *Paul and Paulinism* (London: SPCK, 1982).

Horbury, W., 'The Benediction of the Minim and Early Jewish–Christian Controversy', *JTS* NS 33 (1982), pp. 19-61.

Houlden, J.L., *The Johannine Epistles* (HNTC; New York: Harper & Row, 1973).

—'The Purpose of Luke', *JSNT* 21 (1984), pp. 53-65.

—*Backward into Light* (London: SCM Press, 1987).

Howard, W.F., 'The Common Authorship of the Johannine Gospel and Epistles', *JTS* 48 (1947), pp. 12-25.

Hubbard, B.J., 'Luke, Josephus and Rome: A Comparative Approach to the Lukan "Sitz im Leben"', in Achtemeier (ed.), *SBLSP*, 18 (1979), pp. 59-68.

Hunkin, J.W., 'St Luke and Josephus', *CQR* 88 (1919), pp. 89-108.

Jackson, F.J. Foakes, and K. Lake (eds.), *The Beginnings of Christianity* (5 vols.; London: Macmillan, 1920–33).

Jeffers, J.S., *Conflict at Rome* (Minneapolis: Fortress Press, 1991).

Jeremias, J., 'Beobachtungen zu ntl. Stellen an Hand des neufund. griech. Henoch-Textes', *ZNW* 38 (1937), pp. 115-24.

—*The Eucharistic Words of Jesus* (New York: Charles Scribner's Sons, 1966).

—*The Parables of Jesus* (London: SCM Press, 1972).

—*Die Sprache des Lukasevangeliums* (KEK; Göttingen: Vandenhoeck & Ruprecht, 1980).

Jervell, J., *Luke and the People of God* (Minneapolis: Augsburg, 1972).

—*The Unknown Paul: Essays in Luke–Acts and Early Christian History* (Minneapolis: Augsburg, 1984).

— 'The Church of Jews and God-fearers', in Tyson (ed.), *Luke–Acts and the Jewish People*, pp. 11-20.

Jewett, R., *Dating Paul's Life* (Philadelphia: Fortress Press; London: SCM Press, 1979).

Johnson, L.T., *The Literary Function of Possessions in Luke–Acts* (SBLDS, 39; Missoula, MT: Scholars Press, 1977).

—'On Finding the Lukan Community—A Cautious Cautionary Essay', in Achtemeier (ed.), *SBLSP*, 18 (1979), pp. 87-100.

—*Sharing Possessions* (Philadelphia: Fortress Press, 1981).

—*The Writings of the New Testament* (Philadelphia: Fortress Press, 1986).

—*The Gospel of Luke* (Sacra Pagina; Collegeville, MN: Liturgical Press, 1991).

Johnston, E.D., 'The Johannine Version of the Feeding of the Five Thousand: an Independent Tradition?', *JTS* NS 8 (1961), pp. 151-54.

Jones, C.P.M., 'The Epistle to the Hebrews and the Lukan Writings', in Nineham (ed.), *Studies in the Gospels*, pp. 113-43.

Jonge, M. de (ed.), *L'Evangile de Jean* (BETL, 44; Leuven: Leuven University Press, 1977).

Joynes, C., *Elijah, John the Baptist and Jesus in the Gospel Tradition* (MSt dissertation, Oxford University, 1995).

Juel, D., *Luke–Acts* (Atlanta, GA: John Knox Press, 1983).

Karris, R.J., 'Missionary Communities', *CBQ* 41 (1979), pp. 80-97.

—'Windows and Mirrors: Literary Criticism and Luke's "Sitz im Leben"', in Achtemeier (ed.), *SBLSP*, 18 (1979), pp. 47-58.

—*Luke: Artist and Theologian: Luke's Passion Account as Literature* (New York: Paulist Press, 1985).

Käsemann, E., 'Ephesians and Acts', in Keck and Martyn (eds.), *Studies in Luke–Acts*, pp. 288-97.

—*Essays on New Testament Themes* (London: SCM Press, 1966).

—'Ministry and Community in the New Testament', in *idem, Essays on New Testament Themes* (London: SCM Press, 1966), pp. 63-94.

—'Paul and Early Catholicism', in *idem, New Testament Questions of Today* (London: SCM Press, 1969), pp. 236-51.

Katz, P., 'The Early Christians' Use of Codices Instead of Rolls', *JTS* 46 (1945), pp. 63-65.

Keck, L.E., and J.L. Martyn (eds.), *Studies in Luke–Acts* (Philadelphia: Fortress Press; London: SPCK, 1966).

Kee, H.C., *Good News to the Ends of the Earth* (Philadelphia: Trinity Press International, 1990).

Kelber, H., *The Oral and Written Gospel* (Philadelphia: Fortress Press, 1983).

Kennedy, G.A., *A New Testament Interpretation through Rhetorical Criticism* (Chapel Hill, NC: University of North Carolina Press, 1984).

Kilgallen, J., 'Persecution in the Acts of the Apostles', in O'Collins (ed.), *Luke and Acts*, pp. 143-60.

Kilpatrick, G.D., *The Origins of the Gospel According to St Matthew* (Oxford: Clarendon Press, 1946).

Kimelman, R., '*Birkat Ha-Minim* and the Lack of Evidence for an Anti-Christian Jewish Prayer in Late Antiquity', in E.P. Sanders (ed.), *Jewish and Christian Self-Definition*, II, pp. 226-44.

Kingsbury, J.D., *Conflict in Luke* (Minneapolis: Fortress Press, 1991).

Klein, G., 'Lukas 1:1-4 als theologisches Programm', in Dinkler (ed.), *Zeit und Geschichte*, pp. 193-216.

Klein, H., 'Die lukanische-johanneische Passionstradition', *ZNW* 67 (1976), pp. 155-86.

Kloppenborg, J.S., *The Formation of Q: Trajectories in Ancient Wisdom Collections* (Philadelphia: Fortress Press, 1987).

—'Jesus and the Parables of Jesus in Q', in Piper, *The Gospel Behind the Gospels*, pp. 275-319.

Knox, J., *Marcion and the New Testament* (Chicago: University of Chicago Press, 1942).

—'Acts and the Pauline Letter Corpus', in Keck and Martyn (eds.), *Studies in Luke–Acts*, pp. 279-87.

—*Chapters in a Life of Paul* (Macon, GA: Mercer University Press, 2nd edn, 1989).

—'Some Reflections', in Parsons and Tyson (eds.), *Cadbury, Knox and Talbert*, pp. 107-13.

Knox, W.L., *St Paul and the Church of the Gentiles* (Cambridge: Cambridge University Press, 1932).

Kodell, J., 'Luke's Use of λαός, "People", Especially in the Jerusalem Narrative (Lk. 19:20–24:53)', *CBQ* 31 (1969), pp. 327-43.

Koester, H., *Ancient Christian Gospels* (London: SCM Press; Philadelphia: Trinity Press International, 1990).

Kopas, J., 'Jesus and Women: Luke's Gospel', *TTod* 42 (1986), pp. 192-202.

Kraabel, A.T., 'The Disappearance of the "God-fearers"', *Numen* 28 (1981), pp. 113-26.

Kremer, J. (ed.), *Les Actes des Apôtres: Tradition, Rédaction, Théologie* (BETL, 48; Leuven: Leuven University Press, 1979).

Krenkel, M., *Josephus und Lukas* (Leipzig, 1894).

Kümmel, W.G., *Promise and Fulfilment* (London: SCM Press, 1957).

—*Introduction to the New Testament* (Nashville: Abingdon Press; London: SCM Press, 1975).

Kurz, W.S., 'Luke 22:14-38 and Greco-Roman and Biblical Farewell Addresses', *JBL* 104 (1985), pp. 251-68.

—'Hellenistic Rhetoric in the Christological Proof of Luke–Acts', *CBQ* 42 (1980), pp. 171-95.

Kysar, R.D., 'The Source Analysis of the Fourth Gospel', *NovT* 15 (1973), pp. 134-52.

Lake, K., 'The Apostles' Creed', *HTR* 17 (1924), pp. 173-83.

Lampe, G.W.H., 'The Holy Spirit in the Writings of St Luke', in Nineham (ed.), *Studies in the Gospels*, pp. 159-200.

—'"Grievous Wolves": Ac. 20:29', in Lindars and Smalley (eds.), *Christ and Spirit in the New Testament*, pp. 352-68.

Lampe, G.W.H., and U. Luz, 'Post-Pauline Christianity and Pagan Society', in Becker (ed.), *Christian Beginnings*, pp. 242-82.

Landis, S., *Das Verhältnis des Johannesevangeliums zu den Synoptikern* (BZNW, 74; Berlin: W. de Gruyter, 1994).

Lane Fox, R., *The Unauthorized Version* (Harmondsworth: Penguin, 1991).

Layton, B., *The Gnostic Scriptures* (London: SCM Press, 1987).

Leaney, A.R.C., 'The Resurrection Narratives in St Luke', *NTS* 2 (1955), pp. 110-14.

—'The Johannine Paraclete and the Qumran Scrolls', in Charlesworth (ed.), *John and the Dead Sea Scrolls*, pp. 38-61.

Lee, E.K., *The Religious Thought of St John* (London: SPCK, 1950).

Legault, A., 'An Application of the Form-Critique Method to the Anointings in Galilee and Bethany', *CBQ* 16 (1954), pp. 131-45.

Levick, B.M., *Roman Colonies in Southern Asia Minor* (Oxford: Clarendon Press, 1967).

Lieu, J.M., 'Gnosticism in the Gospel of John', *ExpTim* 90 (1979), pp. 233-37.

—*The Second and Third Epistles of John: History and Background* (Edinburgh: T. & T. Clark, 1986).

Lincoln, A.T., 'The Use of the Old Testament in Ephesians', *JSNT* 14 (1982), pp. 16-57.

Lindars, B., 'The Composition of John 20', *NTS* 7 (1960), pp. 142-47.

—'Traditions Behind the Fourth Gospel', in de Jonge (ed.), *L'Évangile de Jean*, pp. 107-24.

—'Capernaum Revisited: Jn. 4:46-53 and the Synoptics', in van Segbroeck (ed.), *The Four Gospels*, III, pp. 1985-2000.

Lindars, B., and S. Smalley (eds.), *Christ and Spirit in the New Testament* (Cambridge: Cambridge University Press, 1973).

Logan, A.H.B., and A.J.M. Wedderburn (eds.), *The New Testament and Gnosis: Essays in Honour of R.McL. Wilson* (Edinburgh: T. & T. Clark, 1983).

Loisy, A., *L'Évangile selon Luc* (Paris: Emile Nourry, 1924).

Longenecker, R.M., and M.C. Tenney (eds.), *New Dimensions in New Testament Studies* (Grand Rapids: Eerdmans, 1974).

Lüdemann, G., *Paul, Apostle to the Gentiles: Studies in Chronology* (Philadelphia: Fortress Press; London: SCM Press, 1984).

—*Earliest Christianity According to the Traditions in Acts* (London: SCM Press, 1989).

—*Opposition to Paul in Jewish Christianity* (Minneapolis: Augsburg–Fortress, 1989).

Lummis, E.W., *How Luke Was Written* (dissertation, Cambridge University, 1915).

Luz, U., 'Erwägungen zur Enstehung des "Frühkatholizismus": Eine Skizze', *ZNW* 65 (1964), pp. 88-111.

—*Matthew 1–7: A Commentary* (Minneapolis: Augsburg, 1989).

MacRae, G.W. (ed.), *SBLSP*, 12 (Cambridge, MA: Scholars Press, 1973).

—'The Jewish Background of the Gnostic Sophia Myth', *NovT* 12 (1970), pp. 86-101.

Maddox, R., *The Purpose of Luke–Acts* (FRLANT, 126; Göttingen: Vandenhoeck & Ruprecht, 1982; Edinburgh: T. & T. Clark, 1985).

Mahoney, R., *Two Disciples at the Tomb* (TW, 6; Bern: H. Lang, 1972).

Malina, B.J., and J.H. Neyrey, 'Honour and Shame in Luke–Acts', in Neyrey (ed.), *The Social World of Luke–Acts*, pp. 25-66.

Manson, T.W., *The Sayings of Jesus* (London: SCM Press, 1949).

Marshall, I.H., *Luke: Historian and Theologian* (Grand Rapids: Eerdmans, 1970).

—'Early Catholicism in the New Testament', in Longenecker and Tenney (eds.), *New Dimensions in New Testament Studies*, pp. 217-36.

—*The Gospel of Luke* (Exeter: Paternoster Press, 1978).

Martin, R.P., 'An Epistle in Search of a Life-Setting', *ExpTim* 79 (1967), pp. 296-302.

Martyn, J.L., 'Source Criticism and Religionsgeschichte in the Fourth Gospel', in Miller (ed.), *Jesus and Man's Hope*, I, pp. 247-73.

—'Glimpses into the History of the Johannine Community', in de Jonge (ed.), *L'Évangile de Jean*, pp. 149-75.

—*The Gospel of John in Christian History* (New York: Paulist Press, 1978).

—*History and Theology in the Fourth Gospel* (Nashville: Abingdon Press, 2nd edn, 1979).

Massaux, E., *Influence de l'évangile de S. Matthieu sur la littérature chrétienne avant S. Irénée* (Leuven: Leuven University Press, 1950).

Mattill, A.J., 'The Purpose of Acts: Schneckenburger Reconsidered', in Gasque and Martin (eds.), *Apostolic History*, pp. 108-22.

—'The Jesus–Paul Parallels and the Purpose of Luke–Acts: H.H. Evans Reconsidered', *NovT* 17 (1975), pp. 15-46.

—'The Value of Acts as a Source for the Study of Paul', in Talbert (ed.), *Perspectives on Luke–Acts*, pp. 76-98.

McLean, B.H., 'On the Gospel of Thomas and Q', in Piper (ed.), *The Gospel Behind the Gospels*, pp. 321-45.

Meeks, W.A., *The Prophet King* (NovTSup, 14; Leiden: E.J. Brill, 1967).

—'The Man From Heaven in Johannine Sectarianism', *JBL* 91 (1972), pp. 44-72.

—*The First Urban Christians: The Social World of the Apostle Paul* (New Haven: Yale University Press, 1983).

—'The Social Functions of Apocalyptic Language in Pauline Christianity', in Hellholm (ed.), *Apocalypticism in the Mediterranean World and the Near East*, pp. 687-705.

Meier, J.P., *Law and History in Matthew's Gospel* (AnBib, 71; Rome: Pontifical Biblical Institute, 1976).

Mendner, S., 'Zum Problem "Johannes und die Synoptiker"', *NTS* 4 (1951), pp. 282-307.

Merk, O., 'Das Reich Gottes in den lukanischen Schriften', in Ellis and Grässer (eds.), *Jesus und Paulus*, pp. 201-20.

Metzger, B.M., *The Text of the New Testament* (Oxford: Clarendon Press, 1964).

—*A Textual Commentary on the Greek New Testament* (London: United Bible Society, 1971).

—*The Canon of the New Testament* (Oxford: Clarendon Press, 1987).

Miesner, D.R., 'The Missionary Journeys: Narrative Patterns and Purpose', in Talbert (ed.), *Perspectives on Luke–Acts*, pp. 199-214.

Miller, D.G. (ed.), *Jesus and Man's Hope*, I (Pittsburgh: Pittsburgh Theological Seminary, 1970).

Minear, P.S., 'A Note on Lk. 22:36', *NovT* 7 (1964), pp. 128-34.

—'Luke's Use of the Birth Stories', in Keck and Martyn (eds.), *Studies in Luke–Acts*, pp. 111-30.

—'A Note on Lk. 17:7-10', *JBL* 93 (1974), pp. 82-87.

—'Jesus's Audiences, According to Luke', *NovT* 16 (1974), pp. 81-109.

—*To Heal and to Reveal* (New York: Seabury Press, 1976).

Mitchell, S., *Anatolia*. II. *The Rise of the Church* (Oxford: Clarendon Press, 1993).

Mitton, C.L., *The Epistle to the Ephesians: Its Authorship, Origin and Purpose* (Oxford: Clarendon Press, 1951).

—'The Authorship of the Epistle to the Ephesians', *ExpTim* 67 (1955), pp. 195-98.

—*The Formation of the Pauline Corpus of Letters* (London: Epworth Press, 1955).

Moessner, D.P., 'Jesus and the Wilderness Generation: The Death of the Prophet like Moses', in Richards (ed.), *SBLSP*, 21 (1982), pp. 319-40.

—'Luke 9:1-50: Luke's Preview of the Journey of the Prophet like Moses of Deuteronomy', *JBL* 102 (1983), pp. 575-605.

—'The Ironic Fulfilment of Israel's Glory', in Tyson (ed.), *Luke–Acts and the Jewish People*, pp. 35-50.

—*The Lord of the Banquet: The Literary and Theological Significance of the Lukan Travel Narrative* (Minneapolis: Augsburg–Fortress, 1989).

Momigliano, A., *The Development of Greek Biography* (Cambridge, MA: Harvard University Press, 1993).

Morris, L., *Studies in the Fourth Gospel* (Grand Rapids: Eerdmans, 1969).

Moule, C.F.D., *An Idiom Book of New Testament Greek* (Cambridge: Cambridge University Press, 1959).

—'The Christology of Acts', in Keck and Martyn (eds.), *Studies in Luke–Acts*, pp. 159-85.

—'Neglected Feature in the Problem of the "Son of Man"', in Gnilka (ed.), *Neues Testament und Kirche*, pp. 423-48.

—*The Origin of Christology* (Cambridge: Cambridge University Press, 1977).

Moule, C.F.D. (ed.), *The Birth of the New Testament* (Black's New Testament Commentaries; London: Adam & Charles Black, 3rd edn, 1981).

Moxnes, H., *The Economy of the Kingdom* (Philadelphia: Fortress Press, 1988).

Muddiman, J., 'A Note on Reading Lk. 24:12', *ETL* 48 (1972), pp. 542-48.

Mussner, F., '"καθεξῆς" im Lukasprolog', in Ellis and Grässer (eds.), *Jesus und Paulus*, pp. 253-55.

Neirynck, F., 'John and the Synoptics', in de Jonge (ed.), *L'Évangile de Jean*, pp. 73-106.

—*Jean et les synoptiques* (BETL, 49: Leuven: Leuven University Press, 1979).

—*Evangelica*, I (BETL, 60; Leuven: Leuven University Press, 1982).

—'John and the Synoptics: The Empty Tomb Stories', *NTS* 30 (1984), pp. 161-87.

—'John 21', *NTS* 36 (1990), pp. 321-36.

—'John and the Synoptics, 1975–1990', in Denaux (ed.), *John and the Synoptics*, pp. 3-62.

—'The Minor Agreements and Q', in Piper (ed.), *The Gospel Behind the Gospels*, pp. 49-72.

Neusner, J. (ed.), *Christianity, Judaism, and Graeco-Roman Cults*, I (Leiden: E.J. Brill, 1975).

Neyrey, J.H., 'Jesus's Address to the Women of Jerusalem (Lk. 23:27-31): A Prophetic Judgment Oracle', *NTS* 29 (1983), pp. 74-86.

—'The Forensic Defense Speech and Paul's Trial Speeches in Acts 22–26: Form and Function', in Talbert (ed.), *Luke–Acts*, pp. 210-24.

—*The Social World of Luke–Acts* (Cambridge, MA: Harvard University Press, 1991).

Nickelsburg, G.W.E., 'Riches, the Rich, and God's Judgment in 1 Enoch 92-105 and the Gospel According to Luke', *NTS* 25 (1978), pp. 324-44.

—*Jewish Literature between the Bible and the Mishnah* (London: SCM Press, 1981).

Nineham, D.E. (ed.), *Studies in the Gospels: Essays in Memory of R.H. Lightfoot* (Oxford: Basil Blackwell, 1955).

Nock, A.D., *Conversion: The Old and the New in Religion from Alexander the Great to Augustine of Hippo* (Oxford: Oxford University Press, 1933).

Oakman, D.E., 'The Countryside in Luke–Acts', in Neyrey (ed.), *The Social World of Luke–Acts*, pp. 151-79.

O'Collins, G. (ed.), *Luke and Acts* (New York: Paulist Press, 1993).

Odeberg, H., *The Fourth Gospel* (Uppsala: Lundeqvist, 1929).

O'Fearghail, F., 'Rejection in Nazareth: Luke 4:22', *ZNW* 75 (1984), pp. 60-72.

O'Hanlon, J., 'Zacchaeus and the Lukan Ethic', *JSNT* 12 (1981), pp. 2-26.

Oliver, H., 'The Lucan Birth Stories and the Purpose of Luke–Acts', *NTS* 10 (1963), pp. 202-26.

O'Neill, J.C., *The Theology of Acts* (London: SPCK, 2nd edn, 1970).

Osty, E., 'Les points de contact entre le récit de la passion dans S. Luc et dans S. Jean', *RSR* 39 (1951), pp. 146-54.

O'Toole, R.F., 'Luke's Position on Politics and Society', in Cassidy and Scharper (eds.), *Political Issues in Luke–Acts*, pp. 1-17.

—*The Unity of Luke's Theology* (GNS, 9; Wilmington, DE: Michael Glazier, 1984).

Painter, J., 'The Enigmatic Johannine Son of Man', in van Segbroeck (ed.), *The Four Gospels*, III, pp. 1869-87.

Palmer, D.W., 'Acts and the Ancient Historical Monograph', in Winter and Clarke (eds.), *The Book of Acts in its First Century Setting*, pp. 1-30.

Parker, P., 'Luke and the Fourth Evangelist', *NTS* 9 (1963), pp. 317-36.

—'The Former Treatise and the Date of Acts', *JBL* 84 (1965), pp. 52-58.

—'Mark, Acts and Galilean Christianity', *NTS* 16 (1970), pp. 295-304.

Parsons, M.C., and R.I. Pervo (eds.), *Rethinking the Unity of Luke–Acts* (Minneapolis: Augsburg–Fortress, 1993).

Parsons, M.C., and J.B. Tyson (eds.), *Cadbury, Knox and Talbert: American Contributions to the Study of Acts* (SBLBS, 18; Atlanta, GA: Scholars Press, 1992).

Pearce, K., 'The Lucan Origins of the Raising of Lazarus', *ExpTim* 96 (1985), pp. 359-61.

Pearson, B.A., 'Jewish Sources in Gnostic Literature', in Stone (ed.), *Jewish Writings of the Second Temple Period*, pp. 443-81.

Pelling, C.B.R., 'Plutarch's Method of Work in the Roman Lives', *JHS* 19 (1979), pp. 74-96.

—'Plutarch's Adaptation of his Source Material', *JHS* 20 (1980), pp. 127-40.

Perkins, P., *Gnosticism and the New Testament* (Minneapolis: Fortress Press, 1993).

Perry, A.M., *The Sources of Luke's Passion Narrative* (Chicago: University of Chicago Press, 1920).

Pervo, R., *Profit with Delight: The Literary Genre of the Acts of the Apostles* (Philadelphia: Fortress Press, 1987).

Pilgrim, W.E., *Good News to the Poor* (Minneapolis: Augsburg, 1981).

Piper, R.A. (ed.), *The Gospel behind the Gospels* (NovTSup, 75; Leiden: E.J. Brill, 1995).

Plümacher, E., 'Lukas als griechischer Historiker', *PWSup* 14 (1974), cols. 235-64.

Powell, M.A., *What Are They Saying about Luke?* (New York: Paulist Press, 1989).

—*What Is Narrative Criticism?* (Minneapolis: Augsburg–Fortress, 1990).

Praeder, S.M., 'Luke–Acts and the Ancient Novel', in Richards (ed.), *SBLSP*, 20 (1981), pp. 269-92.

Price, J.L., 'Light from Qumran upon Some Aspects of Johannine Theology', in Charlesworth (ed.), *John and the Dead Sea Scrolls*, pp. 9-37.

Quinn, J.D., 'The Last Volume of Luke: The Relation of Luke–Acts to the Pastoral Epistles', in Talbert (ed.), *Perspectives on Luke–Acts*, pp. 62-75.

Quispel, G., 'Qumran, John, and Jewish Christianity', in Charlesworth (ed.), *John and the Dead Sea Scrolls*, pp. 137-55.

Räisänen, H., *Paul and the Law* (Tübingen: J.C.B. Mohr [Paul Siebeck], 1983).

Rajak, T., *Josephus: The Historian and his Society* (London: Gerald Duckworth, 1983).

Ramsay, W.M., 'Professor Blass on the Two Editions of Acts', *Exp*, Fifth Series I (1895), pp. 129-42; 212-25.

—*The Bearing of Recent Discovery on the Trustworthiness of the New Testament* (London: Hodder & Stoughton, 1915).

Ravens, D.A.S., 'The Setting of Luke's Account of the Anointing: Luke 7:2–8:3', *NTS* 34 (1988), pp. 282-92.

—'Luke 9:7-62 and the Prophetic Role of Jesus', *NTS* 36 (1990), pp. 119-29.

Reicke, B., 'Instruction and Discussion in the Travel Narrative', in Aland (ed.), *SE I*, pp. 206-16.

—*The Roots of the Synoptic Tradition* (Philadelphia: Fortress Press, 1986).

Rese, M., 'Das Lukas-Evangelium: Ein Forschungsbericht', *ANRW* II.3 (1985), pp. 2358ff.

Rhoads, D., and D. Michie, *Mark as Story: An Introduction to the Narrative of a Gospel* (Philadelphia: Fortress Press, 1982).

Rice, G.E., 'Luke's Thematic Use of the Call to Discipleship', *AUSS* 19 (1981), pp. 51-58.

—'Lk. 4:31-44: Release for the Captives', *AUSS* 20 (1982), pp. 23-28.

—'Lk. 5:33-6:11: Release from Cultic Tradition', *AUSS* 20 (1982), pp. 127-32.

—' "Western Non-interpolations": A Defence of the Apostolate', in Talbert (ed.), *Luke–Acts*, pp. 1-16.

Richard, E., 'The Divine Purpose: The Jews and the Gentile Mission (Acts 15)', in Talbert (ed.), *Luke–Acts*, pp. 188-209.

Richards, K.H. (ed.), *SBLSP*, 20 (Chico, CA: Scholars Press, 1981).

—*SBLSP*, 21 (Chico, CA: Scholars Press, 1982).

—*SBLSP*, 22 (Chico, CA: Scholars Press, 1983).

—*SBLSP*, 24 (Atlanta, GA: Scholars Press, 1985).

Richardson, N. *The Panorama of Luke* (London: Epworth Press, 1982).

Robbins, V.K., 'By Land and Sea: The We Passages and Ancient Sea Voyages', in Talbert (ed.), *Perspectives on Luke–Acts*, pp. 215-42.

—'Prefaces in Greco-Roman Biography and Luke–Acts', *PRS* 6 (1979), pp. 94-108.

—*Jesus the Teacher* (Philadelphia: Fortress Press, 1984).

—'A Socio-Rhetorical Look at the Work of John Knox on Luke–Acts', in Parsons and Tyson (eds.), *Cadbury, Knox and Talbert*, pp. 91-105.

Robinson, D.W.C., *Selected Material Common to the Third and Fourth Gospels* (MLitt dissertation, Oxford University, 1979).

Robinson, J.A.T., 'The Destination and Purpose of the Johannine Epistles', *NTS* 6 (1960), pp. 117-31.

—*Redating the New Testament* (London: SCM Press, 1976).

—*The Priority of John* (ed. J.F. Coakley; London: SCM Press, 1985).

Robinson, J.M., 'On the Gattung of Mark (and John)', in Miller (ed.), *Jesus and Man's Hope*, I, pp. 99-129.

—'The Johannine Trajectory', in Robinson and Koester, *Trajectories*, pp. 232-68.

—*The Future of our Religious Past* (London: SCM Press, 1971).

Robinson, J.M., and H. Koester, *Trajectories through Early Christianity* (Philadelphia: Fortress Press, 1971).

Robinson, W.C., 'The Theological Context for Interpreting Luke's Travel Narrative', *JBL* 79 (1960), pp. 20-31.

Rohrbaugh, R.L., 'The Pre-industrial City in Luke–Acts: Urban Social Relations', in Neyrey (ed.), *The Social World of Luke–Acts*, pp. 125-49.

Ropes, J.H., 'The Text of Acts', in Jackson and Lake (eds.), *Beginnings*, III, pp. ccxv-cclvi.

Rowland, C., *The Open Heaven* (New York: Crossroad, 1982).

—*Christian Origins* (London: SPCK, 1985).

Ruckstuhl, E., 'Johannine Language and Style', in de Jonge (ed.), *L'Évangile de Jean*, pp. 125-47.

Russell, D.A., ' "De imitatione" ', in West and Woodman (eds.), *Creative Imitation and Latin Literature*, pp. 1-16.

Russell, D.S., *Divine Disclosure* (London: SCM Press, 1992).

Ryan, R., 'The Women from Galilee and Discipleship in Luke', *BTB* 15 (1985), pp. 56-59.

Sabbe, M., 'The Arrest of Jesus in Jn. 18:1-11 and its Relation to the Synoptic Gospels: A Critical Evaluation of A. Dauer's Hypothesis', in de Jonge (ed.), *L'Évangile de Jean*, pp. 203-34.

—*Studia neotestamentica* (BETL, 98; Leuven: Leuven University Press, 1991).

—'The Footwashing in John 13 and its Relation to the Synoptic Gospels', in Sabbe, *Studia neotestamentica*, pp. 409-41.

Salmon, M., 'Insider or Outsider? Luke's Relationship with Judaism', in Tyson (ed.), *Luke–Acts and the Jewish People*, pp. 76-82.

Sanday, W. (ed.), *Oxford Studies in the Synoptic Problem* (Oxford: Clarendon Press, 1911).

Sanders, E.P., 'The Argument from Order and the Relationship Between Matthew and Luke', *NTS* 15 (1968), pp. 249-61.

—*Paul and Palestinian Judaism* (London: SCM Press, 1977).

—*Paul, the Law and the Jewish People* (London: SCM Press, 1983).

—*Jesus and Judaism* (London: SCM Press, 1985).

—*Jewish Law from Jesus to the Mishnah* (London: SCM Press, 1990).

—*Judaism: Practice and Belief 63 B.C.E.–66 C.E.* (London: SCM Press, 1992).

Sanders, E.P. (ed.), *Jewish and Christian Self-Definition*, II (London: SCM Press, 1981).

Sanders, E.P., and M. Davies, *Studying the Synoptic Gospels* (London: SCM Press, 1989).

Sanders, J.T., 'The Salvation of the Jews in Luke–Acts', in Talbert (ed.), *Luke–Acts*, pp. 104-28.

—*The Jews in Luke–Acts* (Philadelphia: Fortress Press; London: SCM Press, 1987).

—'The Jewish People in Luke–Acts', in Tyson (ed.), *Luke–Acts and the Jewish People*, pp. 51-75.

Satterthwaite, P.E., 'Acts against the Background of Classical Rhetoric', in Winter and Clarke (eds.), *The Book of Acts in its First Century Setting*, I, pp. 337-79.

Schmid, J., and A. Vögtle (eds.), *Synoptische Studien* (Munich: Beck, 1953).

Schmidt, D.L., 'Luke's "Innocent" Jesus: A Scriptural Apologetic', in Cassidy and Scharper (eds.), *Political Issues in Luke–Acts*, pp. 111-21.

—'The Historiography of Acts: Deuteronomistic or Hellenistic?', in Richards (ed.), *SBLSP*, 24 (1985), pp. 417-27.

Schnackenburg, R., *The Gospel According to St John* (3 vols.; New York: Crossroad, 1968–82).

—'On the Origin of the Fourth Gospel', in Miller (ed.), *Jesus and Man's Hope*, I, pp. 223-46.

Schneider, G., 'Zur Bedeutung von καθεξῆς im lukanischen Doppelwerk', *ZNW* 68 (1977), pp. 128-31.

Schnelle, U., 'Johannes und die Synoptiker', in van Segbroeck (ed.), *The Four Gospels*, III, pp. 1799-814.

Schniewind, J., *Die Parallelperikopen bei Lukas und Johannes* (Leipzig: J.C. Hinrichs, 1914; repr. Hildesheim: G. Olms, 1958).

Schramm, T., *Der Markus-Stoff bei Lukas* (Cambridge: Cambridge University Press, 1971).

Schreckenberg, H., 'Flavius Josephus und die lukanischen Schriften', in W. Haubeck and M. Bachmann (eds.), *Wort in der Zeit: Festgabe für K.H. Rengstorf* (Leiden: E.J. Brill, 1980), pp. 179-207.

Schubert, P., 'The Structure and Significance of Luke 24', in W. Eltester (ed.), *Neuetestamentliche Studien für Rudolf Bultmann* (BZNW, 21; Berlin: Töpelmann, 1954), pp. 165-86.

Schürer, E., *The History of the Jewish People in the Age of Jesus Christ, 175 B.C.–A.D. 135* (revised by G. Vermes, F. Millar and M. Goodman; Edinburgh: T. & T. Clark; Naperville, IL: Allenson, rev. edn, 1973–87).

Schürmann, H., 'Sprachliche Reminiszenzen an Abgeänderte oder Ausgelassene Bestandteile der Spruchsammlung im Lukas- und Matthäusevangelium', *NTS* 6 (1959), pp. 193-210.

—*Das Lukasevangelium*, I (HTKNT, 3; Freiburg: Herder, 1969).

Schweizer, E., *Church Order in the New Testament* (London: SCM Press, 1961).

—'Concerning the Speeches in Acts', in Keck and Martyn (eds.), *Studies in Luke–Acts*, pp. 208-16.

Scott, B.B., *Hear, then, the Parable* (Philadelphia: Fortress Press, 1989).

Segbroeck, F. van (ed.), *The Four Gospels: Festschrift Frans Neirynck* (3 vols.; BETL; Leuven: Leuven University Press, 1992).

Sheeley, S.M., *Narrative Asides in Luke–Acts* (JSNTSup, 72; Sheffield: Sheffield Academic Press, 1992).

Sherwin-White, A.N., *Roman Society and Roman Law in the New Testament* (Oxford: Oxford University Press, 1963).

Shuler, P.L., *A Genre for the Gospels: The Biographical Character of Matthew* (Minneapolis: Fortress Press, 1982).

Siegemann, E.F., 'St John's Use of the Synoptic Material', *CBQ* 30 (1968), pp. 182-98.

Smallwood, E.M., *The Jews under Roman Rule* (Leiden: E.J. Brill, 1976).

Smith, D.M., 'John 12:12ff. and the Question of John's Use of the Synoptics', *JBL* 82 (1963), pp. 58-64.

—'John and the Synoptics: Some Dimensions of the Problem', *NTS* 26 (1979), pp. 425-44.

—*Johannine Christianity: Essays in its Setting, Sources and Theology* (Columbia, SC: University of South Carolina Press, 1984).

—*John Among the Gospels* (Minneapolis: Augsburg–Fortress, 1992).

Smith, J., *The Voyage and Shipwreck of St Paul* (London, 4th edn, 1880).

Smith, M., *Jesus the Magician* (London: Victor Gollancz, 1978).

Snodgrass, K., ' "Western Non-interpolations" ', *JBL* 91 (1972), pp. 366-79.

Soards, M., *The Passion According to Luke: The Special Material of Luke 22* (JSNTSup, 14; Sheffield: Sheffield Academic Press, 1987).

Sparks, H.F.D., *The Apocryphal Old Testament* (Oxford: Clarendon Press, 1984).

Stanton, G., *Jesus of Nazareth in New Testament Preaching* (Cambridge: Cambridge University Press, 1974).

—*A Gospel for a New People: Studies in Matthew* (Edinburgh: T. & T. Clark, 1992).

Steele, E.S., 'Luke 11:37-54: A Modified Hellenistic Symposium', *JBL* 103 (1984), pp. 379-94.

Sterling, G.E., *Historiography and Self-Definition: Josephos, Luke–Acts and Apologetic Historiography* (NovTSup, 64; Leiden: E.J. Brill, 1992).

Stone, M. (ed.), *Jewish Writings of the Second Temple Period* (CRINT, 2.2; Assen: Van Gorcum; Philadelphia: Fortress Press, 1984).

Strange, W.A., *The Problem of the Text of Acts* (SNTSMS, 71; Cambridge: Cambridge University Press, 1992).

Strecker, G., *The Sermon on the Mount* (trans. O.C. Dean; Nashville: Abingdon Press, 1988).

Streeter, B.H., 'St Mark's Knowledge and Use of Q', in Sanday (ed.), *Oxford Studies in the Synoptic Problem*, pp. 165-83.

—*The Primitive Church* (London: Macmillan, 1929).

—*The Four Gospels* (London: Macmillan, 2nd edn, 1930).

Styler, G.M., 'The Priority of Mark', in Moule (ed.), *The Birth of the New Testament*, pp. 285-316.

Swartley, W., 'Politics and Peace in Luke's Gospel', in Cassidy and Scharper (eds.), *Political Issues in Luke–Acts*, pp. 18-37.

Tajra, H.W., *The Trial of St Paul* (WUNT, 2.95; Tübingen: J.C.B. Mohr, 1989).

Talbert, C.H., *Luke and the Gnostics* (Nashville: Abingdon Press, 1966).

—'An Anti-Gnostic Tendency in Lukan Christology', *NTS* 14 (1967), pp. 259-71.

—'The Redaction Critical Quest for Luke the Theologian', in Miller (ed.), *Jesus and Man's Hope*, I, pp. 171-222.

—*Literary Patterns, Theological Themes and the Genre of Luke–Acts* (SBLMS, 20; Missoula, MT: Scholars Press, 1974).

—'Shifting Sands: The Recent Study of the Gospel of Luke', *Interpretation* 30 (1976), pp. 381-95.

—*What is a Gospel?: The Genre of the Canonical Gospels* (Philadelphia: Fortress Press, 1977).

—'Martyrdom in Luke–Acts and the Lukan Social Ethic', in Cassidy and Scharper (eds.), *Political Issues in Luke–Acts*, pp. 99-110.

—'Promise and Fulfilment in Lucan Theology', in Talbert (ed.), *Luke Acts*, pp. 91-103.

—*Reading Luke* (London: SPCK, 1990).

Talbert, C.H. (ed.), *Perspectives on Luke–Acts* (Danville, VA: Association of Baptist Professors of Religion, 1978).

—*Luke–Acts: New Perspectives from the SBL* (New York: Crossroad, 1984).

Tannehill, R.C., 'A Study in the Theology of Luke–Acts', *ATR* 43 (1961), pp. 195-203.

—'Israel in Luke–Acts: A Tragic Story', *JBL* 104 (1985), pp. 69-85.

—*The Narrative Unity of Luke–Acts* (2 vols.; I, Philadelphia: Fortress Press, 1986; II, Minneapolis: Augsburg–Fortress, 1990).

—'Rejection by Jews and Turning to the Gentiles: The Pattern of Paul's Mission in Acts', in Tyson (ed.), *Luke–Acts and the Jewish People*, pp. 83-101.

Taylor, V., *Behind the Third Gospel* (Oxford: Clarendon Press, 1926).

—*The Formation of the Gospel Tradition* (Cambridge: Cambridge University Press, 1933).

—'The Order of Q', *JTS* NS 4 (1953), pp. 27-31.

—*The Passion Narrative of St Luke* (SNTSMS, 19: Cambridge: Cambridge University Press, 1972).

Tetlow, E., *Women and Ministry in the New Testament* (New York: Paulist Press, 1980).

Theissen, G., *The First Followers of Jesus* (London: SCM Press, 1978 [= *The Sociology of Early Palestinian Christianity*, Philadelphia: Fortress Press, 1978]).

—*The Social Setting of Pauline Christianity* (Edinburgh: T. & T. Clark, 1982).

Thurston, B., *Spiritual Life in the Early Church: The Witness of Acts and Ephesians* (Minneapolis: Augsburg–Fortress, 1993).

Thyen, H., 'Entwicklungen der johanneische Theologie', in de Jonge (ed.), *L'Évangile de Jean*, pp. 259-99.

—'Johannes und die Synoptiker', in Denaux (ed.), *John and the Synoptics*, pp. 81-107.

Tiede, D.L., *Prophecy and History in Luke–Acts* (Philadelphia: Fortress Press, 1980).

—'Glory to thy people, Israel', in Tyson (ed.), *Luke–Acts and the Jewish People*, pp. 21-34.

Torrey, C.C., *The Composition and Date of Acts* (Cambridge, MA: Harvard University Press, 1916).

Townsend, J.T., 'The Date of Luke–Acts', in Talbert (ed.), *Luke–Acts*, pp. 47-62.

—'The Contribution of John Knox to the Study of Acts', in Parsons and Tyson (eds.), *Cadbury, Knox and Talbert*, pp. 81-89.

Trites, A.A., *The New Testament Concept of Witness* (Cambridge: Cambridge University Press, 1977).

—'The Prayer Motif in Luke–Acts', in Talbert (ed.), *Perspectives on Luke–Acts*, pp. 168-86.

Trocmé, E., 'Jean et les synoptiques: L'exemple de Jean 1:15-34', in van Segbroeck (ed.), *The Four Gospels*, III, pp. 1935-41.

Tuckett, C.M., 'The Beatitudes: A Source-Critical Study', *NovT* 25 (1983), pp. 193-207.

—'On the Relationship Between Matthew and Luke', *NTS* 30 (1984), pp. 130-42.

—'Arguments from Order: Definition and Evaluation', in Tuckett (ed.), *Synoptic Studies*, pp. 197-219.

—'The Existence of Q', in Piper (ed.), *The Gospel behind the Gospels*, pp. 19-47.

Tuckett, C.M. (ed.), *Synoptic Studies* (Sheffield: Sheffield Academic Press, 1984).

Turner, N., 'The Minor Verbal Agreements of Matthew and Luke Against Mark', in Aland (ed.), *SE I*, pp. 223-34.

—*A Grammar Of New Testament Greek*, IV (Edinburgh: T. & T. Clark, 1976).

Tyson, J.B., 'The Lukan Version of the Trial of Jesus', *NovT* 3 (1959), pp. 249-58.

—'The Problem of Food in Acts: A Study of Literary Patterns with Particular Reference to Acts 6:1-7', in Achtemeier (ed.), *SBLSP*, 18 (1979), pp. 69-85.

—'The Jewish Public in Luke–Acts', *NTS* 30 (1984), pp. 574-83.

Tyson, J.B. (ed.), *Luke–Acts and the Jewish People* (Minneapolis: Augsburg–Fortress, 1988).

—The Problem of Jewish Rejection in Acts', in Tyson (ed.), *Luke–Acts and the Jewish People*, pp. 124-37.

—'John Knox and the Acts of the Apostles', in Parsons and Tyson (eds.), *Cadbury, Knox and Talbert*, pp. 55-80.

Vanni, U., 'The Apocalypse and the Gospel of Luke', in O'Collins (ed.), *Luke and Acts*, pp. 9-25.

Van Unnik, W.C., 'Luke–Acts: A Storm Centre in Contemporary Scholarship', in Keck and Martyn (eds.), *Studies in Luke–Acts*, pp. 15-32.

—*Sparsa Collecta* (Leiden: E.J. Brill, 1973).

—'The Book of Acts: the Confirmation of the Gospel', in van Unnik, *Sparsa Collecta*, pp. 340-73.

—'Die Apostelgeschichte und die Häresien', in van Unnik, *Sparsa Collecta*, pp. 402-409.

—'Luke's Second Book and the Rules of Hellenistic Historiography', in Kremer (ed.), *Les Actes des Apôtres*, pp. 37-60.

Vermes, G., *Jesus and the World of Judaism* (London: SCM Press, 1983).

—*Jesus the Jew* (London: SCM Press, 2nd edn, 1983).

—*The Dead Sea Scrolls in English* (Harmondsworth: Penguin, 3rd edn, 1987).

Vielhauer, P., 'On the Paulinism of Acts', in Keck and Martyn (eds.), *Studies in Luke–Acts*, pp. 33-50.

Völkel, M., 'Exegetische Erwägungen zum Verständnis des Begriffs καθεξῆς im lukanischen Prolog', *NTS* 20 (1973), pp. 289-99.

von Campenhausen, H., *The Formation of the Christian Bible* (Philadelphia: Fortress Press, 1972).

Wagner, W.W., *After the Apostles* (Minneapolis: Augsburg–Fortress, 1994).

Wainwright, A.W., 'Luke and the Restoration of the Kingdom to Israel', *ExpTim* 89 (1977), pp. 76-79.

Walaskay. P.W., *And So We Came to Rome* (SNTSMS, 49; Cambridge: Cambridge University Press, 1983).

Watson, F., *Paul, Judaism and the Gentiles* (SNTSMS, 56; Cambridge: Cambridge University Press, 1986).

Weeden, T., *Mark: Traditions in Conflict* (Philadelphia: Fortress Press, 1971).

Weinert, F.D., 'Luke, the Temple, and Jesus's Saying about Jerusalem's Abandoned House (Lk. 13:34-35)', *CBQ* 44 (1982), pp. 68-76.

Weiss, B., *Die Quellen des Lukasevangeliums* (Stuttgart: J.G. Cotta, 1907).

Weiss, J., *Jesus's Proclamation of the Kingdom of God* (London: SCM Press; Philadelphia: Fortress Press, 1971).

Wengst, K., *Pax Romana* (trans. J. Bowden; London: SCM Press, 1987).

Wenham, J., *Redating Matthew, Mark and Luke* (London: Hodder & Stoughton, 1991).

West, D., and T. Woodman, *Creative Imitation and Latin Literature* (Cambridge: Cambridge University Press, 1979).

Williams, F.E., 'The Fourth Gospel and Synoptic Tradition', *JBL* 86 (1967), pp. 311-19.

Wilson, R.M., *The Gnostic Problem: A Study in the Relations Between Hellenistic Judaism and the Gnostic Heresy* (London: A.R. Mowbray, 1963).

Wilson, S.G., 'Lukan Eschatology', *NTS* 16 (1969), pp. 330-47.

—*The Gentiles and the Gentile Mission in Luke–Acts* (SNTSMS, 23: Cambridge: Cambridge University Press, 1973).

—*Luke and the Pastoral Epistles* (London: SPCK, 1979).

—*Luke and the Law* (SNTSMS, 50; Cambridge: Cambridge University Press, 1983).

Wilson, W.G., 'An Examination of the Linguistic Evidence Adduced against the Unity of Authorship of the First Epistle of John and the Fourth Gospel', *JTS* 49 (1948), pp. 147-56.

Windisch, H., 'The Case against the Tradition', in Jackson and Lake (eds.), *The Beginnings of Christianity*, II (1922), pp. 298-348.

—*Johannes und die Synoptiker: Wollte der vierte Evangelist die älteren Evangelien ergänzen oder ersetzen?* (UNT, 12; Leipzig: J.C. Hinrichs, 1926).

Wink, W., *Naming the Powers: The Language of Power in the New Testament*, I (Philadelphia: Fortress Press, 1984).

Winter, B.W., and A.D. Clarke (eds.), *The Book of Acts in its First Century Setting*, I (Grand Rapids: Eerdmans, 1993).

Winter, P., 'On Luke and Lucan Sources', *ZNW* 47 (1956), pp. 217-42.

—*On the Trial of Jesus* (ed. T.A. Burkill and G. Vermes; SJ, 1; Berlin: W. de Gruyter, 2nd edn, 1974).

Winter, P., and V. Taylor, 'The Sources of the Lucan Passion Narrative', *ExpTim* 68 (1956), p. 95.

Witherington, B., 'On the Road with Mary Magdalene, Joanna, Susanna, and Other Disciples (Lk.8:1-3)', *ZNW* 70 (1979), pp. 243-48.

—'The Anti-feminist Tendency in the Western Text of Acts', *JBL* 103 (1984), pp. 82-84.

Woodman, A.J., *Rhetoric in Classical Historiography* (London: Croom Helm, 1988).

Woodman, T., 'Self-imitation and the Substance of History', in West and Woodman (eds.), *Creative Imitation and Latin Literature*, pp. 143-55.

Worsley, F.W., 'The Relation of the Fourth Gospel to the Synoptists', *ExpTim* 20 (1908), pp. 62-65.

—*The Fourth Gospel and the Synoptists: Being a Contribution to the Study of the Johannine Problem* (Edinburgh: T. & T. Clark, 1909).

Wrede, W., *The Messianic Secret* (Cambridge: James Clarke, 1971).

Wright, A., *The Gospel According to Luke [in Greek]* (London: Macmillan, 1900).

Yamauchi, E.M., 'Some Alleged Evidences for Pre-Christian Gnosticism', in Longenecker and Tenney (eds.), *New Dimensions in New Testament Studies*, pp. 46-70.

Ziesler, J.A., 'Luke and the Pharisees', *NTS* 25 (1978), pp. 146-57.

Zürhellen, O., *Die Heimat des vierten Evangeliums* (Tübingen: J.C.B. Mohr, 1909).

INDEX

	136, 141, 160, 177, 192	20.28	210	22.21	211		
		20.33-38	285	22.22	165		
		20.35	164, 195	22.23	223		
19.10	136	20.37	210	22.24-27	65, 133		
19.11–21.38	239	20.42-43	210	22.24	74, 110, 237		
19.11	90, 136, 138, 158, 279	20.44	67				
		20.45-47	104	22.25	39, 134		
		20.46	74	22.26-33	209		
19.12-27	90	21	23, 65, 140, 156, 157, 159, 161	22.26-27	277		
19.12	137, 138			22.27	109, 224		
19.13	137			22.28-30	133		
19.14-15	78, 138			22.31-65	239		
19.15-17	181	21.1-4	179	22.31-34	27, 207, 209, 213		
19.17	137	21.5	157				
19.19	160	21.11	157	22.31-32	109, 214		
19.20-21	137	21.14-15	74	22.31	180, 185, 198, 213, 225, 231, 240, 242		
19.22-23	137	21.14	107, 241				
19.22	136, 254	21.15	263				
19.24	137	21.18	263				
19.25	137	21.19	157, 160	22.32	189, 225, 227, 268		
19.26	74, 136, 137	21.20	157, 191				
		21.21	129	22.33-34	214		
19.27	78, 136-39	21.23	156	22.33	274		
		21.24	23, 54, 157, 159, 160	22.34	213, 225		
19.28-44	136			22.36-37	225		
19.28-31	219			22.36	209		
19.28	90	21.25-26	157, 210	22.37	114, 175		
19.29	219, 228	21.27	157, 165, 210	22.39-71	209		
19.30	219			22.39	228		
19.35	220	21.31-32	159	22.40	156		
19.37-40	209, 210	21.31	161	22.42	110		
19.37	228	21.36	165	22.43-44	110		
19.38	39, 71, 211, 221	21.37	228	22.43	153		
		22.1	208	22.44-45	77		
19.39	48, 219	22.2	220	22.46	156		
19.41-42	140	22.3	75, 179, 185, 205, 218, 240-42, 258	22.47-49	226		
19.43-44	23, 273			22.47	206		
19.44	23, 90			22.49	206, 227		
19.46	151, 211			22.50	206, 265		
19.47	208, 220, 222, 246	22.7-13	209	22.51	206		
		22.14–24.53	275	22.52	220, 227		
		22.14-38	205	22.53	177, 206, 222, 227, 228		
19.48	221	22.14-23	209				
20.1-8	246	22.14	222, 224, 242				
20.1	220			22.55	247, 248		
20.6	221	22.16	208, 279	22.58	75, 247		
20.9	210	22.18	279	22.59-60	218		
20.13	120	22.19-20	207, 270	22.59	75, 247		
20.17	210	22.20	253	22.61	247		
20.19	220, 222						

OTHER ANCIENT REFERENCES

INDEX OF MODERN AUTHORS

JOURNAL FOR THE STUDY OF THE NEW TESTAMENT
SUPPLEMENT SERIES

To the memory of
Colonel Thomas L. Sherburne, U.S.A.

First Printing w

ISBN: 0-395-13525-7
Library of Congress Catalog Card Number: 70-173779
Printed in the United States of America

The Way to
FORT PILLOW

A Novel by

JAMES SHERBURNE

———◆———

HOUGHTON MIFFLIN COMPANY BOSTON
1972

Books by James Sherburne

HACEY MILLER
THE WAY TO FORT PILLOW

THE WAY TO
FORT PILLOW